CULTURE, PLACE, AND NATURE

STUDIES IN ANTHROPOLOGY AND ENVIRONMENT

Devon Peña and K. Sivaramakrishnan,

Series Editors

CULTURE, PLACE, AND NATURE

Centered in anthropology, the Culture, Place, and Nature series encompasses new interdisciplinary social science research on environmental issues, focusing on the intersection of culture, ecology, and politics in global, national, and local contexts. Contributors to the series view environmental knowledge and issues from the multiple and often conflicting perspectives of various cultural systems.

From Enslavement to Environmentalism

POLITICS ON A SOUTHERN AFRICAN FRONTIER

David McDermott Hughes

UNIVERSITY OF WASHINGTON PRESS Seattle and London

in association with WEAVER PRESS Harare

THIS PUBLICATION IS SUPPORTED IN PART BY THE
BY THE DONALD R. ELLEGOOD INTERNATIONAL PUBLICATIONS
ENDOWMENT. ADDITIONAL SUPPORT IS PROVIDED BY GRANTS
FROM THE FORD FOUNDATION AND RUTGERS UNIVERSITY.

University of Washington Press
P.O. Box 50096, Seattle, WA 98145
www.washington.edu/uwpress

Distributed in southern Africa by Weaver Press
P.O. Box A1922, Avondale, Harare
www.weaverpresszimbabwe.com

Library of Congress Cataloging-in-Publication Data
Hughes, David McDermott. From enslavement to environmentalism :
politics on a Southern African frontier / David McDermott Hughes.
p. cm. — (Culture, place, and nature)
Includes bibliographical references and index.
ISBN 0-295-98590-9 (hardback : alk. paper)
1. Land use—Zimbabwe—Vhimba—History.   2. Land tenure—Zimbabwe—
Vhimba—History.   3. Land use—Mozambique—Gogói—History.   4. Land
tenure—Mozambique—Gogói—History.   5. Vhimba (Zimbabwe)—Colonization.
6. Gogói (Mozambique)—Colonization.   I. Title.   II. Series.
HD992.Z8V484 2006   333.3'096891-dc22   2005027615

To my mother,
and in memory of my father

CONTENTS

ABBREVIATIONS

ABCFM	American Board of Commissioners for Foreign Missions
AEF	Africa Evangelical Fellowship
AHM	Arquivo Histórico de Moçambique (Historical Archives of Mozambique)
BCG	Beira Corridor Group
BSAC	British South Africa Company
Campfire	Communal Areas Management Programme for Indigenous Resources
CC	civil commissioner
CIES	Centro Informazione e Educazione allo Sviluppo (Center for Information and Education for Development)
CNA	Companhia Nacional Algodeira (National Cotton Company)
CNC	chief native commissioner
DA	district administrator
DC	district commissioner
DNFFB	Direcção Nacional de Florestas e Fauna Bravia (National Directorate of Forestry and Wildlife)
DPAP	Direcção Provincial de Agricultura e Pecuária (Provincial Directorate of Agriculture and Livestock)
Frelimo	Frente de Libertação de Moçambique (Front for the Liberation of Mozambique)

FSM	Floresta e Serração do Muda (Muda Forest and Sawmill)
GTZ	Gesellschaft für technische Zusammenarbeit (Organization for Technical Cooperation)
INSANI	Fundo da Inspecção Nacional dos Serviços Administrativos e dos Negócios Indígenas
MARRP	Manica Agricultural Rural Reconstruction Programme
NAZ	National Archives of Zimbabwe
NC	native commissioner
RDC	rural district council
Renamo	Resistência Nacional Moçambicana (Mozambican National Resistance)
SAFIRE	Southern Alliance for Indigenous Resources
SIM	Serving in Missions
SPFFB	Serviços Provinciais de Florestas e Fauna Bravia (Provincial Services of Forestry and Wildlife)
VADC	Vhimba Area Development Committee
Vidco	village development committee
WWF	World Wide Fund for Nature
ZANLA	Zimbabwe African National Liberation Army
ZANU-PF	Zimbabwe African National Union–Patriotic Front

LINGUISTIC CONVENTIONS

All translations are mine unless otherwise noted, and the original text or statement usually appears in an endnote. In most cases, I have used Zimbabwean Standard Shona spellings, even for Ndau dialect words that do not exist in Standard Shona (apologies to Michel Lafon). For Portuguese quotations, I have kept with the original despite different spellings and diacritics used in that language fifty or more years ago.

Members of the mapping team in Gogoi, Mozambique in 1997:
(from left) Bernardo Melo Meque, David M. Hughes, and Samuel Dube.
Chief Gogoi sits in the foreground. Photo by Melanie H. McDermott

PREFACE

IN 1995, DURING MY FIRST FORTNIGHT IN VHIMBA, ELIAS NYAMUNDA showed me his map of households and administrative divisions. The map did not surprise me. After all, Elias walked regularly up and down the escarpment of this remote area of Zimbabwe, performing his duties as an officer of two local committees. A map would help him find his way, and I copied Elias's map for the same purpose as I carried out fieldwork in Vhimba. In 1996, Elias made more maps—these showing various possible locations of the disputed boundary of Chimanimani National Park. These cartographic efforts did not surprise me either. The Zimbabwean organizations that had helped place me in Vhimba had warned that land and boundaries were political there. Elias drew his maps to defend squatters inside the Chimanimani National Park and to undermine the government's claim to land. The government, he argued, had unjustly moved the park's boundary to the detriment of Vhimba people. Smallholder farmers had not encroached upon the park. Rather, through a surveyor's sleight of hand, the park had encroached upon smallholders. Since my historical research confirmed Elias's position, I assisted him and his committee to elaborate upon the original maps. We joined together in what is sometimes called "countermapping"—the effort legally to substantiate the use of land and natural resources by groups not represented in the state.

In 1997, a similar engagement led me to direct a project in Mozambique, at a location only thirty kilometers distant from Vhimba. Gogoi—the name of the place and its chief—challenged my assumptions in a way Vhimba had not. The same organizations and some new ones had briefed me again:

Gogoi, they said, resembled Vhimba in every respect—same Ndau language, same structure of traditional leadership—and, so, I should have no problem in functioning there. Thus assured, I opened the project by asking Chief Gogoi to draw a map of his territory. Gogoi understood that this map would help protect his people's sacred forests and farmland from expropriation by South African timber companies. Yet, he could not draw a map appropriate to the task. The problem was not technical. Rather, at a cultural level, Chief Gogoi did not grasp what I meant by "territory." Marking the ground with a stick, he indicated the location of sacred forests and of his headmen's homesteads, but he did not and could not encircle them with a boundary. Chief Gogoi simply did not know where the physical limits of his rule lay. Nothing in my experience in Vhimba or anywhere else had prepared me for this impasse. The project plowed ahead, nonetheless, and in the course of making more maps and walking around the landscape, Chief Gogoi grappled with boundaries and their current importance. By the end of the project, Chief Gogoi had demarcated his zone of control and presented the provincial government with a map to prove it. He and those around him were starting to think about land in Vhimba's terms.

This book attempts to account for the vastly different concepts of territory and geography that I encountered in Vhimba and Gogoi. It also attempts to explain the change I witnessed in Gogoi. How can two Ndau communities view the landscape and the politics of land so differently? To answer this question, the book explores the past hundred-odd years of this region's history—a period in which British-ruled Vhimba became "territorialized" and Portuguese-ruled Gogoi did not. White settlement around Vhimba and wildly different forms of administration, development, and conservation caused Vhimba and Gogoi to diverge from one another. In effect, the wider colonial and state systems—and local reactions to them—created two distinct cultures. Thus, for almost the entire twentieth century, the Zimbabwe-Mozambique border has marked a sharp disjuncture in the politics of land, chiefship, farming, timber, labor, and numerous other factors. In the late 1990s, however, power in Gogoi began to move into line with Vhimba. White South Africans sought to establish timber plantations in and around Gogoi. These loggers—as well as "countermappers"—reoriented the relations between strong and weak parties so that land emerged as the preeminent political object. In large measure, these processes in Mozambique recapitulate the dynamics of white settlement on earlier hinterlands, from Vhimba to the American West to Australia. Ultimately, then, this book describes power on a frontier of colonization.

ACKNOWLEDGMENTS

THIS BOOK GREW FROM THE APPLIED ACADEMIC SCENE OF HARARE IN the 1990s—a remarkable time and place where social scientists and policy-makers collaborated, debated, and learned from one another. This ferment drew together scholars of the University of Zimbabwe—particularly of the Centre for Applied Social Sciences—and NGOs and government departments involved in conservation and development. Despite the government's steady decay into dictatorship, free discourse and mutual respect prevailed. I write of this time and place with great sadness, for the moment has definitely passed and once-open doors are firmly closed. Policymakers with power do not listen to scholars, and those few who do listen have too little power to effect change. At a more basic level, my closest friends and colleagues in Zimbabwe must now concentrate on economic survival and physical secu-rity. Paramilitary bands have assaulted a number of my dear, defenseless friends. With trepidation, I visited Vhimba—the chief Zimbabwean field site discussed herein—in late 2002. Almost as soon as I had driven away, the police arrested and beat one of my hosts. He associated with an American, a white—presumably an opponent of the government and possibly an agent of the opposition. Research, advocacy, and criticism can hardly continue in this atmosphere. These acknowledgments, then, commemorate freedoms and modes of action made impossible by Zimbabwe's current government.

In Zimbabwe, people contributed time and energy to my work in ways that I cannot reciprocate. Smallholders in Vhimba left banana fields and beer drinks to talk to me, lead me around, and feed me. I thank, in partic-ular, Elias Nyamunda, Elias Muhanyi, Ruben Zuze, and D. Mapuisa, and their families. Elias Nyamunda passed away in 2001. His counsel and friendship enriched this book and my life deeply, and, to me, Vhimba cannot be the same without him. At a remove from Vhimba, Naison and Dee Chigogo and Shirley and Ted DeWolf provided further friendship and logistical support. In Harare, I am grateful to have been able to share ideas with and receive support from Gus Le Breton, Gladman Kundhlande, and Cephas Zinhumwa (all of the Southern Alliance for Indigenous Resources) and Champion Chinhoyi (of Zimbabwe Trust). The Centre for Applied Social Sciences of the University of Zimbabwe provided me an intellectual home. I am grateful to Marshall Murphree, James Murombedzi, Calvin Nhira, Nontokozo Nabane, and Elias Madzudzo for their fellowship through the past decade. At a later stage, the Department of Economic History hosted me in a similar way, thanks to Pius Nyambara, Eira Kramer, and Joseph Mtisi. And thank you to Vupenyu Dzingirai for helping me in this work and for sharing with me the sorrow of Zimbabwe's decline.

In Gogoi, I worked closely with Chief João Maquinasse Gogoi, Joseph Maquinasse Gogoi (his son), and headmen Bundua, Hlengana, and Matsikiti. As chapter 6 explains, the land rights project I planned provided both the context and a form of thanks for this collaboration. The project team—to whom I am extremely grateful and without whom I would not have achieved any results in Gogoi—included Samuel Dube, Bernardo Melo Meque, Muíno Amarchande Taquidir, and Melanie Hughes McDermott. The Espungabera trio of Felix Camba, Felix Filemone, and Michel Lafon housed and transported me and made me laugh. In Chimoio, Ana Paula Reis and the staff of Serviços Provinciais de Florestas e Fauna Bravia facilitated my work, academic as well as applied. In Maputo, I am grateful for the privilege of collaborating with Bartolomeu Soto (of the Direcção Nacional de Florestas e Fauna Bravia), Rod de Vletter (of the World Bank), and (although then based in Johannesburg) Ken Wilson (of the Ford Foundation).

In addition to all these people and institutions that gave me their expertise and time, a number of organizations put money into my project. The Joint Committee on African Studies of the Social Science Research Council and the American Council of Learned Societies (with funds provided by the Rockefeller Foundation) supported my fieldwork, as did the Center for African Studies and Department of Anthropology at the University of California, Berkeley. Also "in the field," the World Bank (with funds from the Global Environment Facility) and the Center for Information and Education for Development (CIES) funded my research while employing me in related projects. While finishing my dissertation, I received further assistance from the MacArthur Foundation, from the Institute on Global Conflict and Cooperation, and from the Portuguese Studies Program (University of California, Berkeley). Finally, the Land Tenure Center (University of Wisconsin, Madison) with funds from the United States Agency for International Development supported the last phase of research and writing. The Ford Foundation has provided a grant to Weaver Press to distribute the book in Zimbabwe, for which I am grateful. The Research Council of Rutgers University also provided a helpful subvention. Parts of the book have appeared in *Journal of Southern African Studies* (chapter 4), *Development and Change* (sections of chapters 5 and 6), and *Journal of Agrarian Change* (part of chapter 7), and I thank their editors for allowing me to reproduce that material. As ever, Mike Siegel did a superb job on the maps.

Finally, I owe a debt to readers near and far, beginning with my dissertation committee at the University of California, Berkeley: Christine Hastorf (chair), Elizabeth Colson, Louise Fortmann, and Donald Moore. I owe a similar debt to the "Alcatraz 5.5" writing group of the Berkeley-Oakland borderlands: Sharad Chari, James McCarthy, Melanie Hughes McDermott, and Janet Sturgeon. A large group of friends, relations, and colleagues commented in indispensable ways on one or more draft chapters: Jocelyn Alexander, Simon Anstey, James Bannerman, Sara Berry, Erica Bornstein, Vupenyu Dzingirai, Angelique Haugerud, Gerhard Liesegang, Max Likin, Bonnie McCay, Corey Robin, Thomas Rudel, Richard Schroeder, Jay Singh, Eric Worby, and the late David Beach. At and through University of Washington Press, Lorri Hagman, K. Sivaramakrishnan, and three anonymous readers provided thorough and sensitive guidance. My mother and father read and commented on the entire manuscript and made me a better writer. How I wish my father could have lived to see this book. Thank you, Melanie, for being a companion and colleague in this work from the beginning.

*From Enslavement
to Environmentalism*

INTRODUCTION

Power on African Frontiers

THE TERM *FRONTIER* MEANS TWO THINGS, BOTH OF THEM STRIKINGLY political. The frontier is a zone, a hinterland, lying outside the spatial core of a society but within grasp of adventurers and colonists. Frontiers also bound and demarcate national, sovereign territories (Kopytoff 1987:9; Worby 1998a:55–56). In one meaning, the frontier "opens" as a "territory or zone of interpenetration of two previously distinct societies." So write Leonard Thompson and Howard Lamar in their classic comparison of Southern Africa and the United States, both once expanses for conquest (L. Thompson and Lamar 1981a:7; cf. Lattimore 1962:469–70). Put slightly differently, frontiers are "contact zones"—the term Mary Louise Pratt (1992:6–7) uses to avoid privileging the conqueror's perspective. In the second meaning, the frontier is the fence line where conquest has stopped. In practice, however, the same frontier can both permit and circumscribe conquest, even at the same time. Beginning in the sixteenth century, European or European-descended settlers expanded west and south into zones that were to them terra incognita. By the 1880s, states realized that their personnel, or at least their territorial ambitions, would collide geographically. Through war and diplomacy, they marked their hinterlands with international boundaries.[1] Of course, white settlers continued to colonize zonal frontiers up to the linear frontiers of their various national territories. In some cases, settlers approached the boundary from both sides, closing the two zonal frontiers separately, as part of different national and colonial processes, and at very different rates. Geographically, such a boundary distinguishes one hinterland, with one set of political dynamics, from its twin, joined at the hip and evolving interdependently.

Rather than treat hinterlands and boundaries as interlinked in this fashion, most studies consider them as distinct phenomena. For most of the world effectively colonized and settled by Europeans, this analytical separation, in fact, makes sense. All of the "neo-Europes"[2]—the United States, Canada, Argentina, Australia, New Zealand, and arguably Siberia—occupy islands or, at least, border only a small number of other states. International boundaries hardly constrained or otherwise influenced white expansion in the eighteenth and nineteenth centuries.[3] Pioneering in Southern Africa, however, lasted longer and, in consequence, survived into a different geopolitical era. Whites[4] *began* to leave the original Cape Colony only in the 1820s. As many historians have noted, these *trekboers* variously fought, ruled, enslaved, employed, dispossessed, raped, and married Africans.[5] In the 1890s, they were still doing so on the northward trail across the Limpopo and toward the Zambezi River. Then, between the years 1897 and 1902, borders crystallized. The Anglo-Portuguese demarcation settled the extent of sovereignty in what are now Zimbabwe's Eastern Highlands, and the Anglo-Boer War made the Limpopo the dividing line between South Africa and Zimbabwe. Once circumscribed in this fashion, did pioneering, trekking, and the process of closing hinterlands die out? Yes, they did, most scholars imply. White colonization—as distinct from its legacy—hardly figures in current accounts of either Zimbabwe's or Mozambique's borderlands.[6] "The frontier," write Thompson and Lamar (1981a:7), "'closes' when a single political authority has established hegemony over the zone." Pioneering as a whole would appear to have ended with Africa's partition into administered colonies.

This book argues that, on the contrary, settlers and colonization continue to shape politics in a locale of partition. The Chimanimani-Sitatonga region of the Zimbabwe-Mozambique border—the site of this study—comprises a double hinterland. Whites settled the Rhodesian side in the 1890s. On the temperate, fertile plateaus, they established "white highlands" of intensive agriculture.[7] Together with the timber industry and the Department of National Parks, these land managers expropriated and evicted wave after wave of African smallholders. Nevertheless, Africans continued to farm what I call "black lowlands." Officially designated as "native reserves," the spaces provided an answer to the colony's "native question": "Where are Africans to live and farm?" In the late 1980s, environmental agencies posed that question anew and reexamined the spaces. In effect, programs and projects reopened Zimbabwe's lowland frontiers long considered to have closed. Thus, in the 1990s, land alienation, evictions, and countersquatting dominated local political life. Across the border, by contrast, colonization is only now moving toward a peak. Since 1994, South African–owned timber firms have laid claim to the bulk of Mozambique's half of the Chimanimani-Sitatonga region. White Zimbabwean farmers have sought access to even larger tracts slightly to the north. As in Zimbabwe, state agencies have encouraged these outsiders to settle and invest. In short, the pressure to colonize and expropriate this binational hinterland is a contemporary fact.

A word about power in Africa's hinterlands is in order. Two factors condition hinterlands' political evolution: relative underpopulation and the acts of land-grabbing themselves. Initially, natives and colonists alike barely cover the landscape. Economic wealth and cultural capital depend upon controlling a scarce resource: people. Elites on the hinterland focus on accumulating clients, wives, children, bonded sons-in-law, and sometimes even slaves. Then, land alienation and evictions partition the hinterland, bringing a second matter to the fore. Agricultural and silvicultural estates confine African smallholders on all sides. In this new regime of land scarcity, Africans retain only the "black lowlands," otherwise known as native reserves. Among chiefs and local government agencies in such places, the locus of struggle shifts decisively from amassing and manipulating clients to keeping territory. "The world had been turned upside down," writes John Iliffe (1987:277) in a retrospect on South African poverty. "Labour was abundant, land and work were scarce, and the great transition which has dominated the history of the poor in every continent was taking place." In blunt terms, it was the transition from rule by enslavement to rule by enclosure.

Another transition soon compounds this one. Late-twentieth-century environmental organizations launch what has been called a "new enclosures movement"[8]—the third act of the drama being played out on Southern African frontiers. Beginning in the late 1980s, social and natural scientists reexamined the "native reserves." Such experts have long blamed smallholders for wasting their reserves economically and, what is worse, degrading them ecologically. Now, a new generation of technocrats argues that outside investors can and must bring in knowledge, skill, and finance to transform these backward zones. So goes the narrative I call "settler-led development." It has come to dominate debate on the fate of the reserves and on conservation in Zimbabwe and Mozambique. In effect, this discourse has declared the black lowlands "open," in much the same fashion as earlier settler myths spoke of "empty land" in the neo-Europes. Latter-day colonists have not yet descended en masse, but politicians and intellectuals have blazed the trail for them. The frontier lives again.

ENSLAVEMENT

Igor Kopytoff labels Africa a "frontier continent" of ubiquitous hinterlands (1987:7). Beginning with the prehistoric Bantu expansion in the savanna and continuing to the present, farmers and herders south of the Sahara have continually migrated, colonized, and seceded. In a systemic "frontier process," kin groups and polities ejected members and turned them into frontiersmen. These variously dissenting or destitute groups moved to an uninhabited area and therein founded a new polity. As the polity grew, political authority came increasingly to rest upon length of residence, though these polities did accord a ritual role to the original inhabitants and their ancestral spirits. Yet, unlike the bursts of colonizing whites in most parts of the world, Africans moved continuously from one hinterland to another, advancing outward and backfilling the interstices.

This political geography depended upon what other anthropologists and historians have termed "rights-in-persons," and lately "enslavement."[9] In these systems, patriarchs sought to accumulate control over people, or "wealth in people" (Guyer 1993, 1995). Patrilineages acquired wives, and their "wombs of iron and gold" bore children.[10] Likewise, matrilineages, which are never matriarchal, recruited the fathers of their youngest generation. In either case, marriage was a corporate concern designed to maximize the corporate group's procreative potential and rights over progeny. Lineages concentrated on manipulating the relationships involved in marriage. Specifically, they could best multiply their stock by converting a marriage that would normally be patrilineal into a matrilineal one. For example, patrilineages would normally relinquish daughters and rights in progeny in return for a bride-wealth of cattle, hoes, or cash. If a daughter-taking lineage did not possess these material goods, it might still acquire a bride, but only by foregoing its patrilineal rights to her progeny. In this way, the wealthier lineage would accumulate, rather than deplete, its store of people. Impoverished or orphaned men, refugees or those separated from their kin made cost-effective sons-in-law (Meillassoux 1991:30). Indeed, as precolonial raids, wars, and droughts detached people from kin, they sought refuge as the clients and fictive kin of stronger lineages and eventually married in, freezing that subordinate status for life (even for their descendants). In sum, the slave suffers from what Orlando Patterson (1982:5) identifies as an essential social deficit: "natal alienation," or an isolation from the "social heritage of his ancestors." Dislocated, deracinated people lost their rights.

Such servile individuals and their relationships, rather than land, were the measured, counted resource. As a matter of relationships, political rivals used marriage transactions to gain the upper hand. In the more extreme situations, lineage elders used juniors as assets, exchanging and accumulating them strategically over long and short distances. The exchanges became infamous. Overseas slavers tapped supplies in Atlantic Africa and along the Indian Ocean coast. Especially during the "slave century" of 1730–1830, circumstances forced African rulers to sell, rather than accumulate, clients, captives, and other dependent people. In the interior of Southern Africa, rulers mostly accumulated, rather than exchanged, people. From the 1830s to the 1890s, Nguni states conscripted destitute people and captives into male regiments. By waging war, they acquired further prisoners, orphans, and wives. Nobles did exchange their subordinates, but mostly as an internal, Nguni trade and set of marriage relations. I use the term *ambulatory enslavement* to distinguish this form of accumulation and transfer from ship-borne trade—and also to indicate the coproduction of mobility and servitude. Nguni relationships unfolded in space through certain kinds of traffic, as Nguni goods moved on foot (or on hooves) across the landscape.

What of the territory across which those goods traveled? "Land," as Sara Berry (2001:9) writes with respect to precolonial Ghana, "was valued primarily as a means to attract followers, rather than as an asset in its own right." Additionally, specific burial sites and spiritual abodes commanded religious respect. In any case, Africans marked land in ways that made measurement, counting, and comparison impossible. In what became Zimbabwe, some chiefs used rivers, tolerating the cadastral ambiguities that inevitably arose at their headwaters.[11] Elsewhere, dotted lines sufficed. According to an oral account collected in eastern Zimbabwe, "people . . . were sent by Paramount Chief Mutema. They performed their rituals while naked and possessed and where they sat down became the boundary of the village."[12] The Ndebele state was even less territorial. In 1887, its king wrote the neighboring king of the Batswana: "In olden times . . . we never spoke about boundary lines. . . . It is only now they [the British] talk about boundaries."[13] Thus, Africans did cherish land, but not as discrete parcels of bounded hectares. Colonizing whites introduced such a mentality and, thereby, helped replace ambulatory enslavement with a new political economy.

ENCLOSURE

White expansion shaped the southern subcontinent in ways profoundly different from the rest of Africa. In a fashion more typically identified with the Americas or the antipodes, rural whites have colonized Southern Africa's hinterland. And they continue to do so. *Trekboers*—an Afrikaans phrase best translated as "migrating farmers"—expanded from the original Cape Colony in three major movements. In the 1830s, the Great Trek took them to the Orange Free State (in the center of what is now South Africa) and northward to the Transvaal. In the 1890s, some crossed the Limpopo River to Rhodesia,[14] and, in the 1990s, frontiersmen and women trekked to Mozambique, Zambia, and points further north. Each step of the way, settlers have gained access to hinterlands with minimal interference from states or colonial powers. Pioneering of this sort often led to bloodshed. As Laurens van der Post (1966:56) writes of the first migrants,

> [T]hey penetrated deeply into the interior and took this nightmare of tribal warfare, like a bridal opportunity, into their arms. First they settled with the strongest of their black rivals for the country. They broke the Amazulu, repelled the Matabele, cowed many others and pinned down the formidable Basuto among the hills [later, Lesotho]. . . . When all that was done, they turned to the accepted refinement of conquest in Africa: the extermination of the Bushman.

Extermination was, however, the exception to trekker rule. Unlike frontiersmen of the American Great Plains, Australia, or Amazonia, Southern African whites have mostly managed to take land without wiping out indigenous inhabitants. Dane Kennedy describes this singular circumstance as a "demographic conjunction": descendants of the original inhabitants outnumber white settlers and their descendants.[15] Having survived, therefore, Southern African blacks live with the cultural legacy of dispossession and face contemporary land-grabbing.

In seizing the landscape, frontiersmen both define territory and place a premium upon its control. Colonizers act from two fundamental principles—exclusive ownership and physical boundaries—that together constitute enclosure and a territorial paradigm. In New England, for example, colonists expected unique titles when they acquired land from Indian tribes (Cronon 1983:71). Such control of land demands a *total* claim, that is, the negation and cancellation of any and all overlapping rights. Indian farmers, who operated under a different paradigm, sold or gave access to the same piece of land to numerous white buyers and, additionally, expected to retain access for themselves. The misunderstanding irritated the newcomers and complicated their designs. On other frontiers, where whites

8

did not encounter agricultural natives, settlers simply discounted indigenous grazing, hunting, and collecting. Throughout what became neo-
Europes, settlers rode in with John Locke's theory of property: only improvement and "mixing labor with the land" conferred ownership.[16] Landscapes
used solely for foraging or low-input agriculture remained "empty" and
"unowned"—an open frontier legalized as *territorium nullius*.[17] Many
Europeans, by contrast, intended to transform the landscape into intensive
monocultures. Even if settlers frequently failed, the passage of their plow
negated age-old attachments to forest and grassland. "Unproductive"
natives found themselves fenced out.

Fences and other property lines constitute the second crucial concept of
a territorial mentality. In order to be exclusive, zones of ownership must
occupy space up to an unambiguous demarcation line. The owner must mark
the landscape in a way that signals the geographical terminus of one claim
and the beginning of another—no overlap allowed! Again, the mentality
of boundaries may be quite foreign to the original inhabitants. Especially
where natural endowments have been abundant relative to their economic
activities, prior inhabitants may have felt no need to fence resources in or
fence encroachers out. From the colonial perspective, natives' failure to create boundaries undermined their claims to land. *Territorium nullius* was not
even "territory" until Europeans drew lines across it. So argued a family of
western Australian pioneers in refusing even to *negotiate* with aboriginal
occupants.[18] These frontiersmen and others have implemented a whole range
of bounding practices and technologies. In the American West, in Australia,
and in Southern Africa, the surveyor has marched but a few paces behind
the pioneers—and sometimes in front of the pioneers. Both the lines marked
on the landscape and the property map and register—known together as
a cadastre—justify land-grabbing and the idea of territory itself. "The cadastral map," Roger Kain and Elizabeth Baigent write, "is *active*: in portray-
ing one reality, as in the settlement of the New World or in India, it helps
obliterate the old."[19] Spirit-blessed soil now constitutes hectares, counted,
measured, and contested.

But do land-grabbing and the cadastral map truly obliterate an older mentality of overlapping, shared claims to land? Much of the Africanist literature on customary land tenure and common property insists that such systems are, on the contrary, alive and well (Fortmann and Bruce 1988). The
issue turns on the balance between individual or household rights and the
corporate rights of some larger social unit. For a number of decades, it
seemed as if individuals were gaining rights to land while lineages and chief-

taincies were losing hold (Bohannan 1963). In some countries, the twenti-eth-century growth of a rural cash economy promoted informal, or even formal, capitalist markets in land. Smallholders were not immune, and it seemed as if exclusive ownership and land titles might become the order of the day. Yet, counterposed against the market, chiefs, headmen, and vari-ous native departments defended "customary land tenure." In defending it, of course, they partly invented it.[20] Under these "traditions," chiefs held the land in trust for their subjects and could allocate and reallocate rights among households. In effect, chiefs' tracts constituted a common pool resource (Ostrom 1990), open to members—and all their overlapping claims to soil, flora, and fauna—but closed to outsiders. In this fashion, chiefs maintained their own prominence in agrarian relations, and they kept land off the capitalist market.[21] Or, as in Pauline Peters's (1994) description of cattle grazing in Botswana, local convention has often forced privatization down a path that is complex and uneven in the extreme. It would seem that lineages stopped (or delayed) the surveyors at the gates.

On another level, however, chiefs *appropriated* the cadastral mentality. Precisely in closing the gates to colonists and land merchants, ruling line-ages insisted upon boundaries. They may not have made maps, but their territorial ideals fit the cadastral model. Where colonization confined them to reserves, as in Rhodesia, chiefs coveted those reserves. They did not wish to share land with white settlers. Thus African and European authorities partitioned the country without privatizing all of it. The hinterland closed, not only as an outgrowth of capitalist land ownership, but also as a process of segregation between colonizers and colonized. Recently, scholars have begun to describe similar processes as "territorialization." In Europe, the notion of national territory and separateness evolved from the seventeenth to the nineteenth centuries.[22] The change was most evident in the admin-istration of border regions. There, as Peter Sahlins (1989:7) writes of the Franco-Spanish Pyrenees, principles of overlapping jurisdiction and of strictly demarcated sovereignty coexisted for two centuries—until the lat-ter won out. France and Britain spent the better part the nineteenth cen-tury corresponding, lecturing, and, at last, marching in the woods to explain to the king of Siam what a linear boundary meant. In the end, they suc-ceeded; as Thongchai Winichakul writes, Siam traded its web of ambigu-ous tributary relations for a modern "geo-body."[23] The map and the nation (or territorial chiefdom) were born together.

This twin birth amounted to a closing of the frontier in both senses of the word. The hinterlands became demarcated tracts, and this process, as explained above, continues to this day. What was lost in this transformation? The older system of wealth-in-people, tribute-based polities, and slavery was deprived of much of its strength in Southern Africa. Among chiefs, private interests, and branches of the state, political contestation and compromise have come to depend increasingly on the allocation and bounding of land. In a closed hinterland, clients are not valuable in and of themselves. Indeed, they often remain uncounted until they serve the cause of land-grabbing and landholding. Thus, land displaces people as the locus of political culture.

I write "political *culture*" because the territorialization of political *economy* is necessarily more subtle. In that sphere, control over land can never fully replace control over people because one confers the other. The eighteenth-century English enclosures are the classic case. For Marx, the enclosures ensued from something akin to ambulatory enslavement. Tellingly, he titled his essay on the subject, "The Expropriation of the Agricultural Population from the Land," not vice versa. E. P. Thompson's (1975) account of the enclosures also focuses more on the control of people rather than on the control of land. Capital punishment—the most blatantly embodied power over people—underwrote the whole drive against poaching and tree felling. Finally, Karl Polanyi (1944:42) describes the subsequent industrial revolution as arising from the commoditization of labor *and* land.

How, then, can one usefully separate power over people and power over land? They are distinct, not as material outcomes, but as modes of debate and contestation in long, complex processes. Power over people and power over land are forms of political culture. Moreover, they are ideal types, helping to clarify a social reality that is still more complex. Above all, "power over people" and "power over land"—and cognate terms used throughout this book—refer to struggles over meaning. They are claims and arguments that, in Sara Berry's (1989) formulation, foment, propel, and sometimes help resolve struggles over material resources. Thus, this book submits: as the frontier closes and its inhabitants vie for livelihood and predominance, they shift the cultural terms of their engagement from categories of people to categories of land. What counts as a legitimate or persuasive claim changes. Discourses of enslavement give way to those of enclosure, boundaries, and maps. Then arises an enduring cultural pattern that I call "cadastral politics."

ENVIRONMENTALISM

It is not entirely accurate or fair to label environmentalism anywhere in Africa a "new enclosures movement." At least, it is not becoming such a movement in a straightforward fashion. On the ground, environmentalists and associated interests have seized far less land than did nineteenth-century colonists.[24] They neither endorse nor imagine colonization. Yet, their ideas are creating the political will to enclose black lowlands. In the 1970s, environmentalists revisited physiocratism—or, more aptly, explored the converse of the physiocratic argument. That is, if as the physiocrats claimed, economic activity derives from nature, then the degradation of nature will surely stifle economic activity. This pessimistic insight posited—to quote the title of an influential 1972 document—"limits to growth." Governments previously happy to extract minerals, soil fertility, and biomass began to grapple with the nonrenewable, finite nature of some of these endowments. By 1987, international panels were regularly invoking the need for "sustainable development."[25] According to this doctrine, careful husbanding of the Earth's resources would permit modest economic advancement. It gave rise to a plethora of programs and projects in "conservation and development," and Zimbabwe played a prominent role in the ferment. With greater alacrity than most, Zimbabwean governmental and nongovernmental agencies redirected their attention from agriculture to tourism and other supposedly low-impact enterprises (without altogether ceasing extractive industries, of course). Donors, NGOs, and eventually the same actors in Mozambique became boosters, promoting, subsidizing, and advertising "ecotourism" (even when it would fail financially).

In so doing, they embarked on an intellectual journey of remapping space and nature. On paper, conservation and development agencies have repackaged and recombined white, black, settler, and native spaces as "bioregions." They did so by transforming a third spatial category: parks and protected areas. Earlier conservationists had removed people—as supposed agents of degradation—and fenced these "pristine" zones. By the 1990s, many environmentalists recognized the human-made, anthropogenic qualities of many protected forests and grasslands.[26] They also recognized the potential for wildness outside the parks, for the presence and influence of rainforest and ungulates in farmed spaces. Concretely, programs and projects established new spaces of management and intervention, from the straightforward "park buffer zone" to the increasingly vast and amorphous "conservation area," "transfrontier area," and "peace park" (Hughes 2005). Often loosely tacked onto watersheds, mountain ranges, and other ecological units, the new "conservation territories" (Zimmerer 2000) seemed to expand as far and as fast as funding would allow. They engulfed native reserves and white-owned commercial farms—in four countries in one case—casting over them an unwieldy net of regulations and injunctions to "comanage" natural resources. Under the new rubric, landowners were to cohabit and coordinate with nature and with each other. They fell under what Karl Zimmerer calls the "geographical production of nature-society hybrids" (2000:356). Black lowlands and white highlands became less and less distinguishable.

To the extent that enclosure is taking place in Southern Africa, it emerges from the gray area between environmentalists' liberal intentions and their oversights. Cindi Katz's "new enclosures" are an unintended consequence. Hence, they differ radically in political culture from deliberate, colonial land-grabs or from the English enclosures. Professionals in conservation and development have battled precisely against closure and boundaries. They unfenced and unbounded both parks and nation-states. They also unbounded businesses, permitting partnerships between smallholders and capital. People, investment, and wild animals crossed the escarpment between black lowlands and white highlands. Of course, they did so mostly in one direction—from the white/rich space to the black/poor one. Having invested, tourism firms now derive profits from the natural resources of smallholder spaces—and sometimes seek to expel smallholders from those spaces. To this extent, "ecological capital" and what Katz calls "bio-accumulation" are enabling something close to a new enclosures movement.[27] Yet, in Southern Africa, they are fostering a change that is both more profound and less easily condemned than enclosure: racial integration. Black lowlands are a vestige of colonization, violence, and rural apartheid. Especially in Zimbabwe, environmentalists and other liberals would now like to sweep them away, abolishing the economic and spatial segregation that so marks that country. To their minds, they are, at last, surmounting the inequities of conquest. From a different point of view, they are opening a new frontier and a new era of colonization. How can one bridge the gap between these two positions? This book attempts to do precisely that, using history, ethnography, and criticism to trace the nine lives of the frontier on the Zimbabwe-Mozambique border.

SCENARIO OF THE BOOK

In Southern Africa—and surely elsewhere—polities and elites have occupied, closed, and reopened the frontier in a highly complex and contingent fashion. Rather than present a study of the subcontinent or of Zimbabwe and Mozambique, this book focuses on a narrow, but diagnostic, region and time period: the vicinity of the Chimanimani and Sitatonga mountains from

1890 to 2000 (map 1). The area receives some of the highest rainfall in Southern Africa—an ecological condition that has made it desirable to black and white farmers. Focusing the analysis still futher, much of the book describes processes and indices of change in two sites falling under the authority of two chiefs. Ruled by Chief Ngorima, Vhimba lies just inside what is now Zimbabwe, at the southwestern end of the Chimanimani Mountain Range. Only thirty kilometers away, Gogoi and Chief Gogoi are similarly situated on the western side of the Sitatonga Mountains in Mozambique. Smallholders in both Vhimba and Gogoi speak the Ndau dialect of Shona. Between 1862 and 1889, both areas came under the Gaza Nguni kingdom.[28] Therefore, many observers describe inhabitants of the Chimanimanis and the Sitatongas as "one people." They are mistaken. Throughout the twentieth century, vastly different cultural and political logics governed Vhimba and Gogoi. Vhimba and Gogoi present extreme forms in the range of ways by which authorities rule subjects.

Part 1 examines this historical pattern of divergent evolution for the two sides of the region (and will appeal to a more specialized audience). Chapter 1, on Gogoi, Mozambique, establishes the baseline: a Gaza Nguni kingdom oriented toward the accumulation and circulation of subordinate people—toward ambulatory enslavement. Those fundamentals did not change when the Portuguese took control of the area in 1895. Administrators and private companies taxed the human resources of the Sitatonga region, and they used exactly the same collectors that the Gaza Nguni had—Chief Gogoi, other chiefs, and headmen. Since whites neither alienated nor transformed the landscape, politics began and ended with corvées and forced labor, never quite outlawed in the colonial period. Indeed, Mozambique's postcolonial war (1979–92) revived forced labor and its association with chiefship in the Sitatongas. Chapter 2 describes the strikingly different experience across the border, in and around Vhimba, Zimbabwe, during exactly the same time frame. By 1900, the British South Africa Company had facilitated white settlement of the Chimanimani plateau, created native reservations, and begun to relocate Africans to those reservations. Timber companies and nature conservationists continued grabbing and holding land into the period of Zimbabwe's nationhood. Chief Ngorima and his subjects resisted through arson and squatting. Periodically evicted, they contested cadastral lines by engaging in cadastral politics. At the threshold of the 1990s, therefore, the Sitatongas and Chimanimanis presented a stark contrast: a political culture of personal subordination and a political culture of land tenure separated by the thin line of the border.

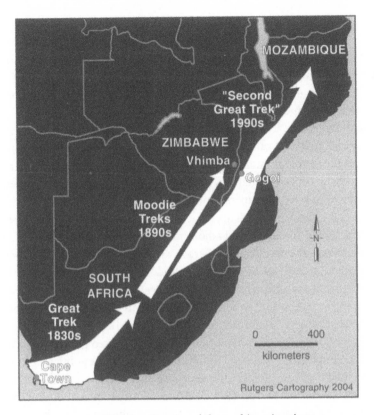

MAP 1. Vhimba, Gogoi, and three white migrations

The border, thus, represents a sharp disjuncture. Part 2 discusses the implications of that "hard border" for border crossers and for the politics of Vhimba and Gogoi in the 1990s. In the early part of the decade, refugees fleeing the war in Gogoi and neighboring parts of Mozambique came to Vhimba. As chapter 3 shows, they approached Zimbabwean headmen (deputies of Chief Ngorima) to pledge themselves as clients. Such pledging followed a wartime custom dating back to the nineteenth century. Vhimba's headmen, though, did not respond in the fashion of a hundred years earlier. Instead, headmen took advantage of refugees' subservience and used them to regain territory from a private estate owner and a national park. Whereas refugees prepared for clientship, they participated in land-grabbing. Chapter 4 explores the political economy of land allocation in Vhimba and its relationship with development projects. In the mid-1990s, NGOs, the Zimbabwean state, and entrepreneurial smallholders in Vhimba

15

tried to implement community forestry and other programs that took the boundaries of the native reservation as given. Headmen sabotaged those efforts. They did so by pursuing turf battles and squatting, a form of "extensive development" that challenged the boundaries of the reservation. In short, an important segment of Vhimba's leadership pursued a territorial notion of prosperity—essentially the enlargement of their geo-bodies.

Chapter 5 returns to Mozambique to witness the birth of eviction and of territorial politics. Again, border crossers are implicated. With the conclusion of Mozambique's war, South African firms and individuals were seeking to establish timber plantations in and around Gogoi. These expatriates, many of whom were Afrikaners, stood poised to reenact the events of the 1890s in the Chimanimanis. This time, however, NGOs attempted to preserve land in the Sitatongas and adjoining regions from alienation. These organizations, many of whose managers crossed the border from Zimbabwe, brought their experience of cadastral politics to the Mozambican hinterland. In the mid-1990s, they began to assist Mozambican chiefs to claim land by mapping the landscape. As one of the consultants, I left Vhimba to direct a project that surveyed and documented Chief Gogoi's "territory." The job was not easy because the territory—in this client-focused polity—did not exist. Like refugees, the mappers initially misconstrued the political culture of their host communities. Yet unlike the refugees in Vhimba, expatriate mappers helped prompt fundamental change. Assisted by central Mozambique's general climate of land and tree claiming, these mappers began to create a cadastre and to make it understood. Politics turned the corner from ambulatory enslavement to territorial (dis)possession. In short, the Mozambican hinterland began to close.

Part 3 elaborates upon that closure. Chapter 6 explains how processes in Zimbabwe contributed. Beginning in the late 1980s, environmentally oriented tourism entered and began to restructure the native reserves. Up to then, administrators had, by and large, honored the original, beneficial intent (among many subsequent pernicious ones) of the reserves: to keep white settlers out and preserve a territorial entitlement for black farmers. A conservation program known as Campfire (Communal Areas Management Programme for Indigenous Resources) overturned that principle entirely. Backed by NGOs, the government of Zimbabwe, and donors, conservationists invited the tourism industry to begin operations in the black lowlands. Blacks lost their right to farm, but could thenceforth appeal to the government and NGOs for the privilege of farming on the basis of their economic productivity and/or ecological sustainability. Campfire redefined and rezoned the reserves. Meanwhile, as chapter 6 further relates, Mozambican civil servants began to ask a version of the question that had first generated Rhodesia's reserves: "Where shall the natives live in relation to investment?"[29] Policymakers looked for examples in neighboring countries, but, by the late 1990s, they could no longer discern entitlement-based reserves in Zimbabwe. They did see—and Zimbabwe's environmentalist intelligentsia showed them repeatedly—the reformulated lowland investment zones. With surprising speed, the bulk of development and conservation agencies in Mozambique opened smallholder spaces to business. In their terms, "communities" and corporations should form partnerships for mutual, ecologically responsible profit making. There were no signs of that happening in central Mozambique. Rather, in early 2001, intensive farmers stood poised to alienate 440,000 hectares. Despite the best intentions, conservation has begotten colonization.

Or, perhaps conservation has begotten colonization *because of* conservation's best, liberal intentions. The book's conclusion reassesses three liberal projects active on the Zimbabwe-Mozambique border: development, democracy, and, from an earlier era, emancipation. As the classic program, nineteenth-century emancipation and abolitionism have undoubtedly achieved the greatest success. Virtually everywhere, including the Zimbabwe-Mozambique borderland, people no longer constitute property.[30] In the course of rooting out Rhodesian enslavement, British administrators considered themselves morally superior to the labor-extracting Portuguese. Surely, one would agree that forcing someone off the land is preferable to forcing him or her to work. But is it preferable by very much? Land alienation compounded emancipation to impoverish African elites. Deprived of both clients and land as stores of wealth, rural Africans had to concentrate on amassing money. Development, the second liberal project, helped them to do so. More recently, both Zimbabwe and Mozambique have pursued the third and final liberal project: democratic empowerment. In this connection, most strategies are territorial; governments decentralize and cede responsibilities, for specific areas, to the people associated with those areas. Known as "communities," these village republics increasingly run their own affairs, but they run very little in the way of national affairs. Having restrained smallholders in space, governments advertise them as "partners" to business. Investors, whom policies have unleashed, swoop down from the highlands. Frontier conditions reign again, and the Chimanimani-Sitatonga landscape lies *open* to settlers.

The value of openness and its close associates, freedom and markets, predates the Zimbabwe-Mozambique border. They lie at the core of liberalism, an ongoing Enlightenment tradition. If John Stuart Mill celebrated the individual, equality, and the possibility of improvement, so do today's so-called neoliberals (Gray 1995:85–96). They would level the playing field so that individuals improve to the limit of their capacity. Lower the barriers, let blacks and whites, peasants and investors, meet and compete equally toward self-betterment! As this book will argue, such an ambition—liberal in root and branch—is dangerous. It would strip black peasants of the unequal, race- and class-based entitlements that have protected them (although only minimally) up to now. Instead, I propose the continuation of Zimbabwe's thoroughly illiberal, paternalistic practice of reserving land for black smallholder communities. (This position is not to be confused with the policy, under South African apartheid, that blacks should live *only* in reserves.) The practice would suit Mozambique just as well. In other words, I argue for maintaining and raising barriers against buying, selling, or investing in smallholder lands—against frontiersmanship in its nineteenth- and twentieth-century forms. Where others support precisely that kind of openness, this book counsels for closure. At the very least, on actual or potential frontiers, liberal projects and good intentions deserve fresh scrutiny.

PART 1

Colonization,
Failed and Successful

The two chapters that comprise part 1 do not attempt to recount the colonial histories of Vhimba and Gogoi. Neither of these places has experienced a "colonial period" of the sort usually imagined: a tight three-quarter-century of European control capped by African self-rule of one kind or another. True, the 1884–85 Congress of Berlin did partition the midsection of Southern Africa among Britain, Portugal, and Germany. Furthermore, formal independence—even if it did not come in 1960 as in more northerly parts—has come. Vhimba and Gogoi felt the reverberations of these events. Yet, in the course of long-distance transmission from the official ceremonies, the various treaties lost much of their original significance. The Anglo-Portuguese boundary delineation of 1898, for example, prompted neither British nor Portuguese actually to settle in the Chimanimani or Sitatonga areas.[1] Instead, imperial partition prior to the delineation itself facilitated colonization by a third white group, South African whites speaking Dutch and English, whose presence in Africa dated back to 1652. If one includes these actors, then the colonial period started long before the Congress of Berlin (1884–85) and reached the region of this study only rather late in the day. The tail end of colonialism is similarly murky. A generation after Mozambique ceased to be a colony of Portugal, Afrikaner-led colonization reached Gogoi. Only in the 1990s were people in Gogoi learning how to resist the seizure of their land by white settlers. Is rural Mozambique, then, somehow stuck in the colonial period? A simplified time line of precolonial, colonial, and postcolonial eras raises exactly these types of contradictions.

Fortunately, historians have improved upon this three-act play and its narrative of states and treaties. As Southern Africanists have long recognized, stateless whites began to *colonize* long before European state rule materialized in the form of *colonialism*.[2] Colonization—or physical settlement for agriculture or silviculture—has often occurred independent of colonialism. Occasionally, colonization has left a more profound mark on African society than has colonialism. Portuguese first settled the Mozambican coast in 1505 and between the early seventeenth century and the Nguni conquest two hundred years later farmed the *prazos* (estates granted by the Portuguese crown) along the Zambezi all the way to Zumbo. Cut off entirely from the metropole, these "transfrontiersmen" intermarried with Africans, becoming chiefs until all visible trace of their origin was lost.[3] Not so the Dutch. Enough of them maintained a separation from Africans—called *apartheid* in some times and places—to establish lasting neo-European enclaves. Thus, a more complicated time line links the Cape Colony to the treks to today's Chipinge Club. Such continuities figure prominently in Zimbabwe's historical record. Indeed, not so long ago that record largely consisted of triumphalist settler narratives about Afrikaners and other pioneers.[4] Yet, later histories and contemporary accounts of the 1980s and 1990s have tended to minimize the influence of whites in favor of African agency. As elsewhere in Africa, accounts of independence movements and wars of liberation have emphasized and/or endorsed African nationalism. Even the more skeptical anthropology of African "postcolonies" implies that the colonial period is past. At the very least, "postcolonial studies" suggest that the flag ceremonies held in 1957 and thereafter changed the cultural face of Africa.[5] The time line of states and treaties may be creeping back in.

Vhimba and Gogoi do not permit this intrusion of "official history." In neither place was national independence an important turning point. Nor was the state often the most important actor. In 1893, whites seized the Chimanimani plateau in an administrative vacuum. The following year, officials stepped in, but they represented a private company—the British South Africa Company—rather than the British state as such. Even after the expiry of that company's concession in 1923, settlers held the balance of power in Rhodesian affairs. This unusual degree of self-government resulted in Zimbabwe's double independence: the unilateral separation from Britain in 1965 and the transfer to a black government in 1980. For the distribution of land in Zimbabwe today, the first, much less recognized independence may have had the greater impact. In Gogoi, private agencies also kept European state rule at arms' length. The Mozambique Company governed Manica and Sofala for fifty years (1893–1943). Portugal ruled it directly for only thirty-two years, until independence in 1975. After independence, however, the Mozambican state hardly governed Gogoi. War and rebel occupation kept the region beyond civil servants' reach for more than a decade. In short, Gogoi is and Vhimba was a hinterland, a place where freebooters, adventurers, and land-grabbers often carry the day.

The two chapters that follow present this frontier history from shortly before white penetration to the start of my ethnographic research. During this period, whites colonized Vhimba more than once. They did not do so because they were *white,* in some essential or "civilizational" sense (as per Huntington 1996). In a more contingent fashion, these European-derived individuals acted with a set of motives, methods, and consequences that frequently accompany long-distance domination, migration, and agricultural settlement. They took land and, in so doing, precipitated far-reaching changes in African society. Chiefs and other powerful African men responded to land alienation, eviction, and timber plantations by holding and expanding their geographical spaces. As described above, polities and political struggle in this part of Zimbabwe became cadastral. The frontier closed. In Gogoi, by contrast, no such changes occurred. Despite several attempts, white settlers did not colonize the area (although they did establish *colonatos* elsewhere in Mozambique). Gogoi became, by default, a labor reserve, in which politics treated the control of people as far more important than the control of land. At least until the arrival of loggers and mappers described in part 2, Gogoi's frontier remained open. Thus, Vhimba and Gogoi span the range of possible outcomes of white colonization—a bull's-eye on the first try versus repeated misfiring.

1

COMPULSORY LABOR
AND UNCLAIMED LAND
IN GOGOI, MOZAMBIQUE,
1862–1992

GOGOI'S DOCUMENTED HISTORY COMPRISES TWO PERIODS OF WARFARE
bounding ninety-odd years of peace. From 1862 to 1889, the Gaza Nguni
empire ruled the area, subjected it to tribute, and raided neighboring polities. From 1979 to 1992, Renamo and Frelimo contested Gogoi, alternately
occupying and attacking it. During both of these periods, political leaders
enslaved smallholder farmers. That is to say, they compelled men and women
to serve as property and/or to perform work in a fashion qualitatively
different from the wage labor form. People functioned as tribute, as soldiers, and as carriers of matériel. War and its associated maneuvers, then,
placed wealth in people at the pivot of power in Gogoi. Yet, war did not
have this effect through any character intrinsic to either African wars or Gogoi
politics. Frelimo and Renamo did not force people to work because, like a
repressed psychological drive, a will to enslave suddenly resurfaced. In fact,
the ninety-year peace had kept the practice of forced labor alive and active.
Portuguese rule perpetuated many of the underlying forms of the Gaza
Nguni kingdom. After 1975, the warring parties—especially Renamo—
capitalized upon people's familiarity with colonial methods of recruiting
forced labor. In this regard, war was merely a harsher form of peace. So, too,
peace under the Portuguese resembled the milder moments of Gogoi's wars.

Portugal, however, had taken power over Gogoi in the 1890s with positive, forward-looking purposes. The first administrators hoped to develop
the region and its people. Located on a fertile upland relatively free of disease, Gogoi could become a center for white settlement and white production of crops and livestock. But Gogoi's location was unfortunate: the Buzi

and Rusitu rivers hemmed it in on three sides, while the international border blocked the only outlet. Both rivers flooded in the wet season, and Rhodesia periodically closed the border to agricultural products. Portugal might have overcome at least the riverine obstacles, but it disposed of scant finances for infrastructural improvement. Gogoi's development, then, depended on inadequate bridges and ferries and was constantly stymied. For reasons ranging from bombs to broken cables, this infrastructure still cannot deliver the goods on time.

Thus, the political history of Gogoi's administration centers on an enduring tension between vision and reality: the ambition of white colonization and the outcome of arrested development. The strain became most apparent during the short periods when whites *did* colonize Gogoi. This chapter presents two such historical junctures, moments when white-run enterprises tried to take land and produce from it. At these times, Portuguese hopes ran high. Would the settlers transform northern Mossurize into a producer of wealth rather than merely an exporter of labor? The answer is no. These failures led the administration to rely upon the only economic activity that consistently worked in Mossurize: forced labor for agricultural and industrial ventures located elsewhere. By default, Gogoi became a labor reserve—the dead end of its development from the Portuguese point of view.

For the Gogoi chieftaincy, however, forced labor was anything but stagnant. This chapter follows that chieftaincy through multiple phases of Portuguese forced labor. Colonial administrators delegated to him and other lineage leaders the task of recruiting workers. Thus co-opted, chiefs occupied a tenuous position: they controlled the labor of their subjects, but, in so doing, they risked antagonizing and ultimately losing followers. Although Frelimo abolished forced labor, Chief Gogoi regained this control under Renamo's occupation. In 1992, however, the system of forced labor finally collapsed. The chapter, then, ends with Gogoi and other chiefs on the threshold of an unprecedented situation: the cessation of the corvée combined with another, more serious intrusion of white settlers. Chapter 5 explores this threat of colonization and Gogoi's equally unprecedented response to it.

PRE-PORTUGUESE POWER, ROOTED AND UPROOTED

Long before 1890, migratory movements had brought new people and new rulers to the Chimanimani and Sitatonga uplands. These early conquests and expansions resembled Igor Kopytoff's (1987) frontier process much more than they did the cadastral politics of the twentieth century. In other words, polities rose and fell as men sought to free themselves from patriarchs in one place and to become patriarchs themselves in another place. The first known revolution of this kind in Zimbabwe occurred in the late seventeenth century when a number of lineages departed from the Rozvi state of the central highlands. Moving east, these *mwoyo*-totem clans conquered the *dziva* clans of the Save Valley and eastward.[1] Under paramount chief Mutema, the conquerors maintained ties with the Rozvi. By roughly 1730, however, they were independent and in the process of creating their own state. Before the end of the century, Mutema had established the Sanga confederacy, encompassing *mwoyo* and *dziva* chieftaincies and spanning the entire area.[2] The two chiefly lineages focused upon in this work derive from this grouping. The Ngorima titleholder, a *mwoyo*, had migrated with Chief Mutema.[3] Much later, a seceding son of Chief Mafussi, one of the original *dziva* dynasties, created the Gogoi chieftaincy.[4]

Secessions and conquests of this nature raised the issue of territorial control in an indirect fashion. Disaffected factions of a lineage could split off easily as long as an "interstitial frontier" (Kopytoff 1987) lay close at hand. No doubt, empty land to the south facilitated Chief Gogoi's defection, and by relocating to it, he gained control of that hinterland. At the same time, the availability of territory made possible a political system focused on non-territorial objectives: the consolidation of a faction at home, the subjugation of frontier dwellers, and the attraction of new adherents and dependents. The survival of Gogoi's polity depended much more upon the number of his adherents than upon hectares or discrete boundaries. There was, however, one sense in which boundaries did matter. Within the Sanga polity, *dziva* dynasties constituted "territorial cults." That is, chiefs bore responsibility for carrying out ceremonies at chiefly gravesites and/or other shrines. Thus associated with specific, immobile locations, the ceremonies and their performers assured the rainfall and fertility of a given area. Conquest by the *mwoyo* dynasties had not destroyed these cults. Indeed, following a well-known pattern, the Mutema lineage and its followers eventually recognized the spiritual power of these autochthons.[5] By the nineteenth century, the leading *dziva* chief, Musikavanhu, received offerings from as far away as the Indian Ocean, thus covering an area exceeding Sanga (Rennie 1978:262). Still, these territorial aspects of *dziva* chiefship fell short of cadastral politics. Boundaries between cults were indistinct, creating the gaps and ambiguities that constituted interstitial frontiers.[6] Moreover, beyond the immediate vicinity of the rain shrines themselves, *dziva* chiefs did not presume to control the land or access to it. Rainmaking did not amount to land management.

In any case, the Nguni *mfecane* (see Introduction) swept away the Sanga polity and many of its territorial elements. Beginning in the 1820s, the *mfecane* was a series of migrations and occupations.[7] They differed in a number of ways from the previous *mwoyo* movements. At the most basic level, Nguni armies moved a longer distance over a shorter period than had any political forces hitherto fore seen in Zimbabwe or Mozambique. Nxaba and Shoshangane emigrated from Zululand in the 1820s; Nxaba invaded Sanga in roughly 1828; and Shoshangane drove him off in 1836, ruling for two years before departing southward to Bilene. Even if these armies dissolved and reformed *en marche,* the sheer geographical scale of Nguni movements dwarfed the Sanga polity and its shrines. Shortly after winning a succession struggle in 1862, Mzila brought the Nguni capital back to Sanga. He solidified a vast kingdom that stretched from Delagoa Bay to the Zambezi. Still, these rulers did not settle down. Mzila moved the capital repeatedly within the former Sanga area—passing near or through Gogoi—and his successor moved to Bilene in 1889, falling to the Portuguese six years later.[8] Virtual globetrotters for their time, the Nguni acted in seeming disregard of the mountains, rivers, and other terrain that had constrained more parochial polities. An itinerant, diasporic people, they were, in effect, Gogoi's first cosmopolitans.

Their kingdom was equally cosmopolitan. In place of the local, territorially based symbols, the Nguni substituted a national identity and state structure. They did so, first and foremost, by disregarding the *dziva* shrines. Rather than make offerings to Musikavanhu—as the *mwoyo* conquerors had done—the Gaza Nguni instituted a system of kingdomwide ceremonies (Rennie 1984:184; cf. Liesegang 1981:178). Farmers from the mouth of the Limpopo to the Zambezi were to seek rain in the same fashion. Language reinforced this uniformity: Nguni rulers, vassal Ndau chiefs, and any social aspirant spoke Zulu. As a further sign of allegiance and acculturation, many Ndau men followed the Nguni practice of piercing their ears—flying, in Chief Gogoi's words, the "flag of Gungunyana."[9] Ndau men also came to identify with the kingdom through service in the army. Age-based regiments carried out raids and performed labor in the royal kraals of the king's wives. Dispersed as they were in space, these duties detached unmarried men from their natal areas, making them national subjects. Finally, the capital itself moved across space. Although always called the Mandhlakazi, it relocated at least five times, passing through Gogoi between 1862 and 1872 (Liesegang 1986:50). In short, the Nguni instituted a portable politics, one that surmounted all preexisting geographical boundaries.

Portable politics, however, required violent forms of power over people.

Having rejected the rain shrines, Mzila forewent the legitimacy of an association with the land's ancestral spirits. Secular power and, in particular, military might would have to justify the state to its subjects. To this end, Mzila deployed Zulu followers, or *nduna*, throughout the kingdom. These regional governors supervised loyal chiefs with particular attention to their recruitment of young men for the army. The system mostly worked. Mafussi submitted to Mzila (Leverson 1893:516), and, even after seceding from Mafussi, Gogoi remained within the Nguni fold. Where chiefs did not submit, however, Mzila's rule turned from threats to outright violence. Unique among the chiefs in the Chimanimani-Sitatonga region, Ngorima resisted incorporation into the kingdom. From 1862 onward, the army repeatedly raided Ngorima's polity. They drove his people into the Chimanimani Mountains, eventually causing the chief himself to flee westward to Gutu (see chapter 2).

Raids generated captives, orphans, and destitute people in general. Once in Nguni hands, such people served a variety of purposes. Some men joined the army. Other men and women worked as slaves for the *nduna*, who could subsequently send them as tribute to the king. Ultimately, these clients, particularly the women, constituted a political currency. Gungunyana accumulated them as wives whose children he subsequently distributed far and wide as wives or workers for loyal notables. Thus, Nguni governance depended upon the subjugation and spatial mobility of rightless people. Such ambulatory enslavement, in turn, derived from the central Nguni institution of *kukhonza*. A Zulu term signifying submission, *kukhonza* encompassed a number of seemingly disparate forms of subservience. At the milder end, Mafussi and other chiefs performed *kukhonza* when they accepted overrule by Mzila and the *nduna*. Vassals thus constituted a group of *vakhonzwa* (singular, *mukhonzwa*), or people who had pledged their obedience. Individuals could also –*khonza*. Orphans and destitutes became slaves by offering their services to an *nduna* or a chief in exchange for protection and sustenance. In this fashion, *vakhonzwa* joined a lineage, as adopted children or other fictive kin, and worked its lands. They swelled the lineage-based enclosures known as *maguta* (singular, *guta*). According to an explorer's account from 1882, *maguta* "contained either 8, 16, 24 or 32 huts according to the wealth of the head man."[10] Clients could switch from one *guta* to another, but only after performing *kukhonza* to a new patriarch (Liengme 1901:124; cf. Junod 1962(1):433). Submission was pervasive.[11]

Personal submission was also multipurpose. As one of the few African firsthand accounts indicates, it linked various sectors of the Gaza Nguni economy. Born to the family of Chief Mapungwana (close to present-day Espungabera), Ngwaqazi remembered Mzila's conquest. Some time thereafter, one of Mzila's cattle died in a game pit dug—in contravention of Mzila's orders—in the vicinity. Male elders could not find the culprit, and so Ngwaqazi's father pledged his son to Mzila. His mother, recalled Ngwaqazi:

> thought I was going to be killed. I was led and handed over to Mzila for being insubordinate. . . . Mzila gave me to his Induna [*nduna*] Magijana and I grew up under him while herding cattle. Though I prided myself on being a great man's slave, I suffered untold hardships for the misdeeds of others. . . . After a long time, Vuso [my father] brought to Mzila a slave to replace me. I was then freed.[12]

In an oddly circular fashion, Mzila's nobility recouped their bovine loss with a rotating herd boy. The *kukhonza* act, thus, detached people from their kin and generated a floating population of clients, sometimes known as *varanda* (singular, *muranda*). Patriarchs then deployed and redeployed *varanda* throughout the empire in fulfillment of personal and corporate obligations.

Not surprisingly, this ambulatory servitude shaded into an outright trade in slaves. Before the establishment of the Gaza Nguni state, other Zulu offshoots as well as indigenous polities of the Indian Ocean coast had sold large numbers of people. In the 1820s and 1830s, French and Portuguese ships had exported workers from Inhambane and Lourenço Marques (Maputo) to plantations on Réunion, Mauritius, and São Tomé.[13] In 1836, however, Portugal outlawed slaving. This legal ban, combined with the much stronger interdiction of the British navy, forced the traffic in people inland. By the time of Mzila's rise to power in 1862, Transvaal Dutchmen were obtaining Nguni subjects from southern Mozambique.[14] When, in the 1870s and 1880s, Natal sugar estates and the Kimberly mines needed workers, the companies recruited men through the leaders of Nguni and subject polities. "By recruiting through powerful sovereigns," according to Patrick Harries, "employers were able to batten onto and feed off non-capitalist forms of labor exploitation."[15] In other words, rulers in the vicinity of Delagoa Bay sold the services of their clients to the plantation and mining economy of what became modern South Africa. To the north, in the Gaza Nguni heartland, migrant labor developed more slowly and involved less coercion. Nonetheless, the wages earned and recruitment fees fed an ambulatory economy. Through *kukhonza*, the slave trade, and voluntary migrant labor, Nguni polities made use of what Harries (1994:13) calls "mobility as a resource."

In the rest of the economy, as well, the Gaza Nguni invested almost exclusively in portable enterprises. Of course, the conquered Ndau continued to practice shifting cultivation and fixed, alluvial or swampland agriculture. They grew maize, groundnuts, peas, beans, sweet potatoes, pumpkins, melons, and cucumbers, among other cultivars (Roder 1965:54–57). Gungunyana showed little interest in these subsistence activities and—except when war and other labor-intensive projects demanded male labor—he allowed subject households to reproduce themselves. He intervened rather more in wildlife exports and in the movement of cattle. According to John Rennie (1973:137), Gungunyana "collected the great majority of animal skins as tax." Further, he created a royal monopoly on the export of ivory, backed with fines and other sanctions (Erskine 1878:27). Hunters, African as well as European, required the king's permission for any off-take. So strict was the royal control of wildlife that in 1872, the explorer St. Vincent Erskine received the following stern warning from an *nduna* right at the edge of the empire, in Chief Mafussi's area: "Here, white man, there are a few hippopotomi in the Lusiti; they are my cattle; you must not shoot them" (Erskine 1875:101). Of course, Mzila and the *nduna* monopolized real cattle as well. Erskine found a thousand head in Mzila's kraal (Erskine 1878:33), plundered from the subject populace and presumably herded by Ngwaqazi and other slaves. In much the same fashion as *vakhonzwa*, cattle circulated from the king to the *nduna* and back again, lubricating the imperial machinery of alliance and obedience. In short, this Gaza Nguni political economy moved on hooves of one species or another and sometimes on human feet.

To a large extent, this economy of hooves and feet functioned independent of a land base. Except for rubber, Nguni trade did not rely upon planted or wild crops. For their own subsistence, moreover, Nguni could levy tribute in the form of food from subjects wherever they went. People, rather than claims to cultivate fixed plots of land, constituted the long-term economic security of the kingdom. Two incidents affecting Mafussi and Gogoi illustrate this convergence of mobile capital and forced labor.[16] Sometime after the conquest, Mzila confronted the problem of tsetse fly and fatal bovine trypanosomiasis. His solution, according to the entomologist and amateur oral historian C. F. M. Swynnerton, entailed "an immense compulsory movement of the population toward the king." Mzila resettled people in a wide arc bounding the worst tsetse area and constituting a *cordon sanitaire* for the cattle. In the bounded space, he ordered people to eradicate tsetse-transmitting animals and to burn their habitat annually late in the dry season (Swynnerton 1921:332, 333). Swynnerton's map shows a portion of Gogoi's people's and of

Chief Macuiana's vacating the crook of the Muchenedzi River (ibid., map). They probably persisted in burning the bush until the second and final dislocation of 1889. At that time, Mzila's successor, Gungunyana, moved the capital to Bilene. He took his cattle, but also—in contrast with early short-distance relocations of the capital—Gungunyana forced thousands of Ndau to go with him. To a large extent, he depopulated Gogoi. *Vakhonzwa*, subjects, wives, cattle—the wealth went south. The land, of course, stayed behind, and, without workers, presumably lay largely fallow. Clearly, Gungunyana's itinerant empire did not place a high value on immovables.

The Gaza Nguni economy and polity thus stand out for their portable, untethered quality. Rulers invested in wealth on the hoof and "on foot." They moved that wealth when and where they desired for reasons that had little to do with the fertility of the soil. So different from the evictions that later characterized Rhodesia, the Gaza Nguni removed people from landscapes they did *not* want. In other words, Nguni politics drew people in as human resources rather than clear them away from some other, natural resources. As a cause or a consequence of this mobility, the Nguni did not invest in the landscape. They did not employ their abundant labor in a plantation system. Nor, on the symbolic level, did the Nguni aristocracy establish a relationship with the ancestral spirits of the land. The empire simply valorized land and territory less than other sources of wealth and power. Mzila's silence at a crucial moment attests to this fact. In 1881, E. H. Richards visited Mzila to seek permission to evangelize his kingdom. The king and his leading *nduna* insisted that missionaries bring gunpowder and their wives. Richard agreed to these (what were to him) minor conditions, gloating that "the king gave us permission to settle where we liked."[17] Mzila simply declined to allocate, manage, or partition the land. Instead, he and the Gaza Nguni denominated their power in heads—of cattle, of elephants, and of people. When it overthrew Gungunyana in 1895, Portugal looked back on this form of governance as a barbaric aberration. Yet, the colonial administration hardly improved upon it. Power over people remained the default condition of Gogoi and its environs.

PORTUGAL SEARCHES FOR A PERCH

Annibal da Silveira Machado, the first long-term Portuguese administrator, arrived in Mossurize in 1897 at what appeared to be a turning point. Portugal had defeated the Gaza Nguni state two years earlier. The earlier Nguni evacuation from Mossurize had left the entire system of wealth in people in ruins[18] (and also had removed the cattle for good[19]). At the same time, white settlers were streaming in from the Orange Free State to the Chimanimani-Chipinge upland of Rhodesia. Could these settlers not move into the land vacated by Gungunyana and his subjects? For a few years, this scenario of colonization and development seemed attainable, and Mossurize appeared useful for wider Portuguese interests. Indeed, colonization seemed to be the only development strategy that stood a chance of success. Portugal could commit no more than minimal resources to Mossurize and had resigned itself to a prolonged period of indirect, subsidiary colonialism. In 1891, it chartered a private concern, the Companhia de Moçambique (Mozambique Company), to administer and develop all of Manica and Sofala for fifty years.[20] A similar concession covered Niassa (under the Niassa Company). Neither company invested significantly in the productive capacity, infrastructure, white settlement, or industry of its hinterlands. Like Portugal itself, they lacked the financial resources to move beyond extractive "corporate feudalism" (Newitt 1981:79–85; cf. Vail 1976). Yet, Mossurize, which lay within sight of white settler highlands, offered the possibility of a foreign subsidy. Since whites tended to attract more whites, European estates—complete with profitable crops and regular employment—would surely spill across the border into Mossurize. In the event, only two white farmers stayed for any time in Mossurize. They were too poor to plant large areas and too disorganized to engage in cadastral politics. The fruits of their land-grabbing wilted on the vine. By 1906, the Companhia de Moçambique had fallen back upon extracting labor and natural resources, in short, upon the business as usual of power over people.

Ten years earlier, however, Machado had had good reason to anticipate fundamental change. Mossurize was, he admitted, economically underdeveloped. "In the whole of the *Circumpscrição* [district]," he reported, "there is not a single tree planted by" the natives.[21] (Of course, people had experienced enough forced resettlement in the previous thirty years to make them wary of investing in the land.) Nonetheless, the land, in at least part of Mossurize, *could be* improved. The south offered only dry, nearly barren soil, but the northern plain, at seven hundred meters and rising to the Sitatonga ridge, held fertile soil, with high rainfall and relatively good conditions for human health.[22] Surely, white settlers would come to this area. Once installed, they would just as surely perform their alchemy. Machado wrote:

> Since the high veld is destined for colonization and settlement, it is not appropriate to tie it to any native property rights, thereby facilitating for the con-

cessionaires the removal of the natives from their farms, taking them to concentrate themselves in "Reserves" intended for this purpose . . . [allowing us]
to obtain practical and useful results in the civilizing mission that falls to us.[23]

Thus, Machado put the north—including Gogoi and Mafussi—at the dis-
posal of any and all land-grabbers who wished to alienate it.

To his satisfaction, white settlers appeared to be moving toward Mossurize to take up this offer. Some had already arrived. Dunbar Moodie had
brought the first group of *Boers*—the Afrikaans term for "farmers"—to the
Chimanimani-Chipinge uplands in 1893, a full five years before Britain and
Portugal agreed upon the delineation of the border. During the intervening period of uncertainty, Moodie had named the area Melsetter and settled many of these and subsequent migrants far to the east. The joint delineation of the border placed several of these homesteads in Portuguese
territory, in the vicinity of what became Espungabera (Edwards 1991:160;
Olivier 1957:59, 139). Concurrent with this fortuitous colonization, the companhia sought deliberately to divert Rhodesia-bound migrants. Officials
steered the Martin trek of 1894 to Macequece (now Vila de Manica), but it
continued south to what is now the northern end of Chimanimani District,
Zimbabwe. Similarly, the Kruger-Bekker party trekked to Mossurize on
Machado's promise of a hundred farms for anyone who could settle all of
them. By 1895, however, the leaders of this expedition had also decided against
the proposition and squeezed themselves into the remaining vacant areas of
Melsetter (Olivier 1957:61–63, 83–85). Still, Machado was not deterred. In 1897,
he wrote from Espungabera, "as soon as the border is demarcated, the 80
Boer families now in Fort Victoria [Masvingo town] will definitely establish
themselves in Portuguese territory which will constitute an important beginning of colonization and which is to be by all possible means encouraged."[24]

Events proved this optimism to be misplaced. The eighty *Boers* never came
from Fort Victoria. Worse still, the delineation of the Anglo-Portuguese border prejudiced existing white settlement. Conditions in Portuguese East
Africa were not nearly as favorable as were those across the border. Although
the regulations of the Companhia de Moçambique demanded that settlers
occupy and use their farms, they in fact limited the property rights of settlers to concessions rather than permanent, transferable titles.[25] Only a handful of companies acquired concessions of up to six thousand hectares. By
1905, all had lost them because of a lack of investment, or as a result of
"beneficial occupation."[26] As for individual holdings, by 1902, all but three
farmers had emigrated, and only two of these appear to have actually

farmed.[27] One of these homesteaders—Edward Dierking, a German, of the Edenburg trek of 1894[28]—became Machado's cause célèbre, a symbol of northern Mossurize's potential and of the companhia's folly. Dierking's farm grew coffee, oranges, eucalyptus, cashews, and bananas—all under irrigation.[29] "The concessionaire," wrote Machado,

> was of all those living in farms on the border the only one who loyally accepted to live under the jurisdiction of the Companhia de Moçambique. Struggling with the difficulties of transport and lack of resources, without even possessing titles to his property in a form with which to obtain credit, he has succeeded in making his property into a model farm, in which are revealed the possibilities of the lands of Mafuci [Mafussi].[30]

Besides Dierking's 9.5–hectare estate, the only active farm lay in the extreme southern end of Gogoi's sphere of influence (Swynnerton 1921: map). In 1902, the Englishman W. Coward established a 5–hectare farm at the southern tip of the Sitatonga Mountains. He planted rubber trees, cotton, and fruit trees, struggling against disease and bankruptcy until his death in 1906.[31]

His passing ended Mossurize's first bid for large-scale white colonization. The exceptional, indefatigable Dierking may have lasted as long as he did (until his death in 1931) only because the location of his farm straddling the border allowed him to smuggle. In 1905, fearing the spread of bovine trypanosomiasis, the British South Africa Company sealed the border against all cattle.[32] The closure effectively cut off Mossurize from its only access to the sea. Despite nearly ten years of pleading from Machado, the companhia had not established even a wagon track—not to mention a road—to or through Mossurize. Agricultural products would have to travel by wagon from Espungabera to Melsetter and Umtali (now Mutare) and then, recross the border en route to markets in Macequece and Beira. In the absence of motorcars, the ban on cattle transit marooned Mossurize, not to mention dashing all hopes of a local stock-raising economy.[33] Faced with this developmental disaster, Machado's successor, Luciano Laure, reiterated his predecessor's arguments for investment in infrastructure:

> The valuable lands that the Companhia de Moçambique now possesses in this region are currently worth very little. However, when this area will be in easy and rapid communication with the seashore, those seeking concessions will not lack, and they will be disposed to pay a high price for them.[34]

Neither the Englishman nor the German altered the landscape or social relations to a degree that would give him a place in oral history. They did not destroy or plant forests; nor did they, in all probability, evict Africans. Indeed, so unremarkable was the turn-of-the-century white presence that an assemblage of Chief Gogoi and his elders in 1997 could only recollect stories of three Swiss miners, all of whom died or disappeared shortly upon arrival. Otherwise, they imagined whites from that time as mere passersby. Proceeding to or from Beira, they traversed Gogoi carried in hammocks called *machila*. As a form of forced labor, this porterage *did* affect the politics and society of Gogoi. Whites, like the Gaza Nguni, concentrated upon ambulatory enslavement and often denominated wealth in people.

In fact, Machado was making calculations of his human resources even while pursuing white colonization. Initially, the figures alarmed him: Gungunyana's forced march had depopulated much of the district. Fortunately, following Gungunyana's defeat, many started to return from Bilene.[35] Some of these returnees remained in Mossurize and replenished its stocks in people. Yet, the onerous Portuguese corvée induced others to pass through Mossurize and resettle in Rhodesia (see chapter 2), where residents of the native reserves owed only a hut tax.[36] "The prudent and practical administrative and colonial science of the English," complained Machado, "succeed[s] in augmenting the intensity of population through the influx of natives from our territory."[37] By "prudent administration," he meant, first and foremost, land alienation—hence, the compelling need to recruit white farmers. Machado also meant an efficient system of taxation, one that would compel Africans indirectly to work for Portuguese. Machado may have lacked sufficient personnel actually to collect and record money. The archival record does not permit a sure judgment, but even if he could have collected tax, residents of Mossurize would not have chosen to earn their tax on Portuguese plantations. South African and Rhodesian enterprises, subsidized by much wealthier states, simply paid much better (Lubkemann 2000:94). Thus, Machado, against his better judgment, was forced to tap labor resources directly. The policy soon defeated itself; between 1912 and 1917, the district lost more than 34 percent of its people (a drop in the total census from 26,677 to 17,535)—mostly men jumping the border (ibid., 80).

The policy also earned Machado and his colleagues international disrepute. Anglophone critics called Portuguese Africa "feudal," "inhumane," and "backward," suggesting that Rhodesia better represented Euro-American modernity. In fact, the respective administrators intended to settle both Mossurize and Melsetter with white farmers employing African workers.

Rhodesia's success in this venture focused political culture on struggles over land. Portugal's failure redoubled the preexisting tensions over the control of people. Later on, Portugal made a virtue of necessity. A 1954 colony-wide report made an implicit and favorable comparison with Britain: "We never . . . usurped [the natives'] legitimate rights of property; on the contrary, we have always defended them scrupulously."[38] Modernity, it seems, lay in the eye of the European beholder.

EXTRACTION

In 1906, as the vision of the white highlands was fading fast, Laure introduced a new form of economic development to northern Mossurize. He compelled people in Chief Gogoi's and other areas to tap indigenous rubber trees. In so doing, he shifted the companhia's agenda from colonization to the extraction of labor and raw natural resources. Rather than lure whites, his administration and subsequent ones concentrated on blacks— on their numbers, on retaining them, and on mobilizing them for rubber tapping and other compulsory employment. *Chibaro*—a term for forced labor used throughout Southern Africa[39]—became the order of the day. In one sense, Mossurize stagnated. It did not develop plantations and industry as Melsetter did during the colonial period. As Malyn Newitt (1980:78) writes, "corporate feudalism" neglected the means of production, such as land, and, instead, derived revenue by controlling the surplus production of Africans. Indeed, the companhia granted only one concession in northern Mossurize after 1906: to the American Board of Commissioners for Foreign Missions. Following the 1881 meeting mentioned above, this group founded a mission station at Mount Selinda, in what became Rhodesia. Later, they sought to evangelize in Portuguese East Africa. Although some of the missionaries wished to establish a plantation, they ultimately devoted their energies to religion rather than cadastral politics. Mossurize did not attract land-grabbers again until the 1960s. Nonetheless, the district certainly accumulated wealth. Through the institution of the colonial corvée, Gogoi and other chiefs refined their power over people. Growth, development, and so on took these familiar, nonterritorial forms. Portuguese colonialism, in other words, perpetuated and amplified ambulatory enslavement. Laure became Gungunyana redux.

Under the companhia, chiefs also fulfilled much the same function they had carried out under the Gaza Nguni. Independent of *chibaro*, they continued to accumulate clients. A German explorer who passed through Gogoi in 1931 recounted:

> From his clan, the chief usually chooses three or four 16–18–year-old youths whom he draws near for his personal services and to whom later as thanks gives girls of his family—daughters or sisters—as wives, without arranging bride-price. . . . One designates these youths, who in earlier times constituted a type of bodyguard, as *muranda*.[40]

In addition, for the Portuguese, chiefs recruited the desired quantity of human arms, or *braços*. Rubber tapping was among the milder forms of forced labor. Tappers worked close to home for relatively short stints. In 1906, Chief Gogoi sent twenty-five men to the nearby rubber groves in Mafussi. They and ninety-five men from other chieftaincies spent three months there, under the supervision of native police and foremen (*cipais* and *capitaes,* respectively).[41] Public works stipulated roughly equivalent terms. Chiefs along the route from Espungabera to Gogoi responded to sporadic corvées for constructing and repairing the road that still does not reliably link these two locales. Other corvées took male recruits further from home. Plantations in Macequece (Vila de Manica) and Vila Pery (Chimoio) required cotton pickers and other unskilled workers. In addition, fledgling industries of all kinds along what is now the Beira Corridor depended upon a readily available and cheap labor force. Contracts with firms, such as Zembe Plantation, the Cereal Growers Association, and Inhasato Sawmill, could last six months and paid very poorly.[42] Chiefs, thus, controlled the careers—and ultimately the social life—of their male subjects. In this sense, forced labor *made* the social position of Gogoi and his counterparts (cf. Allina-Pisano 2003:79).

Forced labor also made that position unstable. Laure's administration had to devote considerable energy to ensuring the labor supply and chiefs' effectiveness as labor suppliers. The companhia paid chiefs by the head. For rubber, chiefs received one escudo for every five paid to workers he recruited.[43] Regarding long-distance contracts, Laure followed Machado's formula—one thousand reis for each three-month contract and twice that for six-month contracts[44]—updating the sums as appropriate. The administration thus provided incentives for chiefs to do their official jobs, and the incentives were necessary. People constantly avoided forced labor in order to avail themselves of better opportunities in South Africa. Since Machado's time, administrators had complained of touts representing the mines who "diverted the current of workers."[45] In response, the companhia tried repeatedly to limit the activities of South African and Rhodesian recruiters— with only limited and intermittent success. The law simply could not compete against what had become a cultural necessity for African men. As the administrator wrote in 1934,

> The native of Mossurize, from boyhood, has only one ambition in life, which is to work for the Rand, and, as soon as he reaches the age of paying tax, he goes out on the path towards "John" [Johannesburg], as they say, given that he who does not work in the mines is not considered a man.[46]

Thus, roughly half the adult men left Mossurize for work elsewhere, some never to return.[47]

Rather than lower labor quotas to reflect this depopulation, the administration forced chiefs to tighten the screws on their remaining male subjects. The companhia established labor quotas as a percentage of the total number of able-bodied men counted in the census. When men included in the census later left—or turned out never to have been physically present in a chief's area—the administration did not reduce the total from which the percentage was calculated. Therefore, the remaining labor-eligible men had to absorb extra shares of *chibaro*. Not only the mines, but also the American Board mission contributed to this injustice. Its employees, who worked voluntarily with good wages and conditions, received an official exemption from forced labor. "Chief Gogoyo," reported the station head, "feels very much grieved because the coming of the Mission has not helped to relieve him from his difficulties in securing men for his labor quota. Instead it has increased his difficulties."[48] Ironically, good employers necessitated greater coercion on the part of Gogoi, other chiefs, and their headmen. In part to address this problem, the administration periodically applied a hut tax and excused taxpayers from some or all labor obligations. Yet, this modification did not change the underlying logic: those with voluntary jobs earned enough income to pay taxes and avoid corvées (if and when they appeared in Mozambique at all)—to the discomfit of the local leadership. Therefore, as one Mafussi-born man self-exiled in Vhimba recalled, "The chiefs made it hard."[49] Responsible for both cash taxes and *braços*, they exacted labor from the penniless. Further, they arrested those who refused to work and sent them to the administration for imprisonment and/or physical punishment. The *palmatória*, or whipping of the palms, awaited anyone who withheld his arms from the colonial labor machine. Or worse: in

1918, a missionary met Chief Gogoi en route to Espungabera with the wives of two absent, tax-defaulting men.[50] The administration, with Gogoi as its agent, was confiscating collateral.

Portuguese rule, therefore, generated within African society conflict over wealth in people. The administration's demand for *braços* turned chiefs' attention and the whole locus of chiefly rule toward *chibaro*. Smallholders set a new standard—or perhaps revived an old one—for judging chiefs. A good chief distributed the obligation to work evenly so that no one family contributed a disproportionate number of sons. By acting in such a fair manner, a chief, at least, could justify his involvement in forced labor (cf. Lubkemann 2000:171). After all, only a local ruler, as opposed to the administrator himself, would know the people well enough to avoid duplications. Yet, even under the best of circumstances, men had every reason to evade Portuguese contracts. The conditions of work in Vila Pery compared unfavorably with those in the Rand. During my fieldwork in Gogoi, men described the difference as "seeing lots of money with good hours and lunch" versus "working pure and simple."[51] Earnings were crucial. Whereas a man returning from Johannesburg ordinarily married—sometimes on a yearly basis—those finishing contracts within Mozambique simply could not afford bride-wealth.[52] The miner quickly accumulated wives and children, and for this reason mining became associated with manhood itself. The field laborer, by contrast, remained empty-handed. Thus forced labor and chiefly power over people ran directly counter to male patterns of accruing wealth in people. The latter tended to win out.

Defeat of this kind could devastate a chief's rule. If a large enough number of men emigrated, the administration intervened. In 1946, the administrator beat chiefs who did not deliver their labor quotas.[53] Despite these measures, the census of 1949 revealed that populations within four Mossurize chieftaincies had declined. Whether through their own mismanagement or excessive colonial demands, these chiefs had lost their labor base. Emigration from their polities had also reduced the projected tax revenue. Therefore, the hard-line administrator Edgar Júlio da Torre do Valle de Lacerda devised a radical solution. Lacerda transferred populations within underperforming chieftaincies to those with better records of success.[54] To do so, it was not necessary physically to move people. Lacerda simply redrew the lines of allegiance between headmen and chiefs. The favored chiefs gained headmen and, therefore, authority over the headmen's subjects. Thus, Lacerda's gerrymandering meted out rewards and punishments in the form of subject people.[55] By such measures of wealth in people, Gogoi fell short and probably incurred the appropriate penalty. In 1997, the current Chief Gogoi recalled a government-sanctioned shift of boundaries in the 1940s, during the reign of his father (see chapter 5). Since we were discussing land claims, he described the adjustment as territorial theft by Portuguese in league with his neighbor, Chief Macuiana. At the time, however, it is more likely that the administrator transferred subjects rather than territory. Lacerda's predecessor, José de Sousa Marques, ended his 1944 census campaign with the following harangue:

> Of all the chiefdoms included in the census, the one where I encountered the greatest deficiencies, worst roads and most difficulty in the execution of the work was in Gogoi, due to the scant prestige that that chief arouses among the populace. In addition to having no prestige whatsoever, he is sloppy, irresponsible, and does not know the people who live in his chiefdom.... Another year has elapsed without being able to carry out a perfect census in the whole area of the *Circunscrição* [district], a job that I regard as of the utmost urgency for a better administration.[56]

According to this critique, Gogoi's incompetence threatened Portuguese interests at numerous levels: within his chiefdom, he did not muster his subjects to build roads; without roads, census-takers could not gain access to the population; without a complete census, the administration could not set an appropriately high quota for labor recruitment and, in a more abstract sense, could not itself become competent. Presumably, as well, a chief lacking prestige sufficient to open roads nearby could hardly mobilize a high number of people for forced labor outside his chiefdom. In response to these failings, de Sousa Marques or Lacerda reallocated some of Gogoi's people. The transfer of land was only incidental. Within the logic of power, territory held importance only as a substrate for resources of far greater significance; or as the son of Gogoi explained in 1997, "A chief rules people. The country is people."[57] The Portuguese rulers of Mossurize clearly felt the same way.

Indeed, while administrators made a fetish out of counting people, they hardly investigated the land.[58] Surveying was the territorial equivalent to census taking. A survey documented the extent of land and location of natural resources and permitted the administration to register nonoverlapping claims. Surveys made the cadastre possible. When American Board missionaries gained the rights to open a mission station at Gogoi in 1916, they sought repeatedly to survey their five hundred hectares.[59] Indeed, the Portuguese concession law required them to do so, and the administration hoped that the farmer-missionaries would replicate the plantations of their Mount Selinda Mission just across the Rhodesian border.[60] Yet, neither the companhia nor the overarching Colony of Mozambique made surveyors available to Mossurize. It appears that the Gogoi Mission Station eventually received a waiver to allow it to use a Rhodesian- rather than a Portuguese-certified surveyor.[61] By that time, however, missionaries had lost their enthusiasm to invest in and transform the landscape. To the administration's chagrin, the mission concentrated on evangelism, education, and on complaining about forced labor. Then, in 1934, official restrictions as well as financial difficulties forced the mission station virtually to close down.[62] Thenceforth, whites crossed the border from Rhodesia only to hunt,[63] and the cadastral offices virtually forgot Mossurize.[64] Detailed maps of the district (at a 1:50,000 scale) did not emerge until the aerial photography flights of 1965.[65]

Long before that, the administration had decided to make the best of a bad situation vis-à-vis white settlers. Shortly before or shortly after the expiration of the companhia's lease in 1941, the colony gazetted most of northern Mossurize as a native reserve.[66] Rather unnecessarily, this designation barred the area from land alienation. Presumably, Portuguese immigrants would thenceforth concentrate in more promising areas. In 1947, the colonial government refined this system. It designated Mossurize as a "closed labor reserve" from which only small-scale settler farmers could draw labor (das Neves 1998:115–16). Thus protected from competition, Portuguese farming mushroomed in Sussundenga and Manica districts, areas just north of Mossurize and well served by the Beira corridor and subsidiary roads. In the 1950s and 1960s, these areas achieved what Laure had imagined for Mossurize. They became Mozambique's white highlands of plantation agriculture and silviculture, complete with land alienation and African resistance.[67] Gogoi and neighboring chieftaincies were spared this form of dispossession just as they escaped land-grabbing by whites. Yet, if they did not have to relinquish land, they still had to contribute their sweat to the white highlands. As that sector expanded, Mossurize became one of the premier reserves of forced labor (das Neves 1998:136–37). Thus, it provided the raw human material with which Portuguese capitalized upon land elsewhere.[68]

The administration, nonetheless, did make some feeble efforts to derive revenue from agriculture in Mossurize. In 1938, the Companhia de Moçambique granted a cotton monopsony for Gogoi and its environs to the Companhia Nacional Algodeira (CNA) (Isaacman 1996:44–45). The arrangement continued under the colonial government until the liberal reforms (and de jure abolition of forced labor) of 1961. Under this corporate partnership, the administrator set cotton production quotas on a per-household basis. In much of the country, the administration further assisted by meting out violent punishment to underproducers. However, CNA preferred the carrot to the stick. It exempted successful producers from *chibaro* (Isaacman 1996:129; cf. Vail and White 1980:321). In this fashion, CNA sought to redeploy wealth in people from the white highlands to smallholders' own fields, breaking the spirit if not the law of the closed labor reserve. It probably got away with this ambiguous form of recruitment because it set cotton quotas in hectares rather than in workdays or output. The production standard of one hectare per household (das Neves 1998:138) constituted Mossurize's first form of land-use planning. The plan, however, was fundamentally flawed. In order to cultivate this labor-intensive cotton, men required wives and children, and the availability of these field hands depended on bride-wealth earned in the Rand. Thus, (female) cotton cultivation backfired: it contributed indirectly to (male) clandestine emigration and the general labor crisis.[69] In 1946, Chief Gogoi himself complained that he could not locate sufficient personnel to grow cash crops in his own fields. The labor—and it is unclear whether Gogoi was referring to relatives or all subjects—had gone south.[70] The authorities of all kinds were right back where they had started.

This kind of gravitation toward politics of labor typified Mossurize's mid-century development. Every effort to develop or profit from the land base eventually veered off into issues of forced and free labor. When white settlement collapsed early in the century, northern Mossurize became a source for rubber, tapped by forced labor. When whites settled nearby, Mossurize contributed its most desired resource, people. Finally, land-use planning resulted in consequences that were unintended but could have been predicted: rather than bring land into production, the cotton system helped drain Mossurize and the white highlands of labor. Efforts to invest in the land degenerated into a calculus of wealth in people. By this measure, moreover, the Portuguese and Chief Gogoi constantly came up short. People, as on-foot assets, simply took to their feet and went to "John." Mobility was, thus, simultaneously the key to success and the downfall of the entire colonial-traditional political economy.

LAST-DITCH COLONIZATION AND THE RETURN OF WAR

Portugal had one last chance to transform northern Mossurize into a white highland. This time silviculture, rather than agriculture, offered the possibility of a breakthrough. The existing white highlands already contained a number of tree plantations, notably at Penhalonga. Could investors not expand these tree farms to the north and south, along the mountainous belt? They could, indeed, if—as was hoped for in the 1890s—they copied Rhodesia's latest experience of land-grabbing (cf. Pinto 1961:35). Companies would merely have to accomplish in Gogoi what Border Timbers, Limited, having bought the pioneer farms, did to Chief Ngorima's people in the 1950s: push the people elsewhere, plant exotic species, and fight arson (see chapter 2). In accordance with this vision, the timber industry entered Mossurize in 1963. Possibly as many as three companies operated in the northern part of the district.[71] Of those, the first and most important was Floresta e Serração do Muda (FSM). In 1963, FSM gained a concession to 25,100 hectares, including almost all of Gogoi's chieftaincy. Shortly thereafter, the company installed a heavy sawmill along the Muchenedzi River.[72] This investment already departed from a pattern common outside the white highlands: using lightweight, mobile sawmills. Had it continued in this vein, FSM would have pursued scientific forestry: it would have planted eucalyptus and pine and necessarily evicted a large number of Gogoi's people.

Yet, as before, the impracticalities of Mossurize forestalled cadastral struggles before they had even begun. Trucks could cross the Rusitu River only by ferry and only at their peril when the water was high. Across the Buzi River, FSM itself helped install a usable bridge, thus connecting Gogoi and Espungabera. In addition to these transport problems, FSM encountered the usual labor shortage. "The autochthons of Mossurize," recalled the company's directors, "only knew and accepted Rhodesian currency. In Rhodesia, they found work by crossing the border without documents."[73] Furthermore, FSM could not compel people to work. The closed recruitment zone would have prevented them from doing so, but, more generally, the formal abolition in 1961 had marginalized (though not eradicated) *chibaro* everywhere in Mozambique (Vail and White 1980:382ff). The company was obliged to bring sawmill workers from Gorongoza. The additional costs of shipping field crews—necessary for pine or eucalyptus cultivation—would probably have reached prohibitively high levels. Therefore, FSM did the only sensible thing; it concentrated on high-value (per truckload and per worker hour) indigenous species. In line with this extensive, rather than intensive, land use,[74] FSM requested the expansion of its concession to the east, west, and south, bringing the total area to forty-seven thousand hectares.[75] The company grew as an extractor, not as a planter, of trees. Although it damaged some forests considered to be sacred (see chapter 5), selective cutting evicted none of Gogoi's people. Indeed, in the mid-1990s, such people counted themselves fortunate; whereas the timber industry had dispossessed people across the border to a massive degree, Gogoi people "farmed where they wanted to."[76]

Portuguese rule in Gogoi ended and African rule began on this high note. By 1975, forced labor had virtually disappeared. The cessation of corvées deprived the private sector of the best solution it had known to labor shortages. At least in Mossurize, then, whites' development of natural resources came to a standstill. Hence, no outsiders alienated land, and smallholders were able to keep their fields. Also to their good fortune, residents of Mossurize were not affected by the war of liberation. The fighting stayed far to the north. Indeed, residents of Gogoi were probably not affected directly by the war and independence until, in 1979, Frelimo (the Front for the Liberation of Mozambique) nationalized all rural land (Sachs and Welch 1990:27–45). With that, the timber firms and the threat of land alienation evaporated. Frelimo did engage in some land-use planning, in the late 1970s, creating "communal villages," or *aldeias*. Yet, Gogoi's people mostly evaded them. More important, Frelimo also did away with the last vestiges of forced labor. For the first time since 1862, no external power was demanding *braços* from Gogoi. Nor were any white settlers or black technocrats taking land. It seemed as if Gogoi could follow a third path—unprecedented in the written history of the region—between ambulatory enslavement and land alienation.

War thwarted that intriguing possibility and returned Gogoi to more familiar politics. In 1979, with heavy Rhodesian support, Renamo (the Mozambican National Resistance) opened a guerrilla campaign against Frelimo (Flower 1987; Minter 1994:33). Along the border, Rhodesia acted directly as well. In 1979, its air force bombed all the bridges between Espungabera and Gogoi, effectively undoing the fruit of eight decades of administrators' efforts. As war unfolded, Frelimo established a military base at the site of the abandoned FSM sawmill. It also redesigned the communal villages as internment camps to separate Renamo from the populace (cf. Borges Coelho 1993, 1998). Gogoi people remember this forced confinement as the worst sin of Frelimo. Yet, they did not interpret their relocation away from their fields as a theft of land. Rather, the oral history I collected in 1997 dwelled on issues related to the homestead. One man from Mafussi summed up Frelimo's principle as follows: "Your wife is mine."[77] The politics of wealth in people were back.

The corvée also returned with a vengeance. Both parties to the war instituted forced porterage, called *chikoroka,* but they did so in different ways. Frelimo, which had declared chiefs to be "obscurantist," recruited laborers directly from the population, rather than via chiefs. In line with much of socialist thinking on this issue, decrees shortly after independence had deprived chiefs of their official status and salaries. At the same time, because no other means of administration was feasible, rural civil servants continued many of the practices of indirect rule.[78] The army, however, did not face such constraints. While it could have recruited porters and other laborers through chiefs, it disposed of means of force sufficient to compel people to work immediately. The sawmill base simply press-ganged men on sight. As one of Gogoi's headmen recalled, soldiers were particularly likely to find laborers in the *aldeias.*[79] Villagization really *was* an indirect means of concentrating and exploiting wealth in people. This method of recruitment also struck Gogoi residents as unfair. Only chiefs and headmen could distribute the demands for porters equally among households. Direct recruitment, people informed me, was not *pamutemo,* or according to law and custom. To its discredit, Frelimo had broken with the (invented) tradition of Portuguese rule.

When Renamo captured the sawmill base in 1987, it restored a sense of order. Local commanders recognized chiefs and headmen. They refrained from committing massacres and mutilating large numbers of people, activities typical of Renamo occupation elsewhere.[80] To use Robert Gersony's (1988) terms, Gogoi was a "tax area" rather than a "control" or "destruction area."[81] Renamo, then, instituted a regime of indirect rule concentrated on the recruitment of *chikoroka* and provision of food for the base. People compared this governance favorably with the one that had come immediately before: Renamo acted *pamutemo.* Nonetheless, Gogoi residents experienced tremendous hardship under Renamo. The rebels' complete lack of vehicles placed heavy demands on porters. They often carried loads of weapons two hundred kilometers to the regional base in Gorongoza. As regards food, Renamo's demands cut deep into household supplies. Furthermore, the destruction of the roads—and mining by both sides—obliterated the commercial network for food. Along with these constraints on home use and purchase, the drought of 1991–92 brought basic livelihood into question. As chapter 3 details, starving people and orphans resorted to time-hallowed means of seeking sustenance. They pledged themselves as clients; they performed the *kukhonza* act of self-enslavement. Renamo brought Gogoi and his people full-circle, back to Nguni-style politics of personal subjugation. In terms of his impact on Gogoi, Afonso Dhlakama, the enigmatic leader of Renamo, was Gungunyana redux.

Did time—for better or worse—somehow forget the Mozambican hinterland? In fact, Gogoi and other remote areas have maintained a surprising degree of continuity over the past hundred-odd years: until the cease-fire of 1992, the substance of politics remained the collection and distribution of unfree labor, that is, ambulatory enslavement. From war, to peace, to war again and from Nguni, to Portuguese, to Renamo rule, chiefs and headmen have managed this system of wealth in people. Of course, in other ways, Gogoi *has* changed. Certainly, the imposition of an international border brought new possibilities and constraints to the region, as part 2 will discuss. Furthermore, people unaffected by the border have experienced evolutions and ruptures in commerce, ideology, education, the rights of women, and other fields too numerous to detail.

Yet, even if *time* did not forget Gogoi, white settlers did. Pioneer homesteaders once ventured into the district but withdrew. Portuguese farmers stayed to the north. The major currents of land alienation, thus, left an eddy around Gogoi and its neighbors. Africans lost control of their labor, but, to their great fortune, they stayed on the land. They also stayed in place politically, treading water while nearby Vhimba rode the cadastral tide. As the next chapter explains, land-grabbing and African resistance to it revolutionized power in Vhimba. Its chief, headmen, and commoners emerged from a system of wealth in people to one of wealth in land, territorial struggle, and the cadastre. Africans lost most of the land. Colonization succeeded in Vhimba whereas it failed in Gogoi, and such failure can be sweet.

2

FROM CLIENTSHIP
TO LAND-GRABBING
IN VHIMBA, ZIMBABWE,
1893–1990

CADASTRAL POLITICS ARE NOT INTRINSIC TO VHIMBA. PEOPLE *MADE* Vhimba into the hornet's nest of turf battles that it is today. As much as events and processes maintained forced labor in Gogoi, Mozambique, a quite different historical sequence institutionalized cadastral politics on the northern bank of the Rusitu River. This chapter recounts that transformation and distinguishes it from the continuity of ambulatory enslavement in Gogoi in the same period.

Vhimba residents identify three transformations in landholding that progressively dispossessed them. The first began with the arrival of white settlers a few years before uprisings convulsed much of Mashonaland and Matabeleland. In 1892–93, Dunbar Moodie and four other families trekked from the Orange Free State. Eight additional, larger treks followed in quick succession (Olivier 1957:146, 156–57), and the administration of the British South Africa Company formalized their land-grabbing with a cadastre, or property map, and compensatory native reserves.[1] Complete though it was, the seizure of the Chimanimani upland did not directly displace African smallholders. Those able to tolerate labor tenancy continued farming the unused parts of the undercapitalized pioneer estates. It was not until the 1950s that a second transformation destroyed smallholding on the plateau. After buying the failing farms, the Border Timbers corporation and the government Forestry Department planted the plateau with pine, eucalyptus, and wattle (a commercial acacia species). Afforestation, then, finally forced the remaining smallholders into the reserve. Conservation instigated the third and final wave of land alienation. In 1965, the Department of National Parks gazetted almost half of the Ngorima reserve as an extension of Chimanimani National Park. The annexation and delayed efforts to implement it drove another batch of smallholders into Vhimba. These seizures of land and the eviction of inhabitants put a premium on territorial control.

In addition to the three phases of land-grabbing, other processes promoted the territorialization of Vhimba in less direct ways. Native commissioners and missionaries outlawed forms of marriage connected to male and female clientage. With the spread of cash for bride-wealth, chiefs and other lineage heads became increasingly unable to use marriage as a means of accumulating wealth in people. Similarly, destitute people ceased pledging themselves to affluent families as the Rhodesian government instituted permanent mechanisms to alleviate famine. These seemingly disconnected policies made Vhimba's leadership poor in people and, thereby, encouraged it to value territory. A second set of socioeconomic developments produced more mixed results. British administration legalized and implemented a variety of forms of labor, ranging from forced to free and involving chiefs in different degrees. *Chibaro*, as it was known, could have reinforced chiefs' control over and wealth in people, as it had so decisively in Mozambique. Yet, each Rhodesian variant of *chibaro* fell short of its Portuguese equivalent. These distinctive policies and practices reflected Portugal's and Britain's vastly unequal ability to collect information about the landscape and to administer it and its people. For example, no map of property existed for Gogoi and its environs until the 1960s. Across the Rusitu, however, Rhodesian settlers, as discussed, created a cadastre in 1894, a year after their arrival. This chapter tallies up the changes in landownership, labor, and marriage in Vhimba and in Chief Ngorima's area and traces how, under these influences, the focus of local politics gradually shifted from accumulating clients to contesting territory, turf, and hectares.

1892: THE BALANCE OF FORCES

On the eve of white colonization, the Ngorima chieftaincy was ripe for such a transition. The Gaza Nguni had drastically weakened the Ngorima chieftancy. Kufakweni Ngorima fought Mzila and lost. In the 1870s, he fled to Gutu and died in exile. Those of his people who remained behind sought refuge from the frequent raids in the caves and ravines of the Chimanimani range. It is unclear whether any leader arose in Kufakweni's absence. Keith-Falconer's expedition of 1890 found that, "About fifteen months ago the paramount chief was raided by Gungunyana and the whole of his tribe broken up and ruined . . . and there is now no headman of any importance from the Lusiti to Shimanimani [from the Rusitu River to the Chimanimani Mountains]."[2] In consequence, "the natives were evidently really really very poor."[3] Other accounts omit this attacked (and apparently murdered) chief and describe the return of Kufakweni's son, Mushanembeu, in or around 1890, as the restoration of long-absent leadership.[4] Whatever the political chronology, Ngorima's people remained poor. In 1892, J. J. Leverson noted: "More than three or four huts are seldom met with together, and these are of the most wretched description. Very little is obtainable in the way of food supplies. The natives have no cattle and appear to live in dread of a raid by Gungunyane" (Leverson 1893:515). In 1899, Ngorima's area still compared unfavorably with Mafussi's, in Portuguese East Africa. Leaving his base at Ngorima's, a pioneer missionary noted Mafussi's "very fat lands, fine crops, good large huts and altogether . . . better people than [at] our present place."[5]

Ngorima's was, in fact, a one-sided form of poverty. It was poverty in people. The land, in this high-rainfall and sparsely populated area, could have fed the people. In 1897, Melsetter as a whole grew maize, sorghum, millet, pumpkins, watermelons, cucumbers, manioc, bananas, and four kinds of beans—mostly under shifting, or slash-and-burn, agriculture.[6] Moreover, as a 1914 report noted, "Crops have never been known to fail in this [the Rusitu] valley during the last 20 years."[7] What Mushanembeu Ngorima and his people lacked were hands for hoeing. (Agriculture had never depended upon cattle in an area where soil was soft enough for hand tilling.) If, as Leverson wrote, homesteads seldom exceeded three or four huts, then there were few of the patriarchal *maguta*, village-like enclosures packed with wives, children, and clients (see chapter 1). Clients would have been few in number, in part because Ngorima's polity had little to attract them. Poor and plundered, the area would have propelled destitute people outward rather than attracting them inward. Poverty in people thus reproduced itself. It also created a political vacuum. The small size of households indicated that lineage heads had not nucleated people beneath them. As long as leadership was defined as control over people, rather than territory, authority simply lacked the appropriate raw materials. At the same time, colonial politics altered the fundamental basis of leadership for Ngorima. By taking most of the African-farmed land, Rhodesians gave to land a political meaning previously unknown.

In May 1892, a group of Dutch- and English-speaking whites left the Orange Free State to settle a promised land. This colonization of the Chimanimani-Chipinge area in the 1890s is deservedly famous. For decades, the nine treks featured prominently in settler, triumphalist historiography (e.g., Burrows 1954; Olivier 1957). Historical scholarship now cites them as among the worst examples of colonial injustice in Southern Rhodesia (Moyana 1984; Palmer 1977). To recount the main events very briefly, the geopolitics of the 1890s thrust Gazaland suddenly into the imperialist limelight. In 1891, as the European scramble for Africa drew to a close, Britain and Portugal signed a treaty partitioning the Gaza Nguni kingdom of Gungunyana. That agreement, however, did not specify the precise line of partition, so that by the end of 1891, a mission of the British South Africa Company had undertaken to negotiate a separate understanding with Gungunyana himself. Dennis Doyle, accompanied by L. S. Jameson (director of the British South Africa Company for Mashonaland) and Dunbar Moodie, extracted rights to the northern parts of Gazaland from its king. This agreement, which Portugal denounced and the British Foreign Office recognized only in part, became the basis for a wider British interest in the settlement of the Chimanimani-Chipinge region (Warhurst 1962:106). Scoffing at the Portuguese, Moodie vowed, "I will make possession nine points of the law and be damned!" (Burrows 1954:121). By late 1895, he and his fellow immigrants from the Orange Free State and adjoining areas had claimed virtually all of the Chimanimani-Chipinge highlands. As Moodie was supposed to have later reflected, "Once you are in possession of the African forests, they are yours . . . and the Melsetter colonists are now in possession of this territory" (Olivier 1957:139).

TAKING OWNERSHIP OF THE LAND

If occupation was nine points of the law, then maps were the tenth point. Cadastral thinking, in fact, underwrote all of Moodie's bluster over grabbing land. Dunbar Moodie and his uncle, Thomas Moodie, who led the first trek, grew up in an atmosphere of mapmaking. Among Dunbar's three paternal uncles, one had become surveyor general of the Transvaal Republic and another trained in Europe and then surveyed the Transvaal–Delagoa Bay rail line (Burrows 1954:109). Moodie's grandfather, the father of Thomas Moodie, had settled the Orange Free State under the Cape Dutch system of land tenure. Free State farmers were entitled to three thousand morgen (approximately twenty-five hundred hectares), calculated as a square each side of which a horse could ride in one hour (Christopher 1971:3; 1974:213). This format permitted occupation prior to survey—at the cost of fast horses and wild errors of measurement. Where land was plentiful and frontiers expanding, neighbors could move elsewhere rather than quarrel (W. Hancock 1958:334). In areas of higher population density, surveying, of course, could settle disputes, but such bureaucracy ran against the grain of self-sufficient trekking. Given his background, however, Moodie was probably disposed toward surveying, and he could not have been unaware of the possibility for conflict between farms that were cheek by jowl smack against the Portuguese border.

In the event, Jameson anticipated the need for cadastral surveying. He hired a surveyor general who empowered Moodie to "show beacons" to incoming trekkers.[8] The "allotment of farms," Jameson wrote to Moodie in early 1892, would proceed on the basis of three thousand morgen per head of household (increased from the company's standard of fifteen hundred morgen so as to compensate for the risks of trekking to remote Melsetter) bounded by four-feet-high beacons. A representative of the British South Africa Company would eventually inspect the beacons and enter the farm into the company's land register in Salisbury. Eventually, the owner would pay twenty-six pounds, one shilling, for "surveying and framing of diagram."[9] These procedures created a proper, durable cadastre (map 2.1).[10] Drawn in Moodie's hand, the property map of 1894 survives in its essential form today. The estates have new owners, of course, but their nearly quadrilinear boundaries are unchanged. Even the quaint names pioneers gave them—Clearwater, Waterfall, Groenvleis—appear on all 1:250,000– and 1:50,000–scale government maps today.[11] The cadastral discipline, then, marked the landscape and helped keep the legal rights to it in white hands. As Surveyor General R. W. Sleigh later reflected, without a hint of irony, "Surveyors and their discipline . . . have served Rhodesia well in the past and continue to do so with notable success as an important pillar in the creation of prosperity for all" (Sleigh 1976:4).

In fact, surveys and beacons permitted what the historian Robin Palmer calls a state of "exploitation pure and simple" (1971:51). As a cost-saving measure, London had ceded control of the colonial frontier to a motley but large crew of profiteers, speculators, gold diggers, and mercenaries. During this lapse in governmental oversight, South Africans and other whites had grabbed an amount of land wholly out of proportion with the mainstream of British colonial endeavor. Beginning in 1894, therefore, the newly created Native Department tried to put brakes on Jameson's uncontrolled demarcation of white land. Now, through the office of an imperial resident commissioner sent to Salisbury (over Rhodes's objections) in 1894, administrators sought to impose proper conditions for long-term development

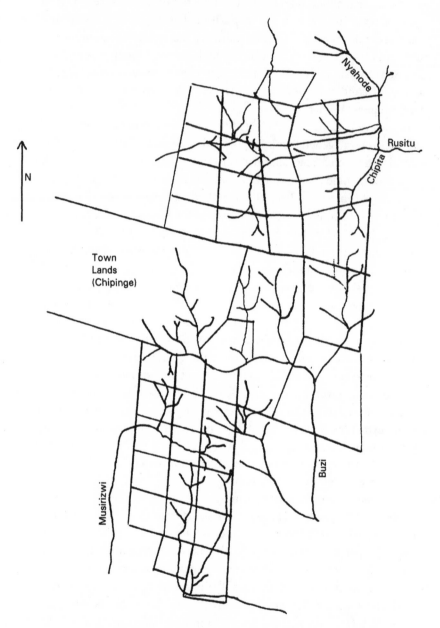

MAP 2.1. "Map showing approximate position of farms taken up in Melsetter, Gazaland," 26 January 1894. Adapted from NAZ file L 2/2/95/25

and for the protection and eventual "civilization" of the natives. At the same time, the settlers were realizing that Rhodesia did not contain a "second Rand" of gold, the motivating factor for much of the immigration in areas less well suited for agriculture than Melsetter. Thus, casting about for means of capital accumulation besides mining, settlers opposed any limits to the alienation of land. Debate stretched on for two decades, London flexed its muscles, but the settlers won important concessions. There is no need to summarize these controversies so admirably described elsewhere (Palmer 1977). What they demonstrate is that colonialism was no bureaucratic monolith. It had many faces in various places and at various times.

In Melsetter, colonial and postcolonial politics have been a rearguard action against Moodie's legacy of rapid alienation and occupation. So alarmed was Native Commissioner J. D. Hulley by the land seizures that he began the process of demarcating native reserves in 1895–96, even before the Native Department instructed him to do so. Moodie's allocation, of course, had left the native commissioner with very little room for maneuver. Settlers had passed over the western approaches to the upland. They had left the dry, tsetse-infested Save Valley to Africans—a phenomenon repeated for the low veld around the Zambezi and Limpopo rivers. The Save lowlands thus became four reserves all bearing the names of pertinent chiefs: Mutema, Musikavanhu, Muwushu, and Mutambara. To the east, settlers had also stayed out of the low veld, that is, the Rusitu and Haroni river valleys. Like the others, these valleys harbored tsetse-born bovine trypanosomiasis.[12] Yet, their high rainfall probably would have compensated for the risk of cattle disease, which was relatively small for these pioneers, who owned few cattle anyway.[13] In all likelihood, uncertainty regarding the Portuguese border prompted Moodie's uncharacteristic restraint. The Portuguese had not recognized J. J. Leverson's British-backed delimitation of the border in 1892 (Leverson 1893). The company suggested to Moodie, "you will be safe in treating the whole of the High Veldt as British South African territory, and the [sic] Mozambique the Low Veldt."[14] In this fashion, three anomalous reserves—anomalous because they were mostly fertile—entered the gazette: Ingorima North (map 2.2), Ingorima South, and Mafusi. Nine thousand morgen (7,650 hectares) in total, these reserves amounted to three white farms for an estimated African population of 1,348.[15]

Demarcation, however, continued in numerous iterations. Endowed with a considerable ability to map, the administration surveyed and resurveyed the Rusitu Valley into the 1920s and has never entirely stopped.[16] Borders gelled only slowly, provoking what Donald Moore (1995:245–47) terms a gen-

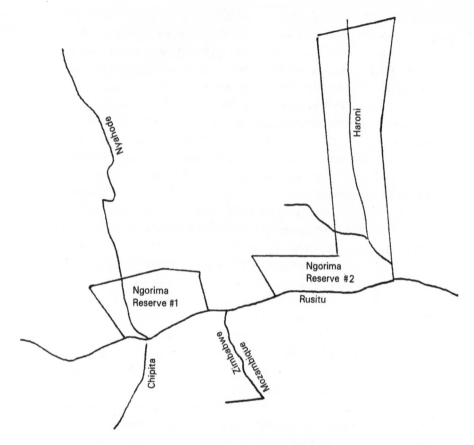

MAP 2.2. Ngorima native reserves.
Adapted from NAZ file N 3/24/20, approx. 1914

eral Rhodesian feeling of "cartographic anxiety." With regard to the
Ngorima Reserve, two particular anomalies gave rise to this uncertainty. First,
in 1897, the South African General Mission applied for a 500–morgen property close to Chief Ngorima's home inside Ngorima South Reserve. Learning
of the application only after the civil commissioner had assented, L. C.
Meredith tried to revoke the decision. He also attempted to locate the mission elsewhere. In the event, Meredith succeeded in reducing its size dra-
matically, from 500 morgen (425 hectares) to 6 acres (2.5 hectares).[17] Second,
and more serious, the Glencoe farm divided Ngorima's area into northern
and southern portions (#2 and #1, respectively).[18] The administration found
that bisection to be inconvenient and, since the owner had neither occu-

pied nor cultivated the valley portion, designated it a Native Purchase Area in 1925 (Palmer 1977:263).[19] This land tenure category permitted freehold by Africans, but it appears that none bought parcels in the area.[20] Thus, by the 1920s, the native territorial endowment was fixed: a long, narrow, fertile but mostly quite steep strip of land snaking along the Mozambican border. The boundaries would not change again until 1965, when the Chimanimani National Park halved the reserve territory (discussed below). Even before this final wave of alienation, white farm owners had grabbed almost half the district and by far the more fertile portion (Palmer 1977:263).

Having settled the boundaries of the reserves, the native commissioner turned to the subject of their governance. Again, he confronted territorial issues. In principle, each reserve corresponded to a tribal "division," headed by a "paramount chief." This "ethnic-spatial fix," to borrow another phrase from Moore (1995), did not obtain in any of the three reserves in the Rusitu Valley. Chief Ngorima did not live inside Ngorima North. As the reserve was said to be nearly uninhabited, his absence was not unduly problematic. As mentioned above, he resided in Ngorima South, but only until 1907. At that point, he decided to move north to the area of the plateau where his father had lived before fleeing from the Gaza Nguni (Young 1970:58). The owner of the Tilbury farm accommodated Ngorima (presumably exempting him from labor obligations) until afforestation necessitated his great grandson's return to the reserve in 1956. The third reserve, Mafussi, presented the biggest obstacle to "fixing" territory and chiefs. Chief Mafussi lived across the international border. The native commissioner hoped, however, that the burdens of Portuguese rule—constantly compared unfavorably to British administration—would drive his people into Rhodesia.[21] Some did immigrate, but, despite Meredith's inducement, Chief Mafussi himself stayed put;[22] so, the administration had to invent a chieftainship for the Mafussi Reserve. In a familiar strategy of tinkering with tradition, Meredith elevated to the rank of chief one of Mafussi's headmen, Ndima, who already resided in the desired location.[23] In effect, Meredith succeeded in giving each reserve a chief and, more important for the sake of cadastral politics, giving each chief a set of geographical boundaries.

Were African politics, then, suddenly cadastral? Palmer interprets Africans' verbal opposition to colonization as land based. "Dunbar Moodie," he writes, "was nicknamed *Dabuyazizwe*, the one who divides the land" (Palmer 1977:41).[24] Moodie certainly did divide the land, but the Nguni phrase refers to the "nation" (*izwe*), an ambiguous entity of people as much as land. The evidence seems to indicate that that nation did not become explicitly territorial or act on territorial imperatives in this period. For a variety of reasons, Melsetter's smallholders refrained from contesting white demarcation and settlement. They did not take part in the 1896–97 "First *Chimurenga*" revolt in which Africans killed whites and interrupted communication in much of Mashonaland and Matabeleland. Gaza Nguni occupation had separated Melsetter chieftaincies from neighboring polities west of the Save River,[25] while Gungunyana's evacuation had undercut their authority. Worse still, in Ngorima, Nguni raids had shattered the polity beyond any ability to coordinate a response to the whites.[26] As an exception, residents of Mutambara Reserve did steal white-owned cattle. Yet, the white response was much more cadastral than the cattle rustling itself: the North Melsetter Farmers Association resolved that "the adjustment of boundary would remove an awkward and *unnatural* wedge [of native reserve] between farms."[27] What was natural to whites was, in fact, still new to Africans. To the small extent that Africans could and did resist Moodie and others, their logic of dissent still embodied notions of power over people.

LABOR, FREE AND FORCED

White settlers gave Africans reason to continue conceptualizing politics as power over people; for the colonists also sought that power and valued wealth in people. In the 1890s, settlers and administration devised four separate means of alienating the labor power of African smallholders. In Gogoi, Portuguese district administrators used violence to compel chiefs to recruit all or nearly all resident male subjects in rotation for long stints of work at a distance. Alternatively, failure to pay tax constituted the method of recruitment, again implemented via chiefs with the threat of force. In Rhodesia, farm owners compelled Africans to work for them, but here recruitment was based on tenancy independent of chiefs' authority.[28] Native commissioners did find labor through chiefs, but that work—mostly road building—took place in the district, was of short duration, and touched a limited portion of the African population. Men who worked at a distance, such as in the mines, found their employment voluntarily and independently of chiefs. Finally, chiefs did collect hut tax, but defaulters were not obligated to work. Thus, labor and taxation in Rhodesia did not conform to the Portuguese type so characteristic of wealth in people.

Forced labor on white farms—the first of four colonial forms of labor—bore the stamp of cadastral politics. In seeking labor, settlers confronted a difficulty that still plagues estate owners in Chimanimani and Chipinge districts: the problem of persuading smallholders, who are unusually self-sufficient in this fertile, high-rainfall area, to work for someone else. In the 1890s, "kaffir-farming" was the solution. As the metaphor suggests, settlers harvested the human resources on their farms, forcing blacks to work for them. The amount of labor and the level of violence involved were striking. As Meredith, the native commissioner, later recalled,

> [T]he farmers did not pay for Native labour but compelled the Natives to work for them gratis, not, indeed, at intervals, but almost daily, and at least three days per week, and if they did not do the work, they were flogged. They found it useless to complain to the then Authority, because by so doing they got another flogging for daring to complain of a White man. . . . They were constantly harassed and persecuted by the Colonial Native Police who were serving under the late Mr. G. B. D. Moodie.[29]

Moodie's system organized forced labor according to the cadastre. Within the logic of "kaffir farming," beacons and straight-line boundaries delimited not only arable land but also labor recruitment areas. Meredith wrote:

> The farmers, in some cases, built their houses, in the midst of what may be called small native locations. That is, where there were a dozen or more small villages, within a radius of about two square miles, the farm houses in some cases were surrounded by Native gardens.[30]

In brief, whites placed their homesteads in such a position as to best obtain and discipline native labor. Forced labor on the farms, thus, depended crucially upon territorial ownership and spatial relations.

Meredith clarified these relations by instituting a legal, rational system of labor tenancy. He also undercut much of its coercive force. First, he informed landowners and African residents that labor requirements would be limited to one week per month. The farm owner, Meredith found, appreciated his efforts to "make [the natives] understand that he was the owner of the farm and that they must respect his rights."[31] Equally Pollyannaish, "in all cases . . . the natives appreciate to give a week's labour per month for the privilege of living on the farms."[32] Moodie, however, resented these regulations, and in late 1896, the magistrate convicted him of assaulting a tenant who had dared complain to the native commissioner about daily exactions of labor.[33] Eventually, by using the stick and the carrot, Meredith convinced the bulk of the Melsetter farmers to sign a standard "labor agreement" with their tenants. That contract, a version of which the Native Department promoted throughout Southern Rhodesia, limited rents to labor and limited labor to three consecutive months per native man per year.[34] The agreement benefited landlords by requiring tenants to give one month's notice before departing a farm. Further, a 1924 amendment of the Private Locations Ordinance (1908) made such desertion a criminal offense (Rennie 1973:189). Yet, Africans violated this provision at will (as did landowners with regard to the entire contract). Meredith and the Native Department had created the reserves as an escape valve from labor tenancy, and Africans increasingly did escape. Cadastral lines thus collected farm labor, but at the same time circumscribed and limited it.

The second form of forced labor depended less on geography and somewhat more upon chiefs. The native commissioner could and did call upon African men for work on local infrastructural projects, particularly, road building. Meredith wrote, "I send my messengers to the Chief of the District [tribal area], and he sends his messengers out with my men."[35] In this fashion, Meredith adopted Portuguese tactics to pry labor out of the reserves, but chiefs assisted only up to a point. "When I said the work was at Salisbury," related Native Commissioner J. D. Hulley in 1895, Chief Nyakufere "refused to give me any more hut tax or any more natives and in consequence, I have made him come into my camp with me and will remain there as my guest until the first hundred boys from his country arrive in Salisbury."[36] When the going got rough, chiefs stepped aside. In 1899, Chief Ngorima apparently absented himself from a mass kidnapping in his vicinity. As reported by an early missionary—no admirer of the chief—"The police [were] making a raid today for boys to work on the new Umtali [Mutare] road. They were holding the women prisoners until their menfolk turned up . . . they took over 50 boys."[37] Native commissioners, thus, knew how to wield power over people. Yet, they did not know how to (or chose not to) graft chiefs onto a colonial system of ambulatory enslavement. Neither chiefs' involvement nor the work itself compared with Mozambican exactions. Rhodesian forced labor was sporadic, of short duration, and almost always relatively nearby. In short, this "soft" *chibaro* could not and did not become a way of life in Ngorima's polity.

The third form of labor, the type most often identified by the name *chibaro* in Rhodesia, *was* a way of life and did involve coercion. Even before the trekkers arrived, recruiters from the Transvaal mines had been seeking laborers in the Chimanimani-Sitatonga area (see chapter 1). In the 1890s and in the following decades, so-called touts recruited labor on behalf of South

African employers and the Rhodesia Native Labour Association. The formation of the native reserves, in fact, greatly assisted them. Men on the reserves owed labor to no local, competing employers. At the same time—but more typically in less fertile areas than Chief Ngorima's—the reserves lacked adequate soil and rainfall to support yeoman farming. In order to support their families, men had to work elsewhere (Arrighi 1970). Nonetheless, neither the touts, nor chiefs, nor headmen *compelled* men to sign up.[38] The management applied physical coercion not at the point of recruitment but at the point of production, in the workplace and in the mines' dormitories. Once recruited, workers could not easily break their long-term contracts.[39] Back in Melsetter, this form of labor did not add to chiefs', headmen's, or native commissioners' power over people.

This local cast of characters *did* manage the hut tax, but this fourth and final method of extracting African labor power also fell short of its Portuguese equivalent. The native commissioner demanded an annual cash payment of all African men in the district, regardless of their residence with respect to cadastral lines. Chiefs collected the tax from their subjects. To this extent, the tax resembled Portuguese *chibaro*. However, taxation and wage work correlated quite differently on the two sides of the border. In Mossurize, as discussed earlier, tax defaulters went to the plantations, and chiefs sent them there under the threat of physical punishment. In Melsetter, however, taxation only encouraged Africans to join the labor force; it did not absolutely compel them to do so. Many, of course, did join the mining proletariat to earn money for, among other purposes, paying tax. When the administration set producer prices high enough, other smallholders earned their tax by selling produce.[40] Still, people defaulted on the tax without serious consequences so that, even when their salaries were pegged to the number of tax-paying subjects, chiefs did not accumulate wealth in people through the tax.[41] Since the administration wielded no means of violence—no *palmatória*—to punish tax evaders, defaulters simply defaulted.[42] The obligation to pay tax represented a weak form of clientage at best.

Meredith, of course, recognized the problem of tax evasion. He proposed two means of boosting tax receipts, which although nonviolent, epitomized the principles of wealth in people. Head taxes and hut taxes necessarily depended upon population and population density. Assuming a fixed rate of compliance, a higher population yielded more tax. A denser population, where surveillance was easier, also yielded enhanced returns. Meredith tried both to increase the African population in Melsetter and to concentrate it. In 1898, the British South Africa Company attracted to its side of the border a large number of Africans returning from the southerly movement of 1889. To Meredith's delight, they constructed 567 taxable huts in Melsetter District. The violence of Portuguese rule promised to send additional natives across the international line. These accretions, however, did not offset the loss of 996 huts (256 in Mafussi's division alone) caused by the final demarcation of the border farther to the west than Meredith had expected.[43] The native commissioner's efforts to villagize people in the reserves proved to be no more successful at augmenting his administration's wealth in people. Meredith tried for years to nucleate African settlement in the reserves. In 1899, he reported optimistically:

> I spent much time in concentrating the Natives and forming larger villages under sub-chiefs. I cannot say it was entirely satisfactory to all but the majority are satisfied, and the chiefs expressed their entire approval as it gives them more direct authority over their people. It will facilitate my work and enable me to collect the hut tax in one half the time it has taken hitherto and will enable more boys to go away and work in the mines.[44]

Meredith, however, registered no such partial success or common interest with Chief Ngorima.[45] The Rusitu Valley's topography of deep canyons and narrow ridges would have made dense settlement particularly unsuitable. As with the whole of the district, the native commissioner's later reports appear to have relinquished the plan of villagization.

To sum up the discussion of four means of taxation in cash and labor, colonial policy simply did not succeed in accruing wealth in people. In Melsetter, *chibaro* gave neither administrators nor chiefs significant added leverage over the labor of Africans. Did the British South Africa Company simply lack the financial and European human resources—as in Sara Berry's (1993) description of "hegemony on a shoestring"—to imprint its will upon African society? In part, yes. Given the scarcity of trained, trustworthy whites, the Native Department relied upon local messengers, police, and the likes of Moodie, individuals over whom it could not exercise full supervision.[46] Native messengers often sabotaged the intent of *chibaro* by using it to their own advantage. In 1918, for example, the messenger Biyeni raped a woman among a group of tax defaulters and other miscreants he was taking to Chipinga for what should have been a mild interview with the acting native commissioner.[47] In extreme cases like this one (and Moodie's conviction for assault), the administration did shorten the leash.[48] It disciplined messengers and farm owners just enough to impede the formation of classes of client- or slaveholders in Melsetter's civil society. Yet the magistrates disciplined these people too little to prevent them from disrupting the state's and chief's own system of clientage. As a result, the total coercive system of ambulatory enslavement never crystallized in Chief Ngorima's area as it did in Mossurize. Whereas Portugal opted to subordinate people in the Chimanimani-Sitatonga region, the British South Africa Company and Rhodesia ultimately concentrated their energies on taking and keeping the region's land.

MARRIAGE AND OTHER MEANS OF CLIENTAGE

If Melsetter's administration limited the extent of slavery in its own and in other Europeans' affairs, it also diminished Africans' wealth in people. In Ngorima's post-1890 restored chieftaincy, accumulative strategies concentrated more on relationships—and less on outright control of bodies—than they had under the Nguni. Male lineage heads exploited inequalities within lineages, principally their own dominance over junior women. Given the weak position of daughters, patriarchs married them strategically to establish alliances or hierarchies between lineages. As in any patrilineal and virilocal system, the marriage of a daughter normally deprived her father of her services and of rights in her children. Daughters were, thus, a long-term liability. If, however, it was possible to marry on the basis of bride-service and on other forms of male clientage—as opposed to bride-wealth—daughters could actually serve as assets. By "giving" a wife, her father could obtain a permanent client (or, as acknowledged publicly, an ally). What is more, he (and, later, his sons) could secure rights to that woman's children. In other words, the usage of bride-service and clientage smuggled a matrilineal practice into a supposedly patrilineal system.[49] Most important, this maneuver converted what would otherwise have been the marriage of a daughter *out,* into the marriage of someone else's son *in.* At the very least, a lineage head could maintain an equilibrium level of wealth in people by receiving bride-wealth in the form of boys or girls. The latter case would constitute a daughter-for-daughter, or *mutenga-tore,* exchange marriage.[50] In Melsetter, Chief Mutambara married his daughter (or client) out and eventually acquired, as a ward, the couple's daughter.[51] Such strategies tended to make the rich richer and the poor poorer. A family that could not meet subsistence requirements had to accept hoes or cash, goods that did not reproduce themselves. A family with labor power sufficient to produce surplus food, however, could refuse hoes or cash and demand bride-service or payment in people.

Colonial intervention increasingly ruled out such refusal. The British South Africa Company, prompted by missionary ideology, interceded in matters of bride-wealth and bride-service. (Recall that the Companhia de Moçambique eventually all but expelled the Gogoi Mission Station, reducing the American Board of Commissioners for Foreign Missions to the status of a supplicant.) Elopements and "runaway girls" brought the issue to a head. Chief Mutambara's adopted daughter stole away with a man. Thereupon, Mutambara and her biological father brought a case of abduction against the suitor. The magistrate settled the matter, not by returning the girl, but by requiring the bridegroom to pay bride-wealth.[52] The following year, 1901, the Native Marriages Ordinance formally outlawed bride-service and bride-exchange, designating cattle and cash as the only acceptable terms of transaction (apart, of course, from Christian marriage).[53] Young women, themselves, assisted greatly in the implementation of this rule. They fled, and Christian missions provided them with their first reliable exit option from *mutenga-tore* and other forced engagements. By 1916, the Rusitu Mission harbored five girls from Ngorima's homestead. All daughters of men to whom the chief had provided wives,[54] they presumably represented the latter half of exchange marriages. Although the chief petitioned for their return, the mission was not inclined to relinquish such young converts upon whom it thrived. Christian marriage served the mission's interests in more ways than one.

Six years later, Chief Ngorima's management of female resources again came to the attention of the Rusitu Mission. A convoluted set of family relations brought marriage and clientage into direct conflict with the new means of cash bride-wealth. To simplify, a man in the structural position of Ngorima's son-in-law offered Ngorima money in lieu of labor. An earlier *mutenga-tore* marriage somewhat complicated the dynamics, however, and Rusitu's missionary in charge had to describe the facts at length (further explained by my own appended chart, figure 2.1):

Pikirisi has been a *muranda* (servant) of the old Chief Ngorima. And evidently not too pleased with the position. But as he was given his wife [B] by Ngorima he wants to pay for her and have his liberty. He has already put in some considerable time working for Ngorima but when he offered twenty pounds to pay for his wife and to be free the old Chief refused and . . . told him to clear out. He Ngorima then took the girl [C] from the kraal where she had been given in exchange for Pikirisi's wife. And as a result the head of that kraal [A] took his daughter, Pikirisi's wife [B] away from him. . . .

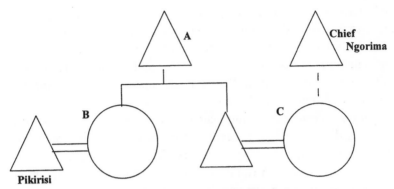

FIG. 2.1. Chart of Ngorima family relations

Pikirisi . . . has offered to pay Ngorima twenty pounds for the girl [C] who was given in exchange for his wife or to give his wife's father [A] the twenty pounds but neither of them will listen to him.[55]

In effect, Ngorima gave a ward (who may or may not have been his biological daughter) so that Pikirisi could marry without paying bride-wealth. Pikirisi, then, assumed a permanent debt to Ngorima and became a *muranda,* or servant/slave (see chapter 1). Wishing to rise above that low status, Pikirisi tried to make a single payment to erase his debt to Ngorima. Since the marriage was in fact a *mutenga-tore* exchange, he also offered the payment to A. Why did neither man accept? Ngorima presumably preferred a *muranda*'s perpetual services to cash. A, who benefited from no such services, might well have accepted the cash, but, it seems reasonable to suppose, both lineage heads would have preferred payment in the form of one of Pikirisi's two children. (Perhaps, Ngorima originally acquired custody of C in this fashion.) Yet—again to make an educated guess—the native commissioner would have insisted, as he did in the Mutambara case, that Ngorima take the money and be done with it.

By the 1940s and 1950s, cash bride-wealth was ubiquitous.[56] Men earned money in the mines or elsewhere and paid for their sons' wives or for their own. Chiefs, such as Mushanembeu's grandson, Shangwa, who ruled from 1939 to 1955, lost out. Shangwa inherited a least one well-known client from Mushanembeu.[57] This man, Dinda, had lost his parents in Gaza Nguni raids and had sought protection in the Ngorima homestead. In the late-nineteenth-century fashion, he married a daughter of Shangwa, without bride-wealth, and performed services for the chief until his death. By rights, his children should have belonged to Shangwa. Yet, according to a contemporary, Dinda's sons-in-law "did not perform bride service. They were able to pay money that was given for them by their parents to the Chief. . . . Thus these people could pay money to leave the clientship of their [fictive] father [the chief]—to stand for themselves."[58] Bride-wealth, therefore, eroded Shangwa's patrimony in people and replaced it with a cash income.

Money was, however, not equivalent to wealth in people, and, for a chief, it was decidedly inferior. Money was more ephemeral than children or clients: in African hands, it could not reproduce itself in capitalist fashion; for colonial laws barred almost all Africans from buying businesses or making other long-term investments. In less remote parts of Rhodesia, upwardly mobile parents invested in the education of their children and, ultimately, boosted the latter's pay grade as migrant laborers (Jeater 1993:221–22). Melsetter, however, contained few schools and very few that admitted blacks. For the most part, money was simply dissipated among relatives and the thousand necessities and luxuries available in growing markets. Lineage heads, of course, recognized this slipperiness of money. In their strategies of marriage, they tried to maintain what James Ferguson describes as a one-way door between reproducible wealth and money.[59] They endeavored to pay a cash bride-wealth for daughters marrying in, but tried by all means to avoid marrying daughters out for cash alone. In the absence of other kinds of income, cash created poverty in people. Chiefs had the most wealth to lose.

If the money economy thus undermined chiefs' endowments in absolute terms, it also leveled them relative to the general rural populace. Money was democratic—a fact that wage earners would have appreciated immediately. Any able-bodied man could sign a contract with the Rhodesia Native Labour Bureau. The touts did not discriminate in favor of chiefs' relatives. Nor did the managers pay the native nobility a higher wage. In fact, the availability of money almost eliminated the only source of clients apart from marriage—rural destitution. Already in the 1903 drought, Meredith reported, "All the Natives [in the Save Valley] who are short of food are sending their young men out to work."[60] In 1908, Save Valley residents traveled to the Rusitu Mission to buy food.[61] A decade or two earlier, they might have sent their sons or daughters in the same direction, but as pledges to Ngorima. At the same time, peace imposed by the British and the growing rural market in foodstuffs made raids both unlawful and unnecessary. By the 1930s, as John Iliffe (1990) writes, a capitalist system of scarcity and relief had replaced the precolonial forms of poverty and wealth.

The Ngorima nobility was stuck between a rock and a hard place.

Missionary morality, political stability, and economic opportunity were cutting off the supply of clients. Southern Rhodesia's piecemeal, comparatively toothless version of forced labor could not resuscitate ambulatory enslavement. Old forms of wealth and status were slipping away. Ngorima and similar lineages might soon become indistinguishable from their subjects. They had feared as much. In 1905, as Ngorima's *mutenga-tore* agreements began to unravel, the Rusitu Mission found "the old man . . . quite in a state of uneasiness about this new development. The missionaries are going to convert all of his girls and he will be left alone in the midst of the land" (Wood 1905:253). How could the Ngorima leadership maintain power and respect? It would have to turn the background—land—into the polity's focus of interest. No one consciously planned such a maneuver, but land alienation propelled it forward and gave the nobility a new raison d'être.

AFFORESTATION OF THE PLATEAU
AND LAND ALLOCATION IN THE VALLEY

The second alienation of the Chimanimani Plateau reworked and deepened the territorializing effects of the first. Occurring in the 1950s, it represented a new relationship among land, people, and capital—one that handicapped African smallholders to an even greater degree. To start with capital, the trekkers had arrived with little livestock. While they and their descendants had built up herds, few obtained the farm machinery necessary to turn substantial profits. In the midst of Rhodesia's post–World War II boom, these capital-poor, land-rich farmers went bust. In the space of a decade, some of the wealthiest firms in Southern Africa acquired that land and capitalized it as plantation forests for pulp and sawn wood. The British South Africa Company—still in business after the transition to settler government in 1923—bought Welgelegen while Tilbury incorporated itself as Border Forests. Both estates eventually merged into Border Timbers Limited, under the ownership of South Africa's Anglo-American corporation (Innis 1984:282). Meanwhile, the Rhodesia Wattle Company bought a huge tract more or less along the Melsetter-Chipinge Road. Lonhro, another major owner of Southern African capital, eventually acquired the Wattle Company (Godwin 1996:165). Finally, in the biggest purchases by land area, the government's Forestry Department gained more than eighteen thousand hectares abutting Ngorima Reserve. The Forest Act of 1954 established five new "forest estates"[62] and created the parastatal Forestry Commission to manage them.

The management of the new forests depended directly upon assessments of the value of land and people. From a forester's point of view, the trekkers had underutilized land and overutilized labor. Owing to the aforementioned lack of livestock and other capital, the trekkers had never cultivated the entire arable portions of their three thousand–morgen plots. They had cultivated that portion for which they had obtained native hands for tilling, harvesting, and so forth. This labor-limited agriculture had left plenty of space for natural vegetation and, as required by the Private Locations Ordinance, for tenants' family crops. It also left plenty of room for increased profits: according to the Forestry Commission's calculations, Melsetter's exotic softwood plantations would generate far greater profit per acre per year than did agriculture (Rhodesia Forestry Commission 1968:145–47). In Melsetter, a per-acre calculus—typical of *scientific* forestry[63]—dictated that the Forestry Commission, Border Timbers, and the like should plant every acre possible. (Since wattle, pine, and eucalyptus will grow on steep slopes, this acreage exceeded even the maximum arable area the previous owners could have cultivated.) Yet as large as they were, these plantations required less labor than had the three thousand–morgen farms. The corporations offered paid, uncoerced jobs for planting, thinning, and felling, but much of such employment required men with skills in operating chainsaws and other machinery. The unskilled and mostly female tenants (female because so many men were engaged in migrant labor), who had been the landlords' main asset, suddenly became the corporations' liability. They could contribute little while each acre of their crops diminished corporate revenues.

Eviction was the obvious solution. Forced removals jump-started the Melsetter timber industry. Among African smallholders, they stirred the first distinctly territorial resentment and, simultaneously, provoked resistance in the form of materialist faits accomplis. One Vhimba resident recalled, "Tarka Forest drove people off. . . . We had a big place. It was taken from us. We were left with a very, very small place."[64] Planting trees consolidated that seizure of land. Indeed, the stands of pine made cadastral politics more visible than they had ever been before. Smallholders responded in kind: they burned the forests. According to Shirley Sinclair's triumphalist *The Story of Melsetter* (1971:173), "a handful of fire-raisers [in the unusually dry winter of 1962] defied the organised and armed forces of the law and threatened Rhodesia's timber industry." Indeed, arson militarized Melsetter, bringing helicopter patrols, paratroops, the Rhodesia Light Infantry, and the Special Air Services (ibid.). Yet, this militia apprehended fewer insurgents than it may have deterred. Arson achieved the maximum damage with the smallest risk of detection. Like many others, Peter Godwin, who as a boy partic-ipated in the fire brigades, thought the fires to be accidental. Only later did he associate the "*moto mukuru*"—"the big fire"—with rebellion and the infa-mous Crocodile Gang that had killed a Melsetter Afrikaner in the name of *Chimurenga*.[65] In a sense, the 1896–97 war of resistance to white settlement—and the pattern of losing—had finally taken hold in Chief Ngorima's polity. This time, though, the basis of struggle was undeniably cadastral.

Forced removal wrought even more powerful and lasting changes in the internal dynamics of Ngorima's polity. Like the timber economy as a whole, the compaction of Ngorima's subjects into the reserve recalibrated the rel-ative value of land and people. New strategies of accumulation focused on the control of land, and, unlike arson, these tactics worked. On the most obvious level, evictions completed the "spatial fix" Meredith had begun. Most of Ngorima's people found themselves in the reserve bearing his name. Kicked off Tilbury in 1956, Chief Garayi Ngorima himself installed his court on the Rusitu Mission (Young 1970:59). Jiho, the sacred site of Ngo-rima graves, remained as a singular cadastral anomaly. The Monuments and Relics Act of 1936 protected the site from afforestation, and a fence excluded intruders. Border Timbers granted Ngorima's people yearly access to Jiho for *kudira* (rainmaking) ceremonies, and Jiho became a potent and visible symbol of Ngorima's geographical disconnectedness. This tiny sacred enclave epitomized the new political logic of territorial loss and confinement.

Confinement, by itself, required the leadership to perform two duties: allo-cate land to newcomers and adjudicate land claims among existing residents. Did Ngorima and his headmen assume these cadastral functions for the first time in the 1950s, or did such preexisting roles simply become more mean-ingful and controversial than they had been previously? Common historical wisdom points to the latter answer. According to J. F. Holleman (1952:13–14), nineteenth-century chiefs disposed of rights to their subjects' labor and land. Yet, the quality of authority was quite different in these two arenas. Chiefs controlled clients, wives, and progeny directly and tangibly. Their authority over land, however, was much more abstract: through *kudira* and other reli-gious practices, chiefs and other leaders bore responsibility for the fertility of a nebulous zone, but they did not allocate farmland as such. Recall Mzila's seeming lack of concern regarding the precise location of the Mount Selinda Mission (see chapter 1). Even when raids forced Nguni-era chiefdoms to con-centrate for safety in hilly redoubts, land scarcity did not necessarily gener-ate a political culture of land allocation.[66] By accomplishing the same task, the *kukhonza* procedure substituted for explicit land management. *Kukhonza* allowed newcomers to gain access to land in the process of pledging themselves as clients. In short, land allocation did not stand *on its own;* it was a by-product of chiefs' accumulation of wealth in people.

If land allocation in the Ngorima Reserve remained abstract, indirect, or latent until the 1950s, demographic movement suddenly made it come alive. Forced removals presented Chief Ngorima and his headmen with a multitude of subjects who needed land immediately. Although coerced to leave their homes, these people were not destitutes or *vakhonzwa.* They were not asking to be incorporated into the leading lineages as clients. Thus, leadership and migrants had to find a new means of putting the latter on the land. The result was by no means preordained. Migrants could have settled themselves, or headmen could have ordered them where to live. Or state technocrats could have demarcated plots for them. In fact, technocrats largely demurred. Vhimba's steep slopes invalidated their conventional ecological criteria for planning land use. Also, during the 1960s, colonial policy favored lineage-based authority, as a counterweight to growing nationalist agitation (Alexander 1993:69–87). Coincidentally, much of the migration to Vhimba corresponded with Rhodesia's only phase of true indirect rule. Under these conditions, a pattern of negotiation emerged in which migrants and headmen examined parcels until they agreed upon a site (chapter 3 reviews cases of land allocation in Vhimba from the mid-1940s to the 1990s). In practice, then, the headmen's role as land allocators might be ambiguous, but their ideological claim to that role became increasingly well articulated. When asked in the 1990s what were "the jobs of the headman," most Vhimba residents listed first, "to give land" (*kupa nzvimbo* or *minda*).

Headmen's allocation of land emphasized territorial lines and cadastral authority. Newcomers negotiated with the headman in whose *territory,* within whose *boundaries,* they wished to settle. Ngorima at some point had established an unwritten cadastre: his headmanships extended as long lots, bounded to the south by the international border of the Rusitu and to the east and west by its tributaries.[67] Many of these lots extended onto the private land of the plateau. Forced removals underscored the illegality of the headmen's claims to the plateau and more palpably denied them the ability to manage people or land there. The director of lands, in fact, ended debate on precisely this point in Melsetter, pronouncing:

Any suggestion that European farming land should come within a Chief's jurisdiction, or that a Chief should have any responsibility for the allocation of a "labour tenant[']s" lands, would imply a measure of permanency in the tenant[']s rights of occupation, and would also detract from the landowner's right and *obligation* to control his labour force.[68]

From then on, fireguards and the wall of pines behind them left no doubt as to the northern boundary of the headmen's authority. Headmen whose lands had been wholly situated on the plateau fared even worse: they simply vanished from the cadastre. In the 1950s, the Forestry Commission pushed Headman Parara and his people into Tiyekiye's, Chikware's, and Matwukira's areas. Parara lost any practical authority over his former subjects and, as an allocatee, became the subject of another headman. "My country was taken by an estate," he said, ". . . I [then] lived in the area of Matwukira . . . I am ruled. [When told], 'do it,' I do it right away."[69] People still clap respectfully for Parara, but it is clear that a headman without territory is no headman at all. As if to underscore that point, the district administration mapped the headmen's areas in 1976. It established five "wards"—based on the same north-south streams—each bearing the name of a major figure. Tiyekiye's ward covered all of Vhimba.[70]

This kind of surveying accompanied another, contemporaneous territorializing process: state-led land-use planning. Rhodesian technocrats had been trying to conserve the soil and grassland of the reserves since the 1930s. These efforts, which were often very poorly conceived,[71] hardly touched the Rusitu Valley. In the 1990s, few Vhimba residents recalled colonial land-use planning—a far cry from accounts of other communities still obsessed with "the lines." The most interventionist planning program, the Native Land Husbandry Act of 1951, simply could not work in Ngorima Reserve. Large parts of the reserve exceeded the 12 percent maximum arable slope dictated by the act (Alexander 1993:53–54). At the same time, sticky dolerite soils permitted hillside cultivation (of millet, maize, and many fruit trees) without the predicted consequence of massive erosion.[72] Had the administration implemented the act in Ngorima Reserve, it would have severely curtailed the headmen's powers to allocate farmland. In the event, however, conservation policies became feasible only when, in the 1960s and 1970s, an administration fearful of nationalist agitation decided to cooperate with chiefs and headmen. The administration had created a *dare revhu,* or "council of the soil," under the chairmanship of Garayi Ngorima. A reputed antinationalist,[73] this chief and his headmen assisted the Department of Conservation and Extension to plant trees and peg contours. Despite local opposition, wrote the district commissioner, the *dare* "appear to be trying to bring about some sort of control over land by preventing the indiscriminate opening of new lands and cutting down valuable trees."[74] In a common pattern, head-men, then, used their collaboration with the Rhodesian government to con-solidate power within the reserve—in this case, to create a monopoly over land management and allocation.

And their monopoly position was strengthened as the population in the reserve became more and more dense. As in many parts of Zimbabwe, evic-tions outside Ngorima Reserve forced large numbers of people into it. In other words, the African person-land ratio rose as its denominator (land area for smallholding) fell.[75] (The common, Malthusian perception, of course, holds that a rise in absolute population—the numerator—has over-crowded the reserves.) Between 1962 and 1969, the population of Ngorima Reserve shot up at least 60 percent (far above the natural rate of increase) to reach a density of 40–50 persons per square kilometer. By 1982, the den-sity had reached the range of 80–120 persons per square kilometer, making Ngorima Reserve among the most tightly packed rural areas in Zimbabwe.[76] How would this human compaction affect the power of chiefs and head-men? In a study of the East African Great Lakes region, Parker Shipton (1984b) predicts that concentration will weaken, rather than fortify, chiefs' powers of land allocation. As population becomes denser, Shipton argues, lineages hold on to their parcels and redistribute them internally. One could expect such an outcome in the Rusitu Valley, particularly, in view of the prevalence of permanent crops. At the time of the Native Land Husbandry Act, writes Jocelyn Alexander (1993:54), "the density of settlement in Ngorima and the investment in coffee, tea, and fruit trees had . . . created conditions in which almost all land was considered to have an 'owner,' mak-ing it virtually impossible to reshuffle settlement patterns and fields." Yet, headmen did reshuffle such patterns. Continued in-migration provided them with occasions to allocate land to newcomers, and, in contradistinction to Shipton's model, headmen did not "turn applicants away from their villages" (Shipton 1984b:622). Indeed, as chapter 3 explains, Vhimba's headmen wel-comed newcomers in the 1990s precisely because of their usefulness in fight-ing turf battles.

High population density added to the chiefs' authority over land in fur-ther ways. As in-migrants surrounded long-standing residents, kin clusters found they could not expand freely. This new, spatial constraint com-pounded the challenge mounted by junior men against the patriarchal *maguta*. In-migration stripped senior men of peripheral lands they might have allocated to sons-in-law. Perhaps chiefs and headmen intended to weaken rival lineage heads in this way. In any case, grooms—who already might have wanted to pay bride-wealth and establish their own homesteads—found themselves *compelled* to move away from kin. "People can no longer live together because there is no land," explained Wilson Manase, who came of age in the 1950s. "It may be that my son may stay in Shamiso, which is far from me here in Chikware. Another may go to Muchadziya. So the *guta* of the father is no more."[77] As the other patriarchs' power waned, chiefs' and headmen's authority waxed. Once living cheek by jowl, smallholders engaged in frequent disputes over farmland both between and within lineages. A plaintiff brought his quarrel to the headmen, and the latter frequently referred it upward to the chief's court (the *dare* proper). Over the decades, these courts institutionalized their role in reallocating contested land, particularly in cases of inheritance. They did not always support lineage heads or rule according to the government's interpretations of African law and "communal tenure." In 1997, for example, Chief Peter Ngorima ruled against an elder brother and awarded his father's land to the younger brother.[78] More systematically, many courts dispossessed widows of spousal inheritance (Cheater 1990). Upon the death of her husband, a woman looked to her sons for access to land—or to the chief's court for support against their stinginess—or to the headman for an entirely new allocation independent of her husband's lineage. Her desperation would rise as population rose and arable land became increasingly scarce.

The land tenure system established at mid-century thus victimized some and empowered others. It was, as Angela Cheater writes, a far cry from the colonial vision of "communal tenure." Tossed off ancestral lands, and packed into tiny reserves, leaders and followers increasingly acted along a cadastral imperative. Land allocation emerged as an invented tradition. Eviction-induced population density manufactured dissent among smallholders (cf. Carney and Watts 1990). It even turned smallholders against the Rusitu Mission. In 1969, Chief Garayi Ngorima obstructed the mission's attempt to survey its tract. He placed a smallholder inside the purported survey line and then reportedly insisted, "No beacons are needed. The Chief and his men are the beacons and the boundaries."[79] Headmen later refined this cadastral strategy of remaking borders with people (chapter 3). Like land allocation in general, these disputes and maneuvers enlarged the power of chiefs and headmen (Colson 1971:197). Thus, the nobility turned the evictions from the Chimanimani Plateau to their own advantage. They overcame the early-twentieth-century loss of clients and similar wealth in people. Instead of ruling people directly, they ruled them *through land*. In terms of the culture of rural politics, chiefs now held wealth in land.

CHIMANIMANI NATIONAL PARK

If land alienation in the 1950s turned Chief Ngorima's people against one another (and eventually against the mission), further seizures turned them against the state—both Rhodesia and Zimbabwe. By enlarging the Chimanimani National Park in 1965, the state, for the first time, played a direct role in taking land from smallholders under Ngorima. The Department of National Parks and Wildlife Management (hereafter, the Parks Department), in fact, had wished to gazette the northern half of Ngorima Reserve when it created the Chimanimani park in 1950. Yet, the Native Land Board demurred, and the Parks Department settled for nonarable land on Welgelegen, Chamois, and Stonehenge estates.[80] Africans, therefore, retained the right to cultivate in the Haroni River Valley and on the western slopes of the main Chimanimani Range. Shortly, however, conservationists' alarm, backed by the scientific and cartographic capacities of the Rhodesian state,[81] brought the boundaries of Ngorima Reserve again into question. In the 1950s, government-sponsored aerial photography (Whitlow 1988:140) revealed the full extent of moist evergreen forest in Rhodesia.[82] Most of these high-canopy rainforests consisted of small patches and riverine galleries of 100 hectares or less. The Haroni Valley of Ngorima Reserve contained two such enclaves, while others lay within the adjoining Forestry Commission estates and the Hayfield B farm (Crook 1956: map). On the basis of these data, botanists and ecologists called upon the Parks Department to protect the woodland in Ngorima Reserve posthaste. In short, the logic of conservation dictated that smallholders be removed from the Haroni Valley, and the Parks Department made it so (for the rest of this chapter, see map 3.1, p. 93).

That logic, it is worth noting here, rested on three erroneous assumptions. First, calculations of forest area treated Rhodesia as an island. They excluded huge areas of forest in Mozambique—not photographed by air until 1965—and therefore vastly underestimated the extent of rainforest within even 100 kilometers of Rhodesia's Eastern Highlands.[83] Second, scientists misidentified the patchiness of Rhodesia's rainforest as evidence of deforestation caused by smallholder agriculture. In the late 1950s and early 1960s, scientists possessed no historical evidence of forest decline. Like the ecologists criticized in James Fairhead and Melissa Leach's (1996) restudy of West African "deforestation," Rhodesian experts extrapolated diachronic conclusions from synchronic evidence. In fact, the 1963 aerial photos showed a marked *expansion* of the Rusitu Forest since 1950.[84] Yet, by that time, Rhodesian conservationists had jumped to the third and final faulty assumption: among categories of land users, smallholders were the least likely to protect rainforest. The Parks Department gazetted only those rainforests whose existing users seemed unwilling to conserve them. The Forestry Commission and the owner of Hayfield B escaped interference because, scientists judged, they would protect forest. The law, however, neither forced these owners to conserve nor guaranteed the continuation of their ownership. (As explained in the conclusion, the owner of Hayfield B lost de facto control of his land in 2001.) The Forestry Commission, moreover, was in the very process of eradicating most of the native vegetation of the Chimanimani Plateau in favor of pines. As opposed to these actions in bad faith, Vhimba's headmen had demonstrated a commitment to at least one rainforest that would have been evident to any scientist who made enquiries.[85] Headman Chikware administered and still administers the Rusitu Forest as a sacred area. He had kept smallholders from settling in the forest, and his son exercised the same authority in the mid-1990s. The active preservation of this forest is all the more remarkable given its documented duration of forty-seven years (1950–97) and population pressure in orders of magnitude above that of the plateau and the national average. In short, Vhimba smallholders supported more people on less land while conserving more forest for a longer period of time than any other land user in Melsetter District. The Parks Department punished Vhimba residents for their good behavior.

The department, in fact, punished them twice, with two distinct bursts of land alienation. The first expropriation came, of course, in 1965 when Chimanimani National Park engulfed the Haroni Valley and the Matsenderero Forest. These areas may have been uninhabited, although smallholders probably collected fuelwood and wild foods there.[86] In its southeastern corner, the expanded park certainly encroached upon smallholders. The gazettement had marked the southern boundary of the park by extending the southern boundary of Hayfield B estate westward to the Haroni, from which point it followed the Haroni. The artificial line, then, took in the southern bank of the Chisengu River, a rocky area of no botanical singularity called Mukwiratunhu. This accident of surveying displaced a number of families and remained a flashpoint for turf battles into the 1990s.[87] The second spate of expropriation targeted the two remaining identified rainforests of the Rusitu Valley. Again based on conservationist alarm, the Parks Department gazetted the Rusitu and Haroni botanical reserves in 1973. This time, however, the Parks Department could evict no one, for the war had reduced Haroni and Rusitu as well as the southern part of Chimanimani to unenforceable, inhabited "paper parks."

During Zimbabwe's war of independence, Vhimba residents embraced a narrow, hectare-focused form of nationalism. Those who personally inhabited the parks, in particular, remember the conflict primarily as a squatters' movement against state-backed conservation. Vhimba's topography and its proximity to the Mozambican border spared them much of the brutality and social upheaval associated with the war in other districts. Rhodesia simply ceded this indefensible wedge of low-lying territory. From Mozambique, ZANLA (Zimbabwe African National Liberation Army) guerrillas effectively occupied Vhimba in 1978 and used it as a base for frequent attacks on white farms.[88] In this semiliberated zone, relations between guerrillas and residents appear to have been easy.[89] If so, then Vhimba did not suffer the internecine "struggles within the struggle" that Kriger (1988, 1992) found in embattled Mutoko District: violent opponent-collaborator conflicts that pitted women against men, youth against elders, and poor against rich in Mutoko.[90] In short, Vhimba residents concentrated on overrunning and overturning the boundary of Chimanimani National Park. "We want a big area,"[91] one smallholder recalled telling his family. The guerrillas promised him, "You may live where you wish to."[92] In the late 1970s, therefore, his family and four others crossed the Haroni River to live and farm in the Matsenderero Forest. Anticipating the overthrow of the government, they treated their tenure as secure and beyond administrative meddling.

After independence, Vhimba residents faced severe disappointment on both counts. First, the new government installed in 1980 hardly reformed Melsetter's colonial cadastre. Recognizing earlier legislation, it revalidated the national park and botanical reserves. In 1981, scouts of the Parks Department tossed the five squatter families out of Matsenderero. With less success, scouts also attempted to enforce the boundaries of the Rusitu and Haroni botanical reserves. Vhimba residents, who had previously been unaware of the existence of these reserves, still accuse the guerrillas—known as Comrades—of having alienated that land. More accurately, the Comrades, who while fighting in the 1970s had downgraded parks all over the country to paper parks, reinstated them as real parks. Private land similarly remained the property of its colonial owner. Only in relation to farms abandoned by their owners did the government show some flexibility. In Chimanimani, however, the Forestry Commission had first pick of the best parcels relinquished on the plateau. The two small farms designated for smallholders in the Nyahode and upper Rusitu Valley lay far away from Vhimba—too far for Vhimba residents to gain a foothold on them in the scramble for resettlement. Measured in hectares, Vhimba's smallholders gained nothing from the change of government.

Headmen in Vhimba and from closer to the resettlement areas had further reasons to complain. Various branches of the state attempted to take back from headmen the power of land allocation. In other words, the state actually tightened administrative control in comparison to its relatively laissez-faire approach to "traditional" land management in the 1960s and 1970s. All over Zimbabwe, resettlement officers set the criteria for choosing families and subplots within the new resettlement areas. In parallel, agricultural extension agents in the reserves attempted to villagize smallholders and replan their use of grazing and farmland. In Chimanimani, both of these attempted coups against headmen met with popular resistance. As with the Native Land Husbandry Act forty years earlier, neither headmen nor commoners in the Rusitu Valley cooperated with land-use planning. The Village Development Committees instituted in 1982 never managed land in Vhimba. In Chimanimani's resettlement areas, chiefs and headmen allocated land, and some migrants simply moved in on their own authority (Alexander 1993:249–82). The government spent the early 1980s trying to regain control of the resettlement process. The age of focused, hectare-by-hectare turf battles had begun.

On one level, Vhimba's turf battles of the 1990s—to be discussed in chapters 3 and 4—were the continuation of the war by other means. They constituted the unfinished business of a failed revolution. Yet, the war itself, as Vhimba people experienced it, was the continuation of a material and cultural sea change under way since the 1890s. Moodie had first made land a focus of capital accumulation and exploitation—on the part of whites. In the first decades of the twentieth century, the Native Marriages Ordinance had eroded blacks' source of wealth and power— control of daughters, sons-in-law, and progeny. With the help of missions and the Native Affairs Department, young men—more so actually than women—emancipated themselves from senior men. The evictions of the 1950s precipitated a double-edged counterrevolution. By settling the evictees, headmen gained tangible control over land in the Ngorima Reserve. Black male elders had found a new means of accumulating wealth and power. At the same time, blacks elaborated means of resisting Moodie's legacy: they asserted their claim to the land taken from them by burning the tree plantations. Literally a scorched earth policy, this rebellion died down as headmen and their subjects turned inward, to the management of field and forest in the reserve. The war shifted attention again, outward to the lost lands. Squatting was possible on lands not planted to pine, and this form of rebellion persisted into the 1990s. In sum, Vhimba residents created a political culture that was foreign, if not unimaginable, to their forebears and to smallholders a short distance away, in Gogoi. Mozambicans of Gogoi entered the 1990s prey to a forced labor system essentially unchanged for a century. In the same century, Vhimba residents had learned how to value land; they had learned how to fight for land. In the 1990s, they learned how to win back land.

PART 2

The Border

The rest of this study addresses contemporary social processes in Vhimba and Gogoi. The data derive principally from my ethnography carried out in those two areas between 1995 and 1997. Much of that ethnography centered on the importance of the Zimbabwe-Mozambique border, a frontier in the linear sense. Upon my initial arrival in Vhimba, however, I had considered the border to be of little consequence. It is, after all, what Africanists constantly term, an "artificial border." That is, the Zimbabwe-Mozambique border cuts across the Ndau ethnolinguistic area and across numerous binational kindreds (Alexander 1993:54). Related to a minority of residents, the border also cuts across the local congregation of the Zion Christian Church. (A labor migrant brought this independent, apostolic faith to the area in the early 1950s.)[1] I expected such ties of religion, ethnicity, language, marriage, and blood to weigh rather more heavily than citizenship in the minds and actions of my subjects. Many Africanists would support such a hypothesis. A. I. Asiwaju (1985a:4), for instance, declares, "Judged . . . from the viewpoint of the border society life in many parts of Africa, the [European imperial] partition can hardly be said to have taken place." This "reality of border-lands where communities merged into one another" explains Donna Flynn's recent finding that people living along the Benin-Nigeria boundary call each other "border" (Nugent and Asiwaju 1996b:9; Flynn 1997). In spite of the centrifugal pull of two capital cities, these and similar partitioned populations have established a common interest and identity. The people of Vhimba, it seemed, could easily have done the same.

In fact, initial signs pointed to the strength of transnational ties. In 1995,

Vhimba contained a large number of Mozambican refugees. They had crossed the border during their country's war, and Vhimba people had given them land to farm. In some cases, Mozambicans' Zimbabwean relatives had assisted them in this process. And the behavior of both parties, again, seemed to resonate with scholarly opinion (Zartmann 1970:144; Hansen 1979:369; Kambudzi 1997:28–29). As the book's introduction mentioned, many anthropologists describe the world as "deterritorialized," such that people move and adapt readily to new places. Refugees would appear to possess the same capacity. Ken Wilson documents that Jehovah's Witnesses chose when to leave Mozambique during its civil war, where to go in Malawi, and when and how to return. They exercised "refugee initiative" such that "[f]light, far from simply disrupting existing social networks, had been a deliberate movement that actually utilized and strengthened them" (Wilson 1994:237, 241). For such people, emigration as a "refugee" was but one instance in a wider pattern of opportunistic cross-border activity. In this view, refugees are migrant laborers, smugglers, and other cosmopolitans fortuitously involved with the United Nations. In Vhimba's Mozambicans, had I not found another group of binational, border people?

Further research proved their citizenship to be rather more rigid. In fact, headmen's method of allocating land to refugees stemmed directly from the difference in the two parties' nationalities and national histories. Northern Mossurize and Vhimba stood at opposite ends of the transformation described in the previous chapter: the shift from a political culture of wealth in people to a political culture of wealth in land. Mozambican forced labor, both contemporary and historical, had prepared its citizens to suffer or evade ambulatory enslavement. In a way few Zimbabweans did, these noncitizens submitted to the personal authority of their hosting headmen. Headmen, in turn, slotted these vulnerable people into Vhimba's multiple cadastral disputes. From 1991 onward, headmen settled refugees on contested pieces of land, on the Hayfield B estate and in Chimanimani National Park. They exploited these vulnerable people in order to take back lost territory. Vhimba's headmen turned border crossers into boundary beacons, to the surprise and dismay of the latter. The Parks Department evicted them and thereby triggered another round of cadastral politics (see chapter 4). By virtue of their citizenship, refugees did not get what they bargained for.

The Zimbabwe-Mozambique border, then, is "hard." People cross it, but emigration strips at least some people of rights and securities they regularly enjoy at home. This conditional, prejudicial permeability characterizes much of Southern Africa. As Ranger (1994:287) notes, Britain, Portugal, and France drew Africa's borders as "sifters of labour rather than as barriers to its movement." In the process of permitting travel, these borders create and differentiate among categories of people.[2] Elites may suffer nothing worse than cultural disorientation upon crossing a border (cf. Wilson and Donnan 1998:2). Even among refugees, groups with preexisting advantages may adapt more easily to exile. The Jehovah's Witnesses described by Wilson possessed organization and leadership to a striking degree. Similarly, Anita Spring (1979) finds that female Angolans in Zambia rose in social position much more readily than did their male counterparts. They divorced their Angolan husbands and remarried wealthier Zambians while their ex-husbands could not afford the higher Zambian bride-wealth and remained single. Immigration, thus, can accentuate privilege and weakness. For some, "deterritorialization" is virtually a form of tourism. International businessmen may very well experience it as such. For others—such as the Mozambicans in Vhimba harassed by the Parks Department—travel may bring terror.

My own crossing of the old Anglo-Portuguese line more closely approximated tourism. As the preface mentioned, I embarked upon fieldwork in Gogoi in 1997, after the better part of a year spent studying Vhimba and prior work elsewhere in Zimbabwe. I, in fact, had joined in the politics of Vhimba. As chapter 4 explains, I assisted Vhimba people to claim land formally inside the Rusitu Botanical Reserve. Gogoi, I thought, would present similar conflicts over land. After all, South Africans had recently crossed their own border with Mozambique and were cutting timber in Gogoi. The South Africans, moreover, were grabbing land. I expected to find Chief Gogoi battling over boundaries and territorial rights. In the event, he was doing no such thing. Even when asked directly, he had little idea where some of his territorial boundaries were or should be. I was disoriented, and I reacted in the Zimbabwean fashion. I led a mapping project that helped Chief Gogoi to draw boundaries of his "territory" and to protect it from alienation. This project, combined with the South African threat, introduced cadastral thinking and cadastral politics to Gogoi. Thus, my ethnography, especially in chapter 5, addresses my own role, as a border crosser. As an anthropologist-mapper, I joined and even pushed forward the territorializing processes I set out to study.

3

REFUGEES, SQUATTERS,
AND THE POLITICS OF LAND
ALLOCATION IN VHIMBA

IN VHIMBA, THE BORDER DELIMITED IN 1898 BECAME IMPORTANT IN
local social relations within little more than a generation.[1] As a bizarre case
of arson reveals, the borderland nurtured its own form of transnational parochialism. In 1929, a Vhimba woman testified before the magistrate, "[The]
Accused said to me if I keep making beer across the Portuguese Border he
would burn our hut. He wanted me to make beer this side so that he could
join in."[2] The alleged arsonist lived in Vhimba, but he may have avoided
Mozambique because he owed taxes there. Portugal and its chartered
Companhia de Moçambique imposed a particularly onerous form of *chibaro*, payable in cash, but failing that, demanded in labor. By mid-century,
de facto corvées, carried out by chiefs and native police, were regularly
provoking Mozambicans to emigrate (see chapter 1). Fleeing residents of
Mossurize simply traded one set of obligations to their chief for a less severe
one to his Rhodesian opposite number. Those Mozambicans who stayed
endured harrowing stints of work in Manica Province's plantation sector.
To make matters worse, they received no formal education, rendering
them, in Vhimba's view, backward and uncouth. "They have not studied.
They are used to war,"[3] Zimbabweans explained in reference to benighted
Mossurize.

In the early 1990s, Vhimba's headmen also considered Zimbabwe to
be different, and they knew how to turn the border to their advantage.
Zimbabwe's history of land alienation and technical land-use planning had
directed rural conflict not toward forced labor but toward cadastral boundaries and claims to land. The Native Land Husbandry Act of 1951 trained

smallholders in resisting official intrusions into their use of land.[4] More generally, in the course of periodic dispossessions in Chimanimani District, chiefs, headmen, their subjects, and branches of the state created a system of power and legitimacy based on struggles over agricultural land. Headmen learned to use their capacity as land allocators against threats from outside and from within the community. Vhimba's commoners also learned how to protect their interests in negotiating with headmen over access to land. Nearby Mozambicans, however, acquired no such skills: their fortune in losing no substantial parcels to white settlers simply made them naïve in cadastral matters. For this reason, Vhimba headmen followed different conventions when allocating land to Mozambican migrants than when allocating to Zimbabwean migrants. Particularly with regard to recent inflows of refugees, Vhimba's headmen treated immigrants not only differently but also *worse* than they did Zimbabwean internal migrants. Refugees settled on the most vulnerable, contested slices of territory. Moreover, notwithstanding their kin and ethnic ties to Vhimba, the newcomers had no choice in the matter of their residence. Unwilling squatters in national parks and elsewhere, these Mozambicans served as transnational pawns in Zimbabwean turf wars beyond their ken.

LAND ALLOCATION IN VHIMBA, 1946–97

During the colonial period, land allocation became the gateway through which all male migrants entered Vhimba. Since the 1890s, expropriation, in-migration, rising population density, and state conservation policies had directed conflict toward land and placed headmen at the center of managing and participating in land-related disputes. As long as migrants continue to arrive in Vhimba, land allocation remains headmen's principle responsibility. Men come to Vhimba in order to establish homesteads and farm, or they come in order to establish homesteads where their wife or wives farm while they work elsewhere. Women come to Vhimba either in the company of their migrating husbands or to marry and live with men already resident in Vhimba. The women who migrate alone to Vhimba are widows. In these cases, a male relative or acquaintance usually speaks with the headman regarding the widow's parcel of land. Land allocation, then, is the mechanism by which headmen discuss with other men so as to locate new homesteads and fields in Vhimba.

Analyses of settlement and land tenure in Zimbabwe often treat these discussions as an unknowable "black box." Such accounts tend to focus on the outcome, rather than the process, of settlement. In so doing, they reduce land allocation to a single decision taken by a single actor, usually the headman. For example, in J. F. Holleman's classic *Shona Customary Law* (1952:6), the headman drives a stake into the ground he has chosen for the new household. Migrants necessarily submit to his fiat. In an alternative scenario, migrants drive their own stakes, figuratively speaking: they allocate land to themselves.[5] Both models envision one active party and one passive party. Neither approach grapples with the real nature of much decision making, the muddling of multiple protagonists who do not know each other well. More in this vein, Shimmer Chinodya's novel *Dew in the Morning* (1982:160) contains a scene in which an older brother, visiting from town, secures more land for his rural siblings:

> At sunset . . . he remained with us to show us the area he wanted earmarked for our fields when we grew up. . . . The area was about thirty acres in extent, and along each border he cut down the bushes and laid them out in a rough line. "Tell headman Simon tomorrow that I propose this area for your fields." . . . We laughed at the determination that was blind to the gathering dusk and to the fact that he was assuming the role of the headman.

Interestingly, this fictional land-grabber still seeks the approval of the headman. He is engaging in the kind of murky maneuvers that lie in between allocation by the headman and self-allocation by the migrant, between a dictate from above and a fait accompli from below.

Although Chinodya's story concerns an existing, expanding family in Headman Simon's area, newcomers can play the same tricks. Still, it seems more reasonable that current subjects, like those in the story, should enlarge their holding unilaterally than that absolute newcomers should try to do so. Are not strangers, especially those without relations in the area, completely at the mercy of headmen? In fact, migrants have some leverage: headmen want more subjects for greater prestige, tax revenues, and better services— quite apart from the possibility of using certain migrants as boundary beacons. In many cases, migrants do bargain with headmen over the sites where they should live and farm (Dzingirai 1994:172–73). A migrant may pick his own spot and subsequently ask for the headman's permission (the strategy in Chinodya's tale), he may reject the first location offered and ask for another, or he may consult two adjoining headmen and take the best offer. Like James Scott's (1985) "everyday forms of peasant resistance," these tactics have the advantage of being covert. Both parties can eventually cover up their bargains and respect the accepted hierarchy. Everyone, including many academic observers, holds to this narrative: the headman allocated the land—full stop.

In Vhimba, however, a particular class of migrants actually conforms to the narrative. These newcomers accept the first parcel headmen offer them. Twenty-nine heads of households, of a larger number I interviewed in 1996–97, are suitable for an analysis of bargaining in land allocation.[6] The heads of these households migrated to Vhimba between 1946 and 1997. Fourteen of them received, with or without requesting it, a choice of parcels. In the remaining fifteen cases, the headman offered only one site. What accounts for the different ways in which these headmen—Chikware, Tiyekiye, and Muhanyi—treated arriving people? Migrants' kinship ties to Vhimba or birth or prior residence in Chief Ngorima's polity could affect the outcome. In fact, none of these variables is as important as the national origin of the migrants. By and large, Zimbabweans chose among two or more possible parcels whereas Mozambicans conceded to headmen's first and only proposal. To be precise, 77 percent of Zimbabweans chose whereas only 25 percent of Mozambicans did so; or 71 percent of those who chose were Zimbabwean and 80 percent of those who did not chose were Mozambican.

Table 3.1 summarizes these data and the influence of common kin, a common chief, and common nationality. Kinship does appear to play a role in land allocation to Zimbabwean migrants. All the Zimbabweans with relations in Vhimba were able to choose their plots. Among the Mozambicans, however, headmen treated Vhimba's kin no better than they treated non-kin. Despite the limitations of a very small sample, Zimbabweans appear to benefit through their Vhimba relatives, whereas for Mozambicans the prejudice against foreign citizenship overwhelms all mitigating factors. A comparison of the households purely on the axis of kin ties reveals (table 3.2) no clear relationship of blood and marriage with negotiating room. A similar comparison, this time purely on the basis of prior residence in Ngorima's polity, appears to indicate that natives of Ngorima's area fare rather better upon arrival in Vhimba (as in table 3.3).[7] Since Ngorima's border coincides with the national border, however, this distribution is misleading. *All* Mozambicans are foreign to Ngorima's area, so a test that controls for nationality in order to measure the bias based on chiefly affiliation must include only Zimbabweans. Table 3.1 shows that, among this group, Ngorima's subjects had hardly more choices than those from outside the chieftaincy. Headmen, then, hardly discriminated on the basis of a migrant's kin or chief. The basis for favorable or unfavorable treatment was nationality (as shown in table 3.4).

TABLE 3.1. Land Allocation in Vhimba, 1946–97

		Choice (n = 14)	No choice (n = 15)
Zimbabwean-born Ngorima natives	With kin	2	0
	Without kin	3	1
Zimbabwean-born Non-Ngorima natives	With kin	1	0
	Without kin	4	2
Mozambican-born	With kin	0	2
	Without kin	4	10

TABLE 3.2. Land Allocation in Vhimba Analyzed by Kin Ties of In-Migrant

	Choice (n = 14)	No choice (n = 15)
Kin ties	3	2
No kin ties	11	13

TABLE 3.3. Land Allocation in Vhimba Analyzed
by Chiefdom of In-Migrant's Birth

	Choice (n = 14)	No choice (n = 15)
Birth in Ngorima's area	5	1
Birth outside Ngorima's area	9	14

TABLE 3.4. Land Allocation in Vhimba Analyzed
by Country of In-Migrant's Birth

	Choice (n = 14)	No choice (n = 15)
Zimbabwean-born	10	3
Mozambican-born	4	12

From their fortunate position, Zimbabweans applied a number of strategies to open and conclude negotiations with Vhimba's headmen. S. M. arrived in 1994 from Shurugwi wanting space to plant fruit trees in the lowland of Vhimba. After the intercession of his wife's sister's husband, Headman Tiyekiye offered S. M. a plot close to the Rusitu River. S. M., however, found this field too small, so he went alone to Chikware who proposed a larger field high up, close to the escarpment. In effect, S. M. shopped with two headmen and took the better of two not entirely satisfactory alternatives. M. C. preferred to live high up and chose the more elevated of the two sites Chikware presented him in 1972. In 1981, C. K. B. chose among three alternatives. Further back, probably in the 1950s and 1960s, Chikware virtually permitted self-allocation: with his blessing, two arriving heads of household scouted the territory themselves. "My family and I looked for a place,"[8] recalled said Z. M. as I interviewed him. M. M. reported a similarly conciliatory attitude on the headman's part: "I want a place," he demanded, and Tiyekiye queried, "Which place do you want?"[9] In sum, give-and-take—and sometimes just *give*—has characterized the interactions between Zimbabwean land seekers and Vhimba headmen.

To Mozambicans, by contrast, the very same headmen made take-it-or-leave-it offers. I. R .M. tried to bargain after Chikware showed him a spot on the western side of Nyakwawa Forest. Chikware told him the spot he desired was not available since the family who previously occupied it might still have a claim. In another case, a headman offered claimed land and only claimed land to a Mozambican migrant. Tiyekiye showed M., who crossed the Rusitu from neighboring Chief Mafussi's area in 1991, a slice of E. N.'s fallow fields. According to M.'s recollection, Tiyekiye then announced: "You have now seen the place to hoe."[10] Having no other choice, M. farmed there and tolerated an uneasy relationship with his neighbor. Almost all the remaining fourteen land allocations to Mozambicans were equally unilateral. Whereas Zimbabweans virtually "wheeled and dealed" their way into Vhimba, Mozambicans came, they saw one place, and they settled immediately.

Interestingly, money was not an issue. The noncommoditized nature of land allocation is all the more striking because deals could so easily include finance.[11] Most migrants did offer a token of respect to the headman upon receipt of a parcel. In earlier times, people gave him a chicken, or *huku*, and the current monetary substitute is still called *huku*. Thus, land allocations could provide headmen with financial resources as well as social and political capital, which is discussed below. A mercenary headman would do well to place *huku* payments at the center of negotiations over land and get the most he could from weak bargainers. Indeed, a number of third parties told me, in confidence, that they suspected Tiyekiye, Chikware, and Muhanyi of doing precisely this and of selfishly "selling the land."[12] Yet, virtually all of the subjects of the migration study quoted *huku* amounts within an order of magnitude of the local price of a live, adult chicken. Indeed, the Mozambican refugee migrants, who haggled the least, got their plots cheapest, that is, as free relief goods. If land allocation was a real estate deal—in which Mozambicans did *not* deal—the sticking point was location, not price.

Why did Mozambicans acquiesce? My field assistants thought Mozambicans were ill treated because many arrived only in recent years, when land had become scarce. These informants cited 1990 as the turning point. In the 1980s, they said, migrants chose their places, but from 1990 onward, free spaces were increasingly unavailable. In this view, time and population density, not the nationality of migrants, affected the degree of flexibility in headmen's allocation of land. To a certain extent, the distinction between these variables is a false one: most of the migrants who came in the 1990s were Mozambican refugees from the 1991–92 drought (ten of thirteen), and most of those who came before were Zimbabwean (ten of sixteen). Mozambican migrants encountered the unfavorable conditions of high population density and uncompromising headmen much more frequently than did their Zimbabwean counterparts, and, predictably, headmen told almost all of them exactly where to live. Yet, the minority figures, small as they are, reveal that headmen exercised a bias against Mozambicans and in favor of Zimbabweans in both periods. Zimbabweans arriving in the 1990s had more choices than Mozambicans. Similarly, in the 1980s, Mozambicans negotiated to a much lesser extent than did Zimbabweans. It is true, however, that conditions were tougher for everyone in the 1990s. Mozambicans chose their plots less often than before, and so did Zimbabweans, but before and after 1990, Zimbabweans had consistently more autonomy in land allocation (as shown in table 3.5). Nationality matters after all.

LAND ALLOCATION AS PERSONAL PLEDGING

Nationality matters because land allocation meant something very different in the case of Mozambicans in the 1990s. A history of land alienation and of resulting high population densities in the communal lands had conditioned Zimbabweans to view land as a political issue. Arriving in a new communal land, they *expected* to bargain with headmen over the location and quality of

TABLE 3.5. Land Allocation in Vhimba Analyzed
by Country of In-Migrant's Birth and Year of Arrival

	1946–89 (n = 16)		1990–97 (n = 13)	
	Choice	No choice	Choice	No choice
Zimbabwean-born	8	2	2	1
Mozambican-born	2	4	2	8

allocated fields. Yet, what was a real estate deal for Zimbabweans was perhaps closer to a "personal estate" deal for Mozambican refugees. Until the mid-1990s, conflict in Mossurize had turned on the allocation of (forced) labor rather than the allocation of fields. There, people viewed their headmen through the lens of Portuguese-era *chibaro* and, in reference to an earlier time, through the experience of *kukhonza*. This latter form of servitude dated from the precolonial Gaza Nguni kingdom. During the Nguni raids and related famines, people pledged themselves to lineage heads, exchanging labor and rights over progeny for physical and economic security. At least in the oral tradition, Mozambicans understood that flight from one's home to a new area incurred a change of status. Integration among hosts would depend, not on negotiations over land, but on personal pledging to a headman.

Now, after a peaceful hiatus of a century, conditions similar to those associated with Gaza Nguni *kukhonza* reappeared in northern Mossurize. The Renamo rebel movement conquered the area in 1987 and established a system of forced labor that came to be known as *chikoroka* (see chapter 1). Chiefs and headmen thereupon stepped into their colonial roles: they recruited porters and other workers for external demands. *Chikoroka*, then, rescued a relationship of servitude that, under Frelimo's socialist rule, was atrophying. *Chikoroka* also created an enabling environment for the efflorescence of that relationship in the course of the 1991–92 drought. Even before rainfall collapsed, the labor corvée and similar taxes in food had diminished households' agricultural capacity. Meanwhile, a strategy of semi-hiding in forested areas had reduced the space under cultivation. Finally, instability and Frelimo's policy against migrant labor impeded travel to South Africa (Schafer 1999:68). The little money workers did remit could not have significantly improved food security: war had interrupted road transport and, therefore, suspended nearly all grain markets in Mossurize. (Zimbabwean smallholders did sell grain to Mozambicans, but at a particular price, which is discussed below.) In sum, smallholders disposed of nearly no economic or productive resources. Like all refugees, they were poor, vulnerable, politically suspect, and transient, but some managed to *use* those qualities. The one resource they possessed in abundance was their position of servitude. Tapping into cultural mechanisms that integrated poor, vulnerable, outsiders, Mozambicans put that resource to good effect across the border, in Zimbabwe.

In the minds of Vhimba residents, Mozambicans' acts of *kukhonza* conformed to old and new models of subordination. Elders associated personal pledging with suspensions of the usual patrilineal conventions of bridewealth. For example, they recalled Shangwa Ngorima's (chief from roughly 1939 to 1955) "orphan" (*nherera*), a man whose parents had died in Gaza Nguni raids in the previous century. He fled to Ngorima's, married the chief's daughter without bride-wealth, served as the chief's assistant, and, in theory, ceded to Ngorima rights over his children (principally the right to negotiate *their* marriage payments).[13] This type of bride-service, however, had mostly died out by the 1990s (see chapter 2), and Mozambican men did not engage in it in Vhimba. A second "free" form of marriage mirrored the events of the 1990s more closely: distressed families offered their unmarried daughters gratis, or the woman herself appealed to a man who could feed her. During the drought, a destitute Mozambican woman pledged herself to M., a Vhimba man, beseeching: "Please take care of me. Please marry me."[14] M., who recalled the event with moral ambivalence in our private conversation, refused this responsibility. He wanted no trouble from the woman's relatives, should they eventually appear. W. C., however, accepted an identical offer from a girl fleeing from the vicinity of Beira. Finally, in cases only reported secondhand, Mozambicans offered their daughters in exchange for food. To Zimbabweans, these practices indicated great hardship (*kusvupika*), the lack of basic means (*kushaya*), and *kukhonza*. These drought-era marriages represented, in other words, a kinship idiom for issues that were, at root, economic.

By contrast, a second set of meanings for *kukhonza* centered on (to put it awkwardly) a "border idiom." Whereas the marital interpretation of pledging focused on common, cross-border kindred, this more political understanding treated the border as distinctly "hard." *Kukhonza*, then, meant to subject oneself to another polity.[15] For example, during Mozambique's war of the 1980s and 1990s, the worst-off residents of Mossurize exhausted sources of support from kin and neighbors and then fled to Zimbabwe.[16] Crossing the Rusitu River, these destitute people could proceed to camps where relief food was available or remain in Ngorima Communal Land where it would be possible to farm in safety. In either case, they were technically and legally refugees, and Zimbabweans and Mozambicans translated this circumstance into a new meaning of *kukhonza*. For example, "One who does not have relatives is called a *mukhonzwa* [someone who has performed a *kukhonza* act] . . . it is similar to refugees."[17] Other observers identified a *mukhonzwa* more broadly, as any undocumented alien: "We say he has -*khonza* because he does not have identity papers from here."[18] Finally, a Mozambican resident of Chief Macuiana's area defended himself from my suggestion in an interview at his homestead that he had -*khonza*, saying, "I do not -*khonza*. I am in Mozambique. I was born in Mozambique."[19] In short, to -*khonza* was to cross the border in desperate circumstances.

More precisely still, the definition applied much more readily to Mozambicans entering Zimbabwe than vice versa. With peace and an efficient state system of famine relief, Zimbabweans could hardly imagine fleeing to a land they identified as backward, violent, and poor. Indeed, informants reported that only a handful of Vhimba families had taken refuge in Mozambique during Zimbabwe's war of the 1970s. Ironically, the relief apparatus that allowed Zimbabweans to stay put rendered Mozambicans doubly vulnerable as long as they stayed in Vhimba. Refugees who wished to avoid deportation to Tongogara Camp depended absolutely upon the collusion of headmen.[20] Yet, headmen had many reasons to eject foreigners from their communities. Unlike most Zimbabwean internal migrants, these Mozambicans came with no letter from the district government attesting to a clean criminal record. With a war under way, Vhimba residents suspected that people were fleeing Mossurize not only as victims of violence but perhaps as wanted perpetrators. One headman confessed that he distrusted refugees for precisely this reason and, therefore, did not let them choose their places of residence. Ordinary citizens were disinclined to extend networks of support, information, and the like to such shady characters. Refugees were, therefore, ultimate strangers and outsiders.[21]

Did Zimbabwean headmen and Mozambican migrants consider their interaction as a form of pledging? Did they understand themselves to be making a personal estate deal, rather than the real estate deal conventional between Zimbabweans? In discussions regarding land allocation to Mozambicans, *kukhonza* constituted at least a strong undercurrent, politically charged and personally embarrassing. M. M., a Zimbabwean man, admitted Mozambican land seekers into his definition of *mukhonzwa*: "A person arrives and says, 'I want a homestead site,' . . . this person has no relatives and comes from elsewhere."[22] At least one of the three headmen also saw land allocation in this way. "If I -*khonza*," Muhanyi told me in an interview, "I want a homestead site" for a short period.[23] The transient nature of this land allocation was important: these fields might be considered short-term relief goods for people who needed to plant immediately. Headman Muhanyi gave such temporary plots to numerous Mozambicans in 1991–92, most of who had returned to Mozambique by 1995. Other headmen and the Mozambicans themselves shared a general confusion regarding *kukhonza* and land allocation. They concurred, however, that Mozambican refugees were especially vulnerable outsiders to a degree equivalent to that of a *mukhonzwa*. In the 1990s, headmen allocated land to these refugees, as to earlier Mozambican immigrants, on unfavorable terms. Refugees, for their part, do not appear to have attempted any of the bargaining strategies familiar to Zimbabwean migrants. In land deals, they submitted to headmen's first proposals. The outcome for these Mozambicans was a striking form of manipulation in the land politics of Vhimba.[24]

VULNERABLE PEOPLE IN PERILOUS PLACES

When refugees started arriving in Vhimba, land politics were heated and likely to become more so. Structural conflicts existed on three levels, and all involved land to a greater or lesser degree. Foremost was the series of grievances against those who had alienated land from Ngorima's polity. Other conflicts based directly on control of land pitted headmen against each other. Finally, headmen needed to justify their positions to commoners in Vhimba. Allocating land was one way to do just this. Headmen, then, *could* employ land allocation in order to strengthen themselves first against the state, second against rival headmen, and third against their subjects. In the early 1990s, headmen *did* manipulate land allocation in all of these ways. They succeeded in doing so precisely because, at the right time, the right kind of migrants arrived—Mozambican refugees.

By 1990, resentment toward the government on the issue of past land alienation had been building for a decade. When conversation turned to the lost lands, Vhimba smallholders often recalled that the guerrillas had promised them personally, "You may live where you want to."[25] That is, after independence, smallholders could and should return to estates and other expropriated lands. With such encouragement, Headman Muhanyi and four other families moved back inside the section of Chimanimani National Park from which they had been evicted in the 1960s, a forested area known as Matsenderero. They farmed there only until 1981, when the Parks Department reasserted control over the margins of the park. Rangers of the new, black-ruled Zimbabwe simply implemented colonial-era legislation and tossed the "squatters" out of Matsenderero (see chapter 2). "In what way have those without a place to live been liberated?"[26] an evictee asked me rhetorically as we noted that the following day was Zimbabwe's Independence Day. On that very anniversary, a meeting of the Village Development Committee (Vidco) addressed the status of Mukwiratunhu, the adjoining area of the park annexed in 1965 (see chapter 2). Again, the postindependence state was reaffirming colonial policy. "The border was taken by the heroes [of the liberation struggle],"[27] accused one man at the Vhimba meeting. Acts of omission compounded the state's guilt: the land redistribution program of the early 1980s gave the parastatal Forestry Commission first pick of the best parcels on the main Chimanimani Plateau. The two small farms designated for smallholders in the Nyahode and upper Rusitu Valley lay far away from Vhimba—too far for Vhimba residents to gain a foothold in the scramble for resettlement on them. Finally, the state's postindependence revival of technocratic land-use planning threatened to marginalize headmen from the process of settlement.[28] Measured in hectares, Vhimba's headmen and commoners gained nothing from the change of government. Together, they formed a searing sense of betrayal by a government verbally committed to land redistribution (Hughes 1996).

Vhimba residents, however, lacked a means to express and act upon their land claims. Obviously, the best—and perhaps the only—way to claim the land was to establish huts and crops on it. Chief Garayi Ngorima had used this cheap form of countersurveying against the Rusitu Mission (chapter 2). Squatting was also smallholders' weapon of choice in postindependence land wars nationwide, and, once squatters were installed, the government had a hard time politically dislodging them.[29] Nonetheless, existing Vhimba residents were understandably wary of opening fields or sending their sons into a forbidden zone. Zimbabwean internal migrants were equally prudent. Through social networks, they learned of the existence and location of these areas. They then bargained their way out of disputed zones and onto safer parcels. Mozambican migrants, as seen here, had less room to maneuver than did Zimbabweans in land allocation. Headmen might have deployed them inside the alienated areas, but very few Mozambicans arrived in the 1980s (only one family in the sample). Enter refugees. These particularly afflicted Mozambicans would live nearly anywhere. Headmen must have sensed that they could send refugees, like infantry, over the trenches and into disputed ground. In the event, headmen settled refugees a small distance inside Chimanimani National Park and the Hayfield B property. While thus expanding the collective perimeter of their Ngorima Communal Land, these headmen also used refugees to counter threats from within Ngorima's polity. The boundaries between headmen's areas were as contested as were those delimiting Ngorima Communal Land. In these headman-to-headman disputes, land allocation was doubly effective. It constituted both a seizure of land and an extension of political jurisdiction. This correlation rested on the association of control over people with control over land in Zimbabwe. Colonial-era evictions, migration to the communal land, and subsequent land allocation in Vhimba had forged that link. In the 1990s, as in the past, migrants owed beer to the land allocator and, in some cases, passed state taxes through him as well. The beer drinks, especially, affirmed the headman's position as social dean and land manager. As a form of thanks to the headman, each migrant family invited its new neighbors—and the headman—to a "housewarming" celebration. Having thus extruded a permanent base of clients and allies, therefore, one headman could erode the sovereignty of another. Yet to live as a protégé of one headman on land claimed by another was not comfortable. Someone who knew enough and could negotiate to avoid this predicament would try to do so. As expected, the people thrown by one headman into another's area in the 1990s were overwhelmingly Mozambican.

A second threat to headmen from close to home concerned the office of headman itself. The English term *headman* encompasses the Shona terms *sadunhu* and *sabhuku* (plural, *masadunhu* and *masabhuku*). The title *sadunhu* dates from the precolonial period, while *sabhuku* is a more recent creation. Native commissioners unintentionally begat the latter term when, at the turn of the twentieth century, they invested certain *masadunhu*[30] with tax books, hence the English-derived root *bhuku* in *sabhuku*. Throughout the colonial era, the new rank stirred uncertainty and contestation. Did a book-bearing *sabhuku* rank above, below, or equal with a *sadunhu* who had never acquired a tax book? (In many other parts of Zimbabwe, the *sadunhu* clearly outranks the *sabhuku*.) At independence, the question became doubly vexed: the new government abolished direct taxation in the communal lands, but the title *sabhuku* persisted nonetheless. Thus, in 1995, respondents disagreed strongly on the proper hierarchy between, say, *sabhuku* Tiyekiye and *sadunhu* Chikware. One factor that swayed these popular political judgments was land allocation. Some Vhimba residents based their order of ranking upon the accomplishments of a given headmen in settling migrants, especially when migrants lived close to the respondent. Of course, since all the *masabhuku* and *masadunhu* in Vhimba and its environs hosted refugees in the early 1990s, land allocation produced a stalemate. By 1997, however, nearly everyone knew of the Rural District Council's "development levy" introduced four years earlier and payable directly to one's *sabhuku*. Although most people continued to evade the tax, the clear majority now placed the *sabhuku* above the *sadunhu*.

Notwithstanding this affirmation, Vhimba's *sabhuku*—as well as its *masadunhu*—still had to watch his back. A final internal threat stemmed from the recurrence of succession disputes for the office of headman. Colonial intervention in chiefly polities was again partly to blame. Pax Britannica had suppressed the use of fratricide and banishment as tools for settling controversy over succession. In place of these effective, if ruthless, methods, district administrators substituted their own principles and ceremonies for official installation.[31] Yet, no headmen in Ngorima's polity had received such an official imprimatur; under the Chiefs and Headmen Act (1982), they were not headmen, and *sabhuku* Tiyekiye bemoaned his deprivation of salary, medallions, and the coveted pith helmet.[32] Without these official endorsements, headmen were exposed to brothers and cousins— ominously alive and close at hand—who would reveal or concoct a past misapplication of the "traditional" rules of succession. As in the bride-service marriages mentioned in chapter 2—which resulted in de facto matrilineage— strategies for seeking power focused on exploiting the loopholes in patrilineal conventions. If successful, aspirant headmen would convert the patrilineal succession of titles into a de facto collateral system, allowing the younger brother (or cousin) to succeed the older one.[33] To forestall this outcome, officeholders needed constantly to assert their legitimacy (John Comaroff 1978). In effect, they waged continual succession disputes against the possibility that they might be demoted to mere regents.

Both Tiyekiye and Chikware found themselves in this precarious position, and both tried to use land allocation to their benefit. Tiyekiye's father assumed office in 1948 as a regent for his younger cousin (his mother's brother's son), the son of the headman originally invested by Chief Ngorima. This regent, however, reigned until his death and succeeded in passing the office to his son, the present Tiyekiye. Neither Tiyekiye nor his deceased father belonged to the clan of the original headman and of Ngorima himself, *mwoyo*. To make matters worse, Tiyekiye worshipped in the Zion apostolic church and, hence, did not deliver offerings to (heathen) ancestral spirits of the sacred forest lying within his domain. His nonconverted younger brother performed this *kudira* ceremony, but many of Tiyekiye's subjects found the substitution less than ideal. Tiyekiye's incumbency, therefore, hung in the balance: at any moment, his subjects could decide that his father's cousin, still living within Ngorima Communal Land, could do a better job.[34] Chikware's grasp on power was even weaker. He took the office in 1990 in place of his older brother, who was absent on migrant labor. For Chikware and Tiyekiye to retain the respect of their people, it was essential that they be seen to perform well. What better device for this effort than land allocation? Through land allocation, Tiyekiye and Chikware demonstrated that they, indeed, could perform as headmen should perform. By extruding a perimeter of settlement, they claimed the interstitial territory for themselves, their subjects, and their subjects' children. Their strategy was additionally effective because much of the land allocated was once confiscated by the state. On this front, headmen were fighting a struggle widely supported by their constituents. Only an improvident public—to extend the metaphor—would unseat successful generals in the midst of winning a popular war.

In summary, headmen used refugees in multiple ways to advance on numerous fronts. Against private and public landowners, refugees were a beachhead. They served the same purpose against neighboring headmen. Finally, toward commoners, the allocation of land demonstrated a headman's efficacy and legitimacy as a ruler. Each of the three headmen in Vhimba—Tiyekiye, Muhanyi, and Chikware—benefited from these manipulations of refugees. In spatial terms, the allocations that benefited them most occurred in three areas: in the Mukwiratunhu section of Chimanimani National Park, in the Hayfield B estate, and in a disputed slice of communal land I will call the "Chisambavarongo wedge" (map 3.1). The remainder of this chapter discusses these cases in turn.

The first allocations in Chimanimani National Park conjoined internally and externally directed conflicts. In 1991 and 1992, Headman Tiyekiye settled four households in the Mukwiratunhu area (map 3.1). Three of these families had left Dombe, Sussundenga District, Mozambique, because of drought and war, and the fourth arrived from Chipinge.[35] None had any choice in the matter of land allocation. As a site for external deployment, Tiyekiye picked Mukwiratunhu because, as he told an officer of the Vhimba Area Development Committee and me, "It was inhabited before. Mafatu died there. Maparara died there too."[36] Matsenderero had also been previously occupied, but the Parks Department was particularly vigilant with regard to moist forest—rather than the rocky upland of Mukwiratunhu—in southern Chimanimani District. Tiyekiye, therefore, thought he could make his claim to Mukwiratunhu stick and, of course, that that claim was legitimate.

In the event, Tiyekiye's allocations provoked opposition from within

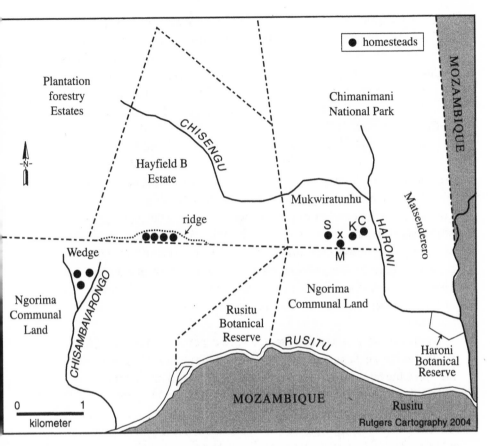

MAP 3.1. Vhimba land disputes, 1995–97

Vhimba even before the Parks Department intervened. By allocating in Mukwiratunhu, Tiyekiye may have overstepped his authority with regard to another headman. Muhanyi claimed to rule Mukwiratunhu, Matsenderero, and the immediately adjoining stretch of communal land. (Muhanyi and his younger brother were two of the household heads evicted from Matsenderero in 1981.) Muhanyi, however, is a *sadunhu* rather than a *sabhuku*, so his subjects were in the colonial "book" of Tiyekiye. Did the responsibility to tax residents of Mukwiratunhu confer on Tiyekiye the privilege of settling people there? (The question was made still murkier by the facts that there had not been a tax in eleven years and that noncitizens in hiding from the law would not have paid tax anyway.) The Muhanyi family thought not; the *sadunhu*'s nephew protested to me, "Tiyekiye wants to rule areas that are not his."[37] In a more public campaign against Tiyekiye, Muhanyi had posted a sign in Mukwiratunhu declaring: "Let us try to do the wishes of the owner of this place, David Muhanyi. Live well with others in this place. Care for your livestock."[38] Eventually, the Muhanyis and wider Vhimba opinion forced Tiyekiye to "hand over" these four families.[39] It was agreed retroactively that Muhanyi had allocated the land in Mukwiratunhu.

Concurrent with the "invention" of these allocations, Muhanyi was actually distributing plots in Mukwiratunhu to migrant families on his own account. Indeed, it was essential for him to do so when he did. Until the protocol between himself and Tiyekiye was formalized, Muhanyi was in a "use it or lose it" situation: if he did not exercise his duties as headman, Tiyekiye might take them from him altogether. During the 1991–93 period, Muhanyi stuck four families into Mukwiratunhu. Again, three of these were Mozambicans; one was Zimbabwean, from Bikita District; and none of them chose their parcels. These allocations—combined with the handover from Tiyekiye—established that Muhanyi was in charge of Mukwiratunhu. All of the eight families there owed their continued residence in Vhimba to Muhanyi.

By 1995, however, six of these families had departed, and Muhanyi faced another set of challenges to his authority. In 1993, the Parks Department identified the removal of "squatters," especially "illegal immigrants," from Chimanimani National Park as a priority (Kawadza and Rogers 1993:2). It undertook a campaign of evictions too complex to be given full treatment here. As part of this effort, threats and intimidation from scouts may have influenced the six families, all Mozambican, to return to their home country. At the same time, the end of the drought, the 1992 peace accords, and the nonviolent conclusion of the 1994 elections made repatriation to Mozambique much more appealing. Whatever the cause, the refugees' desertion was a blow to Muhanyi: the flags he had planted in Mukwiratunhu were now gone. Shortly thereafter, however, a small influx of migrants gave Muhanyi another chance. This time he did not thrust settlers deep in Mukwiratunhu toward the Chisengu River, as before. Instead, he used them to make a compromise, as markers of the conciliatory boundary he wished to establish between his territory and the park. In late 1996, he placed C., who arrived from Gogoi and did not negotiate, in Mukwiratunhu (map 3.1). Together with the two families who remained of the original eight (S.[40] and K.), C. formed a roughly east-to-west line, parallel to but two hundred meters or so north of the official park boundary. When M. immigrated from Dombe,

Mozambique in early 1997, Muhanyi sought to complete that line by siting him at a point (marked with "x" on map 3.1) directly between S. and K.[41] The plan was not entirely successful because M. did not want his wife exposed to wild animals and other insecurities of the bush while he worked in South Africa. M. negotiated for a stand just slightly to the south (where "M" is now marked on map 3.1). Thus, Muhanyi created a zigzag rather than a straight line, but he created a boundary nonetheless.

Inside the Hayfield B estate, Headman Chikware undertook an analogous "counterdemarcation" (map 3.1). The expulsions of the early 1980s had spared one household, K. C., located just south of the ridge between the Rusitu and Chisengu valleys. Chikware appeared to have decided that this ridge would make a fair border between the communal and estate land. Rather than repopulate the Chisengu Valley, therefore, Chikware settled three families in the amphitheater-shaped area around K. C. In these cases, as opposed to those in Mukwiratunhu, the issue of choice in land allocation was not salient. E. C., who received his allocation in 1992, already had farmed at a primary residence in the lowland part of Chikware's area. Migrating from elsewhere in Ngorima Communal Land in 1994, K. M. was a formal-sector worker and not particularly concerned about the location of his fields. Finally, V. M., who arrived in 1995, was a widow and could not be expected to bargain over land. Thus, these migrants did not have strong reasons to oppose their use as Chikware's boundary beacons. By refraining from bargaining—even when some of them could have—these Zimbabweans put themselves in the position of Mozambicans. They became a second row of boundary beacons in the creeping reannexation of Ngorima's lost lands.

Surprisingly, C. L., the white owner of Hayfield B, has accommodated Chikware's push northward. He is aware of the families squatting on his land. Indeed, he insists that the border does not follow the ridge, but approximates a line slightly south, what would be the edge of the amphitheater before the ground slopes steeply toward the Rusitu. Yet, he has taken no steps to evict those four families, having only informed them that they are trespassing. When I visited one of E. C.'s wives at the homestead, she recalled having been notified: "We are in the yard of the white man."[42] The estate owner, furthermore, warned her not to allow fires to escape. More tolerant of squatters than the ZANU–PF-led government, C. L. was considering granting the four families long-term leases on Hayfield B. In effect, this landowner acceded to Chikware's cautious redemarcation of the boundary. For him though, that line was firm. Encroachment farther north would have placed people in the

Chisengu watershed, which C. L. planned to reserve as a butterfly sanctuary. "No way!" responded C. L. when, in the aftermath of a ceremony and feast he had sponsored, evictees grew bold enough to petition him directly.[43]

The final disputed area of land allocation in the 1990s lies along the border between Chikware's and Headman Muitire's areas. The Chisambavarongo stream separates their jurisdictions. High up the escarpment, however, it becomes difficult to distinguish the true Chisambavarongo from a tributary (map 3.1). Based on self-serving interpretations, both headmen claim an almost uninhabited wedge of territory lying between the Chisambavarongo and another watercourse. Prior to 1991, Muitire had settled only one household, a Zimbabwean family, in this area, and Chikware had no presence there. In 1991 and 1992, however, Chikware inserted two Mozambican households, one headed by a widow, from Dombe. Both families were refugees, and neither negotiated in the course of receiving their parcels. As a result, the majority of households living in the Chisambavarongo wedge owe their land to Chikware, and all of them, in fact, contribute to the offerings that he makes to his spirits. One would conclude, as does the head of the Zimbabwean household residing in the wedge, that "Chikware snatched Muitire's land."[44]

Two factors stand out in the cadastral struggles discussed above: the particular people and the particular land at stake. Chikware snatched land, Tiyekiye reappropriated land, and Muhanyi reclaimed land by proxy. The foot soldiers in every one of the turf battles described above were migrants and largely Mozambican refugees. Mozambican migrants were schooled in politics that were based on the control of people. Forced labor, from the *chibaro* of Portuguese administrators to the *chikoroka* of the civil war, had imprinted submission as the model for relations between chiefs and commoners. Submission, moreover, was doubly appropriate for those rendered destitute by war and drought, and it was expected, on both sides of the border, as the concomitant of immigration. Mozambicans knew how to -*khonza*, and Zimbabwean headmen knew what to do with them when they did -*khonza*. Chikware, Tiyekiye, and Muitire used refugees to claim territory and fight for the lost lands around and within Vhimba. Mozambican settlers, in effect, became the pegs of new boundaries, expanding the zone of smallholding and shrinking Chimanimani National Park and the Hayfield B estate. Indeed, Mozambicans helped hold the country even after their departure. When I last visited Vhimba, in late 2002, the Mozambicans of Mukwiratunhu had returned to their country, but they had left some things in place. Zimbabweans were occupying their abandoned homestead sites and fields and growing a crop introduced by refugees: upland rice. Such cross-border interaction actually underscores the enduringly political nature of borders and territory. The Rusitu River and the Zimbabwe-Mozambique border separated those who negotiated for land from those who simply accepted terms given them. Vastly different colonial and postcolonial histories, again distinguished by the border, prepared Zimbabweans to bargain over land and Mozambicans, instead, to pledge themselves to headmen. The border—and its associated identity papers, refugee camps, and the like—made Mozambicans illegal and vulnerable in Vhimba. Their birth in a particular national territory shaped the fact and manner of their integration in Vhimba. In a second sense, as well, the hosting of Mozambicans was fundamentally geographical because headmen acted from territorial desires. Their history of dispossession and spatial compaction kept politics focused on place. Apart from tourists and anthropologists, those who lived in or passed through the Rusitu Valley in the 1990s were thoroughly territorialized.

4

COMMUNITY FORESTRY
AS LAND-GRABBING
IN VHIMBA

MUCH OF WHAT CURRENTLY PASSES FOR "DEVELOPMENT" IN RURAL
Zimbabwe is, in fact, cadastral struggle by other means. Cadastral struggle,
of course, has a much longer history than development in the modern sense.
To recap chapter 2, white settlers and their government alienated 58 percent of the area of what became Zimbabwe.[1] They took most of the fertile
high veld, leaving the dry, malarial lowlands to African smallholders. In the
Kalahari sandveld and in the Zambezi, Limpopo, and Save valleys, "native
reserves" barely sustained previously dynamic agro-pastoral systems. To
the east, where Zimbabwe's rainfall peaks, the seizure was most complete.
Colonists grabbed the Nyanga-Vumba-Chimanimani highlands as a body.
They packed smallholders into the handful of narrow valleys whose epi-
demiology, if not their pluviosity, made them undesirable. The Rusitu and
Haroni valleys became one such enclave. In 1896, the Native Department
gazetted them as the Ngorima Reserve, named after the area's chief. The story
did not end there, however. Chief Ngorima and his people suffered an extreme
form of Rhodesian land alienation, for they inhabited one of the very few
areas of the country that was both fertile and scenic. In 1965, the Chimanimani National Park expanded into the Haroni Valley, annexing half the
Ngorima Reserve and displacing its inhabitants. Finally, in 1973–74, the government gazetted the Haroni and Rusitu botanical reserves. Conservation,
thus, rounded out eight decades of state-backed land alienation.

In the course of these dispossessions and evictions, development became
cadastral in two senses. First, smallholders came to value that which was
scarce—land —and they supported a leadership of headmen who sought

to regain lost land. In other words, smallholders identified as progress and improvement, but never explicitly as "development," the enlargement of the Ngorima Reserve (now known as Ngorima Communal Land). Anticipating that their sons would need farmland, they pressed for a "claim on the future"[2] across the boundary of the communal land. Squatting constituted a bottom-up economic project. Second, the Rhodesian state responded to this land scarcity—interpreted as overpopulation—with a suite of programs explicitly described as "development." "Land husbandry," as it was called in a detested 1951 act, intended to justify the unequal distribution of land by making the reserves more productive. If successful, this and subsequent efforts would demonstrate the adequacy of the reserves for truly efficient African farmers. Intensive agriculture, rather than extensive boundary jumping, constituted colonial top-down development. Viewed from both sides, therefore, economic advancement centered on access to land and on a property map rooted in expropriation. The difference, of course, was that smallholders wanted more land; the state wanted them to make do with less.

In Ngorima Communal Land, community forestry of the mid-1990s represented precisely this kind of cadastral business as usual. Zimbabwe's new government chose not to carry out the guerrillas' promises of returning the Haroni Valley to smallholders. Therefore, squatting continued as before. Like Rhodesia, the new government had to find a way of evicting smallholders and stuffing them into the communal land. "Development"—in the sense of intensification—became all the more urgent. This chapter discusses two organizations created in the 1990s to pursue this kind of development inside the communal land's boundaries and specifically in Vhimba. The first of these organizations, the Chimanimani Rural District Council, coordinated the government's efforts to boost Vhimba's agricultural productivity and marketing. The second organization resulted from an NGO's efforts to reconcile Vhimba residents and the Department of National Parks and Wildlife Management. Elected from within and trained from outside, the Vhimba Area Development Committee oriented itself toward a forest-based tourism enterprise. Loosely associated with the Communal Areas Management Programme for Indigenous Resources (Campfire), this form of community forestry promised to solve Vhimba's land question by reducing the comparative value of squatting. It would do so by permitting Vhimba residents to earn revenue from nonconsumptive tourism in the Chimanimani National Park and Rusitu and Haroni botanical reserves. The structure of incentives would then, on the one hand, discourage the community from squatting in and clearing the forests and, on the other hand, encourage residents to restrict their agriculture to Ngorima Communal Land. Boosted by off-farm tourist revenues, intensive land use would replace extensive squatting. By mid-1997, the project had begun to fail. The latter part of this chapter traces its tortuous career and that of the Vhimba Area Development Committee in three stages: from training on a grinding mill, to negotiations over tourism, and finally through the committee's return to extensive claims on the future. Ultimately territorial claims—defended most fiercely by Vhimba's headmen—proved stronger than any business drive. Community forestry dissolved into a meter-by-meter turf battle.

THE CHIMANIMANI RURAL DISTRICT COUNCIL

In 1993, Zimbabwe created a unified and increasingly controversial system of local government. Since independence, a "rural council" in each district had run the affairs of the commercial areas where (almost exclusively white) landowners and black farm workers lived. In the reserves, black smallholders fell under the purview of a "district council" (and beneath it, under the mostly defunct ward and village development committees). Both bodies reported to the Ministry of Local Government and Rural and Urban Development, but their activities and finances were quite separate—much to the detriment of the district council. In 1993, the Rural District Councils Act amalgamated these two bodies into one and, in theory, enhanced the democracy, auton-omy, financial solvency, and responsibility of local government. In the 1990s, scholars focused on the extent to which the new "rural district councils" were, in fact, democratic, solvent, or independent of the ministry or of the ZANU–PF party. On every count, they found that councils fell short of expec-tations.[3] Chimanimani District, especially in its activities in Vhimba, was no exception. Some elected councilors made decisions without consulting their constituents, financial constraints were inescapable, and the council deferred to line ministries. These observations, for which evidence appears below, accord with Mahmood Mamdani's (1996) view of a decentralized despotism that deprives smallholders of civil and political rights. Clearly, some of Zimbabwe's rural district councils did not do what many liberal democrats would have liked them to do. If so, what *did* councils do?

Chimanimani's politicians—who were in the best position to describe the rural district council positively—explained the organization in two ways, one related to development, the other to territory. According to the coun-cilor who represented Vhimba, Steven Mutiracha, council allocated devel-opment projects within Chimanimani District. (People tend to refer to "council" with no article.) Indeed, the Rural District Councils Act conferred on council the power to "promote the development of the council area."[4] These definitions construed the rural district council as an institution capable of and devoted to elevating Vhimba's economic production. Yet, a second formulation—much more common among the appointed council officers—pointed in a cadastral direction. To the district administrator, who had been acting chief executive officer of the council from 1993 to 1994, "Council was the Local Land Authority."[5] What did this status mean? Most obviously, amalgamation had created a local government entity that presided over commercial areas and reserves. (The district councils had previously administered land but only in the commercial areas.) Of course, council's writ carried more weight on the reserves than in the commercial areas owned by large timber and tea companies. In the reserves, council could determine the use of land, even without consulting the relevant chief. In fact, council began drafting a set of conservation bylaws in 1994 designed, like all previous similar national legislation, to prevent erosion and overgrazing.[6] By 1996, the revised draft gave council the power to "reserve against human occupation or cultivation" any degraded land and to issue renewable "tillage licence/permit[s]" to worthy smallholders.[7] This document ran counter to a movement in Parliament to restore chiefs' "traditional" powers. (In the event, the Traditional Leaders Act of 1998 recognized chiefs' role in arbitrating disputes but not in allocating land.) But it worked: council wished to assume powers of land allocation, and it clothed itself in headmen's robes.

In Vhimba, the rural district council pushed this land authority quite far quite early. It did so by misrepresenting as development a project whose outcome, for Vhimba, was distinctly territorial. Established in 1994, the Haroni banana project proved to be an iron fist in a velvet glove.[8] According to the project plan, thirty families would receive inputs and irrigation to cultivate two hectares each of hybrid commercial bananas for their own profit.[9] Eventually, the project would "include the people in the privilege of such necessary social infrastructures as a clinic, business centre, roads, bus-service."[10] By 1995, however, council had planted a wide swath along the Haroni, evicting seven families who stood in the way. Those individuals had received no compensation from council,[11] although many had taken jobs working on what turned out to be a large plantation under council's management. These workers reported salaries of about Z$100 per month, far below the national rural minimum wage. The situation was a public scandal in Vhimba, and one night in 1995, a peasant protestor destroyed roughly 250 banana plants. The council thus reenacted Vhimba's history of land alienation, and, like the arsonists who burned Border Timbers' pines in the 1950s, opponents to eviction decimated the exotic flora that had displaced people.

Beyond this incident, the banana plantation generated lasting cadastral disputes on two fronts. In the first dispute, the plantation may have encroached upon the Haroni Botanical Reserve, property of the Parks Department. If it did, it crossed the line by only a few meters, into a slice of the protected area already cultivated by smallholders. Nonetheless, as the Parks Department director wrote the council chairman, the evictions and further compaction of smallholders would increase the pressure on all park boundaries. The chairman admitted to having violated the Haroni Reserve but justified this choice of location as having placed a buffer between small-holders and the forest. Thus, the "land authority" of the district came head-to-head—boundary-to-boundary—with the Parks Department.

The second ongoing cadastral dispute involved the local land authority *not* recognized by law—Headman Tiyekiye. According to rumor in Vhimba, Tiyekiye had initially supported the banana scheme. He may have author-ized council to displace smallholders for the plantation. His subsequent appointment as project foreman seemed to confirm some kind of shady deal. Yet, in Tiyekiye's defense, council had probably assured him—as it had the funder—that the project would benefit Vhimba.[12] He and other Vhimba residents, however, soon realized that council was retaining its banana rev-enues. Many suspected personal corruption on the part of council's appointed officers, but even those who believed that council spent the money on projects, noted that those projects took place outside of Vhimba. This extraction of revenue, of course, reflected very poorly on Tiyekiye, and pop-ular outrage eventually compelled him to redeem himself. Tiyekiye could not hope to pry money out of council, but he could assert territorial authority. Periodically, he did exactly that and weakened council's claim to both banana planting and tourism development. As with the Parks Depart-ment, council found itself locked in debates over meters and square meters. Development played second fiddle to the older, intractable cadastral poli-tics of the Rusitu Valley.

THE VHIMBA AREA DEVELOPMENT COMMITTEE

Tiyekiye's reemergence damaged the second new organization much more than it did the Chimanimani Rural District Council. In intent and deed, the Vhimba Area Development Committee (hereafter, "the committee"), rep-resented entrepreneurship, investment, and cooperative production. It came into existence largely because, in 1994, a Harare-based NGO formulated a strategy to overcome the park boundary disputes mentioned previously. The Southern Alliance for Indigenous Resources (SAFIRE) held both Vhimba residents and the Parks Department responsible for ecological degradation. In the NGO's view, Chimanimani National Park and two botanical reserves had abrogated people's "traditional rights of access to the forest," and, in response, smallholders had reclaimed the forest with a vengeance (SAFIRE 1994:3). The solution to this impasse lay, not in evictions or other cadastral ploys, but in a form of development that would discourage smallholders from farming in the protected areas.[13] Specifically, SAFIRE believed that the option of earning money through tourism in the forests would convince smallholders to spare those forests. Known as "community-based natural resources management," this approach aimed to conserve biodiversity by making conservation profitable to local people. From the experience of a much larger effort in Zimbabwe—the Communal Areas Management Programme for Indigenous Resources (Campfire)—SAFIRE had learned that local people were most likely to undertake conservation if they, themselves, ran the business and determined the use of earnings (Murphree 1991). The right incentives and the right leadership could bring success. In Vhimba, therefore, development required a competent local body. With this business aim in mind, SAFIRE helped form the Vhimba Area Development Committee.

The committee drew together many of Vhimba's most entrepreneurial men.[14] In the early 1990s, many had begun experimenting with sweet bananas, avocado-pears, and other fruits. Some had become rich (see chapter 6). Indeed, in 1995, the richest man in Vhimba owned a store there, as well as one in the town of Chipinge, and three vehicles (not all of them working, however). He claimed that sellers of bananas on Harare street corners would know his name. Naturally, this man became the treasurer of Vhimba's committee. Among the other office bearers, two men assumed the bulk of the committee's work. Both had prior leadership experience, but the aims and styles of their leadership differed radically. Charles Tungamirai,[15] the eventual chair of the committee, had been a ZANLA guerrilla. He had also been arrested and personally assaulted by Parks Department scouts for planting bananas within the Rusitu Botanical Reserve. A fiery, mercurial public speaker, he railed against the Parks Department and for the return of *dunhu redu*—"our area." Elias Nyamunda, the committee's secretary, differed from Tungamirai in nearly every respect. In agriculture, for example, Tungamirai farmed his bananas extensively. Nyamunda, by contrast, experimented with small plots of the latest available orange hybrids. Whereas Tungamirai first became a leader while fighting the white regime for land, Nyamunda entered community service by managing a branch of the Rusitu Valley Fruit Growers Association, to which Tungamirai did not even belong. Finally, whereas Tungamirai embodied the drama of leadership, Nyamunda insisted upon transparency and the committee's responsibility to communicate through regular, well-run public meetings, with their minutes in English. Despite these major differences, both Nyamunda and Tungamirai were democrats: they acted upon the expressed wishes of their constituents. Only a community wavering on the cusp of some fundamental change would put forward two so different representatives—an explosive land claimant and a sober man of letters and numbers.

Initially, SAFIRE induced the committee to follow Nyamunda's procedures and business interests. At the first meeting, in December 1994, Nyamunda's minutes recorded: "It was . . . clear that to speed up the development there should be somewhere to look at and be guarded. The need of a Constitution is one great thing that enables the smooth moving of clear events."[16] Under the constitution, the community elected five officers, of whom two made the crucial decisions. Tungamirai became chair, and Nyamunda secretary. These leaders, then, wielded "overall responsibility for the development of the Vhimba area," including "initiating projects" and "sound management of the area's natural resources for the benefit of the community."[17] Specifically, SAFIRE hoped that the committee would conjoin development, projects, and natural resources in the form of businesses to profit from Vhimba's forests. The committee, Nyamunda, and, to an extent, Tungamirai endorsed this strategy for a while. As the minutes recorded, "It is [the] right time for everyone to understand development which enables us to show the difference between the modern and the oldern [sic] years."[18] Yet, flaws in the composition of the committee and in its mandate eventually diverted it from "the smooth moving of clear events."

In part, development veered off course because the committee antagonized two groups it meant to include. Although the constitution named headmen and Vhimba's rural district councilor as ex officio officeholders, none of them participated in the meetings. The councilor's absence, in particular, cast doubt upon the committee's legal legitimacy. The district administrator had authorized the establishment of a committee in Vhimba under the express condition that it include Vhimba's rural district councilor and serve as a subcommittee of council. When the councilor withdrew from this arrangement, he broke the line of communication between the committee and council. Council therefore gradually grew distrustful and suspicious of what it increasingly viewed as a rogue body. On a joint field visit, a council staff member warned the committee: "[T]here is no right for any local community intending to do projects without the knowledge of the council."[19] By 1997, the district administrator was of the opinion that "[t]here has been too much emphasis on the Vhimba Area Development Committee . . . at the expense of legally recognized committees."[20] By legally recognized bodies, he meant the village development committees, arms of government that had never functioned in Vhimba. In any case, the district administrator effectively suppressed all committees in Vhimba when, in mid-1997, he prohibited any public meeting not attended by his representative.

If the district administrator perceived the committee as having usurped power, headmen felt doubly this way. When the committee eventually decided to establish a campsite for tourism, headmen reacted vigorously. Reasserting their right to allocate land for any and all projects, they brought down the committee's house of cards. They did so because their activism raised the question, especially in Tungamirai's mind, of whether the committee should develop business or fight for the lost lands. This question rankled through 1995, 1996, and 1997 as the committee, particularly Nyamunda, struggled to sustain businesses, and the Parks Department tried to evict "squatters" from the Rusitu Botanical Reserve. The rest of this chapter recounts these efforts as three somewhat overlapping phases of the committee's career: management of the grinding mill, negotiations over tourism, and, at last, demarcation of the Rusitu Botanical Reserve. In essence, the committee made two attempts at new-fangled development before falling back upon Vhimba's dependable old steady: the politics of turf.

MANAGING THE GRINDING MILL

No one involved in the formation of the Vhimba Area Development Committee had expected it to take charge of a grinding mill. As already mentioned, SAFIRE had hoped that the committee would make money from the forests, either through tourism or by selling medicinals and other species. The director later wrote, SAFIRE "seeks . . . to promote economic development . . . based on sustainable and productive use of natural resources" (Grundy and Le Breton 1997–98:15). Vhimba people, however, did not share the same goal. At the initial participatory rural appraisal of mid-1994, "the community were no longer willing to discuss issues relating to [commercial] forest product use because of their recent conflict with

National Parks and the fear this had instilled" (SAFIRE 1994:7). Challenging boundaries explicitly on behalf of Vhimba smallholders is not what SAFIRE wished to do (although, as is explained below, it did negotiate diplomatically with National Parks). The appraisal, therefore, shifted to the provision of services, and, happily, the audience asked for a grinding mill, clinic, improved road, and bus route. Among these options, a grinding mill seemed the best bridge toward forest-based business. Therefore, SAFIRE agreed to donate a mill in the expectation that the committee would eventually expand its business into tourism. Development, SAFIRE hoped, would take off and fly in the desired direction.

Vhimba's new leadership seemed committed to making money and reinvesting it to make more. A fieldworker from SAFIRE explained the most fundamental and novel of entrepreneurial ideas, that is, that money should function as a storable, reproducible form of wealth, and Nyamunda, at least, understood. His minutes record: "When the money from the grinding mill is soon banked interests are expected and therefore more income generating projects can be started. Everything was clear."[21] But was it really so clear? In practice, the committee failed adequately to store and reproduce earnings from the grinding mill. The committee opened an account at Barclays Bank and made plans to buy a second grinding mill and a truck for transporting produce.[22] Soon, however, a flawed system of bookkeeping interfered with basic financial storage: the treasurer both receipted the daily revenue and transported it to Barclays. He soon came under suspicion for diverting funds, and the committee increased its level of supervision. In addition, the committee had budgeted transport expenses of Z$200 for each semiweekly trip to and from Chipinge for filling diesel drums. After deducting this and other expenses, Nyamunda and his colleagues expected monthly profits of Z$1,649. The owner of one of the only two working trucks in Vhimba, however, demanded Z$450 per trip, raising the monthly cost of transport by Z$2,000 and making the mill technically unprofitable. Given the monopsonistic market for motorized transport from remote Vhimba, the committee could not and did not run a successful, business-minded grinding mill.

To Vhimba residents, this economic miscarriage signaled the committee's *political* defectiveness. According to the committee's minutes, "Chairman and treasurer had problems of [being] not in good books according the constitution."[23] Yet, the source of disaffection was more profound: the committee, the constitution, and SAFIRE had raised the community's expectations of an economic takeoff. They foresaw shared growth and investment that would improve the road and solve many of Vhimba's problems aside from those related to territory. The committee's failure to store and reproduce money deferred those dreams and stoked resentment. In early 1996, only a year after the opening of the mill, the community elected new officers to manage it. Technically, the voters did not turn out the Vhimba Area Development Committee; they elected a subordinate body, the Grinding Mill Committee. This face-saving improvisation on the constitution allowed the original committee to pursue other aims (discussed below) while the subcommittee continued to manage the decline and bankruptcy of a development dream.

TOURISM

Tourism, the committee's next development project, provoked Vhimba's territorial anxiety for three reasons: whites were involved, the rural district council was involved, and tourism had the potential to raise issues of land allocation. The tourists were white, and so were the tour operators. Their interest in opening Vhimba to tourism recalled the long history of land alienation. In at least one respect, the connection was real and current: the Chipinge Branch of the Wildlife Society of Zimbabwe, a group of tour operators, bird-watchers, and estate owners, had transported Parks Department scouts to Vhimba deliberately so that the scouts could enforce the boundary of the Rusitu Botanical Reserve. Such cooperation, of course, helped protect the tour operators' source of revenue, their stake in the cadastre. Council's banana plantation had earned it the reputation of a land-grabber. In 1995, council appointed a "Campfire officer" to promote tourism in scenic parts of the district's native reserves. This new interest raised the question, Would council manipulate tourism—in the way it had the banana "cooperative"—in order to seize land from smallholders? In fact, rural district councils have dominated Campfire projects elsewhere in Zimbabwe, making a mockery of local control.[24] Vhimba's committee decided to take no such chances; *if* the committee undertook tourism, then the committee would run it.[25] Finally, tourism was a cauldron of cadastral politics because, unlike a grinding mill, it *did* require land, specifically, an area for chalets and/or camping. No one knew how much land was at stake, or where, but already in early 1995, "certain members of the committee felt that this project was meant to grab land from them."[26]

In spite of these fears, the committee actually occupied a middle ground between some male elders opposed to tourism and a set of organizations promoting it. Many Vhimba residents, especially headmen, insisted that the committee settle outstanding turf battles with the Parks Department before engaging in any tourist venture. Nyamunda felt this popular pressure. "In the introduction of the CAMPFIRE," he opined in the minute book, "the community is not satisfied if [convinced that] CAMPFIRE is worth living for. We are in trouble on the displacement of people from their stands [homesteads] and their fields."[27] The grievance with the rural district council was equally pressing and equally disruptive of the work of Nyamunda and the committee. Tiyekiye, who was already implicated in the plantation, wanted to settle that issue prior to *any* development. When the committee considered an irrigation scheme, it found that "[t]he people of Tiyekiye's village . . . prefer boundary issues to water."[28] Vhimba's preferences were known to SAFIRE. At the initial appraisal, "The development of tourism under CAMPFIRE was debated. There is interest in this, but not before outstanding grievances have been resolved with National Parks" (SAFIRE 1994:8). Nonetheless, in early 1995, with the committee's assent and that of council, SAFIRE submitted a proposal for funding. When, a year later, the committee lost its authority over the grinding mill, SAFIRE urged it to prepare to implement this proposal. Ultimately, the committee never decided for or against tourism. Events dictated its course of action.

In late 1996, a British investor made a tourist facility in Vhimba, for the first time, a real possibility. Henry Oberlander[29] had worked in banking in Hong Kong. Tiring of this frenzied life, he decided to establish an "adventure company" in Chimanimani. He joined forces with Collin Walker, a Zimbabwean white raised on an estate in Nyanga District and associated with the Heaven Lodge in Chimanimani town. The two of them hoped to bring backpackers from "Heaven" to Vhimba via steep trails in the Haroni Valley. Once in Vhimba, the tourists would raft on the Rusitu, hike in the Matsenderero Forest, mountain bike on the road, and visit smallholders. In contrast to Zimbabwe's luxury hotels and safaris, Oberlander and Walker imagined a simpler ecotourism embedded in the local community. In order to realize this dream, however, the two entrepreneurs needed, first, to satisfy the rural district council. In late 1996, Oberlander explained his vision to a council meeting. Impressed, council agreed to grant him a business license contingent upon his payment of the standard application fee of Z$50. In effect, council torpedoed SAFIRE's proposal that the Vhimba Area Development Committee conduct the same enterprise in the same area. Later asked in public to account for his authorization of two competing ventures, council's chief executive officer responded, "It's a question of survival of the fittest—dog eat dog."[30] Oberlander's dog, though, had a territorial bite.

Council's deal with Oberlander raised troubling cadastral questions. Did a business license confer rights in land? In late 1996, Oberlander told me it did. Specifically, he claimed to be negotiating with council for the purchase of a small patch of secondary woodland next to the "corner store" (given that name because of its proximity to the ninety-degree bend in the Zimbabwe-Mozambique border). The store had passed though a variety of owners before falling into council's hands. Now, it served as the storage shed for equipment used in the adjacent banana plantation. Associated in this way with council's primal sin, the store was a remarkably poor choice of location for a business in need of Vhimba's support. To make matters worse, council proceeded to act as a land allocator. Authorities within or outside that body had led Oberlander to believe that the land next to the store lay within a business center, an area over which council supposedly exercised full authority. On this assumption—and against my express advice—he decided to pursue access to the area through council and only later to introduce himself to Vhimba's headmen, the committee, and other residents. This delay spawned rumors and, in the end, greatly undercut local support. By March 1997, when Oberlander and Walker held their first meeting in Vhimba, the audience was already treating them as white land-grabbers.

That encounter gave Vhimba residents further reason to interpret tourism as a cadastral claim. Oberlander hoped to win the committee's agreement to a profit-sharing venture. Then, he planned to invite provincial government planners to "peg" the edges of the campsite in preparation for construction of an "ablution block" (toilets and showers). Tungamirai, who knew that land and boundaries were at stake, would meet with Oberlander and Walker only in the presence of a headman. To do otherwise would expose him and the committee to charges of allocating land and of selling out. Finally, Tiyekiye appeared and the meeting—almost a dialogue of the deaf— began as follows:

> *Oberlander:* We have always wanted to work closely with the people of Vhimba. . . . Tourism should be to the benefit of all concerned. Our tourism can be low-impact in a holistic sense, on people, mountains, resources, etc.
>
> *Tiyekiye:* How does this relate to CAMPFIRE? Which site have they pegged with Council? . . .

Tungamirai: We are the people of the area who have conserved this area. We want equal shares of the project.

Man A: They [Oberlander and Walker] have been looking after [for] the place all along—how they spend the money is up to them. . . .

Tungamirai: Where is the place Oberlander wants to put the camp?

Oberlander: The area close to the corner store.

Man A: Who showed the place?

Oberlander: Chimanimani Rural District Council.

Man B: You have done well to come here to tell us what you want. We will tell you now what we want. Council has no right to establish a place.

Walker: The corner store was attractive because of the picturesque nature of village life. It is pointless to displace people because people from elsewhere [tourists] want to see how people live here.

Man A: Not right for Council to point to a place. Council does not know the area.[31]

By the end of the discussion, smallholders were angrier with council than they were afraid of the two whites. Council, it seemed, was evicting people again—and ironically doing so under the banner of "village life." "Where will we farm now," asked one farmer, "[across the border] in Chief Mafussi's area?"[32]

The particular grievance of that meeting and of a subsequent one centered as much on the fact of eviction as on its manner: Council was acting as a headman. In the normal course of events, Tiyekiye, Chikware, and other headmen wielded the particular responsibility of "showing a place" to all newcomers. In the mid-1990s, of course, they had used that role to particular effect in reclaiming parts of Chimanimani National Park and of the Hayfield B estate. Now the Chimanimani Rural District Council was usurping their power. The Z$50 fee Oberlander admitted to having paid to the council seemed to prove this trespass. It fell well within the range of *huku* gifts presented by newcomers to headmen in return for land allocation. Worse still, council had done a bad job of allocating land. Because it did not "know the area," it had given to Oberlander fallow fields technically owned by T. (see map 4.1). In a second meeting, held one month after the first, T. protested. The business center, he argued, extended east from the corner store, not west to his field. Furthermore, Tiyekiye's father had assured T.'s father of this boundary; so council must be mistaken. In relation to Oberlander, this misallocation of land engendered both sympathy and resentment. "You were shown a place that is not yours," said one smallholder to Oberlander in absen-

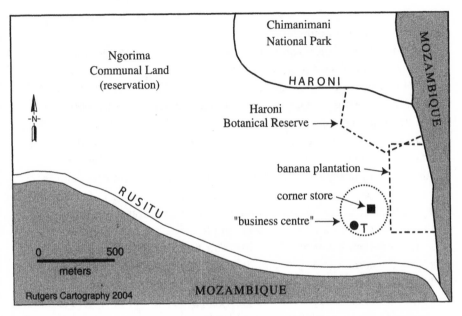

MAP 4.1. Vhimba's "business centre"

tia, "council is insulting him."[33] Perhaps more prevalent was the fear that, as one farmer put it, "[h]e will take our land from us."[34] Council's blunder left Oberlander no means with which to clear his name.

Difficult to falsify, the suspicion of land-grabbing arose from two oddly cadastral interpretations of the facts in Oberlander's case. First, Vhimba people understood the granting of a business license as land allocation.[35] Oberlander appeared as a newcomer, someone from outside Vhimba who wanted to establish himself there. Since the wave of evictions and in-migration in the 1950s, outsiders had inserted themselves into Vhimba by only one means: requesting and receiving land from the headmen on whose land they wished to live. Oberlander wished to construct his "stand" in Tiyekiye's area, but he had spoken and even exchanged money with council. In effect, he and that body had usurped Tiyekiye's power of land allocation and taken the land. The second misunderstanding created boundaries where there were none. Legally, the business center was merely a store. Unlike Vhimba's official business center seven kilometers to the west, the store had never been surveyed and appeared on government maps as simply "store."[36] Issues of boundaries, moreover, appeared natural to small-holders and, it is likely, to a good many of the councilors themselves. All the players except Oberlander were thoroughly prepared to instigate and fight a turf battle over tourism.

In the event, Oberlander salvaged his proposal only by surrendering his piece of land. Under siege at the March meeting, he declared his preference for collaboration with the "Campfire tourism project." He, thus, averted an unpopular "dog-eat-dog" competition—in which he was sure to triumph—and in the process managed to trade his site for a better one. The Vhimba committee and SAFIRE had selected for their proposed campsite a view-point overlooking the Haroni River and the Matsenderero Forest. Far from the disturbances of the store and banana plantation, the committee's site offered the "picturesque" setting that was attractive to tourists from Heaven Lodge. A transfer to this location, moreover, would exonerate Oberlander from charges of land-grabbing. Other people had allocated the site for tourism more than a year before he first came to Vhimba. He was merely accepting the committee's allocation in a way visible to all, not engaging with council in a territorial subterfuge. The rural district council, SAFIRE, and other NGOs encouraged this merger. A month later, in May 1997, the committee decided to cooperate with Oberlander conditional upon an agreement on profit sharing. Oberlander had definitely gambled in ceding his official parcel, but the chances for success seemed good.

Unknown to Oberlander, however, Headman Tiyekiye had reached the point of reasserting his authority over land in a dramatic fashion. He had done so before, of course, when he settled refugees in Chimanimani National Park. In that instance, he had demonstrated his power to outside agencies, specifically to the Parks Department (see chapter 3). Within Vhimba, these allocations proved his suitability to rule and downgraded neighboring headmen and rival claimants to his own headmanship. This time Tiyekiye needed to defend himself against the rural district council. In May, police arrested him on charges of embezzling money from the banana plantation of which he was foreman. In his defense, he argued that council had never paid him his salary. Additionally, he mobilized his cadastral rights to excuse the crime: "Who is the owner of the field?" a Vhimba man quoted him as having asked rhetorically.[37] The question indicated the ambiguity surrounding the headman's role in the banana plantation. Legally, Tiyekiye was the foreman, but, by its first official description, the plantation was a cooperative. In that case, Tiyekiye would be the cooperative manager, a position that ought to give him some authority over the field. Certainly, he had a stronger claim to revenues from a cooperative in Vhimba than did the rural district council. If, however, council admitted to running the plantation as a parastatal business, then Tiyekiye could treat it as another instance of encroachment upon the reserve. Vhimba's small-holders, especially those veterans of the squatter wars with the Parks Department, would sympathize with a landgrab against council's putative field. Even if Tiyekiye might have actually stolen money, in so doing, he was still vaguely waging a longstanding and locally legitimate struggle against the government's seizure of land. In this context, Tiyekiye was not disposed to support the entry of someone whom council had helped to circumvent his authority over land. On the contrary, he opposed any joint venture involving Oberlander, and he helped push the committee into a dramatic about-face in which Tungamirai declared publicly, "Death before partnership!" The joint venture was over before it had begun.

To the extent that Tiyekiye contributed to this reversal, he also acted to defend his interests against the committee itself. As mentioned above, he and the other two headmen of Vhimba had mostly stopped attending regular meetings two years previously. Headmen's ex officio seats effectively stood empty. Given the "traditional" leadership's nonparticipation, the committee ran the risk of exceeding its remit if it cooperated with Oberlander. Like the council before it, the committee would be authorizing an outsider's use of land—taking the headman's job. Tiyekiye, in whose area the joint tourism project would be located, had the greatest reason to feel offended. Yet, other headmen objected more vocally. "There is no plan without a headman. . . . There is no area in Vhimba without a headman!" warned Matwukira (who had succeeded Headman Muitire) at a meeting in July 1997.[38] If Tungamirai did not include headmen in every decision, he continued, "We will refuse him!"[39] Chikware's brother added, "We want seats [on the committee], all of us!"[40] Finally, another Chikware brother, seriously drunk, denounced council to the dwindling audience: "They have eaten us," but now there will be "*Chimurenga* number two."[41] In short, the headmen staged a coup.

By the middle of 1997, when I finished major fieldwork in Vhimba, both the committee and development were crippled. In the wake of the "death before partnership" declaration, the Campfire Association intended to fund a community-run tourism project in Vhimba independent of Oberlander. Tungamirai and Nyamunda still met and, with other officers, constituted the committee. Thanks to the headmen, the constitution itself—as a road map for tourism, development, and "the smooth moving of clear events"—was defunct. Headmen had lambasted the committee for having excluded them, but, in reality, they had transferred the locus of power to behind the scenes, to murky arenas of rumormongering and alliance building. There, especially among elder men, suspicion and loyalty centered on claims to land and efforts to regain the lost lands. The rural district council and the Parks Department, of course, enflamed these grievances by repeatedly taking land from Vhimba smallholders. These politics diverted and strangled "development" in 1997. Unless land alienators returned their booty—or, at least, refrained from grabbing more—there was every reason to believe that territorial struggles would continue to override development projects in Vhimba.

RUSITU BOTANICAL RESERVE

At the time of SAFIRE's 1994 appraisal, the turf battle over the Rusitu Botanical Reserve was already raging. The Parks Department had arrested and assaulted some of Vhimba's most respected men—Tungamirai among them. His visible indignation and desire for redress may well have inspired Vhimba to select him as their committee chair. When I first met Tungamirai in early 1995, he railed against the Parks Department and its conservationist conceit: "When National Parks arrived the trees were already here. There is nothing that they know about trees. National Parks came with food to give to the birds in Nyakwawa, but the birds are eating my food. So the birds are mine."[42] Surprisingly, Tungamirai's metaphorical and inflammatory speech made common cause with the restrained, liberal-minded Nyamunda. More so than in any other turf battle, the protagonists of the Nyakwawa boundary dispute relied upon cartography, and the committee's minutes taker could also make maps. In 1994, as a branch manager for the Rusitu Valley Fruit Growers Association, Nyamunda had mapped all the member households in his jurisdiction as well as the boundaries of the village development committees (Vidcos). This latter feature—gratuitous because Vidcos's boundaries did not affect the association or the functioning of the Vidcos themselves[43]—indicated Nyamunda's preparedness for cadastral politics. Thus, the drama of retaining Nyakwawa cast Nyamunda as scribe, Tungamirai as rabble-rouser.

Even more astonishing than having united this odd couple, the dispute over Nyakwawa allied the committee with Headman Chikware. Chikware's territory encircled Nyakwawa. In addition to its spatial centrality, this forest also represented the core of Chikware's legitimacy to rule. He claimed descent from the Sabunga, a group of inhabitants that predated the arrival of the Ngorima dynasty probably in the late seventeenth century.[44] According to this oral tradition, the reigning Chikware fled after this conquest, but, following a series of droughts, Ngorima asked him to return. If

Chikware would perform the rituals necessary to maintain the land's fertility, then he could serve in Ngorima's nobility.[45] This incorporative bargain, typical of precolonial conquests in Southern and Eastern Africa, gave Chikware the eventual rank of headman (although the state never recognized him in the way it did Tiyekiye [see chapter 3]). The bargain also perpetuated Chikware's *-dira* ceremony, which, in the 1990s, was still carried out more or less annually at the gravesite of the sister of an ancient titleholder. The sister and the site, which is now, of course, a forest, both bore the name Nyakwawa. Vhimba residents, especially the Chikwares themselves, identified that forest as a fundamental aspect of the headmanship. "Our life is to take care of Nyakwawa," said the headman's brother.[46] Imagine, then, the ruling lineage's outrage when, in the early 1990s, scouts informed them that the Parks Department had gazetted Nyakwawa twenty years previously.

This landgrab not only insulted Chikware's religion but also challenged his role as headman. Chikware allocated land to every resident of his area, including those in the vicinity of Nyakwawa. In effect, his allocations determined the distribution of forest and fields in the central part of Vhimba. The Parks Department thought he had done a poor job. Specifically, the department charged Chikware with allowing smallholder agriculture to nibble at the edges of the forest until little was left. As one ecologist reported in 1984, eleven years after the gazettement, "Human population pressure is making increasing inroads into the natural resources of the region, and the area of pristine forest is diminishing daily due to clearing by the locals" (Ryan, Cassidy, and Salinger 1984:91). By 1993, the Parks Department was ready to evict people and to make sure that Chikware would not insert more "squatters" into its estate. Scouts assaulted commoners, such as Tungamirai, but their violence struck symbolically at Chikware. They raised the doubt: could this headman defend his subjects and his allocation of land to them? Aided by the committee, Chikware would spend the next four years trying to enforce his previous allocations.

After the assaults, which had not prompted any farmers to move, the Parks Department adopted a softer, but quintessentially cadastral, strategy: marking the forest's boundaries. At the time of demarcation, the department had never indicated those lines in a permanent fashion on the landscape.[47] In 1993, the department's Campfire unit—the division responsible for community-based natural resources management—reasoned that Chikware could not possibly prevent encroachment until he and everyone else knew precisely where the Parks Estate lay. The solution was to survey and fence the Rusitu Botanical Reserve. The Parks Department, however, could not afford the fees; so the Chipinge Branch of the Wildlife Society—whose tour operator members stood to gain from forest conservation—paid for a survey in mid-1994.[48] The surveyor laid a cement cairn at each of the four corners of the botanical reserve. He made no other markings on the landscape, nor did the Parks Department erect a fence. Although unrecognized at the time, the survey suffered from a further deficiency: it strayed from the technical description legislated for the park boundaries in 1973.[49] Of course, it would have been very nearly impossible to ground truth—that is, to retrace on the land—a flat, table survey over terrain with cliffs and an average slope of 35 percent.[50] As an additional problem, the legal technical description relied upon the corner of an island in the Rusitu River whose shape had changed. These distortions opened a gray zone wide enough to swallow the homesteads and fields of a number of so-called squatters. Thus, the survey failed to create cartographic certainty and to justify the evictions that the Parks Department desired: nearly a quarter-century after gazettement, no · unambiguous representation on the landscape or on a map existed for the Rusitu Botanical Reserve.[51]

The survey, nonetheless, did create enough antagonism so that the department temporarily relinquished its policy of demarcation. In early 1995, the Campfire unit reflected that "[t]he recent demarcation of the boundaries . . . has precipitated unprecedented hostility from Chief Ngorima and the local community."[52] The acting chief (Sanyero Ngorima) refused to attend public meetings with staff of the Parks Department and fined those Vhimba residents who did.[53] Finally, the chief's family went "over the head" of the department. At the installation ceremony of the new chief, Peter Ngorima, in March 1995, the lineage's spokesman addressed the minister in the audience: "We ask you Comrade Minister [of Lands, Kumbirai Kangai] for our important places (tribal monuments), which are . . . [six sacred sites and] the forest of Nyakwawa in Vhimba . . . We can care for these places so that our land stays good and is given blessings by the Creator."[54] At the same time and less publicly, SAFIRE began to mediate between the parties with a stake in Nyakwawa. To address the turf disputes uncovered in its appraisal, the NGO formed the Vhimba Collaborative Committee. Under the chairmanship of the district administrator, this body brought together the Vhimba Area Development Committee, the Parks Department, the rural district council, Chief Ngorima, and a good many other, secondary parties.[55] So productive were the discussions inside and outside this forum, that the Parks Department's Campfire unit was ready to degazette the estimated thirty hectares of the Rusitu Botanical Reserve under cultivation.[56] At last, on the verge of regaining some of the lost lands, Vhimba had reached its high-water mark in cadastral politics.

In the event, however, the Parks Department held the territory and returned to traditional tactics of fighting Vhimba's turf battles. A new governing board of the Parks Department disbanded the Campfire unit while, coincidentally, the accommodating district warden was transferred away from Chimanimani.[57] The new warden, who arrived in August 1996, announced his attention to evict the "squatters" in the Rusitu Botanical Reserve posthaste, as he informed me in an interview: "We won't give them time to say tomorrow. Today! Otherwise, we will be wasting time."[58] Subsequently, scouts paid repeated, menacing visits to trespassing families, pausing only when the 1996–97 rains made Vhimba inaccessible. Meanwhile, having ripped out Tungamirai's and other residents' fruit trees in 1994, a representative of the Parks Department told a meeting that it would "replant indigenous species of the [botanical] reserves."[59] The species did not matter to Vhimba. "Why is it," Nyamunda asked in his minutes, "that the people are arrested and the area is planted [with] some foreign trees, e.g., Tilbury Estates?"[60] Other skeptics invoked floral events more recent than the afforestation of the Chimanimani Plateau. As one "squatter" in the botanical reserve predicted to me, "They will drive us out. They will plant bananas."[61] In short, the Parks Department planned to reenact the landgrabs of Border Timbers and of the rural district council. It was going to remove people so as to plant trees.

The threat of eviction embroiled council in another, more immediate cadastral issue—land allocation. Once removed, where were people to go, and who would give them land? The Parks Department urged families "to start looking for alternative land from Council through their local chief."[62] As the Land Authority, council bore responsibility for finding alternative sites, but it was not capable of doing so. It did not acquire land outside the Ngorima Reserve for resettlement. Nor did it wish to exercise its legal right to allocate and reallocate land within the reserve. Council threw the burden of resettling evictees back onto precisely those authorities from whom it had wrested the right of land allocation. At a meeting in 1995, "Mr. [Headman] Tiyekiye was asked by . . . [the council] whether he has gone through with settling the people affected. He said they were not yet settled hence [because there was] no land to settle them."[63] In truth, Tiyekiye or Chikware could have accommodated the evictees only by reallocating the fallow fields of residents outside the protected areas. To take allocated fields would have discredited the headmen in the eyes of a constituency known to judge leaders in terms of their success in turf battles. Instead, in late 1996, Chikware traveled with some of the offending families to appeal their removal at district headquarters. A cadastral stalemate ensued; no one would allocate land outside the protected areas to those on the wrong side of the boundary.

At this point, the committee came to Chikware's assistance in a way that no one else had done: it made a map. A map might break the deadlock and allow the people to stay in place by simply moving the boundary—or, rather, by returning the boundary to its true location. The committee argued that the Parks Department's survey of 1994 had diverged radically from cuts made on trees in 1974. Those markings had followed watercourses, a dry streambed to the west of Nyakwawa and a wet one to the east.[64] As Tungamirai railed at a November 1996 community meeting, "There is no boundary that is a pathway [i.e., artificial]. The boundary is the stream."[65] He was also careful to affirm: "The headman is the one who knows the boundary."[66] At that meeting, therefore, the committee joined Headman Chikware and other residents in vowing "to erect our original boundaries."[67] They gave Nyamunda the cartographic task, and he produced the most detailed map yet of the disputed area (map 4.2). Nyamunda's map showed three boundaries, from the inside out: the edge of the current forest, the 1974 limit of the botanical reserve (which coincided with the forest fringe to the west), and the 1994 (false) limit. Between the two boundaries of the Rusitu Botanical Reserve lay the fields and homesteads of seven families. A further five households resident outside the 1994 boundary held land in the liminal strip. Finally, the map showed four families inside the 1974 boundary but outside the zone of standing forest.[68] The map, thus, demonstrated that Chikware had largely respected the original marked lines of the Parks Estate, and, even when he had violated them, his allocations had not prejudiced the forest. In a fashion few had anticipated, cartography vindicated the headman. For that reason, it had to be suppressed. Council unilaterally canceled the meeting at which the committee would have presented its map,[69] and the rains shortly suspended all action on the issue.

The cadastral, cartographic dispute, therefore, came to a head early in the dry season of 1997. In May, the Vhimba Collaborative Committee, whose meetings had become extremely infrequent, convened at Vhimba's corner store. Despite prior assurances by the district administrator's office, Tungamirai and Nyamunda's map presentation did not appear on the agenda. In the event, the agenda hardly mattered. I had circulated among government officials a version of Nyamunda's map that included the establishment dates of each of the sixteen homesteads.[70] The resulting composite showed

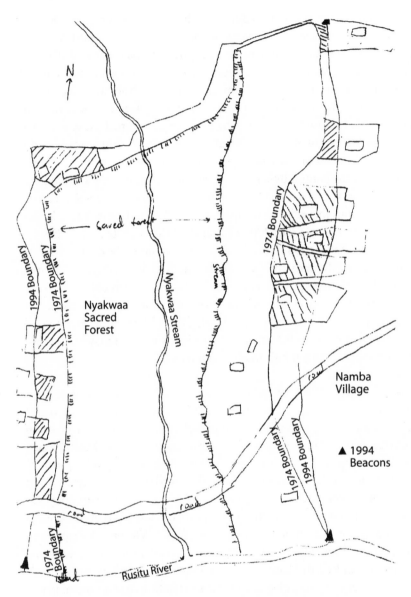

N

Saved forest

1994 Boundary

1974 Boundary

1974 Boundary

Nyakwaa Stream

Stream

1974 Boundary

Nyakwaa
Sacred
Forest

Namba
Village

1974 Boundary

1994 Boundary

▲ 1994
Beacons

road

road

1974
Boundary

Rusitu River

MAP 4.2. Rusitu Botanical Reserve and Nyakwawa sacred forest.
Drawing by Elias Nyamunda, November 1996 (labels added subsequently)

that almost all the residents had lived at the current sites before the park *encroached upon them*. In any event, no map per se was discussed. Strident protest disrupted the meeting before it began. "You have come to chase us out," people shouted at the district administrator.[71] An angry group of men, including some facing eviction from the vicinity of Nyakwawa, demanded to speak with him. He refused to do so at a "closed meeting"—one limited to the invited institutions—and, when the rabble eventually dispersed, he laid down the law on the Rusitu Botanical Reserve. The homesteads could stay, he said, but people must no longer farm in the Parks Estate. In an oblique response to the committee's map, the district administrator affirmed the legal boundary, as described by the office of the surveyor general, regardless of previous markings or mismarkings on the landscape. To back him up, a representative of the Chipinge Branch of the Wildlife Society distributed copies of the 1994 survey. Thus, in his own mind, the district administrator closed the cadastral case. Declaring that all meetings in Vhimba would thenceforth require his approval, he also tried to demobilize the committee. Yet, no banana plants or other crops were uprooted, and no one was evicted. Without a clear winner or loser, this cadastral struggle outlasted my main fieldwork in Vhimba. If the past is any guide, it may well outlast the committee, Tungamirai, and Nyamunda.

The semidefeat of 1997 brought the committee full circle: it had devoted itself almost exclusively to the very debates its formation was meant to preempt. If the committee was intended to deflect the community's attention from turf battles, it had not succeeded. The committee had not accomplished its founding mission: to run one or more businesses, accrue profits, and reinvest them for the development of Vhimba's general productive capacity. The first such enterprise, the grinding mill, failed because ineffective bookkeeping and high transport costs eliminated profits. These kinds of obstacles to development are common in remote areas, such as Vhimba. Perhaps more unusual—but more typical of Zimbabwe—Vhimba succumbed to cadastral politics. Indeed, turf battles did not so much derail development as development, ever so briefly, diverted Vhimba's attention from its ongoing turf battles. Like a stream of water meandering away from an artificial channel back to its accustomed course, the committee slid from the grinding mill into one turf battle after another. The second business, tourism, derailed when the rural district council—and later the committee itself—allocated land to a private investor. The relevant headman interceded and sparred indirectly with council over the placement of a bizarre, little-known boundary. In its final activity, however, the committee cooperated with headmen and affirmed their rights to allocate land. It mapped the Rusitu Botanical Reserve as the area of unallocated land, thus validating the headman's interpretation of a legal boundary that could hardly be otherwise marked on the landscape. The committee, then, became headmen's cartographic defense against national parks. Boundary making and boundary breaking had triumphed over development.

This outcome reveals a fundamental pattern in development writ large in Zimbabwe of the 1990s. Many smallholders wanted the "lost lands" first and development, as defined above, second. To Vhimba people, development appeared as efforts to divert attention from the burning issue of land redistribution. They were dead right in the case of Campfire-style tourism, by which the NGO deliberately sought to reconcile the community and the Parks Department. More generally, the programs of many NGOs and government departments existed precisely to avoid doing what the liberation armies and their peasant supporters fought for. In some cases, this avoidance was quite clear: land-use planning and soil conservation aimed to maintain production within a shrinking per capita land base. More obliquely, Campfire and other programs for the community-based management of natural resources tried to boost rural incomes from the *given* resource base.[72] When they worked, both strategies enhanced the efficient use of the African reserves rather than enlarge them. Vhimba people, however, rejected half measures. Since Zimbabwe's independence, the Parks Department and the rural district council had repeatedly thrown down the gauntlet. Headmen and the committee picked it up, and all parties returned to Chimurenga-era territorial politics. The book's conclusion will revisit this dogged persistence of cadastral disputes in Zimbabwe. Now, I cross the border to examine the first outbreak of such politics in Gogoi, Mozambique.

5

EXPATRIATE LOGGERS
AND MAPMAKERS
IN GOGOI

IN THE MID-1990S, THE LOCUS OF POLITICAL CONTESTATION IN GOGOI began to shift from labor to land. Chief Gogoi and his headmen started to "territorialize" their rule (see Introduction). In many ways, this transformation resembles the onset of cadastral politics a hundred years earlier in nearby Vhimba. There, white settlers seized land in the 1890s. Subsequently, the colonial administration and opportunities for migrant labor undermined patriarchs' methods of accumulating wealth in people. In response to these two developments, headmen took control of the allocation of land and used this power to regain as much alienated territory as possible. This scenario could easily have transpired in Gogoi. In the 1890s the Portuguese administration recruited some of the same South African whites to cross the border from Rhodesia to northern Mossurize. Yet, few came and fewer stayed. In the ensuing decades, white colonists tried repeatedly to claim and transform this landscape. Every time, investors—most recently timber firms in the 1970s—failed to draw reliable profits. Thus, as chapter 1 recounts, the administration perfected forced labor as a means of extraction based on wealth in people rather than wealth in land. Gogoi entered the 1990s in the grip of ambulatory enslavement and without a single notation in the national cadastre. It could not have differed more from contemporary Vhimba. The "hard" Zimbabwe-Mozambique border stood between two worlds of political culture. What changed to make Gogoi more like Vhimba? In part, white land-grabbers came again—crossing the border—and, this time, seemly ready to transform the landscape at last.

In fact, four distinct political and social movements in the aftermath of

Mozambique's civil war[1] brought land to the forefront in Gogoi. First, the 1992 ceasefire terminated the military corvées practiced by Renamo. Second, refugees and displaced people returned to Gogoi or entered it for the first time. These in-migrations gave new prominence to the issue of land allocation. Third, after the 1994 elections, South African and Zimbabwean timber industries scouted Mossurize District. In 1996, one company laid claim to Gogoi itself. Fourth, and largely in reaction to these logging operations, NGOs joined with the provincial government to map chieftaincies and protect their lands from expropriation. In 1997, a team of fieldworkers (including myself) assisted Chief Gogoi to map his *nyika*—his country. This chapter discusses each of the four factors in turn, with particular emphasis on the last two, the loggers and mappers.

The loggers and the field staff of those NGO projects were Zimbabwean, less frequently South African, or, at the very least, had lived and worked for some time in Zimbabwe. Why should these Zimbabwe-influenced people (as I shall call them), rather than Mozambicans, have politicized territory? As grabbers and demarcators of land, Mozambican organizations and individuals were handicapped in relation to their Zimbabwean counterparts in a number of ways. On the practical level, poor roads between Gogoi and the provincial capital (Chimoio), a shortage of qualified provincial staff competent in the Ndau language, and Gogoi's history as a Renamo stronghold kept government personnel at arm's length.[2] In addition, and more important for the purposes of this study, Mozambican civil servants had little experience in land alienation, rural boundary disputes, and squatting. By contrast, Zimbabweans and South Africans were steeped in cadastral culture. Conscious of colonial history, they recognized Gogoi's potential as a hinterland for land-grabbing and land conversion. Loggers wished to realize that potential. Mappers wished to prevent the same from happening. Both groups of border crossers helped push the territorializing process along: the timber firm revealed its intention to plant exotic trees, and mappers (including myself) helped Chief Gogoi to identify his "territory." By mid-1997, the major components of land-grabbing and cadastral resistance were in place. The hinterland had started to close.

A CHIEFTAINCY AT THE CROSSROADS

In the early 1990s, at the onset of peace, Gogoi's chieftaincy reached a turning point unprecedented in its written record. The demobilization of Renamo's rebel army left it free of forced labor. The precolonial Gaza Nguni state and, from the 1890s onward, Portuguese colonials had employed chiefs to extract labor in various unfree ways.[3] Only the interlude of Frelimo's rule between independence in 1975 and the start of the war in 1979 later broke that chain. Frelimo had, however, replaced forced labor with other compulsions related to villagization and then reinstituted forced labor for military purposes. When Renamo conquered Gogoi in 1987, it similarly pressed men into service for porterage. Now, no one from outside Gogoi was attempting to exercise control over the people of Gogoi. Chief Gogoi himself, at last, was unencumbered by external demands for field hands and labor quotas. Of course, his role in Portuguese colonialism and Renamo's corvées had so conditioned his form of rule as to become inseparable from the concept of chieftaincy itself. Now, the sudden end of forced labor detached Gogoi and the meaning of his office from their moorings. Additionally, Gogoi had left his area for a safer region during the waning years of the war. (Two of his three deputies, or headmen, had been absent as well.) After the peace accords, he returned from the Buzi River Valley to resume his duties as chief. What were those duties to be? In the late 1990s, the answer was still unclear. The last three factors mentioned above—the return of displaced people, the entry of loggers, and the intervention of mappers—each played a role in shaping chiefly power and power in general in Gogoi. All of these events were, to greater and lesser degrees, cadastral. Each politicized land and boundaries.

Of these factors, the return of refugees and displaced people was the least prominent. In the immediate postwar years, land allocation of this sort did not appear to create conflict in Gogoi. This finding is all the more surprising given that returnees and other migrating smallholders were stirring up a great deal of trouble in other parts of Mozambique. Jocelyn Alexander (1994:18–26) writes of tangled disputes in neighboring Sussundenga District. There, Portuguese *colonato* settlements from the 1960s and Frelimo's *aldeias comunais* had concentrated people. This in-migration sedimented one layer of counterclaims to land on top of the claims of the original chiefs and subjects. With war, people fled, but others took their place. In 1993 and following, farmers returned to find their fields occupied. Myers (1994) documents the same conflicts in the lower Limpopo Valley (Gaza Province), as do he, Julieta Eliseu, and Erasmo Nhachungue (1993:100) along Manica's Beira Corridor.[4] In the densely populated, demographically turbulent corridor, chiefs and headmen exercised so little authority over land that urban "weekend farmers" cleared plots at will (Effler 1995:7).[5] Even more shocking, displaced people in Mavita (northern Sussundenga) cultivated in sacred groves. Thus, amid arguments from autochthony, colonial and post-colonial legal precedent, and simple occupation, nearly anyone could find a foothold—or reasonably demand one—on the land. In short, smallholders in these areas competed with each other for land, and they competed fiercely.

Conditions in Gogoi and most of northern Mossurize differed markedly. First, since the *colonatos* were intended for commercial agriculture, the Portuguese government had had no reason to install them in this remote area. Second, Frelimo had failed to install the *aldeias:* people refused to move, and Frelimo soon retreated as Renamo advanced. Third, there could be no weekend farmers because the rising waters of the Buzi River obstructed rainy-season commuters from Espungabera. Such urban-based entrepreneurs, moreover, were far more likely to live in distant Chimoio from whence agri-cultural ventures in Gogoi were an absurd proposition. Fourth and most important, the cycle of migration, combined with low population density in Gogoi, simply did not bring wartime residents and postwar migrants into conflict. People certainly fled and abandoned their fields during the war, but new residents did not take their places at that time. As a Renamo area, Gogoi did not offer the security of Frelimo strongholds, such as Sussundenga center, the northern parts of Sussundenga District, the Beira Corridor, and the Limpopo settlements. After the cease-fire, newcomers, mostly from dry Machaze District to the south, *did* mingle with returnees, but land was plen-tiful. Why would a migrating family want to live on a plot with possible claimants when plots with no such liens were available? In the same vein, chiefs and headmen were not constrained to allocate "abandoned" land when undeniably vacant areas abounded. Whereas in the Limpopo Valley and the Chimoio environs smallholders were in conflict, in Gogoi they readily accom-modated one another.[6]

Land allocation in Gogoi in the mid-1990s also differed markedly from that in Vhimba, Zimbabwe. Vhimba headmen, like their counterparts in Gogoi, allocated land in a way that maintained social harmony, but, because of Vhimba's high population density, they achieved that result by different means. Headmen settled some migrants, especially Mozambicans, inside Chimanimani National Park and the private Hayfield B estate (see chapter 3). Although not entirely intended to do so, these allocations helped limit crowding within the communal land. Thus, in neither Vhimba nor Gogoi did the claims of migrants overlap substantially with those of more long-standing residents. In Vhimba, of course, these allocations revived and intensified a different kind of conflict, the turf battles between "squatters" and state and private titleholders of Ngorima's "lost lands." Headmen had intended to do just that and, moreover, hoped to win their turf battles. As a result of these kinds of conflicts, Vhimba residents associated in-migration with categories of land—communal, national park, and private—and with their corresponding borders. Indeed, the meetings and speeches of Vhimba leaders focused on land and completely ignored any issue of distinctions among the inhabitants (notwithstanding the practical significance of the nationality of the migrants for choice in land allocation). The Zimbabwean cadastral political culture twisted migration into a territorial issue.

Gogoi residents, by contrast, associated migration with categories of *people.* In fact, informants in Gogoi did so to a much greater degree and with much less prodding than did even headmen in Vhimba. Most obviously, people in Gogoi use a special term for newly arrived migrants: *muhlafa* (plural, *vahlafa*). This word was not known in Vhimba. Nor did people in Vhimba use any synonym for it. A *muhlafa* is a new resident (not a returnee), and the term implies a probationary status. After some time—variously cited as a month, a year, or one harvest—the *muhlafa* ceases to be denoted as such. He or she then enters the residual category of commoners resident in Gogoi. Both officeholders and commoners talked excitedly about the arrival of numerous *vahlafa* from points north and south of Gogoi. Indeed, Headman Bundua regretted very much that his colonial-era salary had been abolished, for it would have increased as the number of his subjects increased. For Bundua, *vahlafa* augmented wealth *in people.* Postwar in-migration, thus, did not substantially stimulate cadastral politics in Gogoi.

Nonetheless, demographic turmoil could not fail to raise challenging questions. Such a mass exodus followed by mass return had not occurred in Mossurize since Ngungunyane, the last Gaza Nguni king, evacuated in 1888. The return of refugees and displaced people forced Gogoi's headmen to consider the status of abandoned fields. Headman Hlengana found a rule of thumb: after four or five years, the original occupant forfeited the land, although, upon return, that family was entitled to an equivalent parcel nearby. As explained above, headmen could and did avoid repossessing fields. Yet, the apparent possibility of reallocating fields shifted attention to headmen's powers over land. What was previously implicit became more explicit. In-migration also, at least, raised the specter of land-based conflict that was scarcely known before. Unexpectedly, then, the *vahlafa* prepared headmen and their subjects for forms of rule and contestation based on the control of land—for a political culture of enclosure and cadastral politics. These faint imaginings were to become vivid as the timber industry moved into Gogoi.

INVENTING A TIMBER CONCESSION

Continental Timbers, Limited was not entirely new to Gogoi. In 1946, this South African firm had established two subsidiaries—Companhia de Madeiras de Moçambique and Serração Portuguesa de Revue—with head offices in Mozambique's second city, Beira. These companies held concessions in Sofala and Manica provinces, including one in or close to Chief Gogoi's area (next to or overlapping with the FSM concession discussed in chapter 1). The companies cut hardwoods and contracted with sawmills located in the concession areas to mill the logs for Continental's subsidiaries. In this way, and by handling exports of other outfits, the companies became two of the largest exporters of timber from Mozambique (Pinto 1961:29). Although Frelimo nationalized both the Companhia de Madeiras de Moçambique and the Serração Portuguesa de Revue, postwar market reforms gave the former new life. In 1995, Continental teamed up again with a newly privatized Companhia de Madeiras de Moçambique and began cutting hardwoods in Manica and Sofala provinces. In 1996, Continental Timbers[7] installed a mobile sawmill in Gogoi (at the site of FSM's now-derelict permanent sawmill). Although equipment and transport problems had prevented the company from breaking even as of 1997, it was also assembling a heavy, fixed, high-capacity mill. Despite disease, despite landmines, these South Africans were implanting their business on the frontier.

For Afrikaners, this kind of colonization invites comparison with earlier drives to the north. References in 1997 to the "second Great Trek"[8] recalled the first white migration from the Cape Colony to the interior—accompanied by much bloodshed—in the 1830s. Six decades later, another generation of trekkers came to what is now the vicinity of Vhimba with an oral tradition of "war and land" (Palmer 1971). Now, a hundred years after that, South Africans were obtaining land on a massive scale in Mozambique.[9] For the most part, their acquisitions were peaceful.[10] Rather than forceful land-grabbing and evictions, what tied Continental Timbers to the trekkers was the settler's elementary concept and intention—to demarcate and own the land. John, the manager of the Gogoi mill—a non-Afrikaner white who grew up on an estate in Nyanga District, eastern Zimbabwe—expressed the strongest interest in owning land. Employed as a family friend of the owner of Continental Timbers, he remembered the ninety-nine-year lease granted under the Portuguese government. So did Piet, the owner's son, then based in Continental Timbers' Beira office. In 1997, Piet and John both believed that the National Directorate of Forestry and Wildlife had reactivated that lease. John, therefore, considered himself to be managing a sizable and nearly permanent forestry concession.[11]

Factually wrong in every respect, this interpretation led to massive misunderstanding between Continental Timbers and provincial forestry and wildlife officials. Ana Paula Reis, *chefe de serviço* of the Provincial Services of Forestry and Wildlife, had granted Continental Timbers a one-year cutting license for certain volumes of six species of timber. This license would expire on 31 December 1997, and, Reis affirmed, its renewal would depend upon Continental Timbers' adherence to the forestry regulations. Of course, Continental Timbers might have acquired a multiyear concession by going over Reis's head directly to high-level forestry and wildlife officials in Maputo. This kind of irregularity was not unprecedented, and Reis was known to be the kind of scrupulous regulator that an investor would want to dodge. Yet, Continental Timbers did not appear to have made deals in Maputo. Its executive director, a Mozambican "front man" in Beira, confirmed that Continental Timbers had obtained only a license. The company was, he said, in the process of gaining a concession with the understanding of a "preference" from the Manica provincial governor. At the sawmill itself, the Mozambican bookkeeper likewise knew of no concession or lease. Thus, Mozambicans in Continental Timbers as well as in the government held to one account. John and Piet, Zimbabwean and South African, respectively, believed with equal conviction that Continental Timbers held the land.

In practice, this disagreement centered on technical questions. Most mundanely, Piet and Reis were using different units of measure. When Piet discovered that the mapping project would protect sacred forests from logging, he was incensed. Later, we met by accident at the border post. Had Continental Timbers not paid for each and every hectare of its "concession," he shouted at me from across the customs counter. He was ready to ask for a prorated refund of forest charges based on the land he was losing. Yet, he was wrong: Reis had charged him by the cubic meter of raw logs.[12] He would be entitled to nothing for lost territory. In the event, I calmed him by assuring him that the forests were "small"—in hectares, that is, but certainly not in cubic meters! Reis could not have charged him by the hectare even if she had wanted to. Her office had no figures on the spatial area of Continental Timbers' operations in Gogoi. Neither that office nor the Provincial Services of Geography and Cadastre (Serviços Provinciais de Geografia e Cadastre) could lay its hands on a technical description listing coordinates or natural boundaries of the logging zone. Hence, forestry and wildlife's only map of forestry areas—showing that Continental Timbers, Carlos Venichand (another South African firm), and Madeira Africana de Messica had neatly partitioned northern Mossurize—was largely symbolic. The only copy of the map, at a useless scale of 1:250,000, resided at Chimoio headquarters, more than two hundred kilometers (over dirt roads) from the relevant officer who might have detected felling outside the appropriate zone. Hunting licenses were even less geographical. Denominated in species counts, they followed district lines or had no boundaries at all, and they could have easily overlapped with timber licenses. Obviously, this kind of superimposition of resource rights ruled out any possibility of landownership in an exclusive sense.

How, then, could John be so misguided? Clearly, his cadastral mindset did not prepare him for Mozambique. That territorial sensibility instructed him to buy land—a certain number of hectares within known and demarcated borders—from Ana Paula Reis. Sometime after that exchange, he or a Continental Timbers coworker drew the boundaries on a 1:50,000–scale map and tacked it to the wall of John's sawmill office. Yet, Reis had sold him no land. The two parties to this transaction simply understood it differently. In this way, John and Reis replayed the encounter of Zimbabwean headmen and Mozambican refugees. Those refugees came to Vhimba, Zimbabwe, to seek the rights of a client; the headmen used their submission to grab land. In Gogoi, the disjunction was equally sharp but reversed. The newcomers to Gogoi—Zimbabwean and South African expatriates—came to grab land while the government authorities intended to sell them other rights. Like the New England Indians William Cronon (1983:70) describes, Mozambicans sought to share with outsiders overlapping rights to plants and animals. Cadastrally minded colonists thought the Indians were selling (very cheaply) the land itself. In the same vein, John and Piet ascribed to themselves the position of landowners, ignoring the Mozambican staff above and below them who knew better. Their inability to speak or read Portuguese and their disdain for all Mozambicans—and particularly those in government—helped maintain the delusion.[13]

This misunderstanding had serious political consequences for the residents of Gogoi. As he became suspicious, John warned me: "I am the mayor here. The chief is the chief. . . . This is my land."[14] In ways more decisive than posting his "concession" map, John acted as if Gogoi's chiefdom *was* his. When his dog ran away, he confiscated smallholders' snares that would injure it. As he explained his actions to me, he declared that he had bought the land, the animals, everything. Snares, in other words, were his business: they affected the king's game on the king's estate. Even more threateningly,

John planned to develop his land. He and Piet spoke of eucalyptus plantations in the southwest and a game preserve in the northeast. They assured
me these areas were only secondary forests for which the farmers had no
use. Smallholders, in fact, collected edible plants, building materials, and
the like from precisely this kind of forest; so Continental Timbers' planting of trees would have amounted to an enclosure of the commons. John
recognized this possibility, but, as mayor, he felt he had the right to plant
where he wanted to and evict people if necessary. To Gogoi residents, these
schemes of timber plantations were a nightmare come true. They associated eucalyptus, wattle, and pine with the Border Timbers estates in
Chimanimani and Chipinge districts, Zimbabwe. In their view, Mozambique
was mercifully free of (white-owned) estates and the expulsions they caused.
As one farmer opined at the opening meeting of the mapping project, "We
farm where we want to."[15] For this reason, Mozambique was deemed superior to Zimbabwe. Now, the most ruinous aspects of Zimbabwe were creeping east of the border. If unopposed, a deluded Zimbabwean could easily
grab territory.

MAPPERS IN A WORLD WITHOUT BORDERS

At the same time, however, other Zimbabwe-influenced people were entering Manica Province with the stated or implicit intention of thwarting the
threatened enclosures. Between 1994 and 1997, three distinct development
projects—with German, Swiss, and Italian funding or support—undertook
this work in Mossurize and southern Sussundenga districts. Although they
were influenced from abroad, it would be a mistake to treat these projects,
first and foremost, as transnational institutions, participants in a general-
ized global discourse of development (Escobar 1995). Of course, an international trend in development policy toward the community-based management of natural resources did inform planning in Manica. Elsewhere
this trend has bolstered government control (Ribot 1996). Yet, on the
ground and in personal, idiosyncratic ways, a cadre of specifically Zimbabwe-
influenced people implemented the mapping projects. Past experiences in
Zimbabwe's communal lands had taught these people to think territorially,
even cadastrally. In a distant sense, they were children of the Rhodesian
enclosures. They opposed the enclosures across the border and did so in a
·highly political and sometimes conflictual fashion.

In so doing, these individuals exploited two advantages unavailable to
Continental Timbers: first, the ability to make maps, and second, an alliance

with the Mozambican state agriculture and forestry and wildlife offices. Land-grabbers and counter-grabbers must map. The Rhodesian trekkers, for instance, got their plots by taking them forcefully from Africans, but the land stayed out of African hands, even as the pioneers went bankrupt, because of the property survey. John and Piet seemed not to understand the long-term importance of this cadastral move. The map at the mill office notwith-standing, Continental Timbers had never documented its forests, its own-ership of land, or its boundaries in Gogoi. (Initially, John and Piet hoped that the mapping project would fill these needs.) Continental Timbers neg-lected to make a forest inventory and timber harvest plan, requirements for the concession they thought they already had. Continental Timbers, then, left the field open to other Zimbabwe-influenced people who would fill the cadastre with smallholders' claims. "Maps," as David Turnbull (1989:54) writes, "have power in virtue of introducing modes of manipulation and control that are not possible without them." In Gogoi, the property map could prove mightier than the sawmill.

Maps could also be powerful and legitimate because the Mozambican state supported them. The mapmakers coordinated their efforts and often worked in the field with staff of Manica's Provincial Directorate of Agri-culture and Livestock. In 1994, a loose collaborative group—including the provincial directorate and many Zimbabwe-influenced people— coalesced in Manica and devoted itself to trying to enlarge the role of smallholders in the management of forests and in the enjoyment of their benefits. This alliance was new and quite unusual in comparison with other countries. Elsewhere, in Thailand and Indonesia, for example, the state forestry office has overridden local claims to land and trees, selling huge forests to timber multinationals. In such countries, advocates for local rights engage in "countermapping" against state policies (Peluso 1995). In Mozambique, how-ever, oppositions and alliances are more complex. The very same office and officer who gave Continental Timbers its timber license joined with a foreign-funded project to undermine the expansion of that license into a concession. Additionally, headquarters in Maputo—that is, the National Directorate of Forestry and Wildlife—were taking part actively in debate on the draft land law. Adopted during this project, that law recognized small-holders' rights to land. Continental Timbers, therefore, may have had its secret allies in Chimoio or Maputo, but those alliances were strictly infor-mal. They could not generate official documents or lasting property maps. These maps—essentially a rudimentary cadastre—required the overt, explicit recognition and cooperation of relevant civil servants.

They also required the cooperation of chiefs, headmen, and other small-holders. As explained above, these figures were not nearly as accustomed as were Zimbabweans—say, Vhimba headmen—to thinking in territorial terms. At least until the end of the war, power in these polities depended upon control of people and labor much more than it did upon control of contested hectares. These Zimbabwe-inspired mapping projects, then, confronted misunderstandings and bafflement among precisely the people they intended to benefit. Some tackled the paradigm difference more directly than others did. James Bannerman's single-handed mapping of chieftaincies throughout Manica Province avoided the worst of the issue by not demarcating the boundaries between chieftaincies. Frank Matose and Saiti Makuku's rural appraisal in Sussundenga District probably encountered the problem but, it appears, evaded it by reinterpreting locally drawn sketches. My own mapping project, finally, nearly ran aground on these shoals: Gogoi's leaders delimited their land with only the most vague frontiers of settlement. As is explained in a later section, the project and the impending alienation of their land by Continental Timbers eventually convinced them to discover or invent borders—this is, to territorialize their polity.

Bannerman—to start with the least explicitly territorial project—was and is an aficionado of chieftaincies. Having emigrated from Britain to Rhodesia, he developed this interest as an agricultural officer in Victoria Province (now Masvingo) in the 1970s. On field visits, Bannerman collected oral history and interviewed chiefs and elders of Hlengweni, Zimbabwe. Published in 1978 and 1981, this work focused on chiefly lineages. In the style of his teacher at the University of Zimbabwe, David Beach, Bannerman documented the genealogy, migration, confederation, and conquest of the major dynasties. He also placed every chief on eighteenth-century, nineteenth-century, and current maps. After independence, he served the government of Zimbabwe as provincial resettlement officer for Manicaland. In this capacity, he was tasked with unraveling the legacy of land alienation—that is, with resettling communal land farmers to white estates whose owners were killed or fled during the war. Squatters complicated his job immensely. Before he and his staff could select and physically install farmers who qualified according to official criteria, smallholder families simply moved onto the estates. Bannerman, then, was obliged to take part in the kind of kilometer-by-kilometer turf battles characteristic of Vhimba, Zimbabwe. Disillusioned with the resettlement process, Bannerman left government service in 1987 and applied his agricultural skills to a private nursery in the Vumba Mountains.

Nearby Mozambique soon drew Bannerman back into historical research and back into planning. In 1992, the Manica Agricultural and Rural Recon-struction Programme (MARRP) recruited him for ecological and social stud-ies. Funded by the German agency GTZ (Gesellschaft für Teknische Zusammenarbeit), this program assisted various departments of provincial government in planning nearly every aspect of rural development. Again, Bannerman concentrated on chieftaincies. His maps included every colo-nially recognized chief and many headmen in Mossurize, Sussundenga, and Barue districts. Additional maps show rainfall, soil types, roads, farming sys-tems, ecological zones, and official land-use categories. This comprehen-siveness was all the more surprising given that Bannerman did not gain access to the aerial photographs used by some government departments in Maputo. Driving the length and breadth of the province, Bannerman assembled site-specific geographical knowledge that surpassed nearly a century of Portuguese and postcolonial efforts (see, e.g., Bannerman 1993, 1996). Ultimately, and especially with regard to chiefs, Bannerman's most lasting contribution was to provide basic territorial knowledge for an eventual cadastre.

The Manica Agricultural and Rural Reconstruction Programme itself was as cadastral and roughly as Zimbabwean as Bannerman himself. The deputy director (under a German director) was Zimbabwean. He and other sen-ior staff split their time between headquarters in Chimoio and a second office in Mutare, the Zimbabwean border town where their families lived. Before the hiring of more Mozambicans, Bannerman himself described MARRP's staff as "probably a little too much Zimbabwean orientated."[16] In addition to its personnel, some of MARRP's plans implicated Zimbabwe. In the bor-der area west of Gogoi, a long-delayed scheme for agricultural out-grow-ing proposed one-hectare family tea plots. The Zimbabwean Tanganda Tea Company would purchase the farmers' inputs and then, under an exclusive contract, buy their crops.[17] This program sounded suspiciously like Por-tuguese forced cotton cultivation, but actually, it resembled Rhodesian and Zimbabwean land-use planning. Whereas Portuguese agriculturalists had not cared *where* smallholders planted cotton, their Anglophone counter-parts tried periodically to reorganize production into arable and grazing blocks (reminiscent of the Rhodesian Native Land Husbandry Act described in chapter 2). Hence, the zoning of tea, combined with its Zimbabwean con-nection, led farmers in Mossurize to fear that their land would be taken. In the worst cases, then, MARRP's planning reminded Mozambican civil servants of the Zimbabwean enclosures (although they did not resist the project). In the best cases, even Bannerman's work on the geography of chief-ship, which he distinguished quite clearly from the tea proposal, had something in common with it. Under MARRP's Zimbabweanist umbrella, both projects were vaguely cadastral: in one case for chiefs and in the other for crops, they implied the demarcation of land.

Bannerman's work fell short of land demarcation because he did not map the boundaries of chieftaincies. A second, Zimbabwean-influenced project inaugurated this much more difficult form of geographical research in Sussundenga in 1994. Makuku and Matose, both of the Zimbabwean Forestry Commission's Forest Research Centre, played a leading role in this study. At the plantation-oriented Forestry Commission, they had already opened a Pandora's box of controversy on indigenous methods of forest management. Matose and Makuku were also equally sensitive to property and cadastral issues. Matose (1992:177) had decried smallholders' "annexation" of shared woodland in Shurugwi District. In order to prevent this kind of privatization, Matose wrote, "there is need for greater involvement by traditional leaders like chiefs and kraal-heads [headmen]" (ibid.,178). Likewise, Makuku's short article on Bikita, Zimbabwe, commenced with the declaration: "For many generations past, traditional leadership systems have been the nucleus for preservation and sustained management of resources which occurred within territorial boundaries under chieftain rule" (Makuku 1993:18). This manifesto contained two ideas new to Mozambique: first, that chiefs and headmen could and should manage forests, and second, that chiefly authority existed within discrete spatial limits. In places less thoroughly investigated than Shurugwi and Bikita, the research agenda was clear.

Matose and Makuku came to Sussundenga District, Mozambique, in late 1994 as members of a joint Zimbabwean-Mozambican team. They and other Zimbabweans, in fact, led the team. Earlier that year, the World Bank had selected the Chimanimani uplands in Sussundenga as one of three "transfrontier conservation areas" to be established in Mozambique under the auspices of the National Directorate of Forestry and Wildlife.[18] From Zimbabwe, the World Bank and the directorate sought rural researchers to work with communities and to train Mozambicans to do the same. Because the World Bank could not readily fund such preparatory activities, the Harare office of the Swiss-based World Conservation Union (IUCN) sent ten professionals to Sussundenga.[19] Zimbabweans, who comprised six of the ten, predominated numerically as well as linguistically. Whereas all but one Zimbabwean spoke Shona fluently, none of the Mozambicans could even function in the language. Nor did the Mozambicans possess substantial experience in rural social research. Led, therefore, by Zimbabwean expatriates, the project encapsulated the kind of teacher-student relationship of which Mozambicans soon tired.[20]

Specifically, Matose and Makuku taught the techniques of rural appraisal they had used in Zimbabwe. Beyond those methods, it seemed as if they imported their conclusions from Zimbabwe as well. The group investigated natural resources, resource use, settlement patterns, decision-making structures, and population movements in two areas of the Sussundenga District, Mavita at its northern end and Dombe to the south. The report, written by Makuku, Matose, and one other Forestry Commission employee (P. Mushove), finds that "traditional leaders" allocate land to migrants, restrict the harvesting of forest products in various ways, and conduct ceremonies in sacred forests. Thus, "There is no doubt that traditional institutions have a strong role to play" in the conservation of natural resources. Further, "The state institutions will need to . . . work together with the local institutions [i.e., chiefs and headmen] in a collaborative role as equal partners" (Makuku, Matose, and Mushove 1994:6). Matose and Makuku, then, contributed to a renascent debate on local governance in postwar Mozambique. More accurately, they helped to translate President Joaquim Chissano's post-1987 national liberalization into the context of Manica Province. To some of the old-style administrators still serving there, who had attacked the chiefs as obscurantist, their rehabilitation was revolutionary.

In fact, the maps were as revolutionary—and more so, from the perspective of property—as the report's text. The maps created, perhaps fabricated, territorial entities. Makuku, Matose, and their colleagues asked informants to draw their natural resources and the "areas of jurisdiction of the different local leaders" (ibid., 6). Maps included in the report demonstrate varying degrees of cadastral knowledge and betray varying degrees of authorial intervention. When asked to draw jurisdictions, men in Dombe indicated chiefs with triangles and settlements with dots clustered around the triangles (map 5.1). Do the resulting splotches represent jurisdictions? They do only in the sense of power over people (or power over dots). Since the map shows no boundaries between the chiefs, it is clear that the artists of Dombe did not associate their polities with territory. Another jurisdictional map from Ndongwe, however, is unambiguously and suspiciously cadastral. The map divides Chief Ndongwe's area (just north of Dombe) into seven long lots abutting the Mussapa River (map 5.2). Dotted lines separate the domains, which each bear the name of a *sabhuku*. Did the team members who went to Ndongwe "tidy up" a map that originally looked as territorially vague as the Dombe representation? Yes, a principal later recalled: "One would assume

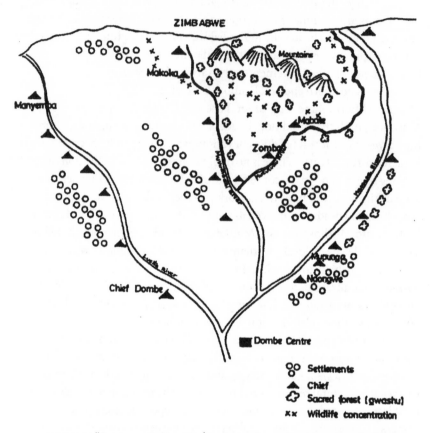

MAP 5.1. "Resource and institutional map drawn by elders, Dombe," Sussundenga District, Mozambique. From Makuku, Matose, and Mushove 1994

[when copying any of the maps from the ground onto paper] that in between [settlements] the boundaries were. The assumption was that half-half [midway] in between the boundaries were."[21] In short, Makuku and Matose's team probably committed the same error as John and Continental Timbers: they intuited that human use of the landscape required its partition into nonoverlapping spaces. They misread Mozambican political geography through a lens of past enclosures elsewhere.

The third and final mapping initiative—my own work in Gogoi—grew indirectly from Matose and Makuku's visit to Sussundenga. In addition to

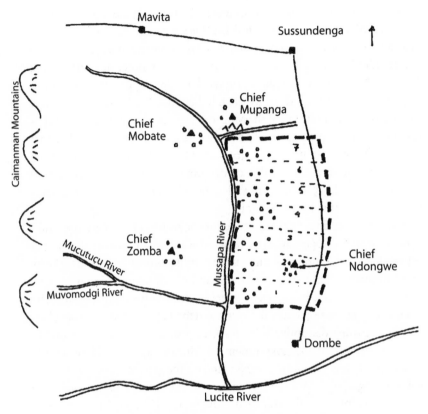

MAP 5.2. Chief Ndongwe's area, Sussundenga District, Mozambique.
From Makuku, Matose, and Mushove 1994

methods of rural appraisal, the Transfrontier Conservation Project imported expertise in community-based resource management from Zimbabwe. Officials imagined that the celebrated Campfire program (see chapter 4) could guide work in the Chimanimani Transfrontier Conservation Area. In mid-1994, the World Conservation Union organized a workshop in Garuzo, Manica, for this purpose (see chapter 6). It invited Marshall Murphree and Calvin Nhira of the Centre for Applied Social Sciences (of the University of the Zimbabwe), the agency most involved in evaluating community-based resource management in Zimbabwe.[22] Marshall Murphree, in turn, invited me. As a result of that workshop, the Transfrontier Project asked me to carry out a "socioeconomic assessment" on both sides of the Rusitu River.[23] Smallholders on the Zimbabwean bank, in Vhimba, taught me the importance of land alienation and cadastral politics. My writings from that initial fieldwork (Hughes 1995a:30–31; 1996:39) advocated the return of alienated land to Vhimba residents. Applying this logic to Mozambique, my next World Bank consultancy report (1995b:10) recommended the guarantee of smallholders' land rights as a precondition to any other activities in the Transfrontier Project. In 1996, I proposed a mapping project in Gogoi to do just that, and the Harare office of an Italian NGO funded it.[24] The project also attracted the attention of the Mozambican government because it represented a trial implementation of those clauses of the draft land law that recognized communities' rights to land. Hence, the Manica Provincial Services of Forestry and Wildlife contributed a fieldworker to the team,[25] and, as soon as the 1996–97 rains ended, he and an Italian-sponsored fieldworker accompanied me to Gogoi.

From its inception, our project fought enclosure. The Italian NGO and I chose to work in Gogoi, in part, because it was the only area of the district actively logged.[26] Continental Timbers was cutting timber there, and we knew that Continental Timbers sought to expand its operations. Under the new Land Law, Gogoi residents could protect themselves from expropriation by documenting their residence on the land and their opposition to timber plantations and other disruptive activities. Our project, therefore, intended to generate maps that the government of Mozambique would recognize. Residents of Gogoi would draw their land on the ground or on paper, and, using a geographic positioning system, we would compile a 1:50,000–scale map compatible with the standard topographical sheets. Our final team member, Melanie Hughes McDermott (my wife), had employed such technology in a similar project that obtained land and resource rights for indigenous people in the Philippines. She trained the team in "geomatics" and oversaw its initial cartographic efforts.[27] Finally, we expected representatives from Gogoi to deliver copies of their hand-drawn maps, the geomatic maps, and other materials to the provincial heads of forestry and wildlife and of geography and cadastre. This complex project confused the team at times and often bewildered Chief Gogoi and subjects completely. Nonetheless, it accomplished what it set out to do.

TERRITORIALIZING GOGOI

In the process, the project territorialized Chief Gogoi's polity. (The same may have occurred in polities affected by the other two mapping projects, but, for obvious reasons, I do not possess equivalent knowledge of them.) Chief Gogoi, his headmen, and others involved in the project came, in fits and starts, to understand the value of turf and the means by which to hold onto it. This transformation took place on two levels. First, Gogoi and some of his people acted: they grasped the idea of enclosures, they took part in the effort to map against them, and, for now, they registered their claim in the cadastre. Second, the maps acted. "All maps," J. B. Harley (1989:11) writes, "state an argument about the world and they are propositional in nature." The maps that Gogoi's leaders drew—and the team elaborated—stated and created the smallholders' claim to land. Like a signpost or a fence, they established property for all to see—including the surprised and pleased people of Gogoi (cf. Rose 1994). Gogoi people were surprised because their politics had not previously focused on bounded territory. Like the "tidied up" map of Makuku and Matose, this project's intervention activated territoriality where it had been only latent before. Up to that point, however, Gogoi residents interpreted and manipulated the mapping project in ways characteristic of their noncadastral politics: first, as a question of labor; second, as one of trees; and, third, as a question of sacred forests.

The project first and unavoidably addressed the need for local staff. To Gogoi residents, we fell into the well-known category of labor recruiters. Upon arrival in Gogoi, we had informed the chief that we would hire a guide, a cook, and a guard, and we asked for his recommendations. He chose a son as our guide, and that son together with our team found a cook and a guard, confirming our selection with Chief Gogoi himself. Without intending to, we thus recapitulated the hiring practice of Renamo and of the Portuguese administration: in a formal sense, we recruited our labor through the chief. Coincidentally, Continental Timbers had also followed this established custom. In its case, the chief had called a popular meeting to announce that Continental Timbers was offering employment. His son later told us that the news had spread in a rather more blunt form as: "The sawmill wants people."[28] Of course, neither our project nor the sawmill was demanding *forced* labor. This distinction regarding the nature of the labor seemed less important than the form of its procurement. We had won local approval by doing what only Frelimo, among labor seekers, had refused to do. We had acknowledged the chief's power over people.

The project, nonetheless, moved rapidly to issues besides labor and distinguished itself from the sawmill. Again, however, the project and Gogoi's people rode on different tracks. The opening meeting, held at Chief Gogoi's compound, turned the attention of the roughly 150 onlookers to natural resources and their ownership. Ana Paula Reis, the provincial head of forestry and wildlife, declared, "We [the government] are not the owners of the land.

You who live here are."[29] Oddly, the remainder of her speech and the public reaction to it focused not on land but on trees. Interrupting Reis, one man asked for clarification: does this talk of community-managed forests mean that he may demand payment for the cutting of trees in the vicinity of his fields and homestead? The audience grew excited at the prospect of charging Continental Timbers by the log. Reis and the other government and NGO officials intended that people should benefit from sustainable commercial use of the forest, but they expected that people would do so as a community rather than individually. Responding to the question of tree sales, Benjamin Gemo, provincial head of geography and cadastre, admonished, "The tree belongs to the community. It does not belong to João [the equivalent of Joe Blow or Joe Bloggs]."[30] Gemo's idealism only heightened the audience's sense of mystification.

In part, the attendees missed Gemo's point because his notion of "community" was foreign to them. Gemo, whose position made him the most sensitive to territory in the provincial government, was referring to a community of place. He assumed that proximity and residence within physical limits gave Gogoi people a common identity and interest. Logically, that interest should include geographical issues and the management of the community's common landscape. Gogoi residents differed with Gemo's notion of community in two senses. First, their community was the *polity* of Chief Gogoi's subjects. In other words, they did not identify, first and foremost, with a geographical community of place. They were members of the collectivity circumscribed by leaders' jurisdiction over people. Given this kind of community, Gogoi residents—differing with Gemo in the second sense—did not associate the resources and activities in and around one's field with Chief Gogoi. Trees and their products were not normally the chief's business; so what could cutting them have to do with the "community" led by him?

The project answered that question by concentrating on religious matters rather than on the ownership and sale of natural resources. Before the first public meeting, the chief had expressed fears that Continental Timbers would cut in sacred forests.[31] As he and his headmen explained, the loggers of the 1960s and early 1970s had done precisely that and, consequently, had caused many forests to cease to be sacred. Chiefs and headmen—the organizers or performers of *kudira* propitiating ceremonies—resented this disenchantment profoundly. Their involvement made sacred forests an issue of the Gogoi polity or, as Gemo had gropingly insisted, a "community" concern. Therefore, I introduced the project as a means for change such that "the company [Continental Timbers] will be required to obey your wishes.

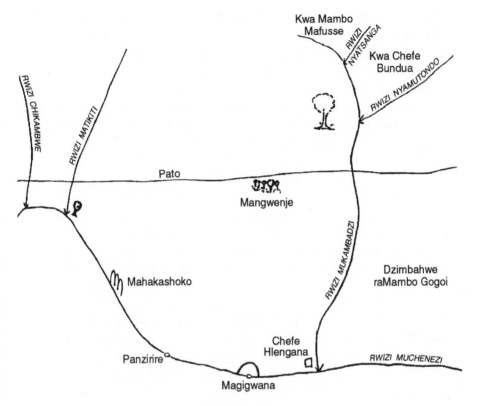

MAP 5.3. Headman Hlengana's area.
Drawing by Headman Hlengana, Gogoi, 9 May 1997 (labels added subsequently)

It will not be permitted to cut in sacred forests or to cut sacred trees or trees that you use."[32] People appreciated this objective immediately. In meetings at Chief Gogoi's homestead and at those of his three headmen, men discussed these forests volubly. Ignoring our additional interest in areas used for fuelwood, hunting, and so on, Gogoi people sketched maps on the ground, in the dirt, or on loose pieces of paper that showed almost nothing but sacred zones (e.g., map 5.3).

These maps of sacred forests were not fully territorial. I had expected—and I had told the rest of the team to expect—that sacred forests would encompass zones of a number of hectares in size within clear boundaries. Nyakwawa, the forest I knew from Vhimba, had been expansive. Although sometimes in a flexible fashion, Vhimba people had demarcated this and other forests using the Rusitu and Haroni rivers and smaller streams. To my surprise, only one of twelve sacred forests in Gogoi corresponded to this model. That forest, known as Mabombe, contained 250 hectares of woodland lying between the Nzuwe, a dry stream, and the Sitatonga mountain ridge. Two of the remaining smaller forests cover at least 1 hectare. More typically, nine of the "forests" are not forests at all. They are stands of trees or even one tree often next to streams or pools. Five *mupanga-panga* (*Milletia stuhlmannii*) trees, for example, sprouted from the grave of Mangwenje; so, the hallowed ground bears his name. Finally, single *muvava* (*Khaya nyasica*) trees constitute the two smallest sites, considered sacred simply because ceremonies are performed there. The team collected one set of coordinates for each of these nine sites and added them as dots to our "cadastral" version of the locally drawn sketch maps. Thus, halfway through the project, we had produced an official representation of Gogoi's "territory" that showed three bounded forests and nine points.[33] We, like so many development workers, had not yet convinced the "participants" in this project to see the world our way.

Our interlocutors also disappointed us on the question of boundaries. On a sketch map where we expected sharp limits, Gogoi encircled his country with a broken, indeterminate frontier. Headmen Hlengana, the only one of Gogoi's three headmen who was able to draw a map at all, likewise left a large gap to the northwest (map 5.3). In response to further prodding, Gogoi and Hlengana named various streams and dry streambeds that would close their circles. Yet, the streams did not connect, they did not flow in the directions indicated, and, given the topography, they could not possibly form an unbroken chain. Gogoi, at last, told us that he did not know his northern boundary and that we must go there to ask Headman Matsikiti. Later, Matsikiti also confessed bafflement. Only the families actually living on the frontier, he said, knew precisely where it was. In the meantime, we had also followed the chain of command upward to the government *chefe de posto* (the lowest level functionary) and district administrator. They had referred us back downward. The knowledge about boundaries, the *chefe de posto* told us, "is there, in the field."[34] Ultimately, the "field" meant, quite literally, the cultivated fields of Gogoi's far-flung subjects. Thus, as far as the leadership was concerned, people—or the remotest hinterland of members of Gogoi's polity—delimited that polity spatially.

This kind of fuzzy frontier came about because settlement preceded demarcation. Gogoi's polity formed and developed according to the pattern of fission and secession common elsewhere in East and Southern Africa. At the turn of the century, Gogoi split from Mafussi and went south. Subsequent Gogoi titleholders prevented secession only by allowing their younger brothers to leave the *dzimbahwe* (the central, capital part of the chiefdom) and assume authority as headmen in the outlying areas. As Igor Kopytoff (1987) writes, this kind of fragmentation slowly populates the "interstitial frontiers" between chiefly seats. In colonial Mozambique, those frontiers did not need to be primarily territorial. Because obligations of forced labor defined the Gogoi polity, Gogoi's chiefdom ended where his ability to compel labor ended. The degree of demarcation, therefore, varied with population density. In Gogoi's heartland, where settlement was much denser, headmen probably agreed on borders in order to avoid overlapping claims to labor. Their sketch maps for the project often placed streams between headmen's areas or between them and the *dzimbahwe*. As a result of dense settlement, frontiers had become solid and physical. In the sparsely populated hinterland, by contrast, physical demarcation was not necessary. Until 1997, the outermost extent of headmen's areas and of Gogoi's chiefdom remained a matter for conjecture.

Frontiers of this kind do not help a chief to wage cadastral battles. In the worst case, the people holding the frontier go elsewhere, causing territory to shrink. Wartime exodus had already affected all of Gogoi's area and probably deepened the leadership's doubt regarding its northern fringe. Now, that lack of specificity threatened to undermine the first cadastral effort to establish and defend Gogoi's land. Gogoi would have been in a much better position if his boundaries had existed prior to or independent of settlement. In Vhimba, for example, Headmen Tiyekiye knew that the Chisengu River was his northern limit. To claim the territory thus encircled, he settled squatters in the uninhabited stretch between his legal border and his desired border. Of course, Tiyekiye exploited his unchecked authority to settle Mozambicans where he wished. Neither Gogoi nor his headmen wielded this kind of authority over land allocation to anyone. Therefore, a history of forced labor rendered Gogoi's leaders doubly disadvantaged in counterdemarcation: their outermost borders were mere frontiers, and they lacked the means to deploy settlers as strategic boundary beacons. The second difficulty was insurmountable in the short term. Gogoi, however, could transform his fuzzy frontiers into cadastral lines, and we hoped he would.

This advantage of physical borders over human frontiers gradually became clear to Gogoi in our discussions over the western delimitation of his land. Here, Chief Macuiana had taken a huge lobe of Gogoi's area in the 1960s. Gogoi and his elders described this theft as a damaging loss of subjects and, consequently, of tribute in tax and labor. Macuiana had expropriated some of Gogoi's power over people. Now, through our project, Gogoi saw a way to regain this part of his authority. Therefore, he sketched the Mbisarutsva Hills[35] as his western limit. This upland, however, did not join up with the Chicambue River, Gogoi's limit to the northwest. Questioned on the exact location of the boundary, Gogoi again stated that the people living in and around Mbisarutsva knew, but, he said, they were too distant to visit. Faced with these difficulties—and perhaps sensing our disbelief— Chief Gogoi opted for clear borders. He simply relinquished his claim against Macuiana. On his sketch, he moved the border roughly twelve kilometers eastward to the Muchenedzi River, where it eventually appeared on the project's official, cadastral maps. He, thus, traded a vague and shifting fron- tier of settlement to lines that could be written down and enforced against Continental Timbers and other resource users.

Yet, Gogoi's maps were not yet serviceable. As they stood, they, in fact, could make matters worse for Gogoi residents. Although the borders had hardened, the interior—the territory itself—was an empty shell. The sketch— cadastral because it had a border—showed only one large forest, two small ones, and nine points. In other words, it showed Gogoi's land as nearly vacant. This map, then, implied that Continental Timbers could plant large tracts to pine without inconveniencing local smallholders. Fortunately and rather suddenly, the chief and headmen perceived this dangerous loophole. In a flash of cadastral insight, they realized that their sketches risked selling the nonsacred parts of the land. To close this loophole, the mapping project changed course. Expanding beyond the male leadership of Gogoi, we worked with groups of men and women to generate matrices of resource use. Using stones and drawings, smallholders made charts showing the usable (some- times saleable) plants and animals that they obtained with land types (Hughes and McDermott 1997:15–21 of app.). They, thus, demonstrated the necessity of fields, mountains, wetlands, primary forest, and a number of secondary forest types for local livelihood. This information, submitted to the government along with the maps, filled Gogoi's vacant lot with actual and potential commercial and subsistence zones, all reserved for the people of Gogoi. Just as important, at least some Gogoi residents knew the value of their work. Rehearsing the presentation of the maps and matrices to the provincial government, a delegation composed of sons and brothers of Chief Gogoi and his headmen declared, "We will not sell the land!"[36]

Did the project, then, protect Chief Gogoi's area from Continental Timbers and other land-grabbers? In July 1997, at the conclusion of the project's fieldwork in Gogoi, the delegation showed its maps and matrices prematurely and unofficially to the Mossurize district administrator. The ensuing discussion, which included a Mozambican representative of Continental Timbers, centered on sacred forests. The district administrator affirmed that Continental Timbers would not be allowed to cut in these zones. Reported to Piet, this remark raised the fears of lost hectares referred to above. At the same time, the district administrator, who shared Piet's mistaken belief that Continental Timbers had a concession, opined that the company could still plant exotics on uncultivated land. The district administrator thus recognized local people's rights of occupation, but he also allowed Continental Timbers to enclose forest commons.[37]

The response of the provincial government will be even more decisive. Ana Paula Reis and Benjamin Gemo accepted the maps and matrices in an official ceremony the following month. The project then moved on (without me) to Macuiana's area and produced the same cadastral documents there.[38] Eventually, under Bannerman's direction, the project mapped the bulk of Mossurize District. Will provincial officials recognize the full implications of Gogoi's, Macuiana's and other areas' documents? These officials (with the exception of Gemo) are, after all, products of Mozambique's non-cadastral politics. To enforce Gogoi's cadastral effort, they would need to start to think in hectares rather than in cubic meters. They would also need to think in terms of exclusive ownership rather than in terms of overlapping use rights. In theory, the transformation is already well underway: Mozambique's Land Law of 1997 recognizes precisely the form of maps and documents produced by the Gogoi project. In practice, however, the Mozambican state is betwixt and between. It is only beginning to retrace the sea change experienced in Gogoi: shifting from rule based on categories of people to rule based on the management of zones of land.

Did the expatriates close the hinterland? This question has two parts. First, there is the issue of quickening frontiers until, in minds and on maps, they are the solid lines of drawn borders. Then comes the possibility of claiming interiors so as to constitute the territory and its ownership. In Continental Timbers, John and Piet believed that the indistinct edge of their timber area was a solid property line, but they convinced no one but themselves. Of course, they succeeded in alarming people, including the Zimbabwe-influenced mappers. In our own minds, we treated frontiers as borders and the interiors as property. By the end of the project in Gogoi, the local leadership had also started to think in this cadastral fashion. On paper, as well, the project and Gogoi's leadership had achieved a cadastral outcome: they had registered the commons against any possible timber or hunting concession. Yet, Gogoi and his people have claimed territory only by the skin of their teeth. By legal means and perhaps by the kind of unofficial land-grabbing already attempted, Continental Timbers will doubtless try to establish a concession. The enclosures, one is inclined to think, are moving, like an unstoppable juggernaut, through Southern Africa.

If they are, then one can expect politics in Gogoi to become increasingly cadastral. In the future, chiefs, headmen, and commoners may struggle with private companies, with the Mozambican government, and with each other over turf and boundaries. Land allocation could become an important weapon in such disputes, and headmen could start to think of in-migration in terms of land rather than in terms of people, such as *vahlafa*. This last conceptual shift would signal that "territorial classification has replaced the old systems based on classification by social category" (Vandergeest and Peluso 1995:400). A polity and political culture of this nature would approximate Vhimba. One would not wish the people of Gogoi to claw, meter by meter—and lose—as do smallholders in Vhimba. Yet, cadastral politics and territorial losses seem preferable to the virtual enslavement of forced labor. Certainly, the Mozambican men who emigrated thought so. Enclosures and battles against them, then, may represent progress in an optimistic sense.

PART 3

Native Questions

Upon independence, University of Zimbabwe faculty virtually banned the use of the term *native* in undergraduate writing. A Rhodesian official term for black African, it recalled the country's experience of racism and discrimination. History students were required to quarantine the offensive word within quotation marks. Without the benefit of punctuation, my own lecture ruffled some feathers in 2000. The past is past, scholars imply, and postcolonial Zimbabwe warrants a new frame of analysis. Did change truly overwhelm continuity?

In important respects, it did not, as I attempt to demonstrate below. The categories of "native," "native question," and "native policy" are as pertinent as ever. Even while the meaning of "native" becomes increasingly difficult to specify, policymakers have perpetuated its key assumptions in the new concepts of "community." There is still a discourse of "native questions." To prove that point, the scope of the book's analysis widens, beyond Vhimba and Gogoi, to discuss the dilemmas of Zimbabwe and Mozambique. Beginning in the late 1980s, state policies toward development and conservation revisited colonial dilemmas. A variety of projects and programs have opened Zimbabwe's communal lands and various Mozambican hinterlands to colonization. Indeed, the projects discussed in chapters 4 and 5 played a part in this process of rezoning, encroachment, and eviction. Throughout, project managers, myself included, employed a new vocabulary: colonists were "investors" or "the private sector," while natives passed as "communities." Despite new terminology, project managers confronted the age-old question: "Where should the natives (or in Portuguese, *indígenas*) live and farm?" The book's conclusion considers how, in the age of black rule, such a high-handed discourse could persist at all. In the 1990s, why were smallholders themselves not in a position to propose answers to the native question? How did officials continue to monopolize national and international debates on this issue? Liberal projects of emancipation, democracy, and development emasculated rural people of the Zimbabwe-Mozambique borderland, impairing their ability to make big demands as a big group. All too frequently, progressives of the 1990s saw smallholders as colonial administrators saw them: tradition-bound people of narrow vision. The "native" concept lived on in agencies' assumptions if not in their assertions. Furthermore, as in the past, colonization threatened to uproot such people and reroot them in smaller spaces. Thus, the persistence of a discourse of the native question—especially when unmasked as such—is troubling. As the dominant answers to that question, expropriation and containment are even more so.

Chapter 6 examines ways in which civil servants, politicians, applied scholars, and the desk and field officers of organizations posed the question and arrived at the answers. How could people in agencies committed to the betterment of rural life ultimately endorse a program to dispossess rural people?[1] My approach is necessarily critical, but I wish to differ in model and method from most critics of development and other state programs. The harshest detractors see organizational officers as either corrupt or ignorant. If corrupt, bureaucrats pursue their own personal and institutional interests at the expense of their stated goals and of the poor. Graham Hancock and Joseph Hanlon, both journalists with a penchant for class analysis, expose such self-serving behavior (G. Hancock 1989; Hanlon 1991:190–202). If ignorant, bureaucrats intervene in social contexts they do not begin to understand, producing unforeseen consequences. According to James Scott (1998), "authoritarian high modernists" "simplify" a messy world, employing grids, surnames, and other standards to make it "legible." The anthropologist James Ferguson writes of the World Bank as less authoritarian than "antipolitical." In his account, deskbound technocrats write plans fantastically inappropriate to the country at hand. Their reports and evaluations, for instance, perpetuate the myth that Lesotho has a national economy independent of South Africa and, therefore, that the government of Lesotho can and should manage it. Projects fail, but, as a "side effect" or an "unauthored resultant constellation," state power marches into Lesotho's mountain fastness (Ferguson 1990:20–21). My critique approximates Ferguson's, and readers of Zimbabwe's and Mozambique's stale memoranda might agree wholeheartedly with him.

In my account, however, workers in environmental projects appear both more eloquent and more discerning than do Ferguson's report writers—and less deliberately authoritarian than are Scott's modernizers. As chapter 5 made clear, I worked in offices and field teams, wherein people spoke and acted in ways that far surpassed their hastily fashioned prose.[2] Their institutions, as Arturo Escobar writes, did employ "textual and documentary forms"—but not always "as a means of representing and presenting a given reality."[3] At least, the printed word did not communicate in any straightforward fashion the values and practices of an organization. My supervisor at the World Bank's Mozambique Mission once thanked me for, as required, composing a report that "makes a 'thunk' when you drop it on the table." Too busy to read, agency staff functioned as nearly nonliterate societies.[4] The oral mode—of presentations, meetings, workshops, and long drives—conveyed much of their thought and intellectual dynamism. Thus, their story is largely *oral* history—and also *intellectual* history. These agencies and employees deliberately assessed the world around them according to theory and systematic observation.[5] Social and natural scientists formed the core of what one participant called a "general Southern Africa cult" of community-based resource management.[6] At the University of Zimbabwe's Centre for Applied Social Sciences, Professor Marshall Murphree supervised numerous doctoral students engaged in research on conservation and development. In common with many if not all scholars, this intelligentsia simplified the world around it. Investigators subjected some variables to scrutiny and knowingly treated others as externalities. They chose their unit of analysis, the "community," deliberately but not blindly. In what Murphree (1997:10–12) later described as a "strategic compromise," he and other scholars downplayed the heterogeneous, fluid nature of rural society in favor of a simpler model accessible to policymakers. Once "legible," rural people would gain authority over flora and fauna. Few did so, but, to the extent the intelligentsia made mistakes, these were smart, educated, liberal-minded mistakes.

Ultimately, development and conservation agencies helped to shape the "constellation" of conditions in which smallholders lost (or failed to obtain) security in land. Although no organization sought that outcome, most understood that their projects entailed the possibility of land alienation. In 2000, the unexpected demise of tourism almost turned that remote risk into a reality. My informants only half understood what was occurring. Thus, in what follows (and already somewhat in chapter 5), I grope toward a genre still emergent: an ethnography of meaning and murkiness within development and conservation agencies and an explanation of how good people sometimes make flawed policies.[7]

6

OPEN NATIVE RESERVES
OR NONE?

ON THE ZIMBABWE-MOZAMBIQUE BORDER, THE EXISTENCE AND
function of native reserves hang in the balance. They now appear to be
obstructing economic development. It was not always so. A hundred or even
fifty years ago, the policy of reserves removed moral and economic imped-
iments to colonization—dilemmas unknown in the eastern United States
and other frontiers of extermination. Administrators from the 1890s onward
felt the moral obligation to shelter natives from the depredations of frontier pioneers; during this "second wave" of colonization, economic concerns
dictated that natives cede ground to intensive agriculture and silviculture.
Native reserves resolved both of these issues; they provided refuge from white
landlords and sequestered space outside the high-potential development
zones. In essence, native commissioners manipulated the cadastre to hin-
der the exploitation of people and to facilitate the exploitation of land. Then,
agro-industrial development and accumulation ensued in the "white highlands." After independence, government and NGOs promoted smallholder
agriculture in the reserves. In the 1990s, however, Zimbabwean civil servants
and NGOs lost faith in smallholder agriculture. The black lowlands, they con-
cluded, should join the economy of the white highlands. Meanwhile, on
Mozambique's frontier, policymakers asked—virtually for the first time—
what sort of reserves to put where. The mapping projects described in chapter 5 tried to establish a model for them: areas designated for smallholder
agriculture—and its development—based on existing chiefdoms. That
model won few adherents.

Both Zimbabwe and Mozambique are opting for less restrictive, less protective reserves. For Zimbabwe, this decision represents the abandonment of an entitlement ideal. Commissioner L. C. Meredith established Ngorima and other reserves as guaranteed zones for black smallholders. By keeping white settlers out, the reserves, at least, maintained the minimum conditions for black families to reproduce themselves. As in Karl Polanyi's (1944:77–85) description of England's Speenhamland Law of 1795, the reserves supplemented the inadequate wages paid in labor markets. Of course, in doing so, the reserves helped to depress wages. Still, life would not have been better without the reserves. They constituted a safety net, an agrarian version of twentieth-century America's welfare policy, and a birthright for even the most vulnerable members of society—women, children, and the elderly—to farm.[1] Today's Zimbabwean reserves no longer serve these functions. Quietly, government has torn up the Rhodesian guarantee of smallholder land. As chapter 4 explained, the Chimanimani Rural District Council licensed Henry Oberlander to take farmland for tourist chalets in Vhimba. Under the banner of Campfire[2] and community-based resource management, further incursions have continued in Vhimba and throughout lowland Zimbabwe. Increasingly, rural district councils solicit outside investment. In the 1990s, they weighed the merits of smallholder agriculture against those of tourism and other businesses. If economic or ecological criteria so dictated, they were not averse to dislodging smallholders. Indeed, government and NGOs began to transform the lowland reserves into subsidized business zones.[3]

This chapter tells the story of Mozambique's rapid evolution toward "open" reserves, accomplished in an uneven symbiosis with Zimbabwe. From one perspective, it is a story of missed opportunity. Policymakers could have replicated and improved upon Meredith's work; for instance, enshrining a political right to one's land and freedom from displacement. Yet, that opportunity was not presented clearly in Mozambique. By the end of Mozambique's war, when civil servants were beginning to think again about rural policy, Meredith's legacy had become nearly unrecognizable in Zimbabwe. In its place, policymakers, NGO workers, and academics in that country elaborated a new rationale for the reserves that ironically suited Mozambique even better than it did Zimbabwe. According to this logic, smallholder agriculture never will serve as an engine for growth; only skilled outsiders with capital can possibly uplift the hinterlands. And venture capitalists rushed to Mozambique at the onset of peace. Firms, such as Continental Timbers (see chapter 5), vastly impressed remote administrators otherwise unable to fund any rural development. Thus, a combination of necessity and belief steered Mozambican policymakers toward settler-driven, investor-led development. The earliest ideals of colonization came back in fashion.

THE RHODESIAN ORDER OF RACE AND SPACE RECONSIDERED

The first treks pricked the liberal conscience and generated the question, "Where to put the natives?" Recall chapter 2: the British South Africa Company initially invited South African pioneers to colonize the Limpopo hinterland. So began the unbridled "age of the fortune hunters, 1890–96" (Palmer 1977). In Melsetter, Dunbar Moodie and his trekkers coupled white landholding with physical control over people—the cadastre with the whip. As Moodie's diary records for an unpleasant day in 1895: "Niggers troubling us. Not coming to work. Brickmaking at critical stage. Had to sjambok several."[4] Such "kaffir farming" epitomized the primordial geography of conquest: settlers and natives lived on the same parcels of land, the former as feudal lords and the latter as indentured serfs. Shortly, however, the Native Department arrived—and with it a limited defense of African interests and space. In 1896, Native Commissioner J. D. Hulley (Meredith's short-lived predecessor) proposed the creation of a native reserve (Palmer 1977:41). The next year, Meredith himself announced, "I pegged off a tract of country for a Native reserve and told the Natives that if they were not content to remain on private farms, they were at liberty to move to the Reserve. . . . I have done the best I could in the selection of this piece of land as there was no choice. The rest of the district was already pegged off."[5] During his tenure, Meredith demarcated the eastern low veld as Ngorima Reserve (as shown previously in map 2.2), along with five other native reserves.

Whites opposed him at nearly every turn. Missionaries objected to his attempts to deny them land in the Rusitu Valley. He cut the lease—granted behind his back by the civil commissioner—by 97 percent (see chapter 2). At the other end of the spectrum, settlers despised Meredith for giving blacks a route of escape from kaffir farming. "The English government pampers the blacks to such an extent as to make the country impossible for the whites," wrote a sympathetic German visitor. "Exeter Hall [the Colonial Office] is ruining Africa."[6] Thanks to Exeter Hall, African smallholders held slightly more than half of Melsetter District (Palmer 1977:262–63). Thus, Meredith's lasting dispensation of race and space enshrined white highlands, black lowlands, and the lines of partition between them. It locked up land, altering the course of colonization midstream. Whites could still extract resources, such as timber, but they could not farm in the reserves. The black refuge thenceforth constituted a forbidden zone to white settlement.[7]

As the colonial political economy evolved, the reserves took on additional, less protective roles. Outsiders and insiders exploited the reserves in multifarious ways, corrupting Meredith's mission almost beyond recognition. Politically, segregation placed rural and rural-based blacks outside civil law and civil liberties and within (colonially invented) "customary law." Chiefs and headmen had free reign to rule the reserves and impose what Mamdani (1996) calls "decentralized despotism" (cf. Ribot 1996, 1999). On the economic front, chief-administered "communal tenure" obstructed ambitious smallholders in obtaining either title deeds or investment credit. Upwardly mobile blacks could neither mortgage nor legally sell their fields in the reserves[8] (although some, such as officers of the Vhimba Area Development Committee, succeeded as capitalist farmers nonetheless). They *could* sell their labor and, perforce, did so cheaply. Because the Rhodesian equivalent of South Africa's "influx control" banned workers' families from the towns, women continued to farm the reserves. Reserves fed the young and old. In effect, women and the reserves reproduced the labor force, lessening the responsibilities of employers. Consequently, black men earned less, and white industrialists accumulated more than either party otherwise would have (Arrighi 1970). In all these ways, the reserve boundary cut off blacks from opportunities for advancement. They epitomized "uneven development": the uplift of rich regions at the expense of poor ones in Zimbabwe and elsewhere (P. Bond 1998; Smith 1984). Yet, even this bleak cloud held a silver lining: the same segregation that stymied black ambition underwrote black security. In 1952, as the timber estates were beginning to evict tenants, the native commissioner revalidated the boundary of the Ngorima Reserve. He refused the Rusitu Mission permission to expand onto 21.25 additional hectares (25 morgen) of "overcrowded" reserve land.[9] In 1962, he tried (unsuccessfully) to restrain the Department of National Parks and Wildlife Management from annexing the Haroni section of the Ngorima Reserve (see chapter 2). To the extent possible, local government's policies toward race and space sustained the black lowlands.

That policy reached a distinct limit. Beginning in the 1930s, governmental practices of conservation infringed upon the sanctuaries. Programs of "technical development" (Drinkwater 1991:40–72; Moore 1995:217–19) sought to prohibit farming on slopes and stream banks and strictly to regulate cropping and grazing throughout the reserves. Still, these laws did not undermine the exclusivity of the black lowlands; they certainly did not open those

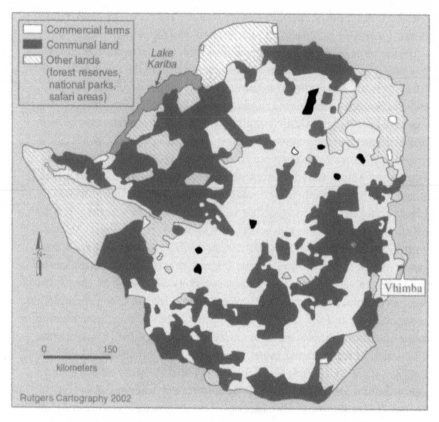

MAP 6.1. Zimbabwe's land distribution at Independence (1980)

zones to nonsmallholders. In the east, moreover, the Natural Resources Act
(1941) and Native Land Husbandry Act (1951) had less impact than elsewhere
in Rhodesia, for the slopes were so ubiquitous and the population so dense
that strict enforcement was infeasible (see chapter 2). A later generation of
conservationists compromised rather less. Backed by the harsh Rhodesian
Front regime, the Parks Department cut the Haroni Valley from the Ngorima
Reserve in 1965. In 1973, the same department established the Haroni and
Rusitu botanical reserves. Thus, otherwise well-meaning ornithologists and
herpetologists accomplished for the sake of birds and lizards what white settlers had not been able to achieve for themselves: in practice, they violated
the ideal of secure territorial entitlements for black farmers. Shortly thereafter, the Rhodesian Front regime fell. The policy and the practice of native
reserves survived—the original, protective intent overlaid with decades of

exploitation. In 1980, the hectares spoke for themselves: native reserves occupied 42.1 percent of Zimbabwe (map 6.1). Together with commercial estates and protected areas, they constituted an order of race, space, and nature.

CAMPFIRE THOUGHT

From its inception, Campfire contested the conventional spatial order. An academically savvy "Campfire intelligentsia" raised ecological, economic, and, in particular, social challenges. To begin with the ecological, reforms leading up to Campfire introduced the concept of bioregionalism. Having started in the United States in the 1960s, the bioregional movement questioned administrative and national borders (Aberly 1999; Berg and Dasmann 1977). Surely, proponents argued, those who wished to preserve nature had to think and act with *ecological* units of analysis—watersheds, valleys, mountain ranges, and so on. Developments in the East African savannah supported this reframing. During the mid-1970s drought, elephants inside Kenya's Tsavo National Park ate the woodland and then starved in enormous numbers.[10] This carnage—the effect of "insularization"[11]—incriminated the entire system of discrete protected areas. Nature now had to exceed its colonially mandated enclaves. Before independence, Rhodesia's Parks Department director, Graham Child, convinced white landowners to "allow space for wildlife on their land, thus providing corridors between the protected areas."[12] Elephants should reconstitute their archaic Zambezi Valley migration. Meanwhile, managers adopted what one principal described as a "landscape strategy":[13] bioregions spanning the escarpment between highlands and lowlands. Ultimately, roaming animals accomplished what trekking colonists had failed to do. They overcame the colonial partition of white, black, and natural zones.

Economic thinking also helped weaken those walls. Unwittingly, Campfire's advocates borrowed the principles and vocabulary of nineteenth-century frontier boosterism. Proponents of investment in the western United States had expounded that the right configuration of natural resources *inevitably* generated wealth. As the story went, soil, climate, and navigable rivers would make (and did make) Chicago and the Great West.[14] Perhaps Zimbabwe's fauna, sunshine, and (to stretch the parallel) air routes and roads could produce a similar success story. This was the thought of wildlife managers in the 1980s and 1990s. Indeed, tourism exploited the "big-five" species, and visitors doled out dollars to photograph and/or kill them. How could it be otherwise? Wildlife, Graham Child later wrote, possessed an "*inherent* financial comparative advantage" (G. Child 1996:358; emphasis added). Development and entrepreneurial possibility seemed to emanate from the very landscape, unmediated by culture. Hayfield B estate, boasted its owner, contained a fail-safe location for a new age spiritual retreat: "spot on" latitude 20 degrees south, longitude 33 degrees east.[15] Deeply flawed, such boosterism assumed the unalterable attractiveness of the region and an unending flow of travelers.[16] When every form of tourism except hunting collapsed in 2000, Campfire proponents would have reason to reconsider their assumptions. Until then, boosterism and bioregionalism freed the Campfire intelligentsia to concentrate on what really troubled it: rural black society.

In the 1980s, various public and private agencies converged on a social analysis: too many people lived in Zimbabwe's reserves. In future, they felt, fewer should reside there, or, at least, the rate of increase should go down. The resettlement program transferred more than seventy thousand families from the communal lands to parcels abandoned or sold by whites (Kinsey 1999:173). With less success, industry created urban jobs, complete with family accommodation. Programs aimed at population growth helped to lower the birthrate, while conservationists consistently bemoaned the "population problem" in Zimbabwe's lowveld. As a result, the reserves, once a place to go *to*, officially became a place to go *from* in search of opportunity elsewhere. At the very least, this unlikely consensus among proponents of industry, conservation, and resettlement stipulated that the reserves' population and the opening of agricultural land should be stabilized (a set of desires at least as old as the Native Land Husbandry Act of 1951). Yet, rural people did the opposite. In the most significant postindependence migration, smallholders moved from the southeast to the northwest lowveld. They filled up communal lands of the cotton frontier in Gokwe, Binga, and Nyaminyami districts.[17] As other government agencies eradicated the tsetse fly, migrants and their cattle advanced toward the Zambezi. Meanwhile, the official resettlement program stalled in 1985, and industry hit its own ceiling around 1990. Contrary to most official hopes, people discovered opportunity in the reserves.

Campfire blossomed in this atmosphere of demographic disappointment. The program identified the reserves as zones of wild abundance and human threat, a longstanding conservationist view (Schroeder 1999b:361–62). As opposed to old-style "fortress conservation," however, the designers of Campfire imagined that local people themselves could reduce the excess population. In support of this belief, conservationists elaborated a historical narrative of the reserves that sanctified local natives and demonized in-migrants (without, however, including that narrative as an explicit component of policy). As Simon Metcalfe, a social scientist and early Campfire organizer, explained, "The traditional roots of communal life are still strong, providing a web of affection and social and material security." Yet, he continued, two problems impinged from outside. First, "the modern state apparatus . . . imposed [itself] on communal Africa" (Metcalfe 1994:185). Campfire found a legal solution to that externality: in thirty-six districts, it transferred control of game from the central government to local people or their representatives in district government. As for the second problem, new settlers— stigmatized as "immigrants"—were overrunning wildlife habitats of the Zambezi Valley.[18] Metcalf (1994:184) warned, "Unless modern and traditional authorities pull together locally, membership of Campfire producer communities will be threatened by a lack of exclusivity, spontaneous unplanned settlement and fragmentation of wildlife habitat. The ability to exclude settlers, if necessary, may be a prerequisite for ultimate success." In other words, headmen, chiefs, and the whole "web of affection" were embracing outsiders too readily. Could technical support reform these institutions, making them less hospitable?

Metcalfe and others certainly thought so, but their reasoning misconstrued the raison d'être for "traditional authorities" and for the reserves as a whole. In Zimbabwe, in-migration constitutes the founding principle of reserves and their leadership. As explained above, the Native Department created reserves as zones of arrival. Headmen rose to power precisely when and because people did arrive in the reserves (in the 1950s in Ngorima).[19] Newcomers petitioned them for access to farmland and, from that moment on, owed their tenure to higher authorities. Each migrant added to the power of headmen—certainly not a "traditional" power.[20] Often longstanding residents resented and still resent the swaggering attitude of migrants and their ability to grab the lion's share of resources (Alexander, McGregor, and Ranger 2000; Dzingirai 1994, 1996). However, migrants contributed to the critical mass of people necessary to obtain a clinic, school, bus route, member of parliament, and other amenities that benefit everyone. As Eric Worby (1998b:567) writes, migrants turned Gokwe from a wildlife-infested backwater into "the pre-eminent cash-crop zone of Zimbabwe's widely-heralded small-holder revolution." To many rural and development-oriented Zimbabweans, migrants mean modernity.

Campfire agencies spent the late 1980s and the 1990s trying to convert rural Zimbabweans to an opposing economic belief. Proponents sought to demonstrate that the "extensification of agriculture" was misguided and self-defeating. Specialists embarked on a process of "identifying options for people, generating information, letting them make . . . choices."[21] That research focused on the finance of reserves—the commodities and markets linked to them. Could the reserves generate more income from the conservation of wildlife than from cattle grazing and other activities that jeopardized wildlife? "Yes," said the economists, and tourism was the answer. Some of the wealthiest North Americans and Europeans would pay US$800 per day to stalk big game and thousands more for the necessary trophy fees. The World Wide Fund for Nature (WWF) calculated that sport hunting would almost certainly generate higher profits than extensive stock raising. If smallholders could only capture the revenues from wildlife, they would gladly and immediately return cultivated areas to wildlife habitat.[22] Surely, they would also prohibit in-migration, both to preserve their own share of the loot and to further protect the habitat. In other words, "rational peasants" would voluntarily relinquish their entitlement to farm and graze the reserves. Utilitarianism would save the day, or, as boosters told me in 1994, "Cash is the best extension agent."[23]

Embodied in "Campfire principles," the theory made eminent sense—except for two seemingly small oversights. First, the economic calculations omitted cotton. As Ivan Bond, an author of the original study, later explained to me, the crop did not lend itself to comparison because of its long-term effects. Cotton might outearn wildlife initially. "If you were modeling over twenty years, [however,] you might get very different answers as crop pests build up and soil fertility declines."[24] Bond was probably correct. Yet, this temporal caveat complicated his and Campfire's utilitarian logic considerably: the idealized peasants should not simply maximize profits but maximize them over the long term *at the expense of short-term utility*. Perhaps, many households would, but one should hardly have expected peasants with less than a twenty-year financial cushion to do so. Indeed, in 1993, Campfire-sponsored research found that Mahenye residents were simply maximizing both options: they collected sport-hunting revenues one day and poached the next.[25] Ultimately, no one could properly generalize or falsify Bond's hypothesis, for Campfire's second oversight invalidated all of its economic predictions. The utilitarian theory had treated local government as an externality, as exempt from (peasants') self-interested thinking. According to the principles, altruistic rural district councils would contract with ecotourism firms, receive tourism revenues, and transfer the bulk of these to local "producer communities." In the event, many councils acted exactly like "rational peasants" and captured the revenue. The more democratically minded local governments distributed those resources to voters throughout their districts (cf. Duffy 2000:109–10). Other councils handled their accounts in a less exemplary—and sometimes quite corrupt—fashion.[26] Nonetheless, a handful of successes buoyed spirits. The program moved forward.

Even in the two Campfire cases widely heralded as successful, however, the economic outcome was ambiguous. Rural people *did* get cash. That money inoculated those projects and much of Campfire from criticism. In the longer term—over the interval that, in a different context, concerned Bond—the program did structural damage to rural security and land tenure. Campfire and its principles rezoned the two reserves. In Masoka, which lay across the Zambezi Valley elephant habitat, residents delineated an enclosure for agriculture. wwf donated an electric fence to protect people and crops from elephants (and vice versa).[27] Leaders of Chikwarakwara, Beitbridge District, drew up a similar plan for villagization and for "retain[ing] remote and wild land which is valuable for tourism and wildlife" (B. Child 1993:290; cf. B. Child and Peterson 1991). Both the relevant district councils returned revenues directly to local people. Proponents inflated these two cases into a general model. A widely circulated diagram from wwf (1997:7) suggested that animal-rich reserves be remapped into two zones: "community wildlife management areas" and much smaller, agricultural "settlement areas" (figure 6.1). Conservationists and the tourism industry, thereby, would enclose the bulk of the reserve. They would convert potential farmland—not necessarily less fertile than existing farmland—into a buffer zone for the adjoining protected area. This "*exclosure* of resident human populations" would prejudice nonresidents to an even greater degree (Schroeder 1999b:365; cf. Murombedzi 2001:254). Rump reserves would surely lack residual space to support in-migrants. Unborn children—wwf seemed to assume—would need to limit their numbers so as not to overcrowd the settlement areas. In short, wwf deftly overturned the inclusionary logic of the reserves—with the full support of Campfire agencies.

On the ground, this type of partition generated irate peasant protest and muted dissent from the Campfire intelligentsia. In 1989, Nyamandhlovu District Council called upon Campfire scholars to help it launch sport hunting. The council and the Parks Department had already zoned a wildlife-rich "buffer zone" within communal land adjacent to Hwange National Park. The affected residents, council hoped, would retreat "voluntarily" from the outer edge of the reserve to a more secure and well-served location. One Campfire fieldworker recalled council officers coaxing, "We want to bring you back into the lines [of Land Husbandry] so it is easier for Council to do what Council is supposed to do." Certainly, the provision of schools,

FIG. 6.1. Campfire's new dispensation of race, space, and nature.
Reproduced with permission from World-Wide Fund for Nature (1997:7)

clinics, and water points was attractive; "it made sense," recalled the social scientist.[28] Another social anthropologist noticed a contradiction: "If wildlife production is to be, as is postulated, a real money-spinner, they [local residents] should benefit from their location. Why move them?"[29] For a more visceral view, authors deferred to local voices: "You have moved us to let your wildlife in," declared one virtual evictee in an unpublished document.[30]

Meanwhile, Campfire-related rezoning provoked an even more blatant conflict elsewhere in western Zimbabwe, in Binga District. Violating an agreement on fencing, Broom Safaris unilaterally encircled a zone for farming much smaller than that stipulated. The fence cut smallholders off from usable lands. When, in 1994, another researcher and I encountered the safari operator in precisely this area, he defended it as "my best hunting ground."[31] Again, a Campfire scholar intervened in print, quoting the lament of a Binga elder: "Campfire is now ransoming everything that we have. First it was the animals. . . . Now it is the land" (Dzingirai 1995:7). In the face of an escalating row, District Administrator Dumisani Ncube clarified the situation to the press: "The Campfire project . . . is, in fact, a people's project. What is being done at the moment is to demarcate the concession area from other parts of the communal land so that safari operators can do their work without any disturbances. People should not panic."[32] This valiant defense of partition calmed no one. Five years later, as discontent still simmered, the Campfire manager for Binga sowed panic himself. Calling migrants "foreigners in inverted commas," he startled a conference with his own update on the conflict: "This issue of migrants is now a needle in the Manager's tongue. It is high time [a] council resolution should be implemented to get the environmental disturbance rubbed off once and for all. . . . This illegal occupation of our promised land will seek an intervention by high ranked politicians."[33] Thus, smallholders, who once enjoyed a guaranteed sanctuary, now squatted precariously on someone else's business district. The logic of Campfire culminated in eviction.

Why did dissenters within Campfire agencies not object more forcefully? Circumstances outside and within this collaborative group imposed considerable pressure to conform. Internationally, the Campfire program faced harsh opposition for reasons having nothing to do with the eviction of smallholders. Throughout the 1990s, animal welfarists and the Humane Society (1997) lobbied the U.S. government ferociously to cut off aid. Meanwhile, the government of Zimbabwe was battling for an exception to the ban on ivory exports under the Convention on International Trade in Endangered Species.[34] Partisans cited Campfire continually as evidence of Zimbabwe's sustainable, locally beneficial management of elephants.[35] Thus, the struggle against animal protectionism—and for sustainable use—overwhelmed other concerns. Although James Murombedzi (1992) sounded an alarm on district councils' "recentralization" of Campfire revenues, most other researchers were loath to attack the program in its hour of greatest need.

Institutional changes within the Campfire agencies also suppressed criticism. In 1988, WWF, the Centre for Applied Social Sciences, Zimbabwe Trust, and the Department of National Parks and Wildlife had formed the Campfire Collaborative Group (Gibson 1999:112). As Campfire expanded, this consortium managed funds, co-opted other agencies, and vetted proposals from rural district councils. Rural district councils themselves soon formed their own body known as the Campfire Association. Often erroneously classified as an NGO, this organ gained control of the enormous American aid pipeline. By early 1999, the collaborative group was dead. A natural resource management conference actually stalled on the question of whether "Campfire" meant anything more than the association.[36] All other parties, especially the intelligentsia, lost clout. When fieldworkers defended residents' interests, safari operators dismissed them, saying—as one NGO manager recalled—"You can tell Zimbabwe Trust to go to hell. According to the law there is nothing they can do."[37] To stay relevant, some NGOs subsumed themselves to rural district councils. One agency director admitted regretfully: "The idea is that government can't do their job; so we do it for them on a contractual basis. . . . Effectively, we are part of the system. We are not change agents anymore."[38] At the University of Zimbabwe, the Centre for Applied Social Sciences took almost the same course. In short, conditions discouraged academic freedom. If whistle-blowers were few, it was surprising there were any.

PIONEERS IN IMPROBABLE PLACES

The most astonishing aspect of Campfire's entrenchment in the mid-1990s was its geographical expansion. In spreading to eastern Zimbabwe, the Campfire Association released itself from the economic foundation so painstakingly constructed by the intelligentsia.[39] Compared with the arid, game-rich west, eastern Zimbabwe benefited far less from tourism and far more from agriculture. The region contained the most fertile land with the highest annual rainfall in the country. For decades, estates had grown tea, coffee, and various fruits. In Ngorima Reserve, a government survey recommended as early as 1962 that, "[i]n the national interest, the bulk of this land should be put down to high value special crops . . . the problem is how to achieve this desirable state of affairs when the bulk of the people are either incapable or unwilling to grow these high value crops."[40] With the right incentives, smallholders eventually changed their minds, and the banana boom took off (cf. Manzou 2000:10–12). In 1994, Vhimba's two fruit marketing groups grossed US$4,388. Each group member earned, on average, US$61, while the top five producers brought in a mean of US$296 each (table 6.1).[41] One household, that of Wilbert and Ester Yaibva, grossed US$307 annually per hectare (table 6.2).[42] (The banana tycoon discussed in chapter 4 operated at too large a scale to sell through the group, and his own, boastful figures could not be trusted.) The accumulation, even if lopsided, was unmistakable. Indeed, so profitable was banana cultivation that the rural district council itself alienated twenty hectares in Vhimba in 1994 for a parastatal farm (see chapter 4). Planners of that scheme hoped to increase production to reach US$4,851 in profits plus local wages per hectare per year (table 6.2).[43] Combined with smallholder fields, the plantation left little room for tourism, even for chalets or campsites. Of course, any such facility, if it truly represented development, would have to top the US$4,851 per hectare mark. Council's wildly optimistic numbers boxed boosters of tourism into a corner.

How could the hospitality industry, especially when limited to bird-watching and hiking, beat the banana? Boosters trusted in a future "eastern circuit" and in travelers' desire to foray into little-known communal lands (Africa Resources Trust n.d.). Would they venture in large enough numbers to Vhimba, in the deep recesses of Ngorima Communal Land, where rains regularly interrupted vehicle traffic? The quixotic proposal for a "Vhimba Eco-Tourism Project" predicted total local benefits of only US$1,924 per annum. According to the proposal, the project committee would then divide this grand sum between a revolving fund and dividends to beneficiaries.[44] At the maximum level conceivable, each of the more than two hundred households would take home at most US$10. Such a pittance could hardly justify any household's opportunity cost of giving up a banana field. Delicately, another study admitted that "the estimated annual income . . . [will] have possible negative repercussions to the [local] people's continued interest to participate in the project" (Matikinyidze 1995:12). Truly, bird-watching amounted to petty cash as against Vhimba's golden fruit! Among Campfire agencies, however, interest remained strong. Tourism, profitable or not, might help protect forests and rezone the reserves for future investment of unknown proportions.

Boosters of ecotourism began by demonizing black/poor newcomers to

TABLE 6.1. Vhimba Smallholders' Revenue from Bananas (in US$)

	1994	1995	1996
Mean of top five producers	296	312	267
Mean of all marketing members	61	54	60

TABLE 6.2. Profitability of Land Uses (in US$)

	Chimanimani Rural District Council's estimates of profit plus local wages per hectare, per year	Actual profit plus local wages per hectare for the year immediately following the estimate
Banana production	4,851	307
Ecotourism	1,471	0
Opportunity cost of ecotourism per hectare	3,380	307

Vhimba and sanctifying white/rich ones. At least some of the blacks migrating to Vhimba had jumped the Mozambican border—sometimes in both directions (see chapter 3). In the early 1990s, the Parks Department sounded its usual alarm with more than the usual doublespeak: "[T]he main cultural and political difficulty is the problem of illegal immigrants . . . [who may] have family in both Mozambique and Zimbabwe [and] hold both Mozambiquan [sic] and Zimbabwean papers" (Kawadza and Rogers 1993:4). The Parks Department blamed these itinerant dual citizens and refugees from Mozambique's war for partially clearing the Haroni and Rusitu botanical reserves in order to plant bananas and other crops. It sought assistance from another outside group with interests in Vhimba: plantation owners and other whites on the highlands. Gathered together under the banner of the Chiping Branch of the Wildlife Society of Zimbabwe, these conservationists provided transportation for armed Parks Department patrols. Then, as chapter 4 related, the Parks Department decided to defer to Campfire-style initiatives and outside investment. In 1996, the only true immigrant involved—a one-time British Hong Konger and stock trader—approached the rural district council. Henry Oberlander envisioned a string of backpacker lodges and adventure outposts anchored at Vhimba and supporting local communities.[45] Council joined in the effort. It hired a British tourism officer, and she advised that Vhimba should "work with an experienced partner" to develop its "tourism product."[46] A white expatriate, thus, obtained a privilege local government had long denied to local whites and even to Mozambican dual nationals: an official invitation to do business in the native reserve.

Once inside the reserve, Oberlander moved from grabbing land to celebrating local culture. As chapter 4 also related, council granted the entrepreneur access to a fictive "business centre." Thereupon, heated debate ensued as to the boundaries of this investment zone (and the parties called upon me to mediate and translate). A smallholder was cultivating along its eastern edge, and his friends and patrons rose to his defense. Trying to make the best of a bad situation, council and NGOs (and myself) urged Oberlander to form a joint venture with a local committee in Vhimba and to operate according to Campfire principles. This marriage between external capital and local entrepreneurship seemed to be made in heaven. It would give Vhimba people money and give Oberlander political legitimacy. A joint venture would also lay the groundwork for the "culture based activities (crafts, music, dance, etc.)" that the tourism officer recommended.[47] Collin Walker, Oberlander's partner and a white Zimbabwean, assessed the potential for cultural tourism in blunter terms: Vhimba, he later reminisced, has "got black people smiling. They wave. It's not like Harlem."[48] Yet, many people in Vhimba and especially the aggrieved farmer continued to frown. Under intense pressure from headmen and the district administrator, council withdrew its invitation to Oberlander in 1997.

Nonetheless, council and allied agencies persevered in rezoning the Ngorima Reserve. For the next three years, it vetted proposals for investment and/or partnership with the diffident people of Vhimba. Council turned first to the Chipinge Branch of the Wildlife Society. Despite their earlier parapolice involvement, members of the branch desired to collaborate with Vhimba residents for tourism and conservation. Terry Eagle, a birder already running the nature-oriented Kiledo Lodge, had thought for years of expanding operations and providing employment in Vhimba. If blacks could only "improve their lot" off-farm, he fervently believed, then they would spare wildlife and forests from the ravages of the plow.[49] He made scant progress and soon ceded the field to others in the Wildlife

Society. In 1999, one of its branch officers met with a consultant to the Campfire Association to discuss the branch's construction of five chalets in Vhimba. Again, nothing came of the idea.[50] In the same year, Rainbow Tourism Group, owner of the nearby Chimanimani Hotel, developed the most ambitious plan. On a detailed map, the company plotted a wide footprint of nine structures, quite similar to Eagle's Kiledo Lodge. In a breathtaking solution to the perennial transport problem, the company also sited a helicopter landing pad. The complex would occupy 36.9 hectares of arable land[51]—at a staggering annual opportunity cost of US$179,002 (based on council's figure for per-hectare banana revenues in its parastatal farm). Then, the Rainbow Tourism Group sold the Chimanimani Hotel and turned its attention away from eastern Zimbabwe. Still, as of mid-2000, the manager of the hotel clung to his Vhimba dream. A black businessman, he spoke more openly about eviction than any other would-be investor in Vhimba: "Talk to him [the local farmer], give something [or] else compensate [him]. Then you can take over there. If he says 'no that is not good enough,' just go ahead and take over."

Such investor confidence rested on nearly blind adherence to the notion of settler-led development. Regarding tourism, the council's Campfire officer explained, Vhimba people "can't just bump into it without the necessary expertise."[52] Thus, local government discouraged Vhimba's committee from building its own campsite while seeking an investor to train the community in "basic tourism management and operations."[53] This form of partnership could possibly generate valuable spin-off effects. Tourists, the boosters claim, would demand a more comfortable road. A new road would stimulate an even bigger banana boom (although the subsequent scheme of flying tourists by helicopter would have made this plan moot). Yet, the numbers did not add up. Through the Campfire Association, the council contracted an economist, and he estimated an appalling loss of US$290,754 over five years.[54] The economist anticipated that international donors would cover such start-up costs of tourism. Even when eventually self-sustaining, however, the chalets would earn only US$54,279 per year, or US$1,471 per hectare.[55] Based on council's own figures, Vhimba smallholders would lose roughly US$3,380 of potential income for every hectare rezoned from farmland to tourism (table 6.2). Shortly after this report, political violence demolished the tourist trade throughout the country.[56] When I visited Chimanimani in July 2000, I stayed at the only hotel (of four) in the district center not closed, and there I was virtually the only guest not attending a workshop. Close to year-end, the Kiledo Lodge was running at

15 percent occupancy, and only 40 percent of these guests were nature lovers. From ecotourism, the lodge's rate of profit (really negative profit, or losses) plus local wages lay at or below zero (table 6.2)![57]

Against these odds, the dream of a Vhimba hotel lived on. How could NGOS, donors, and the investors themselves continue to hope? Campfire's ideology blinded them to the negative economic indicators—including the slump in nonhunting tourism nationwide—and even eclipsed the positive ones. From east to west, utopianism was breaking out. In common with the liberal "born free" (after 1980) generation, idealists inside and outside government were groping toward a new dispensation of race and space. They would shrink exclusionary zones or abolish them altogether. In smaller, WWF-style reserves (figure 6.1), people would live more compactly and perhaps even vertically: "OK," explained a leading Campfire professional, "let us expand upwards, and, if we can, have some five-story buildings, rather than expanding that way [arms outstretched]."[58] His one-story office had not yet run the numbers on this vision. In mid-2000, the council's new tourism officer, a young, black Zimbabwean, articulated an even grander future, completely without reserves: "Why should there be segregation? Whites, blacks . . . we are all out to help each other, to build a better nation. So why should we be segregating?"[59]

Desegregation, however, was and is risky. Long stuck in the rear seats (the reserves), by 2000 some smallholders risked losing their place on the bus (or train or restaurant) entirely. The United States provides a cautionary tale. There, gentrification along what Neil Smith (1996) calls a "new urban frontier" is whitening New York's Harlem and other historically black ghettos. Residents must now petition just to retain the meager spatial concessions of a once-segregationist society. The Campfire program put Zimbabwean smallholders in a similar predicament. It undermined their Rhodesian entitlement to farmland. Although paltry, an income stream from tourism might have helped sweeten that bitter pill, but only if rural people were entitled to that income in perpetuity (and in hard currency!). Even in the animal-rich west, Campfire projects never warranted such confidence. As events showed, moreover, no one in Southern Africa should bank on the tourist dollar. Thus, Campfire's benefits evaporated, leaving a hazardous residue. As in other development schemes, the intended, planned effects gave way to undesirable, only half-anticipated "side effects" (Ferguson 1990). The partial alienation of Vhimba was one of these. No land changed hands, but policy unlocked a door once firmly shut against those who would take land. As a principle, Chimanimani's black lowlands disappeared.

MOZAMBIQUE DISCOVERS "COMMUNITY"

Ten years ago, the principle of black lowlands did not exist in Mozambique. In the short space of a decade, Mozambican planners first discovered and then discarded the ideal of territorial entitlements for smallholders. Why this delayed onset? In Mozambique, neither the colonial nor the postcolonial state had been forced to confront the "native question" nearly as directly as had Rhodesia since its earliest days. Much of the country was a white highlands *manqué*. Administrators, such as Luciano Laure at the start of the twentieth century, tried to promote European colonization and would have gladly tackled the spatial issue of reserves. Yet, as explained in chapter 1, settlers did not come, and politics did not turn cadastral in Mossurize. To the north, in Sussundenga and Manica districts, Portuguese did colonize, and, beginning in 1947, used Mossurize as a "closed labor reserve." This denotation, however, did not affect landholding—black or white—but only the flow of *braços* to European farms elsewhere. Even within the *colonatos* and various white settlements, pioneers rarely passed the land to any "second wave" of intensive agriculture and silviculture. Some pine and eucalyptus plantations hugged the Beira-Mutare road, as did irrigated agriculture to the Limpopo River. At a remove from these corridors, colonial development failed. So, too, did conservation. Portugal demarcated only the flimsiest "paper parks." Thus, Portugal neither converted nor preserved African nature. (It did not even map most of it in detail until after 1965.) Natives held the land, and reserves were patently irrelevant. In short, Portugal did not and could not partition space according to race. Race was not a geographical issue.

Independence did not change this state of affairs—until, in the late 1980s, the state's ideological shifts recast society in spatial terms. The original Mozambican socialists—inspired by Eduardo Mondlane and Samora Machel—had seen rural people as a "peasantry," a single unit of analysis. "Unity," wrote Frelimo's Department of Ideological Work (1982 [1978]:2), "started to come into being because everyone suffered the same way under the same [colonial] oppression." Such universalism discounted local particulars, such as ethnicity, language, and loyalty to chiefs. Machel's policy of villagization strove for a national standard in rural settlement and production. The 1983 Party Congress heralded "the correct development of the Mozambican personality."[60] Idealism soon withered in the face of Mozambique's blatant, bloody disunity. Assuming the presidency at the height of war, Joaquim Chissano abandoned both socialism and the quest for homogeneity. He celebrated Mozambicans' individual dynamism and entrepreneurship first and their common bonds second. On the frontier, that shift in perspective was crucial. To use Scott's terms (1998), the state was preparing to replace the lenses with which it "saw" rural people, the measures by which it counted and categorized them and made their lives "legible" to the state. *Community* was to supplant *peasantry* as a new, much smaller, much more geographical unit of analysis for observing and intervening in rural society. "Community" would also raise the possibility of community-based native reserves.

War assisted in this process of reformulation by establishing a break with past knowledge. In the course of fifteen years, the rural areas became terra incognita to the government. Renamo targeted civil servants, roads were mined, and maps were nearly unobtainable. (Security procedures virtually classified the hard-won 1:50,000–scale maps.) Up to 1994, desk studies relied upon 1980 population figures—at the district level![61] The more daring researchers traveled with aid planes to remote airstrips, rarely spending the night (cf. Finnegan 1992:4–5; Middleton 1994:109–16). Conducting fieldwork under these hazardous, peripatetic conditions, the anthropologist Carolyn Nordstrom simply ruled geography out of her analysis. She concentrated on the "war-scape"—rather than landscape—"a theme and a process . . . not a place" (Nordstrom 1997:41). In part, Nordstrom described Mozambique accurately: millions of rural people were *dis*placed and in motion (of course, more millions were not). Undeniably, she captured the sensibility of professionals, journalists, and aid workers trying to learn what was happening outside the cities: finding out who was where did not seem feasible or even important.

The 1992 cease-fire reopened the investigation of Mozambique's human geography—an uneven process to be sure. Newly mobile, provincial officers and expatriates constantly traded stories of impassible highways, car wrecks, and ambushes, while reports obsessed about roads—muddy, mined, and otherwise encumbered.[62] Some expatriates with experience elsewhere in Southern Africa implied that Mozambique was scarcely penetrable. Border areas—in one telling, if infrequently used, English phrase—lay "inland" from the more navigable sea of neighboring countries. Maps could drive one to distraction. Just acquiring them—and overcoming lingering wartime suspicions— required persistence and personal connections. "Geographers," the geographer Nick Middleton observes only half in jest, "were clearly an odd breed and to be treated with caution" (1994:202). Jumpy officials in Mossurize suspended the mapping project (chapter 5) for using a camera and a global positioning system without authorization.[63] Back in Maputo's ministries, civil servants craved geographical knowledge, and they braced themselves for a steep learning curve. As late as a 1997 national meeting on forestry and wildlife, earnest but rudimentary questions followed my presentation of Gogoi maps: "You mean, there in Manica, they do not live in villages?" asked an officer from the newly created Ministry of Environmental Coordination.[64] Amid booming interest in things rural, Mozambique's capital and southernmost city felt positively parochial (in a way Harare, centrally located and staffed with rural-to-urban migrants, never did). Government officers, donors, and NGO workers pasted national maps to their walls, peered across the Limpopo, and strained to discern what was "upcountry."[65]

Manica Province presented the greatest challenge and the greatest potential for learning. As the birthplace of Renamo, Manica and its Ndau language were synonymous with insurgency. With "tradition" as well: chiefs and headmen had resisted and/or evaded party secretaries and the entire village policy (Alexander 1994:43–58). How could the government administer such chiefdoms and former rebel zones and create something of value for them? More broadly, asked the Ministry of State Administration, how could Frelimo learn to "respect and valorize pluralism" and multipartyism?[66] In late 1992, the ministry dispatched Iraê Baptista Lundin to Manica to address these questions. Her informants showered her with criticisms of Frelimo and of communal villages. They complained, as had my informants in Gogoi, of having been forcibly relocated. According to Lundin, they even objected to Frelimo's invented "toponyms," the new place-names often associated with revolutionary heroes and events. Such alterations were indeed unpopular. To Lundin, fondness for the old toponyms indicated more: an unalterable attachment to the landscape. She inferred, "Even for those who remained at home, the systematic change of names . . . augmented the alienation of the individual who (only) recognizes himself as a man, and thus identifies himself, as a social being in his territory."[67] Lundin effectively revised and territorialized the socialist idea of a "Mozambican personality." Published with similar studies of other provinces, her research suggested some form of state decentralization. More basically, it made human geography a leading field of enquiry. Previously, Portuguese administrators had employed the census mainly to obtain their labor supply (see chapter 1). Now, planning required much greater accuracy and comprehensiveness: what an official of the survey department later described as a "correct spatial localization of 'who occupies what and where.'"[68]

Such knowledge demanded new geographical concepts and methods and outside assistance. Mozambican civil servants reached out to the Campfire intelligentsia—to which I was then affiliating myself—and we rushed to advise and train.[69] In 1994, Marshall Murphree, Joseph Matowanyika, and Ken Wilson[70] organized a weeklong "workshop on indigenous knowledge on natural resource management." Viewed by participants as a turning point, the meeting drew people to the Garuzo Motel outside Chimoio (Manica's provincial capital), where they laid the groundwork for Mozambique's reorganization into "communities." Lectures on "participatory resource-use mapping" and related topics augmented field trips into the bush, where desk officers struggled to apply ethnographic methods. Learning was slow. Upon alighting from her four-by-four, one forester asked the assembled rural folk point-blank in Portuguese, "What do you hunt?"[71] Clearly, the Campfire intelligentsia had to stay involved (despite some local, nationalist resentment). Later that year, Zimbabwean social foresters helped Mozambican counterparts to map chiefdoms in Sussundenga District (see chapter 5). With less success, participants in the Garuzo workshop investigated nearby territories, finding that "these boundaries need clarification and registration."[72] According to the Garuzo imperative, social groups required space, and space required social groups.[73]

This embrace of "community" reshaped the discourse of rural administration much more clearly than it did the practice. On an intellectual level, the civil service had disaggregated the vastness of Mozambique's peasantry into manageable, legible chunks. In "traditional" Manica, those chunks mostly centered on chiefs—a return to the *ideal* of colonial indirect rule (Alexander 1997:5, 18; Virtanen 1999:2–3). Yet, Garuzo produced little political change on the ground. Despite the concerns expressed,[74] Mozambique's programs in community-based resource management did not extend state power into the countryside. Instead, private business often distracted Mozambican civil servants from their jobs. An unknown number of corrupt civil servants enlisted their offices for private gain, rendering the work of whole departments *purely* intellectual (Hanlon 1996). Even among honest civil servants, ambiguity and indeterminacy were the order of the day. For instance, in an effort to safeguard Manica's Moribane Forest Reserve, three Mozambican civil servants conducted doctoral fieldwork intermittently and in Portuguese. As of 1999, the project's objective remained to achieve "a zoning that we [the fieldworkers and the community] would agree upon."[75] On the ground, however, agreement seemed distant indeed. Only some months previously, local residents had held the single Shona-speaking fieldworker at knifepoint, later releasing her.[76] Unrest derailed this "project" and delayed the dissertations as well. "It was remarkable," marveled Wilson (1997:10), "just what capacity

Mozambique retained to absorb and overwhelm [mega-programs], tending to become only differently chaotic rather than less chaotic in consequence."

Rather than take a decisive direction, community-based conservation resulted in a political nonevent: it helped frustrate the possibility of wide-scale rural mobilization.[77] Government planners, Lundin, and donors spoke of popular empowerment and bureaucratic devolution. Meanwhile, the Campfire intelligentsia defined communities in geographically narrow terms in relation to common property and within Elinor Ostrom's influential framework. Ostrom suggested that local political life focused on administering shared, depletable resources, such as wildlife and forests. Institutions for managing common property would work best within "clearly defined boundaries"—a principle readily adopted by Garuzo participants (Ostrom 1990:91; Anstey and de Sousa 2001:196). From this view flowed the rationale for government decentralization: communities should run their wildlife and forests, within their boundaries, in as sovereign a manner as possible (Murphree 1991). They should run what the National Directorate of Forestry and Wildlife called "pilot areas with the participation of the community in the conservation and use of forest and wildlife resources."[78] That was all rural people should influence. Once balkanized by their uncompromisingly geographical identity, village republics lost any purchase they might have had on adjoining or overarching concerns. Peasant movements and wide-scale mobilization were not even imagined at Garuzo. In evening caucuses, the donors built consensus for investor-led growth in three vast, international bioregions. By day, they allowed rural people to paint in the local details of "transfrontier conservation." By night, planners still framed the canvas.

THE INVESTORS ARE HERE!

Mozambican planners rediscovered rural people and foreign investors at virtually the same time—a happy coincidence for backers of settler-led development. Capitalists, of course, had mostly departed Mozambique when Frelimo nationalized all land and most industry. Ten years later, as in Zimbabwe, government, donors, and many NGOs lost faith in state-led, or even peasant-led, growth. For such planners, foreign investors remained the only credible source of economic stimulation. Hence, a slew of post-socialist, post-peasantry reforms provided niches for foreign capital (Hanlon 1991:113–22: Bowen 2000:185–202). Sure enough, after the 1992 cease-fire, capitalists came. South African and Zimbabwean loggers, hunters, and hoteliers, in particular, arrived and immediately raised a central dilemma of liberalizing economies: how should the government of Mozambique regulate investments so as to protect the public good without discouraging investors? A modus operandi emerged indirectly through a series of difficult compromises regarding specific investments mostly in remote places. Proponents of tourism, timber, hunting, and so forth clashed with cultural and social preservationists—and neither party got its way. Instead, policymakers agreed upon various third options. For instance, government terminated plans for an enormous eucalyptus plantation south of Maputo when an American billionaire offered to turn the same place into an "ecotourist's paradise."[79] This scheme won favor because it accorded more closely with the emerging compromise: investor-driven, environmentally friendly development for (or with) local benefits. Provided they hewed to this new party line, venture capitalists could range far and wide in Mozambique. In the new social-geographical lingo, *community-based* capitalism became the order of the day and appeared to solve all problems.

The Directorate of Forestry and Wildlife first tested this multivalent program in negotiations with a Zimbabwean and a South African sport-hunting firm. Deceptively named Mozambique Safaris, the first of these enterprises gained notoriety between the cease-fire and the peace accords by tying suspected local poachers to a tree for three days. Upon hearing of this human rights violation in Mágoè District, Tete Province, the directorate chose neither to annul the hunting concession nor to prosecute officers of Mozambique Safaris in a court of law. Instead, it suspended the concession and dispatched Luís Namanha—a geographical accomplishment in itself given that the Portuguese government had once taken steps to cede remote Mágoè to Zimbabwe.[80] During 1992–93, Murphree and other Campfire proponents visited Namanha in Mágoè. Meanwhile, the directorate "propose[d] an agreement to work with the community as a condition for Mozambique Safaris to resume operations" (Wilson 1997:17). Reluctantly, the company complied. So began the "Tchuma Tchato" (Our Wealth) program in community-based wildlife management. As in Campfire, collaboration generated revenue for a grinding mill and other projects, and it raised the possibility of a fence. In this case—as opposed to Campfire—fencing and partitioning began even before any reserve existed. In 1998, Tete's Provincial Services of Forestry and Wildlife with Ken Wilson advocated a "regional land-use zoning plan."[81] As in Campfire, this limitation of farmland provoked anxiety with regard to children and in-migrants. "The [fenced] land is getting full almost every day," worried an associate of Namanha in 1999.[82] Outsiders, however, continued to treat Tchuma Tchato as a model marriage between community and capital.[83]

As this success story was unfolding, the directorate spied the potential for a similar, but grander, project in Gaza Province. Again, officials embraced ecotourism as the remedy for corporate misbehavior. To start, the World Bank sent two consultants to investigate the activities of Gaza Safaris: Paola Agostini and myself. Both of us were working on doctorates at U.S. universities, and we had met at Garuzo. Yet, viewing the same hunting concession—known as Coutada 16—we came to diametrically opposite conclusions. Agostini, an Italian-born economist, spent much time in late 1994 with the safari executives. She reported: "I . . . tr[ied] to make them understand that it was in their best interest to get along with the communities . . . I was surprised to see how quickly they made these principles their own principles."[84] Three months later, I found no evidence of this quick conversion. Accompanying a famine-relief team, I stayed with the solitary, off-season manager of Gaza Safari's camp. Keenly aware of his status as the only white man resident within 100 kilometers and bored nearly beyond sanity, Johann had been polishing his skills as a tracker of Africans, rifle at the ready. In his view, "kaffirs" entered the bush—with or without cattle—with the intention to poach animals. To the World Bank, I reported on this bizarre individual and the local consternation he provoked.[85] I also noted a looming territorial conflict between safaris and cattle grazing. The director of Gaza Safaris himself had warned, shortly after Agostini's sage counsel, that "land must be set aside for their [the residents'] use for agriculture, grazing, traditional or subsistence, hunting, etc."[86] If he could, surely he would ram zoning and fences down the throats of Gaza stockholders. My skepticism appeared to sway staff at the World Bank and the directorate more than did Agostini's Panglossian attitude. But ultimately, her view won out.

In Gaza, Mozambique's new openness to investment challenged and reshaped the theory of community. Gaza formed the centerpiece of Garuzo's nocturnal agenda: a World Bank–funded megaproject involving three international bioregions.[87] The Gaza "transfrontier conservation area" would encompass South Africa's premier Kruger National Park and parts of Mozambique and Zimbabwe and link this aggregation to the coast via a new road.[88] Boosters spoke of a tourism mecca in the making. "The idea of creating the largest conservation area in the world is so evocative," raved Agostini, "that *by itself* [it] will attract a lot of tourists."[89] She and other promoters acknowledged the need for community participation but also expressed a sense of urgency—in the face of "unplanned settlement as a result of returning refugees" (Environment and Development Group 1994a:28). Such deracinated people, according to Lundin's model, did not belong in the "community of place" or in "community-based conservation." The same study, however, worried that "traditional communities are difficult to identify following their [wartime] disruption" (ibid., 29). Why not then wait for the native-born to return and revive "tradition"? One territorial rationale called for Campfire-style, preemptive planning to preserve communities against alien intrusion. A second, cultural rationale suggested greater patience as repatriating citizens helped communities to coalesce. Never directly addressed, this contradiction contributed to a general unease about rural people. The World Bank, the directorate, and even investors sought reassurance from social scientists, myself included. "I don't know what these anthropologists do," confessed one South African businessman after my remarks at a World Bank meeting in 1995, "but whatever it is, it's important, and we need more of it."[90]

LEGISLATION CATCHES UP

By 1996, investors and their fellow travelers had outpaced Mozambican law. Mozambique's process of postsocialist reform had not yet legislated many of the changes envisioned by the World Bank's and similar projects. Many investors did not know or care—assuming, as did the loggers in Gogoi, that Mozambican officials could be ignored or bribed. But the wiser businessmen recognized a lacuna: no one knew what legal rights and responsibilities rural Mozambicans would enjoy with respect to land and natural resources. The possibilities were broad. If the status quo prevailed, all land would remain property of the state. Neither peasants nor private firms would dispose of secure rights over their farmland. At the other extreme, government could grant titles to individual smallholders and investors. Many investors and donors advocated such privatization—"to cadastre the country up" as one expatriate critic later described the view.[91] Clearly, the transfrontier project depended upon a resolution of the issue. The World Bank meeting that so heartily endorsed anthropologists also pleaded for surveyors. "There is still no national cadastre in Mozambique," averred Chris Tanner, a British consultant on land matters.[92] Government knew this, of course, and never really considered the extreme positions of public or private ownership. The Ministry of Agriculture, the Council of Ministers, and expatriates, such as Tanner, debated various versions of the old idea of native reserves. Without recognizing the parallel, they considered the Rhodesian ideal of territorial entitlement for African smallholders, of no-go zones for investment. In the course of the late 1990s, however, furious dialogue among civil servants, fledgling peasant organizations, NGOs, and investors themselves generated a different ideal: the Campfire-style, rezoned reserve.[93] Mozambique missed a historic opportunity.

In its specifics, legislative reform focused on at least three crucial questions: Were concessions territorial? Did communities possess rights to uncultivated land? And, if so, were those rights transferable or saleable? The first issue regarding the territorial qualities of concessions had already caused confusion in Gogoi. As chapter 5 recounted, Continental Timbers thought it had bought rights to a certain hectarage, whereas Ana Paula Reis of the Provincial Services of Forestry and Wildlife had charged the company for cubic meters of wood and would have been prepared to sell hunting rights in the same area. "What is a concession?" asked the 1997 National Forestry and Wildlife Conference, held outside Maputo—a parcel of land or natural resources alone?[94] Civil servants and NGO representatives, including myself and staff of the Gogoi project, tangled with the few investors attending. "Concessions are a route to development," expounded one official of Entreposto, a large firm that inherited many assets of the old Companhia de Moçambique. She continued, "The definition of a concession cannot be only exploitation" of natural resources but must encompass the management of an entire area, including the building of roads and bridges therein.[95] The draft law of forestry and wildlife, under discussion at the meeting, more or less supported her view. Based on the "Principle of the Forestry and Wildlife Guard," the document accorded concession holders the "rights and duties ... [of] controlling and managing forestry and wildlife resources in the areas conceded."[96] A civil servant from Zambézia Province derided this attitude: "We think that the concession holder is owner of everything, plus animals, plus people."[97] In agreement with him, the Forestry and Wildlife Law of 1999 cut the controversial passage, limiting concessions to specified trees rather than full-scale territorial management. Investors appeared to have lost out.

A concurrent reform seemed to damage their interests still further. In 1996, a draft of the new Land Law conceded to smallholders sweeping rights to land, even to uncultivated zones. A product of immense public debate, the bill overturned the earlier, benchmark of improvement, "beneficial occupation," and the Lockean notion of land rights acquired through labor. Instead, the law defined "local community" as a "grouping of families" that encompassed worked and unworked zones: "fallows, forest, sites of cultural importance, pastures, springs, and areas of expansion."[98] Three of these categories—sites of cultural importance, forests, and areas of expansion—underwrit much activism in the ensuing years. The national directorate focused on "sacred forests." Staffers visited the forests and, employing their growing expertise in social research, tried to discern the related sylvan beliefs and practices. Sometimes the spirits of the forest brought civil servants low. For lack of observing the proper rituals, reported a directorate staffer, "a team . . . was lost for some hours [in a sacred forest in Gorongosa] and even the aerial photograph they brought did not help them to find the exit quickly."[99] By the time of its national meeting, the directorate had converted that trepidation into a clause on "community forests" in the draft law of forestry and wildlife.[100] Timber barons, it seemed, would have to stay off hallowed ground.

The Gogoi project and subsequent "community delimitations"[101] capitalized upon this pro-peasant balance of forces. From 1997 to 1999, they pushed the "zones of expansion" to the furthest extent possible. In so doing, mappers violated an earlier consensus about the place of investors on the landscape: that, as a leading official in the directorate had predicted in 1996, capitalists would operate in the "free areas" between communities.[102] His statement implied that rural geography contained discontinuities—gaps or what Kopytoff (1987) describes as "interstitial frontiers"—between settlements. Perhaps such gaps existed, but mappers did not allow for these in-between spaces. In Mossurize District, Niassa Province, and other locales, projects delimited one community or one chiefdom right up to the edge of another. In part, doing so was simpler than obtaining coordinates for all the pastures, forests, and so on. One could simply treat the "zone of expansion" as equivalent to the territory of the chiefdom, based on whatever boundaries local people cited or crafted in the course of the project. "You've got [the community's] oral rights," recounted one mapper, "and then you've got the putting down of the concrete."[103] In such an atmosphere of finality, chiefs might make last-ditch attempts to claim or reclaim neighboring territory, as did Chief Gogoi (see chapter 5). Nevertheless, delimitations eventually fit communities together like pieces of a jigsaw puzzle, leaving no residual areas for the private sector. Investors were being mapped off the landscape.

Or were they? Just as they were gaining steam, the mappers themselves reappraised their work: they fundamentally weakened the notion of delimitation. Meeting in Beira in August 1998, representatives from NGOs and state agencies involved in demarcation considered the third question mentioned above: Could or should communities sell their land rights to outside concerns or concession seekers? Concessions, civil servants had decided, consisted of nonterritorial rights to trees or wildlife. Communities, by contrast, were consummately territorial—vast, largely uncultivated expanses of land. Precisely the difference between these two units created the possibility for harmony between them: concessionaires could, in theory, buy permission to hunt or cut trees within the nonfarm zones of communities without immediately affecting food security. The conference considered this possibility by asking should the delimitation "protect or isolate" communities from investors and their financial offers.[104] Tanner sketched the options of "open" or "closed" boundaries (figure 6.2). With an open boundary, communities would admit private firms. Communities could even forge "partnerships" with capitalists. A closed boundary, however, would constrain investors to the "free areas," much as Rhodesia's reserves had done. Or as South African Bantustans were doing, said Tanner (Tanner, de Wit, and Madureira 1998:4; cf. Tanner 2002:48). That reference to Apartheid—the rhetorical equivalent of Nazism in Europe and North America—seemed to end the search for regional comparisons. The case for closed reserves was over almost before it was articulated.

Would the mappers have come to a different decision if they had examined Zimbabwe—or really, Rhodesia? They might have appreciated the importance of timing. In the 1890s, Meredith created sanctuaries *from ongoing, incomplete colonization*—a situation very much like that of interior Mozambique a century later. In South Africa, by contrast, architects of Apartheid implemented Bantustans from the 1960s, *long after complete colonization*. Those enclaves really did act as concentration camps, incarcerating blacks.[105] This cross-Limpopo difference was crucial. However, even if it had discussed Zimbabwe seriously, the Beira conference probably would have overlooked the timeliness and enduring value of Rhodesia-style reserves. By 1998, Campfire had redefined and undone the sanctuaries; the program had opened boundaries that Meredith and company once demarcated as closed. At Garuzo and elsewhere, Campfire's intelligentsia had celebrated the new possibilities for investment and joint ventures. At their point of initiation into this forward-looking world of community-based resource management, Mozambican practitioners were not likely to excavate an archaic, segregationist structure. To them, modernity meant capital flows. Finally, political pressures militated against closing off anywhere near 42 percent of the country, the Rhodesian figure. "Government is going to jump up and down," said one major player, if we exclude investors from large areas.[106] Only the tiniest of closed reserves—limited to fields and homesteads—would

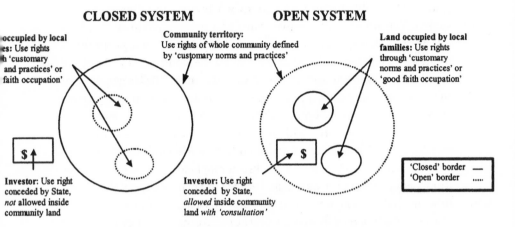

CLOSED SYSTEM **OPEN SYSTEM**

occupied by local
es: Use rights
h 'customary
and practices' or
faith occupation'

Community territory:
Use rights of whole community defined
by 'customary norms and practices'

Land occupied by local
families: Use rights
through 'customary
norms and practices' or
'good faith occupation'

S

'Closed' border ——
'Open' border .....

S

Investor: Use right
conceded by State,
not allowed inside
community land

Investor: Use right
conceded by State,
allowed inside community
land *with 'consultation'*

FIG. 6.2. Reproduced here with permission from Tanner (2000:22).
(For the Portuguese version, see Tanner, de Wit, and Madureira
[1998:3].)

survive such a fracas. In short, political developments on both sides of the
border made the Rhodesian model invisible to most, suspect to many, and
imprudent for the few who would have supported it.

Opinion and strategy then converged on flinging the gates wide open.
Tanner's drawing of the "open system" reproduced the essential lines of
WWF's picture (figure 6.2). Furthermore, Tanner's agenda became policy:
"the creation of conditions favorable for the integration of the community
and the private sector . . . to promote the entry of new capital into the rural
areas for the benefit of all."[107] Retroactively, this manifesto revised the meaning of delimitations undertaken in Gogoi and elsewhere. They had mapped,
in one expatriate's description, "an area of jurisdiction rather than a strong
land right."[108] Recent, ongoing, and future cadastral efforts would serve not
as barriers but as conduits to business. No need to *rezone* the reserves; experts
simply erased the reserve model from the drawing board and instead began
to sketch investment spaces.

OUTCOMES AND SIDE EFFECTS IN MANICA

In the nitty-gritty of projects, this ideological shift produced no immediate effect. A year before the Beira conference, the directorate officially
launched the Chimanimani Transfrontier Conservation Area Project.[109] Like

the two other international bioregions, this project anticipated Tanner's open system. At the ribbon-cutting ceremony in Chimoio, top conservationists spoke of "creating a political environment for private investment" and, for this purpose, engaging in "community mobilization."[110] In 1999, the directorate seemed to have miscalculated: it hired the iconoclastic Richard Bell to write a management plan for the transfrontier area.[111] Bell began the consultancy with a decided skepticism toward rural investment. Meeting me en route to Chimoio, Bell proposed to invite the affected communities to a workshop and to generate with them "a management plan that says 'leave me alone.'"[112] The consultant appeared to be a Meredith in the making. The following month, Bell and the directorate held a two-day workshop. Rural people did attend, although, because of what Bell called the "logistical imperialism" of government, they arrived late, tired, and humiliated.[113] The plan that emerged from this workshop and other activities almost said "leave me alone." Bell's (2000) document focused on obtaining legal standing for rural people and community-level titles to land and resources. Even after these steps, communities would not enact Tchuma Tchato–style zoning and fencing. "Land-use partitioning," he later explained, "can not precede the realization of non-farm products but is a possible consequence."[114] Unwittingly, Bell forced investors into a catch-22: they could not have land until they generated profits, but, of course, investors felt they needed the land first.

This muddled state of affairs did not last. In mid-2000, the directorate convened another workshop in Chimoio precisely to overcome Bell's catch-22. Reis, now heading the Chimanimani Transfrontier Area Project, explained, "We cannot attract the private sector before we have a definition of the land."[115] Zoning and partition, after all, would precede "the realization of non-farm products." From the point of view of communities, circumstances were most unfavorable. In 1999, the Forestry and Wildlife Law had emerged in its final form without any reference to community forests.[116] Moreover, communities in and around the conservation area had not attained anything approaching the legal clout envisioned by Bell. They had no titles; they had not even been officially delimited. In Chimoio, staff of NGOs and government agencies—as well as myself—dominated discussion at the workshop. We considered a map of the conservation area divided into the high mountains and surrounding lowlands. There was little disagreement that the high mountains—where apparently no one resided—should be zoned as a strictly protected national reserve.[117] But what of the lowlands, a district-sized swathe of fertile foothills, grasslands, and forest? The designation of community forest, delimited community, or even native reserve would have pleased many in attendance. In light of legal constraints, participants opted to classify the lowlands as a multiple-use "buffer zone."[118] And it was done. People might later reverse the decision, assured the provincial director (in response to my query). "Subject to approval from Maputo," he neglected to mention. Reis, however, understood the permanence of this zoning all too well. Having overruled Bell's central principle, she thrust his management plan aloft and intoned, "We are deciding upon our Bible."[119]

Adding to this sense of nearly religious fervor, participants—including many smallholders—maintained an unshakable faith in tourism. All were boosters. In 1997, Wilson had written his superiors, "Given the superb resource base in Mozambique, it will be able to attract ecotourists in its own right." To make matters better still, "a nascent tourism industry in Mozambique will also benefit from the resource pressure and resource degradation in Zimbabwe."[120] In other words, natural endowments—touted as the "elephant of Chimanimani"[121]—complemented a saturation model of tourism. Yet, by 2000, when forestry and wildlife staff had cleared a road and built a camp (Reis 1999:5), Zimbabwean tourism was anything but saturated. Paramilitaries had emptied all but the hunting lodges. This political scare might have dampened expectations at the Chimoio meeting. It did no such thing. Despite my skepticism, one community representative attested to "the pressure that one feels" from Zimbabwean investors.[122] Specifically, Collin Walker, whose history in Vhimba hardly recommended him (chapter 4), had expressed interest in transfrontier tourism. Or so said Reis at the Chimoio conclave. Perhaps he would pay communities for access to their scenic trails and yawning precipices. Yet, days earlier, Walker had told me personally that his adventure business was moribund, and, in any case, he was satisfied taking middle-aged Europeans on sedate strolls within Zimbabwe. Leaving the Chimoio meeting, I almost shared the Afro-pessimism Walker had expressed regarding development: "Give it another thousand years."[123]

Yet, Walker was quite wrong. The project had achieved something: the side effect of opening political space for investment. In a process at least as influential as legislation, the planning of conservation and development helped to change the political attitudes of planners themselves. To the agencies that would regulate land, Manica now constituted a frontier for capitalism, a zone of unrealized potential. Current smallholder agriculture, said Reis, "will never bring great benefit to the area."[124] Her statement did not quite declare the land empty, as some settler myths have. Yet, she directed attention away from the people and toward the "area," toward the territorial rather than the social aspect of "community." In her eyes, these hectares cried out for an economy commensurate with an inherent possibility (cf. Hughes 2005). "It's a deal! It's a deal!" declared one exasperated NGO manager to the imaginary, elusive tycoons.[125] My conservationist colleagues preferred investment in tourism, but any capitalist could enter a claim. In 1998, the Center for the Promotion of Investment declared all of central Mozambique a tax-free investment zone.[126] A compact with capital was in the making—if only capital would show up. Thus, the push for ecotourism had portrayed Manica as an economic vacuum, a set of glaringly open reserves. The tourism industry had failed to fill that vacuum and, in that failure, passed the baton along. Perhaps another industry would step in. Above all, Mozambique's new dogma mandated that the vacuum be filled.

In 2000, someone *was* filling it, seizing the figurative baton. As we deliberated in Chimoio, white Zimbabwean farmers were organizing in Harare and lobbying in Maputo to colonize a swath of Manica. Without fully intending to do so, they exploited the exact points of permissiveness established by community-based conservation. The largest of these schemes treated 440,000 hectares on the north bank of the Pungwe River as an open native reserve—a space for investment that would benefit local people.[127] To begin, the project would take pains to avoid displacing people or forest. Roughly 150 farmers would cultivate nonfarmed zones, leaving half of each of their 1,600–hectare parcels to the current occupants and/or to conservation. The director and chief planner read current Mozambican politics correctly: "You've got to get them [local Africans] on your side," he advised me. "If you don't . . . you're not going to succeed at all."[128] Then he described the carrots: a huge soya growing and processing operation, schools, and a university—all employing, educating, or otherwise assisting 300,000 Mozambicans. Community benefits—no problem! Many Mozambicans were suitably impressed. The more grandiose the business plan, the more it accorded with their dim view of smallholder agriculture. Said one community representative from Chimanimani—supporting white Zimbabwean colonization—"By ourselves, we have no development. We have none."[129]

He did not know the full story, however. The logic of open reserves was veering toward eviction, despite the fact that the Land Law of 1997 signaled the possibility of true territorial entitlements. "No one leaves" their home areas, insisted one of the law's leading authors.[130] That commitment not to displace smallholders suffered much in the course of time and travel to the provinces. The shift toward open community boundaries and open reserves permitted displacement, provided that communities authorized it and benefited from it. Voluntary resettlement became an unspoken policy, flowing naturally from the welcome extended to investors. In mid-2000, a leading agricultural official in Manica commented on the Zimbabwean settlement schemes. He insisted, "We will not *force* anyone to leave."[131] What *will* the state do? The National Directorate of Geography and the Cadastre—in charge of certifying all community demarcations—seems caught between land claimants. In early 2001, its chief planner wrote, "The state has a responsibility to mediate between the local community and the investor." By adhering to such a neutral position—between protection and eviction—the state could regulate open reserves. Yet, it is not likely to do so. "The state," clarified the same official, "really has . . . to contact and convince the community to accept investment project[s]."[132] As in Zimbabwe, a public-private partnership was emerging. According to the legislation, rural people could stop that partnership, closing their community boundaries. In practice, their room for maneuver was slight. "If the operator comes from above," predicted one elder from the Chimanimani transfrontier area, "it is no use for the community to say 'no.'"[133] Once policymakers define progress as settler-led development, peasants can hardly obstruct it.

Both the Vhimba hotel and the enormous settlement in Manica are absurd white elephants. Neither venture seems likely to take shape on the ground. Indeed, in 2001, the hotelier withdrew from Vhimba, allowing the local committee to construct its own campsite and one chalet. It did exactly that. By late 2002, having operated for nearly a year, Vhimba's facility had garnered revenues of US$4 and was incurring heavy losses.[134] Across the border, the Zimbabwean colonization scheme was still seeking a major bank loan and insurance.[135] Even as failures, these plans still represent unlocked doors—different from but essential to the person who will enter. These projects are widening the political space for investment in Southern Africa's hinterland. In precisely the same fashion, Zimbabwe's Campfire program created that space in the first instance. The program's early financial success won it allies within local and national levels of government—people who are now all too willing to facilitate the entry of capital into communal lands. Campfire also had the same effect in Mozambique, compounded by the influence of Tchuma Tchato and the Chimanimani Transfrontier Conservation Area Project. The government even gave white colonization a trial run: the infamous Mosagrius Development Programme in Niassa Province. In 1996, a deal between South Africa and Mozambique conceded sixty-four thousand hectares to Afrikaners, who proceeded to endanger local access to land and food security (Braga 2001:211–16). Then, the settlers went bankrupt and decamped. Studied in 1998–99, this debacle did not discredit the *idea* of white settlement. It only cast certain white settlers into disrepute and put provincial planners on guard. Hence, in 2000, Benjamin Gemo of Manica's Provincial Services of Geography and the Cadastre wanted only "the good ones" as settlers. "I mean the best ones," he corrected, "The good ones can stay" in Zimbabwe.[136] As a matter of principle, Gemo unlocked and rezoned black farmland. On both sides of the border, then, settlers *of the right sort* are welcome on longstanding or incipient reserves, and surely, some will eventually come.

They will come bearing claims. "The best ones" will harness the region's soil, flora, and fauna to create local jobs and income with minimal damage to ecosystems. Such "sustainable development" revives and reforms earlier modes of colonization. On the side of revival and continuity, claim making recalls the "age of the fortune hunters." As in the scramble of 1890–96, no boundaries stand in the way of settlers. Precisely by bounding white ambition, Meredith and other native commissioners ended the age of fortune hunters. They constrained white settlement and channeled it away from zones of black entitlement. A century later, Mozambique nearly followed the same course but hastily reconsidered. Before they could even mark most reserve lines, planners "opened" those boundaries to venture capitalism. In both countries, local and national officials did not so much rezone as dezone. They removed a patchwork of entitlements to restore the previous undifferentiated field for making claims. On the side of reform, most current settlers act with goodwill. They do not "sjambok" the natives, as Moodie did. Indeed, many investors and boosters are themselves black, although, where tourism is concerned, virtually all the tourists are white. A business ethic, rather than race, gives these colonizers their unity of purpose.

In some ways, that business ethic is fundamentally new. In the 1890s, whites held land in Southern Africa by cutting trees—the "beneficial occupation" clause. Colonial administrations followed John Locke's model of property: the occupant gains rights by working the landscape, transforming it ecologically, and producing useful goods. In the 1980s and 1990s, postcolonial administrations began to understand the complexities of the common property systems, based on overlapping, usufruct rights to do things to and on the land—in short, to *produce* something. Now, those systems are becoming irrelevant. Many of the would-be investors in rural Mozambique and, even more so, in Zimbabwe have no intention of producing goods. They and like-minded conservationists seek precisely to limit ecological transformation and economic production on those landscapes. Recall that even the putative white colony in Manica, Mozambique, would refrain from cultivating fully half of its hectarage. Such set-asides would provide "environmental services," preserving biodiversity, rare habitats, or scenic zones. If such landscapes produce anything economic at all, they would only support nonconsumptive or low-impact tourism. This shift puts smallholders in an exceedingly difficult position. Their success as agricultural producers constitutes failure as environmental stewards. Nor can they *work* their way out of this problem. Investing more labor only confounds their ecological folly. According to the new logic of land use, black peasants should concentrate on selling their vistas to passing North Americans and Europeans— a task that is nearly impossible for poor, non-English-speakers.

Almost by definition, then, "the best" investors belong to social classes foreign to the black lowlands. They are urban businessmen, highland tourist operators, and commercial farmers, all eager to provide environmental services. They are also frequently white. In the 1990s, in Zimbabwe and Mozambique, local governments actively recruited whites for activities in black smallholder spaces. Racial and economic integration began to outweigh measurable economic development. By 2000, desegregation, alongside the provision of environmental services, had become an unspoken agenda in government circles So it should be, proponents of reconciliation and national unity would say. Perhaps, but only if desegregation does not further weaken the weakest group. The current spatial mingling of classes in the black lowlands threatens to do precisely that. In open reserves, smallholders will lose the minimal territorial security they obtained in Rhodesia and nearly obtained in Mozambique. Investors can only gain. Policy has opened a new frontier for them. Of course, settler-led investment incurs many risks in the black lowlands, but states, donors, and NGOs are willing to help defray initial costs—from feasibility studies to the messy business of eviction. Through Campfire and transfrontier conservation, planners have forged a public-private partnership for latter-day colonization. They give cause for a bizarre nostalgia: once, in what is now Zimbabwe, black farmland was simply, indisputably black farmland.

7

IN CONCLUSION,
THREE LIBERAL PROJECTS
REASSESSED

I ARRIVED ON THE ZIMBABWE-MOZAMBIQUE BORDER AT A TIME OF HIGH
hopes. A century after the Moodie treks, postemancipation, postcolonial
states—bolstered by liberal-minded donors and NGOs—controlled both
banks of the Rusitu. Surely, these well-meaning people and institutions would
prevent a second colonization of Chief Ngorima's territory. Just as surely,
they would bar settlers from Chief Gogoi's domain. Agencies were striving
to improve the political and economic standing of rural Africans. I joined
their efforts. Earlier chapters narrated these and related endeavors. None
of them achieved an unequivocal success. Implementers tended to brush aside
such failures and their own complicity with land-grabbing. Episodic break-
downs in the field did not undermine the soundness of liberal plans. At this
point, however, those plans and agendas deserve reappraisal.

Southern African liberal projects arose as colonial planners confronted
"the native problem." The problem, or, more neutrally, the "question," has
grown to encompass three issues: (1) how to emancipate rural Africans as
individuals; (2) how to enfranchise or empower them in political systems;
and (3) how to advance them economically. These desires led to three liberal projects, all rooted in eighteenth-century Euro-American ideals of freedom, meritocracy, equality, and democracy. To emancipate Africans, missionaries and British native commissioners eradicated bride-service and the
system of wealth in people. Since independence, NGOs and state agencies in
both countries have helped "empower" smallholders through various local
committees and councils. Peasants elected a democratic leadership that began

to displace hereditary monarchs (chiefs and headmen). Finally, in the quest to advance smallholders economically, development programs are recruiting investment for the black lowlands. If successful in Zimbabwe, they will overthrow the segregationist, Rhodesian order of race and space. In Mozambique, they will prevent such an order from ever coalescing. Will smallholders be better off as a result? These liberal projects have undermined structures that provided security—clientship, lineage-based leadership, and native reserves—in favor of structures that give greater scope for ambition. Business firms certainly benefit from this expansion of opportunity. As in the past, *some* smallholders will be able act entrepreneurially, maximizing their wealth and power. Optimists and neoliberals are betting that *everyone* will benefit—a best-case scenario. They misjudge the dangers. In fact, something closer to the worst case is now imaginable: in the "investment zones" of Southern Africa, the weakest, poorest rural people are in danger of losing their claim on charity, their political voice, and their agricultural base.

What alternative exists? Posing this question raises uncomfortable issues for students of Southern Africa. There, liberal projects represent the hard-won principle of equal treatment for whites and blacks, for haves and have-nots (Ferguson 1999:33). Especially in the face of President Mugabe's current antiwhite rhetoric and actions, intellectuals, development practitioners, and conservationists yearn for a multiracial, unitary society. How does one question this liberal ideal? I do so by arguing that, for people at the intersection of underprivilege in race and class—black smallholders—equal treatment and equal protection are not good enough. They fall far short, and a status of equality may undermine minimal, colonial-era guarantees. Below, I argue for a series of entitlements that would recognize smallholders' special needs regarding land. Provisionally, I advocate reviving the earlier notion of separate territorial arrangements whereby smallholders enjoy exclusive access to the black lowlands—without, however, being limited to the lowlands. At the very least, I suggest that cross-class and/or cross-racial partnerships create wide scope for exploitation. Unity, in other words, also deserves a reappraisal along the Zimbabwe-Mozambique border.

But is the time right for such a criticism in Zimbabwe? Since 2000, President Mugabe's government has arguably killed liberalism in Zimbabwe. The paramilitary occupations of 2000 and onward have abrogated rights of private property. In their place, the ruling party has articulated a notion of race- and nationality-based claims to land on the highveld. Variegated groups of peasants, urban elites, and well-placed politicians have replaced white landowners and their workforces. Meanwhile, draconian legislation has restricted nonstate media virtually out of existence. In Chimanimani, security forces run the district and carry out a campaign of persecution against the district's white Member of Parliament, elected in 2000, and those around him. The elected institutions and committees of the 1990s have little power, and their members have suffered human rights abuses at the hands of the state. After my last visit, in late 2002, police beat one of my hosts. They accused (but did not charge) him with associating with a suspicious white American. In sum, the state has fostered a climate of fear, intimidation, racism, repression, and theft. Yet, in so doing, the state has also stimulated, among its numberless critics, a renewed faith in liberal institutions and values. Opponents of the regime demand a restoration of "law and order" and see salvation in a post-Mugabe torrent of foreign investment and aid. Many romanticize the 1990s, overlooking the frustration with liberalism, investment, and aid that led some Vhimba residents to invade private land. Liberalism did not provide the people of Vhimba with sufficient land or security. Mugabe's current policies provide them with even less of both. This is precisely the time to suggest third alternatives for Zimbabwe, Mozambique, and points further afield.

EMANCIPATION

Nineteenth-century abolitionism was slow in coming to Mozambique, arriving in a late-twentieth-century context of enclosure and environmentalism. Under these unfavorable circumstances, freedom presents two moral paradoxes. First, the freed do not seem to appreciate their freedom as much as abolitionists might expect. Gogoi residents, released from forced porterage only in 1992, had suffered corvées under the Portuguese and under Renamo. Through oral history, they knew of Gaza Nguni raids and *muranda* servitude. Vhimba people, across the hard line of the international border, experienced and remembered a different history. Missionaries rooted out brideservice and other vestiges of Nguni and pre-Nguni wealth in people. This suppression, combined with massive land alienation, shifted the locus of power from controlling people to controlling land. Was this shift to cadastral politics for the better? Many Gogoi men anticipated it with dread. In 1997, they felt fortunate in comparison with their land-deprived counterparts across the border (and would have felt the same vis-à-vis evictees from the parts of Mozambique where land was alienated). When a meeting raised the subject of Zimbabwe, one man boasted, "We farm where we want to."[1]

In a discussion of white loggers, Headman Hlengana associated gum tree plantations with Zimbabwe. "We don't want it!" he insisted.[2] Finally, one Gogoi man who fled to Vhimba in 1981 returned at war's end because, as he said, "Here you farm as you wish. . . . There, there are no [homestead] stands."[3] These statements do not reject the fruits of emancipation per se. I cite them not in order to suggest that forced labor is preferable to land alienation but, rather, to indicate a moral ambiguity. By way of silence, my informants' counternarrative raises doubts about two abolitionist assumptions: the priority of labor rights over land rights and the preferability of rule by enclosure to rule by enslavement. My informants most certainly did *not* say, "We would prefer to have our land taken than be to press-ganged and whipped." Perhaps missionaries and other abolitionists strove to confer upon Vhimba people a freedom that was secondary to them.

At the same time, emancipation and subsequent developments took away something of distinct value—security. Herein lies the second paradox: African enslavement offered stronger guarantees to the weakest members of society than do many postemancipation systems. Chiefs Ngorima and Gogoi sought out destitute people and made them clients, wives, or sons-in-law. The institution of *kukhonza*, wherein clients worked for and lived with patriarchs, addressed the problems of unemployment and starvation simultaneously. *Kukhonza* made orphanages and, what is worse, street begging unnecessary. Even Portugal strove to conserve the human resources of Mozambique. Each individual who emigrated represented a transfer of wealth from the Portuguese empire to the gold industry of South Africa. These enslaving systems provided elites with sufficient incentive to support those who failed to support themselves. So too, many systems of emancipated, "free labor" have provided elites with the same incentives—although critics correctly point out their negative sides.[4] As Marx indicated, labor, having been alienated from the means of production, works in servitude to the owners of those means. And, since he or she can, the owner exploits the worker. Yet, in order to keep on doing so, the owner protects the exploited from a harsher fate. Residents of the Zimbabwe-Mozambique border gained minimal guarantees from callous elites as long as elites could wring something from them. Humanitarianism—of a paltry sort—made economic sense.

Now, it is economic *nonsense*. Today's environmentalist elites want nothing from people—or, at least, not from *more* people. Value resides, not in human beings or even in what they produce, but in wild landscapes and environmental services. At best, smallholders are irrelevant. At worst, they threaten the landscape, its diversity and scenic qualities. This thinking pays little heed to the anthropogenic history of forests, such as Vhimba's Nyakwawa. It also discounts the cases in which corporations, such as the Forestry Commission, have destroyed far more indigenous vegetation than have the poor masses nearby. With great tenacity, the ideology and economy of conservation press for removing the poor. Only pure, uneconomic humanitarianism softens the blow—in a limited way. Liberal agencies seek the sustainable development of people living in forested areas of the Zimbabwe-Mozambique border. At they same time, they evict potential residents preemptively: they demarcate human settlement and zone the remaining land for ecotourism. Future generations of smallholders lose the ground their parents planned for them. Born at the wrong time or in the wrong place, they are "surplus people."[5] Recall the Campfire manager who called in-migrants an "environmental disturbance [that must be] rubbed off once and for all" (chapter 6). Fortunately, genocide is not likely in Southern Africa, although Zimbabwe's paramilitaries have driven farm workers and farm owners out of their homes with great violence. These acts share one feature with environmentalism: they minimize human resources and maximize natural resources. They treat a certain kind of people as parasites on a beloved landscape. This set of values betrays what a critic of conservation calls "the arrogance of anti-humanism" (Guha 1997; cf. Bell 1987). Ironically, principles of "wealth in people," when they fell short of chattel slavery, often presented a more human face.

EMPOWERMENT

In the 1990s, Zimbabwe and Mozambique experimented with what agencies called "empowerment." Such programs designed new institutions according to principles of democracy, multiracialism, and republicanism (or, more precisely, antimonarchism). Mozambique's postwar elections of 1994 established genuine multipartyism. In 1997, a law of "Autarquias" permitted the election of local government units.[6] Meanwhile, the Transfrontier Project and similar ventures envisioned elected committees managing the flora and fauna of even the most remote areas. Thus, Mozambicans seemed headed toward enfranchisement at national and lower levels. In Zimbabwe, NGOs could also maintain such optimism by ignoring national politics. Already virtually a one-party state, the country slid into dictatorship during the 1990s. Local government did the same. "Council is as transparent as a brick wall," complained a Chimanimani councilor himself.[7] Hence, NGOs focused their efforts on the grassroots. They promoted the Vhimba Area

Development Committee and similar elected structures elsewhere.[8] Did such "village republics" actually enable rural people to exercise power?

Throughout the 1990s, the format of empowerment limited rural power in two crucial respects. As *villages,* these republics narrowed the geographical scale of rural demand making. As *republics,* they emasculated peasants' existing, hereditary leadership. To start with the latter issue, Mozambican agencies attempted, in a relatively mild fashion, to make chiefdoms constitutional. Bell's plan (2000) recommended "community management groups" composed of seven hereditary leaders or their designates and five "members appointed by consensus." Zimbabwean agencies went much further: they actively sought to *disempower* chiefs and headmen (Singh 2001:101). At root, NGOs wanted to replace a leadership committed to cadastral struggle with one interested in grinding mills and other small-scale development projects. They used liberal notions of meritocracy, accountability, and feminism to denigrate headmen. Headmen, these critics contended, lacked skills in writing and bookkeeping, both necessary for running a grinding mill (though dispensable when settling squatters). Nor were they accountable. Here, republicans failed to appreciate the ways in which constituents removed bad aristocrats—by discovering the "true heirs." Indeed, between 1995 and 1999, three of Vhimba's four headmen ceded their thrones to cousins and brothers (a higher rate of turnover than in any "democratic" institution legislating for Vhimba in the same period). Even so, headmen could not change their gender. Inspired by feminism, NGOs insisted that Vhimba people "elect" a quota of female representatives—who likely would then not dare to appear before male, often domineering, bureaucrats. Only headmen and chiefs commanded respect from government officers. To replace them was to decapitate rural polities—and to demobilize cadastral struggle.

The geography of village republics also undercut rural popular territorial agendas. As a spatial notion, the "village" perpetuated an English feudal tradition, embedded in many democratic systems, of representing estates in appeals to the king (Guinier 1994:133). People belonged to the land they inhabited. Similarly, in Zimbabwe and Mozambique, representation depended upon the demarcation of boundaries. As one NGO manager insisted, recalling an earlier rural meeting: "You guys as a village have to know where your boundary begins and ends so that you can benefit from CBRM [community-based resource management]."[9] Scholars have criticized such efforts elsewhere for drawing the boundaries two broadly—for lumping women with men, one ethnicity with another, and poor with rich purely on the basis of coresidence.[10] In this sense, the villages were too big.

In a geographical sense, they were too small. Agencies recognized the republics' remits only within the native reserves—and only as long as they focused on neighborhood ecotourism rather than on national or regional economic justice. Of course, Vhimba people did not always acquiesce. They tried—in a fashion successful in Southeast Asia—to "invoke community" for the sake of cadastral struggle (McDermott 2001; cf. Li 2001:172–75). Could Vhimba people, organized as a village republic, demand and obtain access to lost lands? They could not. In 1996, when the Vhimba Area Development Committee appealed on behalf of alleged squatters, the Parks Department bluntly refused to meet with it. In 1997, when the same squatters tried to address the district administrator directly, he shut the committee down (see chapter 4). Across the border, experts in community delimitation deliberately dodged political controversy by discussing only local natural resources with committees. "It was a bit of fiction," admitted one advocate, "but it allowed us to stop stirring up this pot."[11] Such studied parochialism undercut possibilities for a national peasant movement.

Meanwhile, the range of "politics" contracted in relation to people's daily lives. During the 1990s, environmentalists worked hard to keep emergent conflicts and coalitions out of the political, democratic sphere. Prior to Campfire, deals between residents of communal lands and white investors were unimagined. When the Campfire agencies did imagine such deals, they faced a choice of forum—although they did not appreciate it as such. They could have adopted the territorial rationale of Zimbabwe's empowerment programs. Under such a format, the investor would have presented his or her idea to the village, and the village would have voted on it. Most proposals—and certainly the original Vhimba ecotourism plan—would have gone down in defeat. Perhaps for this reason, promoters of investment never subordinated it to geographically based, democratic *politics*—the win-lose format of elections.[12] Instead, they established a model for corporatist *economic* negotiation—for reaching consensus and win-win outcomes. "Stakeholders" met through "collaborative groups" and "workshops."[13] Like the prerevolutionary French estates—clergy, aristocracy, and bourgeoisie—the three parties of residents, investors, and civil servants deliberated as notional equals. Nongovernmental organizations lubricated the discussion. Still, Vhimba's delegates, as well as Oberlander and Walker, often strained to break free of this corporatist chamber, to appeal to legislative bodies or to the courts. Environmental agencies recanalized the debate. When, much alarmed, I relayed news of the territorial dispute over the campsite, one NGO manager told me not to worry: "We'll workshop it!"[14]

Workshops began with liberal sentiment and ended with a contrary effect. Investors, who were invariably white, needed to be heard. Surely, a pluralist Zimbabwe would foster communication between the races. To take this principle one step further, investors' claims had to matter. Campfire and the Transfrontier Project gave these individuals greater consideration than their numbers alone warranted. In so doing, they forestalled a tyranny of the (black) majority. Yet, they overcompensated: workshops amplified external, minority voices at the expense of the local majority. They marginalized peasants by adopting English as a primary language—a courtesy to monolingual whites. Moreover, these workshops wrought a political change. When the civil servant minority joined with the investor minority, they constituted an Anglophone majority (or a Lusophone one in Mozambique). Exactly such a coalition emerged in 1997 when the Chimanimani chief executive officer uttered his famous (and untranslated) "dog eat dog" judgment, allowing Oberlander to proceed with a private ecotourism facility. Delegates from Vhimba attended the meeting but followed the English poorly. Thus, Campfire and its affiliated programs attempted to level the playing field between smallholder masses and a handful of white individuals. Their efforts violated the geographical standard of democracy, but they conformed to an illiberal corporatist ethic. Liberal project managers felt no sense of contradiction. In their minds, one standard applied to political empowerment, the other to economic development.

Zimbabwe's explosion over land should scramble such neat distinctions and mental models. In confining debate to local minutia, community-based committees had repressed demands for lost lands. Corporatist, economic workshops had denied peasants the clout of their numbers. Neither forum allowed smallholders to challenge the cadastre in a fashion that mattered (or even to defend the native reserves). Hence, many were prepared to seek land— as headmen and squatters in Vhimba had already done—outside of legal convention. When paramilitaries broke down the farm gates, nonmilitary peasants poured in.[15] They did not "workshop it." Tungamirai himself, the ex-chair of the Vhimba committee and a veteran of workshops, endorsed the paramilitary agenda. His co-militants within Vhimba menaced committee members, whites, and ecotourism in general: "We will torch you. We will beat you, all of you," they reportedly threatened.[16] In 2001, sixty-five families occupied Hayfield B with the intention to farm. "The politics went a bit silly," the estate owner told me, keeping a stiff upper lip.[17] They went silly, or they went serious. These peasants chucked the faulty contraption of democracy and empowerment. They voted with their feet and retook lost lands.

DEVELOPMENT, OR DE-ENVELOPMENT

Emancipation and democracy, the two liberal projects discussed above, entail a "narrowing of vision." Scott (1998) uses this phrase to describe the ways in which states simplify a complex social reality, focusing on certain attributes of people and populations while treating others as externalities. In this vein, abolitionists fought for labor rights while forgetting land rights. Democrats have acted as if, in the American aphorism, "all politics are local." Yet, political desires are also frequently regional or national. Even small-holders care about and make alliances in places where they do not reside— and where geographical democracy gives them little influence. Both emancipation and democracy advance "natives" in a certain sphere but close off other spheres to them. They emancipate and enfranchise people *narrowly*.

Development also confers narrow benefits. In the 1990s, after an abortive program of land reform in Zimbabwe, numerous agencies assisted peasants in both Zimbabwe and Mozambique to accumulate wealth, but only a very restricted kind of wealth. To developers, wealth means money— Zimbabwe dollars and Mozambican meticais. (No project I know of has even tried to enrich rural people with stable, foreign currency.) In Zimbabwe, this narrowing of vision has a long history. At the end of the nineteenth century, missionaries and native commissioners expressly discouraged patriarchs from accumulating wealth in people. The Rusitu Mission even secreted away some of that wealth, in the form of runaway girls. Patriarchs then turned their attention to accumulating land, and state agencies thwarted them there, too. Every phase of eastern Rhodesia's economic development— starting with the Moodies, through commercial forestry, to ecotourism— took land from smallholders. As if in compensation, development and conservation organizations offered the aggrieved parties less land-extensive opportunities. Rhodesian-era soil conservation and, in the 1990s, Vhimba's grinding mill, banana fields, and elusive chalets all promised maximum economic reward on minimal hectares. The path to officially sanctioned prosperity was straight and narrow. It imposed, as Escobar (1995:56) writes in a global critique of development, a single solution on myriad peoples and problems. In other words, this liberal project produced an illiberal effect: it limited the themes and geographical scale of political action on the Zimbabwe-Mozambique border.

Development projects have released other people, however, and, partly for this reason, they remain in favor. On the Zimbabwe-Mozambique border, Campfire and the Transfrontier Project have allowed white and black investors to enter what were once forbidden zones. This form of development recapitulates colonization. Indeed, both programs are cut from the same cloth: a liberal sensibility of opening. As in its literal meaning, "development" implies an unfolding, an "un-envelopment," and a realization of latent potential. In 1893, the trekker Thomas Moodie "opened up this district."[18] (So says his gravestone.) Now, in the midst of a "recolonization" of Southern Africa, investors again push against geographical limits.[19] Latter-day pioneers wrote the business strategy of Continental Timbers and of the Chimanimani Hotel. Hotels and tourism in general are the settler homesteads of a new century. In 1999, magnates in Southern Africa's hospitality industry founded Open Africa, an organization seeking "free movement of tourists across the boundaries."[20] All of these people and institutions want to go farther and to cross boundaries—to incorporate that which is strange, to equalize that which is unbalanced, or to desegregate land and people hithertofore segregated. This perspective treats the criticism of development as an endorsement, the weakness as a strength: precisely by imposing a single solution, agencies and policies seek to overcome the partition between communal and commercial areas, between black lowlands and white highlands. These sentiments are liberal in the colloquial sense of that term. They have shaped the root and branch of Southern Africa's *settler-led* development.

The vision of openness has also shaped its frontiers. As this book observed at the outset, the term *frontier* denotes a zone and a line. Both may be open, and frontiersmen in the 1890s and in the 1990s opened both kinds of frontiers. They opened zones either by judging their occupants to be without merit and/or by physically removing the occupants. Gogoi's smallholders failed the test of "beneficial occupation" a hundred years ago. Hence, Luciano Laure, the first administrator, advertised his putative white highlands to tree-planting white settlers. They did not come. With greater success, the Rhodesia Forestry Commission expelled Chief Ngorima's people and replaced them with tree plantations. In the 1990s, Zimbabwean conservationists heaped scorn on smallholder agriculture. Despite the existence of figures to the contrary, boosters of Campfire treated Vhimba's crops as unprofitable—or as ecologically damaging. These smallholders failed the old standard of beneficial occupation and the revised, "green" one as well. Briefly, Mozambique swung to the opposite extreme, acknowledging smallholders' entitlement to "zones of expansion." Mappers, such as those in Gogoi, allowed cultivators and grazers to claim their hinterlands—but not for long. Tanner's "open system" soon redefined the zones of expansion as merely "within community jurisdiction but . . . not . . . used by local people"

(Tanner 2000:2). Such abbreviated language discounts future generations of smallholders who might use the zones. It assumes that, as in Zimbabwe, residents apparently do not and will not occupy the territory beneficially. They leave an economic vacuum—an opportunity for investors on both sides of the border. Settler-led development has been reborn.

Investors-cum-settlers breach boundaries, opening the frontier in its second, linear sense. In the area of this study, two sets of boundaries previously impeded colonization and investment: on the one hand, the escarpments between white highlands and black lowlands and, on the other, the Zimbabwe-Mozambique border. Black lowlands once excluded white investors in tourism and other sectors. Until Campfire, lines cut the social and economic world. Those lines formed part of what the neoliberal advocate Hernando de Soto calls a global "capitalist apartheid . . . that prevents the majority from entering the formal property system" (de Soto 2000:67). Campfire rezoned the reserves for business and for private property. In Mozambique, as well, boosters now speak of "cross-investment" and "cross-exchange."[21] The demarcated boundaries of communities exert only minimal friction on the movement of capital. Ditto for national borders. The Transfrontier Project and Open Africa delegitimate the customs posts with their very names. In Anna Tsing's (2000:119–20) terms, they are regional, neoliberal "scale-making projects." National insularity is no longer good for business, especially as Southern Africa plans a common market.[22] More emotively, many white Africans, who run much of the tourist trade, have long yearned for social unity and for a kind of pan-Africanism. Even in the 1970s, a tourism expert hoped for "new centers of pilgrimage . . . as an African culture—both white and black—develops and discovers its own past."[23] Having attracted donors' support, boosters now see these symbols and this multiracial, boundaryless society on the horizon. They would remake the continent into one enormous, biocultural region, undoing apartheid and the Rhodesian order of race and space. Lines and locked doors are passé.

Yet, in other ways, lines and locks are already returning. Colonization, as it is conventionally and narrowly understood, enclosed land, as all now acknowledge. Now, increasingly open markets may do so as well.[24] In Zimbabwe, neoliberal reformers call for privatization and "the provision of title deeds in communal areas to enable land to be used as security to attract much-needed investment."[25] In other words, smallholders should mortgage their farms to banks. Upon default—a likely event for the poorest—the bank will own the parcel and attempt to resell it (in order to recoup the lost loan). It is an immoral economy: as Vhimba's biggest banana grower warned, "You may be robbed with a title deed."[26] The Chimanimani hotelier, coveting Vhimba land for his chalets and helipad, assumed a land market already existed. "You can get title deeds there," he assured me.[27] He might acquire a parcel with even greater ease in Mozambique. There, community delimitations serve the purpose of group titles. They allow coresidents to sell access to their cropland, grazing, and forest. Whites whose great-grandparents took land with a gun in Zimbabwe may now take it with a box of cash in Mozambique. Is enclosure close at hand?

It may be, but liberal ideology disguises the seizure of land. In theory, markets are just and meritocratic. As in the test of beneficial occupation, fiscally prudent farmers do well, and the less so do less well. Drought and past or present state subsidies affect the outcome, as neoliberals are often loath to admit. Even to the extent that they *are* meritocracies, however, markets can damage people in ways that are (or should be) undesirable. Nineteenth-century slave markets—wherein destitutes frequently pawned themselves or their children—destroyed lives and societies. (So, too, may current markets in bodily organs and sexual services.) Like good abolitionists, neoliberals have excluded people from their commodity list. People are entitled to their own labor. Also, like good abolitionists, these liberals see no reason to extend that exclusion to land.[28] People, they assume, are not entitled to the land they farm. If allowed, trading houses will see to that. By definition, markets weaken guarantees and entitlements or abolish them altogether. Smallholders who mismanage their assets (or merely succumb to drought) lose them. Then, the buyer of a bankrupt farm justifies his ownership as the result of meritocratic, Darwinian competition. The next buyer does not even remember the original smallholder. In 1997, as the owner of Hayfield B estate shared his ambivalence about a handful of squatters, I sympathized with his problem: "Unfortunately, you are the inheritor of a hundred years of Rhodesian land-grabbing." He shot back in anger, "I didn't inherit this land. I bought it fair and square."[29] The market supplies wrapping paper for stolen goods. It opens avenues of exchange—for the weak and the poor to transfer their goods—and then dispossess them forever. If neoliberals bring land within its orbit, then surely lines will separate smallholders from what was once permanently theirs.

On the frontier, liberal projects breed their antithesis. In Vhimba, Gogoi, and their environs, groups have met and mixed. Capitalists have shaken hands with peasants. Whites and blacks have integrated to a degree with one another. The meeting and mixing ultimately leads to a partition, division, and hierarchy—to an enclosure. There is, however, an interval of equality and tolerance—a moment when liberal projects hold sway. Activists pose and try to answer "native questions." In the wake of Nguni rule, missionaries and native commissioners intervened to root out clientship among Africans. They freed smallholders from external demands on their labor, but ultimately robbed them of an appeal they could make to even the most unsympathetic authorities: their exploitability. Much later, the black rulers of Zimbabwe and Mozambique permitted a level of free speech and democratic expression among the citizenry. Their reforms fragmented that collectivity into a thousand powerless parts. Finally, economic partnership between predominantly white capitalists and black peasants promises to heal Southern Africa's rifts of race and class. Racism and racialism should give way to an economic and ecological meritocracy. Will this renaissance unfold? It may, but probably not as predicted. "Cross-investment" could take from black smallholders the little territory to which their race and class have entitled them. In other words, the removal of entitlements—in the quest for equality— could lead to a far more severe inequality. Early warning signs of this calamity abound. Business plans now arc across a continental scale, while policies assume that smallholders and their children will fold into more and more diminished domains (Hughes 2005). Liberal endeavors helped to produce this bizarre conjuncture: an ideology of (white) gigantism and (black) miniaturization, an opening and closure. Elites enjoy the opportunities of liberal reforms. The poor endure the risks of those efforts.

But the effort cannot be easily dismissed. This book has presented an ethnography of liberal projects along the Zimbabwe-Mozambique border— and an oblique recounting of my own participation in them. Anthropologists frequently take part in liberal projects. In my own fashion, many grapple with the processes, enthuse in them, and, then, from within, discern and describe disturbing trends. This odyssey lacks the ease and brilliance of knowing the outcome from the beginning (or the sense of ease and brilliance conveyed by describing only the outcome). However, the odyssey—the narrative of discovery—permits a fuller ethnography of liberal endeavors. Liberal activists, such as the project managers described above, also embark on journeys of discovery. They are more explorers than surveyors. Their daily work concerns the indices and contingencies arising as a policy advances toward an uncertain outcome. Few have the time or intellectual freedom to tally long-range consequences. This book offers just such "academic" commentary but also illuminates the quotidian practices of implementing liberal ideas. Planners continually make faulty, but reasonable, assumptions while pursuing policies, which seem good to nearly all. For instance, boosters of Campfire assumed that ecotourism would take little land or little land that Vhimba people cared about. They misjudged both the colonizers-cum-investors and the colonized. That story indicates early warning signs that policymakers may already notice—but not appreciate—on frontiers of colonization. In Mozambique, environmentalists wooed a hospitality industry that was taking off. Events brought it suddenly down to earth, leaving a void for agricultural colonists to attempt to fill. That story should alert boosters of ecotourism to the potential for similar denouements elsewhere—for environmentalism's enabling role vis-à-vis enclosure. Thus, workers in development and conservation agencies should see their work and themselves in this book as optimists who plan on best-case scenarios.

In distinguishing myself from them, I have argued for a form of pessimism and conservatism—for *planning on the worst case*. The worst case corresponds more closely to the history related in this book. From Cape Town, Dutchmen and later immigrants trekked northward, claiming land and closing frontiers. So did European-derived people in North America and the antipodes, making these areas neo-Europes. North of the Limpopo, however, whites settlers have closed the frontier only partially. They have not yet extruded themselves and their investments into all black spaces. One might have expected agencies concerned with rural poverty to protect or enlarge those residual spaces. The institutions discussed in this book did no such thing. From the outset, they accepted the status quo in the white highlands. They disregarded demands for business-to-smallholder (or white-to-black) land transfers (ultimately ceding that issue to squatters and paramilitary bands). Furthermore, these agencies assisted gladly in smallholder-to-business land transfers. They did not have to do so. Rather, they could have preserved the status quo of black lowlands—even while restructuring white highlands. However, to a variety of agencies involved in development and conservation in Southern Africa in the 1990s, black lowlands did not appear worth saving.

By 2005, as I revise this book for publication, black lowlands should have proven their worth amply. Or, at least, the leading alternative form of land tenure should appear less attractive. Outside the black lowlands or "communal areas," Zimbabwe is experiencing precisely what policymakers planned against: the worst case of economic insecurity. Since 2000, the state has systematically undermined freehold tenure. Government-backed land invasions and a series of edicts have invalidated the land titles of white landowners without instituting new titles or owners. In 2002, the government suggested the possibility of granting new, black farmers ninety-nine-year leases. It has still taken no steps toward issuing those documents. On the contrary, a second wave of elite black settlers—including government ministers and army generals—has evicted some of the earlier black settlers. Few farmers occupying the white highlands—rich, poor, white, or black—now feel secure enough to plant large hectarages. What is the solution? Opponents of the government argue for the restoration of freehold to the highlands. Many also suggest extending freehold to the communal areas as well. This latter, quintessentially liberal proposal overlooks a central lesson of the current crisis: freehold is weak and violable whereas "communal" tenure is resilient. Although battered by hyperinflation, shortages of hybrid seed, and political killings, smallholders are still sowing and reaping in the communal areas. In 2003, while living in Harare, I observed urban people buying food directly from the communal areas—a practice previously almost unknown. The so-called new farmers of the highlands are also, in many cases, relying upon food from communal areas. In other words, the communal areas are helping to alleviate the suffering of Zimbabweans near and far. These zones—governed by an assortment of hereditary patriarchs—deliver stronger guarantees for black smallholders than any other combination of land and governance in Zimbabwe.[30]

Thus communal areas, natives reserves, or black lowlands provide a better answer to the native questions than does settler-led development—of either Moodie's or Campfire's variety. They represent a semiclosed frontier and a high point between what preceded them and what, in the worst case, could follow them. By providing minimal guarantees, black lowlands forestall the worst, neo-European outcome of total dispossession. Many in Vhimba and Gogoi need and defend just such a bulwark. They need a place where only they can farm—a place they may leave, if they wish, but to which no other class of people may lay claim. In a neoliberal age, they need a refuge from competitions they are likely to lose. Women and men of Gogoi and Vhimba have—set firmly against the market—what David Harvey calls "a right to uneven geographical development" (2000:93). They have a right (that was recognized legally until Campfire) to reserve land. Despite Campfire and equivalent programs, there are spaces where colonization should not unfold. Black lowlands are that space, the marker of an enduring frontier.

GLOSSARY

aldeia communal village created by Frelimo in the late 1970s

braço laborer (lit., "arm")

chibaro compulsory labor and/or taxation

chikoroka forced labor under Frelimo and Renamo

colonato a Portuguese agricultural settlement

dzimbahwe central, capital part of a chiefdom

huku gift made by a migrant to a headman in course of land allocation (lit. "chicken")

kudira (or -dira) ceremony of pouring beer on the ground to propitiate ancestral spirits and ask them for rain and soil fertility

kukhonza (or -khonza) to pledge oneself as subordinate, variously conceived

maguta (singular: guta) lineage-based residual compounds

mfecane a series of migrations and violent occupations by Nguni speakers throughout southeastern Africa beginning in the 1820s

muhlafa (plural: va-) migrant new to an area

mukhonzwa (plural: va-) someone who has performed kukhonza

mutenga-tore exchange marriage

palmatória beating on the palms of the hands

pamutemo according to law and custom

prazo estate in the Zambezi Valley granted by the Portuguese crown in the seventeenth century

sabhuku (plural: ma-) headman

sadunhu (plural: ma-) headman

trekboer Afrikaans-speaking migrating farmer

varanda (singular: muranda) client, indentured servant, or slave

NOTES

1. A small number of efforts toward boundary making had occurred beforehand. Yet, many of these—most notably the Treaty of Tordesillas (1494) between Spain and Portugal—relied upon "table surveys" in the most disconnected sense. Marking the landscape was and is quite a different matter.

2. Alfred Crosby (1986:2) coined this term.

3. This was the case except, arguably, as regards the westward expansion of the United States before the Mexican-American war cleared the path to the Pacific.

4. In using the shorthand term *white*, I am here committing the error of projecting twentieth-century categories back into a different cultural milieu. As Robert Ross (1981:231–32) writes, seventeenth-, eighteenth-, and, to an extent, nineteenth-century South Africa exhibited a surprising degree of ethnic diversity, mixture, and fluidity. For this reason, I avoid the term *Afrikaner* except with respect to current migrations from South Africa to Mozambique. The introduction to part 1 further discusses my usage of the term *white*.

5. Basic works include Crais (1992), Eldredge and Morton (1994), and Ross (1981).

6. The introduction to part 2 reviews this literature.

7. Dane Kennedy (1987:111) refers to the healthier upland climate as a major factor in white settlement and development in Kenya.

8. Katz (1998:47); cf. Watts (2000:44–46).

9. This terminology has provoked intense controversy regarding the relationship between New World chattel slavery and subjugation within Africa. Without entering that debate, I follow Kopytoff and Miers (1977:5–7), Larson (2000:6–23), and Patterson (1982) in adopting inclusive language that respects the flexibility and mutability of African social relations.

10. The phrase derives from Meillassoux (1991).

11. In the early twentieth century, Machiwenyika recalled a quarrel between Maungwe and Manyika people cultivating on opposite sides of a watercourse just to the east of present-day Mutare (Jason Tafara Machiwenyika, "History of Manyika," Shona/Manyika and English versions, Lesson 101, historical manuscripts MA 14/1/1 and MA 14/1/2, National Archives of Zimbabwe [NAZ]). Therefore, I mean something much more specific—involving solid boundaries—than the loose sense in which Maxwell (1999:12, 21, 232) refers to the "territorial" basis of precolonial chieftaincy.

12. Quoted and apparently translated by Carin Vijfhuizen (2002:176). Vijfhuizen describes the ritual as "ancient."

13. Lobengula to Khama, *Parliamentary Papers*, C.5237, 59, 1 March 1887. I am grateful to Terence Ranger (1999:42) for this reference.

14. Afrikaners also migrated to Angola and Kenya (Clarence-Smith 1975; Groen 1974:42).

15. Kennedy (1987:2–3) includes colonial Kenya—before the postindependence white exodus—in this characterization.

16. Regarding Southern Africa, see L. Thompson and Lamar (1981b:17–18) and Wilmsen (1989a:1–2).

17. R. Gordon (1989:147–48); Hiatt (1989:101); Wilmsen (1989a:1–2). Had they been available, findings on the "anthropogenic landscapes" of shifting cultivators would have challenged that view (cf. Fairhead and Leach 1996).

18. Carter (1988:64) elaborates on an account presented in Corris (1968:53).

19. Kain and Baigent (1992:344; emphasis in original). Cf. Noyes (1992:275–84) and Scott (1998:44–45).

20. Colson (1971:196); Cheater (1990); cf. Ranger (1983).

21. The ambiguity and flexibility of African systems of land tenure have insulated them considerably from commoditization. See Berry (1993, 1997).

22. For a discussion of this complex evolution, see Murphy (1996).

23. Thongchai (1994); cf. Vandergeest and Peluso (1995).

24. They have seized much more in the realm of germplasm (cf. Kloppenburg 1988).

25. The foundational treatises on "limits to growth" and "sustainable development" are, respectively, Meadows et al. (1972) (a report of the Club of Rome) and World Commission on Environment and Development (1987) (known as the "Bruntland report").

26. James Fairhead and Melissa Leach (1996) assisted them in this realization.

27. The phrases derive from, respectively, O'Connor (1993:16) and Katz (1998:47).

28. Hence, Britons and Rhodesians often referred to the area and points south as "Gazaland."

29. As the introduction to part 3 explains, I use the term *native* in this context advisedly.

30. Virtually everywhere is not equivalent to everywhere: Mauritania, the overland slave trade in Sudan, slave smuggling in the Bight of Benin, and the bonding of African and Asian labor in the United States all attest to the persistence of unfree labor.

PART 1 / COLONIZATION, FAILED AND SUCCESSFUL

1. The two powers had delimited the border—a preliminary, more approximate step—in 1891 (Grant 1893; Leverson 1893). For a discussion of work on the border delineation slightly to the north, see Schmidt (1998).

2. On a broader geographical scale, see Frederick Cooper and Ann Stoler's (1989) work on "tensions of empire."

3. The term "transfrontiersman" comes from Isaacman and Isaacman (1975). For other accounts of these people and their land grants, known as *prazos*, see Isaacman (1972; 1976:1–8) and Isaacman and Isaacman (1983:14–18).

4. For this region, see Burrows (1954) and Olivier (1957).

5. As Ranger (1996:280) writes, "Colonial Africa was much more like postcolonial Africa than most of us have hitherto imagined" (cf. Werbner 1996). For less nuanced treatments of postcoloniality, see Bhabha (1992) and Mbembe (1992a, 1992b).

1 / COMPULSORY LABOR AND UNCLAIMED LAND IN GOGOI

1. Totems refer to formally exogamous clans associated with taboo foods—heart (of cattle) for *mwoyo* and hippo for *dziva*. Currently, people in both Gogoi and Vhimba tend to use Nguni, rather than Shona, terms for the totems, that is, *nkomo* or *sithole* for *mwoyo* and *muyambo* for *dziva*.

2. On the migrations and Sanga, see Beach (1980:170–71; 1994b:150–51), Bannerman (1981), and Rennie (1973:68–72).

3. As chapter 2 explains, the title was, at that time, Hode and was changed to Ngorima in the 1890s.

4. Oral history that I collected places this secession sometime in the nineteenth century: according to the current Chief Gogoi, João Maquinasse, his great-grandfather, Kandemukanwa (also known as Mandende), was sent by Chief Mafussi to rule in an outlying part of the chiefdom. He accompanied the Gaza Nguni to Bilene in the migration explained below (Gogoi, 1 May 1997). It is probable that he founded the Gogoi chieftaincy upon his return and sought and received recognition from the Portuguese as an independent chief.

5. Mutema's people did, however, kill the incumbent Chief Musikavanhu and otherwise seek to expel and/or control the cult. For the best account of these complicated processes, see Rennie (1978).

6. Korekore of the Zambezi Valley, however, appear to have observed and still observe strictly demarcated "spirit provinces" (Bourdillon 1978:236–38; Garbett 1966:141–44; 1977; Lan 1985:31–34; Spierenburg 1995).

7. See Cobbing (1988) for the best treatment of the controversies surrounding this term.

8. For the details of this chronology, see Liesegang (1967, 1975, 1986:8–12) and Rennie (1984:182).

9. "A bandeira de Gungunyane" (Gogoi, 9 May 1997).

10. E. H. Richards to F. O. Means, 4 January 1882, p. 34, Papers of the American Board of Commissioners for Foreign Missions, 15.2, 12:34, Houghton Library, Harvard University, Cambridge, Mass. (hereafter cited as ABCFM).

11. Bhila (1982:186–91) provides a similar description of Gaza Nguni rule over a longer period in Manyika, north of the area discussed here.

12. Mhlanga (1948:70). The author was the son of Ngwaqazi and wrote down his father's oral account.

13. Harries (1981a:213–14). North of the Zambezi, slaving through the port towns of Moçambique and Kilwa was even more pronounced. Moçambique, in fact, served as a transshipment point for many slaves from southern Mozambique bound for Goa and Madagascar (Alpers 1975; Capela 1993).

14. Eldredge (1994:152–53). An explicitly "Afrikaner" identity coalesced only in the twentieth century.

15. Harries (1994:27). See also his earlier works (Harries 1981a, 1981b).

16. Kandemukanwa, the great-grandfather of the current Chief Gogoi, probably was posted by Mafussi to the environs of the Muchenedzi River sometime during Mzila's reign. It is unclear, however, if he had, at this time, declared himself to be an independent chief (see above).

17. E. H. Richards to F. O. Means, 4 January 1882, ABCFM, 15.2, 12:23–24.

18. Machado reported on his initial trip to Espungabera: "Todas as povoações que encontrei no meu trajecto são insificantes e miseraveis ainda mesmo as que pertencem aos regulos e que em geral não contem mais de 8 a 12 palhotas" (Mossurize report of 18 March 1897, Arquivo Histórico de Moçambique, Maputo, Fundo da Companhia de Moçambique, Relatórios Cx. 259 [hereafter cited as AHM]). [All of the settlements I encountered on my route are insignificant and miserable, even those belonging to the chiefs, which in general do not contain more than from 8 to 12 huts.]

19. On the total absence of cattle from Gogoi, see, e.g., J. Orner, Mt. Selinda, to Rev. James L. Barton, Boston, 1 November 1917, ABCFM 15.4, 34:1. Provincial Veterinary Services reported fewer than one head per square kilometer in 1951–52 and 1967–68 (Weber 1971:141). Personally, I saw not a single head in 1997 in Gogoi.

20. In fact, British and, later, French shareholders controlled the Mozambique Company (Vail 1976:395).

21. "Em toda a Circumpscrição, não existe uma unica arvore plantada por elles" (Mossurize annual report for 1903, 16 February 1904, p. 24, AHM, Fundo da Companhia de Moçambique, Relatórios Cx. 259). (Throughout, I have translated the colonial designation *circumpscrição* as "district" for the sake of clarity. Mossurize

is now a *distrito,* although, before independence, this term applied to the wider administrative unit of Manica and Sofala, now *províncias.*)

22. After independence, Mossurize broke into two districts, its southern part becoming Machaze. I use the term "northern Mossurize" throughout to refer to the area north of the Buzi River, equivalent to roughly a third of the current, much smaller Mossurize.

23. "As terras altas estando destinadas a colonisação de povoamento não convem de forma alguma vincular n'ellas direitos de propriedade aos indigenas, antes facilitando aos concessionarios a faculade de remoção dos indigenas para fora das suas farms levando-os a concentrarem-se nas 'Reservas' para esse fim destinadas, aonde ao mesmo tempo que exerçamos melhor controle sobre elles possamos tirar melhor proveito de uma acção autoritaria prudente e bem regulada no sentido de obter resultados practicos e utilitarios na missão civilizadora que nos cabe" (Mossurize monthly report of November 1903, 5 December 1903, AHM, Fundo da Companhia de Moçambique, Relatórios Cx. 259, pp. 4–5).

24. "Logo que a fronteira seja marcada as 80 familias boers existentes no Forte Victoria veem definitivamente estabelecerem-se em territorio portuguez o que constituirá um importante inicio de colonização que é de toda conveniencia animar"(Mossurize report of 18 March 1897, AHM, Fundo da Companhia de Moçambique, Relatórios Cx. 259).

25. Companhia de Moçambique (1902:211–12); cf. Companhia de Moçambique, "Regulamento sobre concessões de terreno" (ibid., app., 43–47).

26. Relatório Annual de Mossurize de 1902, pp. 2, 10, AHM, Fundo da Companhia de Moçambique, Relatórios Cx. 159; Mossurize annual report for 1904, p. 56, ibid., Relatórios Cx. 260.

27. Mossurize annual report for 1902, p. 2, AHM, Fundo da Companhia de Moçambique, Relatórios Cx. 259. In 1903, L. Kleenj of Melsetter requested ten farms in the vicinity of Dierking with the understanding that he would recruit ten Dutch families from Natal and Orange Free States. Nothing came of this scheme either. Relatório Mensal de Outobro de 1903, 2 November 1903, ibid., pp. 2–3.

28. Olivier (1957:60) lists an E. Dorking as member of that trek.

29. Relatório Annual de Mossurize de 1904, 8 February 1905, p. 55a, AHM, Fundo da Companhia de Moçambique, Relatórios Cx. 260.

30. "Este concessionario foi de todos os que viviamos nas farms da fronteira o unico que lealmente acceitou o viver sob a jurisdiccao da Companhia de Moçambique. Lutando com as dificuldades de transporte e falto de recursos, sem ao menos possuir os títulos da sua propriedade da forma a sobre elles poder obter crédito, tem conseguido fazer da sua propriedade uma *farm* modelo, em que vae revellando as succeptiblidades dos terrenos do Mafuci" (ibid., 55b). Swynnerton (1921: map) suggests that the farm, called Maruma, was actually closer to Makuaiana, although, of course, chieftaincies were not demarcated. As a sure point of reference, Maruma abuts border beacon 90.

31. Mossurize annual report for 1904, p. 56, AHM, Fundo da Companhia de Moçambique, Relatórios Cx. 260; Mossurize annual report for 1906, 14 March 1907, p. 15, ibid.

32. Mossurize annual report for 1905, p. 18, ibid.

33. See, e.g., Mossurize annual report for 1911, 1 January 1912, p. 27, ibid., Relatórios Cx. 262.

34. "Os valiosos terrenos que a Companhia de Moçambique possue actualmente n'esta região tem agora pouco valor, quando esta zona estiver porem em communicação facil e rapida com o littora, os pretendentes a concessões não faltarão e estarão dispostos a paga-las por um preço elevado" (Mossurize annual report for 1906, 14 March 1907, p. 25, ibid., Relatórios Cx. 260). See Arnold (1908:142) for a similar view voiced by the "inspector for development" of the Companhia de Moçambique.

35. Mossurize monthly report for September 1900, 1 October 1900, p. 2, AHM, Fundo da Companhia Moçambique, Relatórios Cx. 259.

36. Mossurize annual report for 1901, 5 January 1902, p. 4, ibid.

37. "A judiciosa practica sciencia administrativa e colonial dos Inglezes, . . . conseguindo augmentar a intensidade da população pelo influxo de indigenas do nosso territorio . . ." (Mossurize annual report for 1902, p. 34, ibid.).

38. "Nunca . . . usurpamos os seus legítimos direitos de propriedade; pelo contrário, temo-los sempre defendido escrupulosamente" ("Relatório do Inspector-Chefe referente a 1954," p. 34, AHM, Fundo do Governo Geral, Relatório no. 497, Serviços Geográficos e Cadastrais). The statement helped support Mozambique's evolving policy of native reserves (see below).

39. For a discussion on the various regional meanings of *chibaro*, see van Onselen (1976:99). Gogoi elders also recalled a term, *jeti*, for early-twentieth-century forced labor. I am unsure of the derivation of this word and of how its meaning might differ from *chibaro*.

40. "Aus seinem Stamme sucht sich ferner der Häuptling gewöhnlich drei oder vier 16–18 jähriger Jünglinge aus, die er zu allerlei persönlichen Diensten heranzieht und denen er dann später zum Danke dafür Mädchen seiner Familie—Töchter oder Schwestern—zu Frauen gibt, ohne für diese den sonst üblichen Heiratspreis zu verlangen. . . . Man bezeichnet diese Jünglinge, die in früheren Zeiten eine Art Leibgarde bildeten, als *muranda*" (Spannaus 1961:633). This observation applied to the whole swath of Manica and Sofala through which Günther Spannaus passed. For a map of his route, see Spannaus (1933). For assistance in obtaining materials by Spannaus, I am indebted to Karin Bautz of the Institute for Ethnology, Leipzig University.

41. Unfortunately, the work—from February to May—occupied much of the peak agricultural season. Mossurize monthly report for June 1906, AHM, Fundo da Companhia de Moçambique, Relatórios Cx. 260.

42. The last two firms were known by their Portuguese names, Gremio dos Cereais and Serrações Inhasato. See, e.g., Mossurize monthly diaries for September

1950, October 1950, December 1950, and January 1951, AHM, Fundo do Governo do Distrito da Beira, A/42, Cx. 216.

43. Mossurize monthly report for July 1905, 16 August 1905, p. 2, AHM, Fundo da Companhia de Moçambique, Relatórios Cx. 260.

44. Mossurize annual report for 1901, 5 January 1902, p. 9, ibid., Relatórios Cx. 259.

45. "Desviar para elles a corrente de trabalhadores" (Mossurize annual report for 1902, p. 35, ibid.).

46. "O indigena de Mossurize, desde rapaz novo, só tem uma ambição na vida que é trabalhar para o Rand e, logo que chega á idade de pagar imposto, ele ai vai a caminho de 'John' como eles dizem, pois quem não trabalha nas minas não é considerado homen" (Mossurize annual report, "Recenseamento da população e arrolamento de palhotas," 1934, p. 8, ibid., Relatórios Cx. 265).

47. In 1946, an inspection found that 47 percent of the men eligible for contract labor had departed for Rhodesia or the Transvaal (AHM, Fundo da Inspecção Nacional dos Serviços Administrativos e dos Negócios Indígenas [hereafter cited as INSANI], "Relatório da Inspecção Ordinária da Circunscrição de Mossurize," 1946, p. 287).

48. Gogoyo Station Report, June 1921, pp. 7–8, National Archives of Zimbabwe, Harare, UN 3/20/1/16/5 (hereafter cited as NAZ).

49. "Vaiomesa, Mambo" (Vhimba, 22 April 1997).

50. W. J. Lawrence, Mt. Selinda, to Rev. Jas. L. Barton, Boston, 26 January 1918, ABCFM 15.4, vol. 33.

51. "Unoona mari yakawanda. *Hours* akanaka ne*lunch*"; "kushanda chete" (Gogoi, 9 July 1997). Cf. Allina-Pisano (2003:80).

52. Stephen Lubkemann's (2000:107) oral history from Machaze, just to the south of present-day Mossurize, indicates that bride-wealth would absorb the earnings from five domestic wage contracts but only one trip to South Africa.

53. For examples, see Relatório da Inspecção Ordinária à Circunscrição de Mossurize, 1946, p. 297, AHM, Fundo da INSANI, Cx. 39.

54. Mossurize monthly diary for January 1949, AHM, Fundo do Governo do Distrito da Beira A/42 Cx. 216.

55. The administration also built a house for Macuiana and other exemplary chiefs. Mossurize monthly diary for August 1947, p. 3, ibid.

56. "De todas as regedorias recenseadas onde encontrei maiores deficiencias, peores estradas e mias dificuldades foi no Gogoi, devido ao pouco prestigio de que este regedor dispreita [*sic:* desperta] entre a população. Alem de não ter prestigio algum, é desleixado, pouco cumpridor e não conhece a população que habita na sua regedoria. . . . Mais um ano decorre sem que se possa fazer um recenseamento perfeito em toda a área da Circunscrição, trabalho este que reputo da maior urgencia para uma melhor Administração" (Mossurize monthly diary for September 1944, ibid.).

57. "Mambo vanotonga vandu. Nyika vandu" (Gogoi, 5 July 1997).

58. Under the Companhia de Moçambique, the Mossurize administrator's annual report included a detailed chart enumerating huts, men, women, and children under each chief.

59. W. J. Lawrence, Gogoyo, to Rev. Enoch Jas. F. Barton, Boston, 2 January 1918, 29 October 1918, ABCFM 15.4, vol. 33; W. J. Lawrence to Rev. Enoch F. Bell, Boston, 14 February 1919, ibid.

60. In 1906, Laure had described the mission as the "only immediate solution for the colonization of Mossurize" [a unica solução imediata para a colonisaçao do Mossurize] (Mossurize monthly report, June 1906, last page, AHM, Fundo da Companhia de Moçambique, Secretaria Geral, Relátorios Cx. 260). See also Arthur J. Orner, Mt. Selinda, to Rev. Enoch F. Bell, Boston, 6 January 1917, ABCFM 15.4, vol. 34.

61. W. J. Lawrence, Mt. Selinda, to Rev. Enoch F. Bell, Boston, 29 September 1919, ABCFM 15.4, 33:1.

62. See Rennie (1973:351–59) for a detailed recounting of this history.

63. Mossurize third trimester report for 1933, p. 6, AHM, Fundo da Companhia de Moçambique, Secretaria Geral, Relátorios Cx. 265.

64. The 1946 Missão Geografica to Mossurize is an interesting exception. The colonial office of geography instructed the administrator to make arrangements for two surveyors to carry out fieldwork in northern Mossurize. His diaries dwell upon the difficulties of recruiting eighty carriers on short notice and then feeding them in Espungabera as they awaited the delayed surveyors. The diaries do not mention the purpose or outcome of the survey. Mossurize service dairies for September, October, and November 1946, AHM, Fundo do Governo do Distrito da Beira, A/42 Cx. 216.

65. For the status quo of Mozambican mapping in 1954, see "Relatório do Inspector-Chefe referente a 1954," AHM, Fundo do Governo Geral, Relatório no. 497, Serviços Geográficos e Cadastrais. The delay was all the more remarkable given that the concession regulations required the Repartição de Agrimensura to produce 1:50,000-scale maps of each concession (Colônia de Moçambique 1931:12), maps that would have been much less useful without a comparable district base map. By 1936, Mozambique had fallen so far behind in geodetic triangulation—having determined no elevations inland from Beira—that Southern Rhodesia decided to base its elevations on readings from Messina, South Africa (Bradford and Gauld 1952:101).

66. The companhia had already designated a strip approximately twenty kilometers wide along the international border (das Neves 1998:134), but this area would have excluded most of Chief Gogoi's people. For a map of the expanded reserve, see "Relatório do Inspector-Chefe referente a 1954," following page 35, AHM, Fundo do Governo Geral, Relatório no. 497, Serviços Geográficos e Cadastrais.

67. Joel Maurício das Neves (1998) has written a seminal work on this topic. Also see Alexander (1994:9–11) and Newitt (1995:465–67).

68. This kind of functional dualism may have had the added advantage of discouraging absenteeism "on the part of workers. In Zambézia, companies, in fact, preferred migrant to local labor for precisely this reason (Vail and White 1980:309).

69. Allen Isaacman (1996:16) rightly emphasizes that "women were the principle cotton growers." In other words, cotton cultivation brought them, for the first time in most of Mozambique, into the forced labor system (cf. ibid., 98).

70. "Foi então dito pelo régulo Gó-Goi que êle mesmo já pensara em aumentar as culturas nas suas terras, mas que não o pudera fazer por a maioria da sua gente ter emigrado" (Relatório da Inspecção Ordinária à Circunscrição de Mossurize, Acta de Audiência, Espungabera, 21 December 1946, AHM, Fundo da INSANI, Cx. 39).

71. The number and identity of these firms remains quite unclear because of their shifting names and subsidiary relationships with one another. The most reliable, consistent information available to me derives from the written document mentioned below and from my interview with Jaime Athoguia, Moçambique Florestal S.A.R.L., Beira, 25 January 1999.

72. Francisco José de Cabedo and Loucastre África de Oliveira, FSM, Beira, to Ministro do Ultramar, 14 April 1970, pp. 1–2. In archives of Serviços Provinciais de Florestas e Fauna Bravia, Chimoio, binder marked " Projecto de Reflorestamento," file marked "Repartição de Agricultura e Florestas da Beira, SABRI, Ltda., pedido de concessão florestal, 1970." The sawmill is visible in Government of Mozambique air photo no. 61–406, taken on 26 June 1965, and some of its broken machinery remains on-site today.

73. "Os autóctones de Mossurize . . . apenas conheciam e aceitavam a moeda rodesiana; na Rodésia procuravam trabalho atravessando, indocumentados, a fronteira" (ibid., p. 2).

74. "Intensive" and "extensive" here refer to the amount of investment per unit of area.

75. Ibid.

76. "Tinorima kwatinoda" (Gogoi, 29 April 1997). A man made this comment as an explicit contrast with Zimbabwe at the opening meeting of the land rights project discussed in chapter 5.

77. "Mukadzi wenyu ndewangu"(Vhimba, 15 March 1995). Schafer (1999:82) associates such statements with Frelimo's policy against polygyny.

78. Alexander (1997:5) links such compromises with post-1987 liberalization under President Chissano.

79. Gogoi, 6 July 1997.

80. See Wilson (1992) for an analysis of "cults of violence" and "power over people" in such places.

81. Roesch (1992:29) describes the area between the Save and Buzi rivers—thus abutting Gogoi—as "Renamo's most stable taxation area—i.e., that part of central Mozambique most solidly under Renamo control." Cf. Finnegan (1992:56–58); and Schafer (1999:74, 119).

2 / FROM CLIENTSHIP TO LAND-GRABBING IN VHIMBA

1. By that time, the government of Southern Rhodesia had changed the terminology in favor of "tribal trust land." I remain with the term *reserve* partly for the convenience of the non-Zimbabweanist reader but also because *reserve* is the most straightforward and honest of all the designations—colonial and postcolonial—for these areas.

2. Captain Henry F. Hosie to the District Commissioner (DC), Massi Kessi, 12 December 1890, NAZ, A 1/6/2. I am indebted to David Beach for suggesting this little-known source to me.

3. Captain Keith-Falconer, British South Africa Company (BSAC) Police, to the Officer Commanding BSAC Police, Fort Salisbury, 1 January 1891, pp. 167–69, NAZ, LO 5/2/7.

4. Delineation Report, Tribal Trust Lands in the Melsetter District, 1965, p. 6, NAZ, S 2929/1/6; Young 1970:56; cf. Rennie 1973:586.

5. "Extracts from the diary of Harry Raney," entry for 4 July 1899, Papers of the Africa Evangelical Fellowship, British Council, box 26, Serving in Missions (SIM), Charlotte, North Carolina, USA (hereafter cited as AEF).

6. L. C. Meredith, Native Commissioner (NC), Melsetter, to the Chief Native Commissioner (CNC), 20 October 1897, p. 2, NAZ, NUE 2/1/2.

7. Report of James T. English to the Surveyor General, 30 May 1914, NAZ, SG 3/1/3.

8. A. H. Duncan, BSAC, to G. B. D. Moodie, 20 October 1892; quoted in Olivier (1957:150); cf. Palmer (1977: 37).

9. L. S. Jameson, BSAC, to G. B. D. Moodie, n.d.; quoted in Olivier (1957:148–49).

10. "Map showing approximate position of farms taken up in Melsetter, Gazaland," January 1894, NAZ, L 2/2/95/25.

11. Triumphalist settler narratives also frequently reprint the earlier colonial register of Melsetter properties (e.g., de Bruijn and de Bruijn 1991:154; Sinclair 1971: frontispiece).

12. NAZ, earlier references; NC, Melsetter, annual report for the year ended 31 December 1955, p. 6, NAZ, S 2827/2/2/3.

13. In 1907, the total livestock for ninety-seven Melsetter farms was 2,040 cattle, 4,984 goats, 7,893 sheep, 265 donkeys, 8 mules, and 17 horses (List of Names of the Farmers and Farms in the Melsetter District, August 1907, pp. 336–37, NAZ, NUE 2/1/6,).

14. A. H. Duncan, BSAC, to G. B. D. Moodie, 20 October 1892; cited in Olivier (1957:150).

15. L. C. Meredith, NC, Melsetter, to CNC, n.d., NAZ, N 3/24/15–20.

16. This process was not uniform throughout Rhodesia. It is worth comparing

Melsetter's experience with that of Sebungwe (now known as Gokwe). Eric Worby (1994:380–81) writes that the administration drew the first three reserves of that district as perfect circles. In other words, it did not bother at all to delimit physical boundaries of the reserve. Why was the administration so uninterested in territorial control in Sebungwe? Perhaps, the unsuitability of this vast, dry, tsetse-infested area for white agriculture puts it in a different category from the majority of Rhodesia. After all, no land was alienated in Sebungwe.

17. Raney (1898:275); Frank Huskisson, Cape Town, to Arthur Mercer, Wimbledon, 4 July 1898, p. 3, AEF, British Council, box 2; L. C. Meredith, NC, Melsetter, to the Civil Commissioner (CC), Melsetter, 30 November 1897, NAZ, NUE 2/1/2; L. C. Meredith, NC, Melsetter, to Mr. Raney, South African General Mission, 26 January 1899, NAZ, NUE 2/1/2. The mission did expand considerably in a later period.

18. L. C. Meredith, NC, Melsetter, to Farm Glencoe, 21 October 1899, NAZ, NUE 2/1/3.

19. A few years earlier, the surveyor general had considered a quite different recommendation. In 1914, James T. English (himself, a large Melsetter landowner) reported on the desirability of regazetting the upland portion of Ngorima B, abutting the Hayfield A farm, for white stock raising. Report of James T. English, 30 May 1914, p. 18, NAZ, SG 3/1/3.

20. Headman Hlabiso continued to inhabit the zone, and in the 1960s, the Land Board annexed it to the native reserve. National "Land Apportionment" maps for 1956, 1960, and 1965 and national "Southern Rhodesia" maps for 1909, 1932–33, and 1949, NAZ, "La Rhodesia," map file.

21. "Native Reserves," p. 7, NAZ, N 3/24.

22. L. C. Meredith, NC, Melsetter, to CNC, Mashonaland, 3 October 1898, NAZ, NUE 2/1/2.

23. L. C. Meredith, NC, Melsetter, to CNC, Mashonaland, 5 November 1907, NAZ, NUE 2/1/6; "Delineation Reports: Tribal Trust Lands in the Melsetter District," 1965, pp. 3–4, NAZ, S 2929/1/6. For a similar issue of cross-border chieftaincy, see Schmidt (1996:184–85).

24. The delineation report on Melsetter chiefs recounts, "The first Europeans to pass through the area were named Dabuyazuze and Nabuyesaka" ("Tribal Trust Lands in the Melsetter District," 1965, p. 4, NAZ, S 2929/1/6).

25. The magistrate for Melsetter later explained the failure to rise as follows: "My district was occupied by mixed tribes—Shangaans, Mandau, a small tribe of Barotses, and others with no connection with the Mashonas" (Longden 1950:187).

26. Terence Ranger's work on the risings minimized the destructive effect of the raids, in part, by omitting Melsetter and other areas in which the people did not resist whites (Ranger 1967:29; Palmer 1977:44, 55).

27. R. Wodehouse, North Melsetter Farmers Association, to W. Longden, Magistrate, Melsetter, 2 May 1914, NAZ, N 3/24/14–20; my emphasis.

28. In other parts of Zimbabwe, landowners may have communicated their demands for tenants' labor through chiefs and/or headmen, but I found no evidence of such a practice in Chimanimani.

29. L. C. Meredith, NC, Melsetter, to CNC, Salisbury, 20 October 1897, NAZ, NUE 2/1/2.

30. Ibid.

31. L. C. Meredith, "Reminiscences," p. 170, NAZ, ME 4/1/1.

32. L. C. Meredith, NC, Melsetter, to CNC, Mashonaland, 6 January 1897, NAZ, NUE 2/2/2.

33. Case of the Queen vs. George Benjamin Dunbar Moodie, 21 December 1896, NAZ, D 3/3/1.

34. L. C. Meredith, NC, Melsetter, to the CNC, Mashonaland, 19 January 1899, NAZ, NUE 2/1/1.

35. L. C. Meredith, NC, Melsetter, to Officer-in-Charge, BSA Police, Melsetter, 22 November 1897, NAZ, NUE 2/1/2.

36. J. D. Hulley, NC, Melsetter, to the Secretary, Native Department, Salisbury, 12 October 1895, NAZ, NUE 2/1/1.

37. "Extract from the diaries of Harry Raney," entry for 16 March 1899, AEF, British Council, box 26.

38. L. C. Meredith ("Report for the half year ended 30th September 1907," NAZ, NUE 2/1/6): "Certain mining companies sent their native employees into the district to recruit boys but were not successful as the majority of boys wishing to go out [to] work had already gone and such boys as were approached by the touts said that they knew where to work without any guidance."

39. Charles Van Onselen (1976) describes these conditions of work thoroughly. He also notes that recruiters, while not exercising force, often deceived potential workers as to the method for calculating pay and the period of service (ibid., 98).

40. For many years, Meredith reports that large proportions of the African population paid willingly. L. C. Meredith, NC, Melsetter, to CNC, Mashonaland, 30 June 1897, NAZ, NUE 2/2/2.

41. A document from the 1930s ("Chief," NAZ, N 8/1/1) gives a standard figure of six pounds for Ngorima's salary.

42. In 1907, for instance, chiefs and headmen confessed to Meredith, "they could not induce the young men to go out to work during the green mealie and harvesting seasons, when the date for payment of tax was almost due" (L. C. Meredith, NC, Melsetter, "Report for the month ending 30th August 1907," NAZ, NUE 2/1/6).

43. For figures and Meredith's comments, see L. C. Meredith, NC, Melsetter, to CNC, Mashonaland, 1 April 1899, NAZ, NUE 2/1/2. In 1902, however, Douglas Wood of the Rusitu Mission found that "the huts and natives there [along the Rusitu River] have increased by over double since I came here, the natives having come over from the Portuguese" (Wood 1903:27).

44. L. C. Meredith, "Quarterly report," 6 October 1899, NAZ, NUE 2/1/3.

45. L. C. Meredith, "Statistical report," 7 October 1899, NAZ, NUE 2/1/3; L. C. Meredith, "List of chiefs and sub-chiefs in the Melsetter District," 28 February 1900, p. 3, ibid.

46. In the first months of his tenure, Meredith found that the messengers in his employ had, in fact, previously caused complaints, and he punished a number of them (L. C. Meredith, NC, Melsetter, to CNC, Mashonaland, 2 April 1896, p. 2, NAZ, NUE 2/1/1).

47. Rex vs. Biyeni, 22 June 1918, NAZ, NUE 3/1/1. Chipinga was the colonial name for the current town of Chipinge.

48. The phrase "shorten the leash" is used advisedly, for Biyeni was only transferred.

49. As Richards (1950:207 n.2), Davison (1997:17), and O'Laughlin (1995) argue, outcomes may depend upon the flexible negotiation of coexisting ideals of patriliny and matriliny, rather than upon the application of any rigid system of rules.

50. L. C. Meredith, NC, Melsetter, to CNC, Mashonaland, 2 April 1896, p. 3, NAZ, NUE 2/1/1. I learned of the phrase *mutenga-tore* in Vhimba, and it translates literally as, "You buy. Take."

51. L. C. Meredith, NC, Melsetter, Quarterly Report, 3 July 1900, p. 5, NAZ, NUE 2/1/3.

52. Ibid. The Queen vs. Willem Bezuidenhout, alias Msorowenzowo, 29 June 1900, NAZ, D3/1/1.

53. See Jeater (1993:197) for a discussion of the difficulties in interpreting this poorly written law—difficulties partially surmounted by the 1917 Native Marriages Ordinance.

54. "Statement by Chief Ngorima re his daughters at Rusitu Mission Station," 24 January 1916, NAZ, NUE 3/1/1; and the Missionary in Charge, Rusitu Mission, to NC's Office, Melsetter, 25 January 1916, ibid.

55. J. E. Hatch, Rusitu Mission, to Mr. Franklin, NC, Melsetter, 25 July 1922, NAZ, NUE 3/1/1.

56. My survey of sixty-five extended families in 1996–97 revealed only eleven non-bride-wealth marriages involving a person alive at the time of the survey. In two or three of those cases, Mozambican refugee women pledged themselves to Vhimba men in the 1990s (see chapter 3).

57. In the years 1936–39, Mwandihamba, Mushanembeu's son and Shangwa's father, held the position of chief (Rennie 1973:586).

58. "Havizi kuzogarira. Vakazokwanisa kubhadhara mari dzakanga dzakukwanisa kubhadharwa ngavabereki vavo kunaMambo. . . . Saka vana avo vakazokwanisa kuchizobhadhare mari kubva muuranda hwaBaba vavo—kuchizvimirira" (transcript of oral history of Wilson Manase, 9 February 1997).

59. With his notion of a one-way door, Ferguson (1990:137) challenges Paul Bohannan's (1955) concept of "spheres of exchange" isolated from one another.

60. L. C. Meredith, NC, Melsetter, Monthly Report, April 1903, NAZ, N 9/4/15 f. 41; cited in Iliffe (1990:34).

61. John Hatch, Rusitu Mission, to Carrie Kofoid, Berkeley, California, USA, 6 November 1908, box 3, folder 30; and John Hatch, Rusitu Mission, to Flora Winter, Berkeley, California, USA, 15 December 1908, box 3, folder 32, Charles Atwood Kofoid Papers, Scripps Institution of Oceanography, La Jolla, California, USA.

62. Lionhills, Chisengu, Tarka, Martin, and Glencoe.

63. Sivaramakrishnan (1999) provides an excellent overview of the origins and contradictions in British colonial scientific forestry.

64. "Vakadzingwa vanhu nge *Tarka Forest* . . . Takanga tine nzvimbo hombe. Takaitorerwa. Tasara nekaplace kadiki-diki." (Vhimba, 15 September 1996).

65. Godwin (1996:199–200). This observation may say more about the experience of a "white boy in Africa" (as Godwin's memoir is titled) than it does about Rhodesian history. Ranger disputes Godwin's assertion that the Crocodile Gang left a note at a murder scene proclaiming "Viva Chimurenga" (Godwin 1996:12; Ranger 1997:671–72).

66. D. N. Beach (1997:18), using the oral history of Jason Machiwenyika, argues that there was competition for defensible mountain land. If so, such contests would have centered on the control of relatively small areas rather than on the demarcation and expansion of territory, the stuff of cadastral politics.

67. Interview with Headman Killion Parara, Vhimba, 24 July 1997.

68. Director of Lands, Salisbury, to Secretary for Internal Affairs, Salisbury, 25 June 1966, NAZ, S 2929/1/7 (emphasis in original); cf. Alexander (1993:146–47).

69. "Nyika yangu yatorwa nepurazi . . . Ndakagara muno maMatwukira . . . Ndinotongwa. Itai. Ndoita" (Vhimba, 24 July 1997).

70. Map, 14 August 1976, Ngorima personnel (PER) file, Office of the District Administrator, Chimanimani. (These "wards" should not be confused with the administrative divisions, also called wards, which exist currently.) Apparently unaware of this mapping, Agritex (the government's agricultural extension service) began to map headmen's areas in the Chimanimani reserves all over again in 1997. Agritex hoped to establish the constituencies for new "village assemblies."

71. Criticisms of Rhodesian and Zimbabwean land-use planning point to ecological mistakes and a dismissal of smallholders' knowledge. See, e.g., Drinkwater (1991); McGregor (1991); Scoones (1989); and Wilson (1989).

72. As noted, e.g., in Annual Report of the Assistant NC, Melsetter, 1952, 5:3, NAZ, S 2827/2/2/2.

73. In the late 1970s, e.g., Garayi Ngorima served on the Rhodesian government's Council of Chiefs.

74. District Commissioner, Melsetter, to Provincial Commissioner, Manicaland, n.d. (ca. 1970), Ngorima PER file.

75. As a rough gauge of the rise in population (during a period of quiescent evangelism), records of the Rusitu Mission indicate a 136 percent rise in church membership (from 716 to 1,690) between 1952 and 1960, after which membership leveled off (file named "Annual Statistics, 1960–1966," AEF, British Council, box 28).

76. The ranges derive from government national maps based on census data: "Rhodesia African population density" (1969), including, as an inset, "African rural population percentage change 1962–69"; and "Zimbabwe rural population density" (1982).

77. Muchadziya is at the other end of Ngorima Communal Land. "Vanhu havachakwanisi kugara pamwepo ngokuti nzvimbo hakusisina. Zvotoite kuti mwana wangu ungakone kugara kwaShamiso kusiyana nekwandiri kwaChikware. Umwe mwana wotoende kugarawo kwaMuchadziya. Saka guta rababa hapasisina" (transcript of oral history of Wilson Manase, Vhimba, 9 February 1997).

78. My observation of Chief Ngorima's *dare*, Rusitu Mission, 27 April 1997.

79. Reginald Green, Field Director, to David Evans, Executive Director, 20 October 1969, box 2; "Report of a meeting with Chief Ngorima to inspect the Mission Boundaries," by Verne L. Reeves, Station Head, 13 October 1969, box 2; and Rusitu Staff Meeting Minutes, 4 November 1969, box 1, AEF, Zimbabwe Council.

80. Minutes of the National Parks Advisory Board, 12 October 1949 and 14 February 1951, NAZ, S 932/66/4, vol. 4.

81. Among the works of government officers, see Crook (1956); Goodier and Phipps (1962–63); and Phipps and Goodier (1962).

82. Tom Müller (1994) has identified twelve types of rainforest in Zimbabwe. According to his definitive work on the subject, the forests of the Rusitu-Chimanimani area are type 12, whose dominant species is *Newtonia buchananii* and canopy height is roughly fifty meters (Müller 1994:10–11).

83. The Moribane Forest in adjoining Sussundenga District, e.g., was later found to cover fifty-three hundred hectares, larger than all the rainforest extant in Zimbabwe in 1994 (Müller 1994:13). Ironically, a substantial amount of this forest—perhaps more than half—burned down in 1995–96. The cause was not smallholder agriculture, but cooking and brush-clearing fires related to the rehabilitation of the Cahora Bassa power lines (another indirect ecological cost of the Cahora Bassa Dam).

84. Jonathan Timberlake's (1994) analysis of aerial photographs finds unilinear shrinkage of this forest only because he starts at 1963.

85. The scientists who gathered evidence in support of gazetting the Rusitu Forest did not investigate its cultural qualities. Müller, the tree specialist of the scientific team, only suspected that it might be sacred (interview with Tom Müller, Harare, 9 April 1997). Donald Broadley, the herpetologist, had no such intuition and learned only in 1997 (from me) that the Rusitu Forest was sacred (interview with Donald Broadley, Bulawayo, 29 March 1997).

86. Based on the 1950 aerial photographs. J. B. Phipps and R. Goodier, however, reported, "Small settlements are to be found on the lower slopes below 4000 ft" of the western Chimanimani ridge (Phipps and Goodier 1962:302).

87. Aerial photos indicate smallholders' presence in Mukwiratunhu in 1950, the addition of some families slightly to the north just shy of the Chisengu-Haroni junction in 1963, and the removal of those latter families by 1968.

88. Rhodesian soldiers were "contacted" by ZANLA 1,053 times, and whites fled in droves (Alexander 1995:180; Caute 1983:271–83; cf. Martin and Johnson: 1981:223–24).

89. The guerrilla army does not appear to have coerced the assistance of local *vajibha*—resident youth who in other places provided food and intelligence to the guerrillas—or to have punished state collaborators. Given the exclusion of the government's army from the area—the road parallel to the Rusitu River became known as *mabinya*, or "bandits" road—such collaborators were probably very few.

90. I owe this useful distinction between Mutoko and semiliberated zones to Alexander (1995:177).

91. "Tinoda nzvimbo yakakura" (Vhimba, 17 September 1996).

92. "Munogona kugara kwamunoda," as recalled by the Vhimba smallholder (Vhimba, 4 October 1996).

PART 2 / THE BORDER

1. Cf. Jean Comaroff 1985:177ff.

2. On the treatment of foreign workers in Zimbabwe's commercial agriculture sector, see Manungo (1996).

3 / REFUGEES, SQUATTERS, AND THE POLITICS OF LAND ALLOCATION

1. Cf. Allina-Pisano (2003:67). For a discussion of the Anglo-Portuguese Boundary Commissions, see Schmidt (1998).

2. Case of Rex vs. Musoreyani, preliminary examination, 12 November 1929, NAZ, S 1071.

3. "Havana kudzidza. Vajaira hondo." Meanwhile, in Mossurize, Jessica Schafer (1999:100) found that "[n]ational identity is surprisingly strong."

4. For a recounting of resistance to the act in Chimanimani District and in Ngorima Communal Land in particular, see Alexander (1993:51–59).

5. In Insiza District, see ibid., p. 120. With regard to women in Nyanga District, see Moore (1995:607).

6. With the assistance of Elias Muhanyi, I interviewed the heads (mostly men) of sixty-seven households separately (although often surrounded by family members) at their homesteads. Of these, there were thirty-seven households whose heads migrated to Vhimba from outside Vhimba for the purpose of farming (rather than for the purpose of creating a home base from which to migrate to formal sector jobs). The figure of twenty-nine is arrived at by making the following exclusions: three households for whom information on bargaining was not available; two who insisted that they approved of the first site offered to them and, hence, did not bargain; one cattle owner who needed a site with grazing land, of which there was a very limited number; and two Mozambican widows who would have had difficulty bargaining and did not try.

7. One could also hypothesize that prior residence, at any time, in Ngorima's area is the explanatory variable. There are, however, no migrants who were born outside Ngorima and lived in Ngorima's area, beyond Vhimba, before coming to Vhimba. Intermediate points between a migrant's place of birth fall into three categories: smallholder areas outside Ngorima Communal Land (in either country); migrant labor sites in Zimbabwe, Mozambique, or South Africa and outside Ngorima's historical boundaries; and migrant labor sites inside Ngorima's historical boundaries but outside the Ngorima Communal Land. These last areas include the Forestry Commission and private plantation forests, areas in which workers, unless born in Ngorima, do not hold any rights or obligations toward the chief.

8. "Takatsvaka nzimbo" (Vhimba, 12 November 1996).

9. "Ndinoda nzvimbo." . . . "Munoda dunhu ripi?" (Vhimba, 13 February 1997).

10. "Watoona nzvimbo yokurima" (Vhimba, 11 November 1996).

11. Andersson (1999:555) makes a similar argument regarding the symbolic and political nature of land allocation.

12. "Kutengesa nyika."

13. Informants on both sides of the border linked this type of subordination to the status of *muranda*. Chief Gogoi, who was nonetheless careful to distinguish *kukhonza* from *muranda*, defined the latter as "someone who takes a child [bride] without paying bride-wealth" [munhu anotora mwana asikasi kuroora] (Gogoi, 17 July 1997).

14. "Mungangondichengete. Mungangondiroore" (Vhimba, 19 September 1996).

15. For this formulation, I am grateful to an anonymous reviewer.

16. With a few exceptions, the warring parties confined their depredations to the Mozambican side of the Rusitu River. In other areas, Renamo crossed into Zimbabwe to rob and kill people.

17. "Usina hama unonzi mukhonzwa . . . akafanika semarefugees" (Vhimba, 20 May 1997).

18. "Tinoti wakhonza nokuti haasi chibarwa chemuno" (Vhimba, 8 March 1997).

19. "Handikhonzi. Ndiri muMozambique. Ndakabarwa muMozambique" (Macuiana, 13 July 1997). The man distinguished migrant labor in South Africa from the circumstances that would lead one to -*khonza* in a foreign country.

20. Mario Azevedo (2002:64) describes the inhospitable conditions of that camp.

21. Even so, these Mozambicans fared far better than did those who fell into the clutches of cross-border slaving circuits. For Zimbabwe, see Chingono (1996:107–8). For South Africa, see E. Koch, "Slave Trade Still a Booming Business," *Weekly Mail* (Johannesburg), 5–11 June 1992, p. 9–10; and P. Stober, "Seeking a Better Life, She Was Sold for R200," *Weekly Mail* (Johannesburg), 5–11 June 1992, p. 9.

22. "Kuuya munhu unosvika unoti, 'Ini ndinoda pokugara,' . . . asina hama, anobva kumwe" (Vhimba, 8 February 1997).

23. "Ndakhonza. Ndinoda pokugara" (Vhimba, 11 November 1996).

24. These findings closely parallel those of JoAnn McGregor (1994:esp. 560–61)

and Jessica Schafer (1999:91). Although, as McGregor observes, Mozambican border residents entering Swaziland in the 1980s did not formally "*khonta*" to a chief, they did become clients of hosting families and, in consequence, endured constraints and abuse in the course of gaining access to land. Schafer documents cases where Mossurize refugees worked for Zimbabwean smallholders in exchange for access to a portion of the hosts' land.

25. "Munogona kugara pamunoda"—recalled by a noncombatant Vhimba resident (Vhimba, 4 October 1996).

26. "Vanhu vasina pokugara vanosununguka chii?" (Vhimba, 17 April 1995).

27. "Muganhu wakatorwa nemakamba" (Vhimba, 18 April 1995).

28. Alexander (1993:360–70) describes this process thoroughly and (ibid., 361–62) recounts headmen's use of refugees to assert authority over land in northeastern Chimanimani District, a process close to that in Vhimba.

29. For accounts of "squatter wars" in Zimbabwe, see Alexander (1993:247ff), Herbst (1990:63ff), and Moore (1993:388–93; 1997:96–101; 1998:358–60). For another narrative of headmen's use of "strategic land allocation," see Andersson (1999:575–76).

30. More tangentially, it also encompasses the Ndau dialect terms *sharuka* and *doda*.

31. To my knowledge, Maxwell (1999:149–86) provides the most detailed academic account of a postmortem succession dispute in independent Zimbabwe.

32. However, it is not clear that recognized headmen, as opposed to chiefs, are legally entitled to any of these perks.

33. In fact, many other chieftaincies in Zimbabwe use collateral succession. It is not clear why or how lineages adopted one rule of succession or the other—and the rule is often contested. A dispute regarding Chief Ngorima himself raged through the early 1990s. When it was settled in 1995, at the installation of Peter Ngorima, the spokesperson for the lineage declared, before a crowd of hundreds: "Yafa; yabara," or "One dies; one is born"—a proverb that advocates patrilineal succession (printed speech of Phineas Philip Ngorima, delivered at Rusitu Mission, 31 March 1995).

34. In fact, Tiyekiye did lose his office to that man in early or mid-1998. Personal communication, Elias Nyamunda, Secretary, Vhimba Area Development Committee, 14 September 1998.

35. The head of household in this case may also have been born in Mozambique. There is extremely little communal land in Chipinge District, Zimbabwe, especially in the eastern part. Except for the tiny Tamandayi Communal Land, commercial tea estates occupy the entire eastern part of the district, and most of the residents of these estates are Mozambican migrant laborers. This migrant could very well have been a Mozambican tea picker who tried to hide his Mozambican nationality for obvious reasons. In one other case, Vhimba residents identified as Zimbabwean a migrant who arrived from the Ratelshoek estate in Chipinge District, but the migrant himself eventually disclosed to me his birth in Gogoi.

36. "Yaigarwa kare. Mafuta akafirei-wo. Maparara akafirei-wo" (Vhimba, 24 April 1997).

37. "Tiyekiye anoda kutonga nzvimbo dzisiri dzake" (Vhimba, 20 March 1995).

38. "Ngatiedze kuita zvido zvemuridzi wenzvimbo ino, David Muhanyi. Kugara nevamwe zvakanaka munharaunda. Chengetai zvipfuyo zvenyu."

39. People used the English expression.

40. S. claimed to have been born on one of the tea estates in eastern Zimbabwe, but his national identity card listed Gogoi, Mozambique, as his place of birth. Probably, his mother lived permanently in Gogoi and gave birth to him during a period of migrant labor in Zimbabwe.

41. A neighbor just outside Mukwiratunhu described Muhanyi as wanting "*kuita* boundary" ("to make a boundary") and desiring that these households "kuti vaite *line* rimwe chete" ("make one line") (Vhimba, 26 July 1997).

42. "Tiri mu*yard* yemungezi" (Vhimba, 23 April 1997).

43. On 16 February 1997, C. L.—having paid for a beer and goat party the previous day—hosted a *kudira* ceremony carried out by Headman Chikware on Hayfield B. C. L. had asked Chikware to perform the ritual in the hope that such spiritual respect would overcome problems plaguing his small sawmill. The sawmill was engaged in the extraction of eucalyptus, which had invaded Hayfield B from the neighboring forestry estates.

44. "Chikware wakabvuta nyika yaMuitire" (Vhimba, 14 April 1995).

4 / COMMUNITY FORESTRY AS LAND-GRABBING IN VHIMBA

1. This figure comprises the "commercial areas," national parks, and safari areas at independence in 1980. See Riddell (1979:20–21), Moyana (1984), Moyo (1995), and Moyo et al. (1991).

2. I borrow this term from Jane I. Guyer (personal communication, 1998).

3. On the democracy of rural district councils, see Murombedzi (1992:19–20). On autonomy from the party, see Dzingirai (1996:23–28). On autonomy from the ministry, see Manyarureni (1995). On financial aspects, see Masuko (1995) and Roe (1995:836–37). For comparisons with decentralization in the 1980s in Zimbabwe, see de Valk and Wekwete (1990) and Helmsing et al. (1991).

4. Rural District Councils Act, sec. 74(1)(a).

5. Chimanimani Rural District Council, Consultative Meeting on Haroni/Vhimba Botanical Reserves, official minutes, 13 June 1995, p. 2 (capitals in original).

6. Chimanimani Rural District Council, "Gazetting of Chimanimani Rural District Council (Land Use and Conservation By-Laws) Draft (1994)."

7. Chimanimani Rural District Council, "Draft Conservation and Cultivation By-Laws," 4 March 1996, p. 1.

8. Project Appraisal Report, Haroni Banana Project (internal document of European Union microprojects, Zimbabwe), September 1994, p. 1.

9. The document also foresaw twenty-four hectares of banana cultivation to raise revenues for council itself.

10. Ibid., p. 2.

11. While local people insisted that they had received no compensation in cash or kind, local government asserted that they had. See Minutes of the Meeting on SAFIRE Activities, held on 27 April 1995, at DA's office, p. 2.

12. In May 2000, Jaidev Singh (2001:93) found the rural district council had still neither compensated the displaced people nor shared revenues with Vhimba residents in any form besides wages.

13. Ibid.

14. In fact, four of the six initial, elected (non–ex officio) officers were men.

15. Charles Tungamirai is a pseudonym.

16. Vhimba Area Development Committee (VADC), Minutes of First VADC Meeting, 8 December 1994, p. 1.

17. "Vhimba Area Development Committee Constitution," p. 2.

18. VADC, Minutes of Community Meeting—General Assembly, 4 March 1995, pp. 1–2.

19. VADC, Minutes of First Look and Learn Tour, 24 January 1995, p. 6.

20. My minutes of Haroni/Vhimba Consultative Group Meeting, 19 February 1997.

21. VADC, Minutes of Community General Assembly, 6 April 1995, p. 1.

22. VADC, Minutes of Committee Meeting, 20 July 1995, p. 4.

23. Ibid, p. 6.

24. Regarding Nyaminyami Rural District Council, see Murombedzi (1992:19–20). Alexander and McGregor (2000) describe the planning of the Campfire project in Lupane and Nkayi districts in which the two councils were preparing to evict people.

25. Zvidzai Chidhakwa, Project Officer for Vhimba, "Report on the Look-and-Learn Tour to Uzumba-Maramba-Pfungwe's Sunungukai Camp by the Vhimba Area Development Committee," January 1995, p. 8.

26. Ibid., p. 4.

27. VADC, Minutes, personal note of Elias Nyamunda, 6 April 1995.

28. VADC, Minutes of Community Meeting, 4 October 1995, p. 2.

29. Henry Oberlander and Collin Walker (see below) are pseudonyms.

30. My minutes of Haroni/Vhimba Consultative Group Meeting, 19 February 1997.

31. I took the official minutes of this meeting (held on 4 March 1997), translating into English those remarks made in Shona.

32. "Tinongorima papi? KwaMafussi?" (addendum to my minutes of 4 March 1997).

33. "Makaratidziwa nzimbo isiri yenyu . . . council iri kumukanganisa." (Vhimba, 21 April 1997).

34. "Anozotitorera nyika yedu" (Vhimba, 26 July 1997).

35. Had Oberlander been already resident in Vhimba, they might not have

jumped to this conclusion. Two wealthy fruit farmers had already opened licensed retail outlets in Vhimba.

36. Nonetheless, the rural district council acted within the law when it apportioned T.'s field to Oberlander. As the "land authority," it could allocate land to a business, a banana plantation, or any user. The notion of a bounded business center merely helped to justify what the council could have done for any reason.

37. "Muridzi wemunda ndiani?" (Vhimba, 20 May 1997).

38. "Hakuna urongwa usina sabhuku. . . . Hamuna nyika kwaVhimba isina sabhuku" (from my Minutes of VADC Meeting, 25 July 1997).

39. "Tichamurambira!" (ibid.).

40. "Tinoda zvigaro tese!" (ibid.).

41. "Vadya isusu." The second phrase was spoken in English. Had he remembered the 1896–97 war of primary resistance, the speaker would have called for "*Chimurenga* number three" (from ibid.).

42. "*National Parks* akasvika miti iripo. Hapana zvaanoziva pamusoro pemiti. *National Parks* akauya nechikafu chekupa kune shiri dziri muNyakwawa. Asi shiri dziri kudya chikafu changu. Saka shiri ndedzangu" (Vhimba, 15 April 1995).

43. At Vidcos elections of 1997, a plenary meeting elected the officers for all three Vidcos.

44. Young (1970:50). The name is probably related to the Bunga Mountain, now on Tarka Forestry Estate.

45. Oral history collected mostly from the Chikware brothers corroborates Young (1970:50) except that Young refers to the lineage or tribe of "Mutsonu" rather than "Sabunga."

46. "Upenyu hwedu ndokuchengetedza Nyakwawa" (Vhimba, 6 September 1996).

47. They may have been marked with a cut line, as the herpetologist who supported the gazettement reported at the time (Broadley 1974:17).

48. "A Report on the Haroni-Rusitu Botanical Reserves following a Visit by Brian Child, Emmanuel Kawadza, and Cathy Rogers on the 24 August 1993," pp. 4–5.

49. The discrepancy was as large as 55 meters for distances and 1.5 degrees for compass bearings. This latter distortion, amplified over a distance of 2,250 meters led to a further discrepancy of 58 meters.

50. This is a rise of 520 meters over a horizontal distance of 1,400 meters.

51. For a more detailed description of the practices that arose from this uncertainty, particularly regarding the use of watercourses as boundaries, see Hughes (2001c).

52. "Report to the Parks and Wild Life Board concerning the Protection of the Haroni-Rusitu (Lusitu) Botanical Reserves," February 1995, p. 1.

53. Ibid., p. 5.

54. "Tinokumbirawo, Cde. Minister . . . nzvimbo dzedu dzakakosha (*tribal monuments*) dzakadai nge. . . . Gwasha rekwaNyakwawa kwaVhimba . . . Tingachengete

idzi nzvimbo, nyika yedu inozogara yakanaka nekuramba yakapuwa donhodzo ndiMusiki" (printed speech of Phineas Philip Ngorima, Rusitu Mission, 31 March 1995). Cf. "Chief Ngorima Installed," *Manica Post* (Mutare), 7 April 1995, p. 12.

55. These included the business interests (Chipinge Branch of the Wildlife Society and Chimanimani Tourist Association), the security bodies (Zimbabwe Republic Police, Zimbabwe National Army, and Central Intelligence Organisation) and the party, ZANU–PF.

56. "Report to the Parks and Wild Life Board concerning the Protection of the Haroni-Rusitu (Lusitu) Botanical Reserves," February 1995, p. 1. The rural district council was also proposing to lease the botanical reserve from the Parks Department, presumably so as to bring the "squatters" under its protective wing. The Parks Department, however, did not permit such a lease.

57. The Parks Board intended to reform the Parks Department so that it would generate greater revenues and take fewer resources from the national treasury. This imperative probably downgraded the priority of community-based initiatives, such as Campfire.

58. Interview with Mr. Mukwebu, District Warden, Chimanimani District, 1 October 1996.

59. Chimanimani Rural District Council, Minutes of Consultative Meeting on Haroni/Vhimba Botanical Reserves, no. 1/95, 13 June 1995, p. 3.

60. VADC, Minutes of Community Meeting, 3 November 1996, p. 1.

61. "Vodzinga. Vosima ma*banana*" (Vhimba, 18 September 1996).

62. Chimanimani Rural District Council, Minutes of Consultative Meeting on Haroni/Vhimba Botanical Reserves, no. 1/95, 13 June 1995, p. 4.

63. VADC, Minutes of Meeting with Chimanimani Rural District Council, Chimanimani, 22 August 1995, pp. 1–2.

64. In fact, a contemporary member of the Melsetter Rural Council also remembered that the first boundary of the Rusitu Botanical Reserve followed watercourses, rather than straight lines (interview with Frank Elias, Chimanimani, 20 July 1997).

65. "Hakuna muganhu wenzira. Muganhu ngechimvura" (my minutes of VADC Community Meeting, 3 November 1996).

66. "Sabhuku ndiye unoziva muganhu" (ibid.).

67. VADC, Minutes of Community Meeting, 3 November 1996, p. 1.

68. He, in fact, had allocated land within the forest to two families in the mid-1990s. He and Chief Ngorima had evicted the first of these before Nyamunda drafted his map. The second family was a special case: a cattle owner who wished to graze his livestock at a remove from other farmers' fields. After Ngorima's intervention, Chikware also evicted this family shortly after Nyamunda produced the map, leaving only three families within the 1974 boundaries.

69. I, in fact, had helped to schedule that meeting with the invited guests from government departments.

70. At the committee's request and with the permission of the heads of the house-

holds, I had interviewed the sixteen families, added their dates of arrival or birth in Vhimba to the map, and disseminated the map (without names) to relevant government agencies and NGOS. Eventually the map appeared in Lucy Welford's (1998:39) cogent and widely circulated report.

71. "Mauya kutidzinga" (Vhimba, 20 May 1997).

72. For comparisons with the Zambezi Valley, see Derman and Murombedzi (1994) and Hill (1996:112–13).

5 / EXPATRIATE LOGGERS AND MAPMAKERS IN GOGOI

1. As in chapter 1, I use the term *civil war* only as shorthand. Renamo received substantial assistance from Rhodesia, South Africa, Malawi, and Kenya.

2. The district administrator described the northern part of his district as a "problem area" [zona que tem problemas] (conversation with José Gimo, district administrator, Espungabera, 8 November 1996). In mid-1995, a Renamo contingent supported by chiefs had held nearby Dombe, preventing government officers from assuming their posts. By late 1995, "chimwenje" bandits were operating in Dombe and in northern Mossurize. So serious was the chimwenje threat (an attack actually having occurred in Vhimba in 1996) that the Mossurize district administrator forbade me absolutely from carrying out any research in Chief Mafussi's area. We compromised on Gogoi—because its location along the national highway improved security—with the condition that the district administrator was not liable for expenses of repatriating my corpse. (See "Dombe Reclaimed," *Beira Corridor Group Bulletin* [Harare], October 1995, p. 7; Víctor Machirica, "Bando armado ataca e assalta Dombe," *Notícias*, 2 November 1995, p. 1; "Situação em Dombe volta à normalidade," *Notícias*, 3 November 1995, p. 1; "Dombe Revisited," *Beira Corridor Group Bulletin* [Harare], December 1995, p. 6; "Suspected Chimwenje Gang Shoots Two Dead," *Sunday Mail* [Harare], 5 May 1996.)

3. For general descriptions of these periods, see Liesegang (1967) and Newitt (1981, 1995).

4. See Gengenbach (1998) for a description of contemporary land conflicts in the similarly densely populated Nkomati Valley.

5. Another element in the corridor—not mentioned in the text because its existence was debatable—is the alleged emigration of Zimbabwean smallholders to farming areas north of Machipanda. (See "Rural Folk Scramble for Land in Mozambique" *Horizon* [Harare], November 1994, pp. 8–9; Severino Sumbe, "Zimbabweanos não estão a usurpar terras em Moçambique," *Domingo* [Maputo], 29 January 1995.)

6. Demobilized Renamo and Frelimo soldiers also appear to have accommodated one another, as Chris Dolan and Jessica Schafer (1997:138–41) find in a study based, in part, on data from Espungabera.

7. I will use the company name "Continental Timbers" in reference to its activities and those of its subsidiary, the Companhia de Madeiras de Moçambique.

8. For example, "Afrikaners on a Second Great Trek," *Economist,* 30 August 1997, 30.

9. It is impossible to estimate the extent of South African landholding. Many data are not centralized, and South African–owned firms often register themselves as Mozambican businesses. The most noted areas are Niassa Province, where the governments of Mozambique and South Africa negotiated for an explicitly Afrikaner settlement, and the scenic coast of southern Maputo Province (on the latter, see Brouwer 1998; Massinga 1996; McGregor 1997).

10. Not always, however: in 1995, in the Coutada 16 hunting concession (Gaza Province), an Afrikaner employee of the concession holder chased herders away from "his" hunting grounds at gunpoint (Hughes 1995a; cf. Massinga 1996:74).

11. I use pseudonyms for both of these individuals.

12. The *Manual de Legislação Florestal* (DNFFB 1987:16) distinguishes clearly between *licenças simples* for which only *taxas de corte* (cutting charges) apply and *concessões* for which *rendas de terreno* (rent for land) also applies.

13. The delusion appears more reasonable if one takes into account three factors. First, the governor might have given some kind of verbal encouragement that a concession would be forthcoming. He did, after all, attend the opening ceremony of the mill. Nonspeakers of Portuguese might easily interpret the "preference" (mentioned above) as consent. Second, it is difficult to underestimate John's and Piet's disregard for legal institutions and contracts in Mozambique. They avoided the district government in Espungabera. For that reason and because they often allowed their visas to lapse, they regularly crossed the border at the police checkpoint at Mpengo rather than the immigration border post at Espungabera. As regards the concession, the moral right of the Companhia de Madeiras de Moçambique to its colonial concession and the fact of the companhia's presence on the land certainly outweighed legal formalities for these "men of action." Third and finally, the legal system of concessions *was* murky in Mozambique, even to those who tried to understand it. The district administrator in Espungabera firmly believed that the Companhia de Madeiras de Moçambique *did* obtain a concession. Central government might have been involved since it must approve the more expansive concessions. Debates in Maputo had confused other concessions mightily—for example, in the prolonged official and unofficial competition between South African Pulp and Paper Industries and James Blanchard III for land in Matutuíne District, southern Maputo Province (cf. Massinga 1996:75). In such contexts, the truth was not plain to see. In the case of the Companhia de Madeiras de Moçambique, nonetheless, the two Mozambican staff members did confirm that the companhia did not have a concession: so their own misunderstanding and willful ignorance probably accounted for John's and Piet's contrary belief to a much greater degree than did government's own politics.

14. Gogoi, 6 May 1997.

15. "Tinorima kwatinoda" (notes of meeting in Gogoi, 29 April 1997).

16. Personal communication from James Bannerman, 1997.

17. The investment was a Zimbabwean-Mozambican joint venture between Tanganda and Citrinos de Manica located in the most populated parts (also those closest to the border) of Espungabera, Chiurairui, and Dacata administrative areas. Each family would use five hectares allocated as follows: one for tea or coffee, one for other crops, and three for grazing. As of late 1996, the legal rights of families to their five-hectare blocks were unclear, as was the form of tenure of the investment (i.e., as a concession or otherwise). (See "Projecto de chá e café occupará um terço de Mossurize," *Diário de Moçambique* [Beira], 12 September 1996, p. 1.) What did seem to be clear was that smallholders would be compelled to participate. Given their apparent assent at meetings organized for that purpose, the district agricultural officer determined, "São poucas as posiliidades de negar" [There are few possibilities for them to refuse] (interview with Benjamin Ngwenya, Espungabera, 13 March 1997).

18. Environment and Development Group (1994a, 1994b). Chapter 6 of this book discusses this program at length.

19. From Zimbabwe were Matose, Makuku, P. Mushove, B. Sithole, B. Campbell, and C. Chibudu. From Mozambique were Alfonso Madope, B. Chande, C. Quilambo, and John Hatton (the last actually a South African–born resident of Mozambique).

20. In particular, they tired of the virtually obligatory use of English as the language of instruction.

21. Interview, Harare, 28 March 2000.

22. The agency was a member of the Campfire (Communal Areas Management Programme for Indigenous Resources) Collaborative Group (see chapter 6). The idea of the workshop, in fact, originated with Joseph Matowanyika, a Zimbabwean who had recently finished a geography dissertation (1991) on territorial cults and indigenous methods of resource management in Nyanga District, Zimbabwe.

23. This segment of the valley actually lay just outside the transfrontier conservation area. However, given the anticipated tourist potential of the Zimbabwean botanical reserves, the World Bank officer in Maputo thought such a study worthwhile.

24. The organization was CIES (Center for Information and Education for Development). It had started activities in Southern Africa with a small project in Bulawayo, Zimbabwe. The head of the Harare office, Roberto Agnoletto, an Italian and former member of a forestry cooperative, had started CIES's activities in Mozambique.

25. The Ford Foundation funded the costs of that fieldworker as a grant to the Provincial Services of Forestry and Wildlife. Again, a Zimbabwe-influenced person was involved. Although born in Malawi and educated in Britain, Ken Wilson had conducted Ph.D. research in Zimbabwe on smallholders' farming systems and use of wild plants and animals (Wilson 1990). He worked for Ford as program officer in Harare, where his interests gradually shifted toward Mozambique. By the time he moved with his office to Johannesburg, he was responsible for all of Ford's activity in Mozambique.

26. The Carlos Venichand firm did not realize its cutting rights in Mafussi and Mpengo because the terrain made the extraction of logs from forested areas impossible. Madeira Africana de Messica held rights in Mossurize and Sussundenga districts but was felling trees only in the latter.

27. Geomatics were already widespread in land rights projects in Southeast Asia and Latin America (see, e.g., *Cultural Survival Quarterly* 1995).

28. "Serasawe inoda vandu."

29. "Os donos da terra não somos nós. São vocês que vivem aqui" (notes of meeting in Gogoi, 29 April 1997).

30. "A árvore é da comunidade. Não é do João" (notes of meeting in Gogoi, 29 April 1997).

31. Gogoi people understood these forests somewhat differently from Vhimba residents. In Vhimba, such forests were sacred (*–era*): they had the same quality of respect owed to totems and objects associated with the dead. Vhimba's sacred grove, in fact, held all the graves of dead headmen or other ancestors. In Gogoi, special forests cause fear (*–tyisa*). People associate them not so much with who was buried there (although some are inhabited by spirits of the precolonial era) but rather by what strange, seemingly supernatural phenomena occur there, such as constant rain, strange noises, strange winds, etc.

32. "*Company* yacho ichafanira kuteera zvido zvenyu. Haichabvumirwi kutema makwasha akakosha kana mimbuti yakakosha kana mimbuti inoshandiswa nemi" (notes of meeting in Gogoi, 29 April 1997).

33. Unfortunately, the map is too detailed to reproduce here.

34. "Está lá, no campo" (interview with Francisco Zianja, chefe de posto, Dacata, Mossurize, 7 July 1997).

35. Serra Bissaluteza on the standard 1:50,000, sheet no. 892.

36. "Hatitengesi nyika!" (Gogoi, 9 July 1997).

37. This statement was, nonetheless, a compromise. A few months earlier, the district administrator had speculated that he would villagize smallholders in southern Mossurize in order to make way for a hunting concession.

38. See CIES (1997). "Inventário participativo dos recursos em Macuiana" (Maputo).

PART 3 / NATIVE QUESTIONS

1. I use the categories "agency" and "organization" to encompass governmental and nongovernmental not-for-profit bodies. Perhaps more so than in the fields of agriculture or health (Bratton 1989), NGO bodies exchange information, funds, and personnel regularly with state entities. Faculty at public universities, in particular, straddles any gap between state and nonstate worlds.

2. During 1995–97, I engaged myself as a consultant twice to the World Bank

and once to an Italian NGO in Mozambique. Meanwhile, I held a research associate-ship at the Centre for Applied Social Sciences (see below) at the University of Zimbabwe. Finally, in 1999, I consulted for a Zimbabwean NGO.

3. Both quotations are from Escobar (1995:108). Escobar makes clear that he is interested in "forms of social consciousness that are . . . the property of organiza-tions" rather than in the discussion and dissension among individuals within organizations (ibid.).

4. Because donors and expatriates wrote many of Mozambique's most cited doc-uments in English, Lusophone civil servants operated with particular independence from the printed page. All documents had difficulty leaving Maputo, frequently arriv-ing with great delay, as a single copy per province (where many offices lacked both a photocopier and funds for photocopying), or simply never appearing. Robins (1994) criticizes Ferguson for the "reification of text," and, in a similar vein, Riles (2000:81–89) describes the ways in which international treaty documents are "used" rather than read.

5. I use "intellectual" and "intelligentsia" in an attempt to include more, rather than fewer, people within those categories. See Feierman (1990) for a more thor-ough effort with respect to "peasant intellectuals."

6. Interview, Washington, DC, 8 January 2001. Haas (1992) would describe this cult as an "epistemic community."

7. Bornstein (2003), Crewe and Harrison (1998), and Riles (2000) are among the few to publish such ethnographies. To appreciate the subtlety of a people-centered stance, compare the "Campfire Thought" section in chapter 6 with its equivalent in an earlier, less ethnographic, and more policy-focused article (Hughes 2001b).

6 / OPEN NATIVE RESERVES OR NONE?

1. I use this concept of "entitlement" in its colloquial sense: goods that one is guaranteed and for which one need not articulate or defend claims. This definition corresponds roughly to Amartya Sen's category of "endowment" (Sen 1981; cf. Leach, Mearns, and Scoones 1999:232–33).

2. Communal Areas Management Programme for Indigenous Resources.

3. Moyo (2000:151–52) makes a similar argument.

4. The *sjambok* is a hippo-hide whip. The diary is excerpted in G. B. D. Moodie, "The Undaunted: The Story of the Moodie Trek and the Early Days of the Melsetter Settlement," p. 138, NAZ, MO 11/4.

5. L. C. Meredith, NC, Melsetter, to CNC, Salisbury, 20 October 1897, NAZ, NUE 2/1/2. Eventually, however, Meredith did repossess all but two of the Moodie farms for want of "beneficial occupation" (Burrows 1954:158).

6. In the midst of a tour of Melsetter estates, this quotation derives from the 29 April 1900 entry in the diary of Carl Peters (1902:252).

7. The claim would apply to all uses of natural resources were it not for fishing, the felling of indigenous trees by the Rhodesia Native Timber Corporation (chiefly in Gwai, western Zimbabwe), and mining (McGregor 1991:452; Vincent Machangaidze, personal communication, 10 November 2000). Only the last of these activities involved permanent installations.

8. With the Land Apportionment Act of 1930, formal racial segregation closed an important loophole: upwardly mobile blacks had been legally (though not practically) able to buy commercial farms. The act limited such acquisitions to "African Purchase areas" set off from white agriculture (Palmer 1977:135–36).

9. Zimbabwe Reports, 1949–72, Rusitu District Conference, 1952, SIM, AEF, British Council, box 28. Native commissioners, nonetheless, were disposed to make exceptions for Missions. The Rusitu Mission did eventually acquire additional land in Muusha Reserve.

10. Beard (1988:235–73) provides a compelling pictorial account of the death.

11. The term derives from the ecological theory of island biogeography, which exerted a strong influence on African conservation (MacArthur and Wilson 1967:176; cf. Western 1994:42). Some experts, however, still subscribe to a minority view that stochastic crashes of the elephant population are normal and could be expected even absent humans (Richard Bell, personal communication, 18 June 2001).

12. In this way, Child (1996:361) initiated Operation Windfall (Wildlife Industries New Development for All), the precursor to Campfire.

13. Interview, Harare, 13 July 1999. David Cumming of WWF-Harare compiled comprehensive maps of drainage basins, species habitats, centers of endemism, and other transboundary "eco-regions" in Southern Africa (Cumming 1999: figs. 2.2–2.20).

14. Many such boosters, however, were also speculators, attempting to manipulate public opinion in order to make their predictions come true (Cronon 1991:31–41). Boosters of Southern African ecotourism, by contrast, believed fully in their assertions.

15. Interview, Hayfield B, 23 July 1997.

16. Patrick Bond (1998:401) argues that many foreigners visited Zimbabwe precisely because structural adjustment had weakened its currency. Tourism owed its boom, in part, to economic woe in most other sectors and in the lives of ordinary Zimbabweans.

17. The migrations had already begun in Gokwe in the 1960s and accelerated in the 1980s (Nyambara 1999:124–95; Worby 1998b:567; Zinyama and Whitlow 1986:373).

18. Even authors sympathetic to migrants use this terminology, helping to conflate foreignness to a locality with foreignness to Zimbabwe (Dzingirai 1994, 2000; Nyambara 1999, 2001).

19. As opposed to Metcalf's "communal Africa," Angela Cheater (1990) (cf. Bruce 1988:24–25) argues that men as well as women had owned and bequeathed land virtually as private property.

20. Nyambara (1999:441). Some migrants, however, settled together with their own chiefs and headmen, thus empowering a transplanted leadership.

21. Both quotations are from an interview, Harare, 28 March 2000.

22. For the cattle-wildlife comparison, see Jansen, Bond, and Child (1992).

23. Versions of this remark also appeared in print (Child and Peterson 1991:39; Murphree 1991:14; cf. Munro 1998:277).

24. Ivan Bond, personal communication, 15 September 2000. Ivan Bond (2001:235–36) shows that, during the period 1989–93, median annual household income from Campfire (in all the wards involved in the program for the given year) varied from 21 percent to 2 percent of the figure from agriculture. Even if one doubles those percentages to reflect the 53 percent of total Campfire revenues absorbed by rural district councils, wildlife underperforms agriculture. Thus, sport-hunting enterprises only benefit smallholder households when they *supplement*—and do not *replace*—agriculture. In Vhimba, land scarcity permits only the latter, zero-sum possibility.

25. D. Gordon (1993:78–82). Reviewing a similar program in Zambia, Gibson and Marks (1996) found that hunters switched to more covert tactics, such as snaring.

26. Scholars and practitioners have amply discussed the ways in which rural district councils centralized funds and power under Campfire (Campbell, Sithole, and Frost 2000; Derman and Murombedzi 1994:125–27; Duffy 2000:107–11; Gibson 1999:113; Hill 1996:114; Murombedzi 1992; Murphree 1997:21).

27. Matzke and Nabane (1996:77–81); Murphree (1991:10). Early on, a Parks Department ecologist expressed the ambivalent nature of these fences as follows: "[T]he project *cannot* promote wildlife management—through *restriction of access to arable and grazing lands*—as a replacement for traditional crop and livestock productions. Instead, it must be viewed as a complementary system which is compatible with the established system. One element of this compatibility is to protect, people, crops, and livestock from marauding wildlife by *fencing the village areas off from the game management areas*" (Murindagomo 1990:130 [emphasis added]; cf. Wunder 1997:261–62; Duffy 2000:98–99).

28. Interview, Harare, 26 March 2000.

29. Interview, Harare, 29 March 2000.

30. Quoted in Madzudzo (1996:7). For an earlier assessment, see Murphree (1989). Alexander and McGregor (2000:621) describe a Campfire-related eviction in nearby Lupane Communal Land.

31. Interview, Kabuba, Binga District, 7 July 1994. I am grateful to Vupenyu Dzingirai for allowing me to accompany him during fieldwork.

32. "ZANU(PF) Intervenes in Binga Row," *Bulawayo Chronicle*, 22 May 1994.

33. The second quotation is from S. L. Lunga's (1999) printed text, and the first from his oral comment during the subsequent discussion (my notes from International Conference on Natural Resource Management, University of Zimbabwe, Harare, 27 January 1999).

34. Adams and McShane (1992:63–66); Bonner (1993). Zimbabwe, Namibia, and Botswana did obtain a highly circumscribed exemption at the 1997 conference of parties, held fortuitously in Harare.

35. In doing so, lobbyists engaged in a ploy. The convention affected only the export of culled ivory, not sport-hunted trophies.

36. My notes from International Conference on Natural Resource Management, University of Zimbabwe, Harare, 26–29 January 1999 (cf. Murombedzi 1997:15).

37. Interview, Harare, 28 March 2000.

38. Interview, Harare, 23 August 1999.

39. In fact, the particular organization that sent its fieldworker to Vhimba in 1994 was motivated primarily by a desire to resolve the political and territorial conflict between local people and the Parks Department (see chapter 4).

40. "Working Party D District Survey, Melsetter," 2 November 1962, National Records Office, Harare, file 5.2.8R/82725. I am grateful to Jocelyn Alexander for sharing with me her notes on this document. The National Records Office appears to have lost the original.

41. Neglected by all previous studies (cited below), these data derive from the "production books" of the Nyakwawa and Marirangwe groups of the Rusitu Valley Fruit Growers Association. Because farmers used no inputs, revenues from sales are equivalent to profit plus the cost of labor. The production books indicate only a portion of each member's harvest of bananas. Depending on price and terms, farmers often marketed outside the association. Hence, total production might have gone much higher. I counted as members only those people who marketed bananas through the groups in a given year. Hence, the total number of producers varies from year to year, as does the identity of the top five producers. Official exchange rates apply to 1 July of the given year (8.21, 8.56, and 9.86 for 1994–96). All figures are in current dollars, and the U.S. dollar was stable during this period.

42. These are pseudonyms. The income figure is for 1995, as recorded in the production books of the Rusitu Valley Fruit Growers Association. The field size (2.3 hectares) derives from my examination of the Zimbabwe surveyor general's 1996 aerial photograph no. 077 (Chipinge series). Wilbert Yaibva himself stated his field size as roughly 2 hectares and his number of banana plants as 2,600 at 3–meter intervals (giving a field size of 2.34 hectares) (interview, Vhimba, 4 February 1997).

43. E. K. Madenyika, "Project Appraisal Report: Haroni Banana Project," Harare: European Community Microjects, 16 September 1994, p. 11. The pretax figure was based on a 1 September 1994 exchange rate of 8.20. Bananas were to be planted at only 2–meter intervals, rather than at Yaibva's 3–meter spacing. The council also assumed perfect transportation and zero spoilage, conditions certainly not experienced by Yaibva. Nonetheless, as the banana plants matured, the chairman of the rural district council announced a comparably high figure: "Chimanimani to Earn $3M from Bananas," *Herald* (Harare), 1 May 1995, p. 6.

44. The figure represents profits plus the wage bill for staff. The author of the report included this cost because jobs would constitute a benefit to the community (SAFIRE 1996:19, 27). Thus, the comparison with smallholders' banana revenue (where labor was the only cost) is exact. The exchange rate refers to 1 January 1996 (9.33).

45. Henry Oberlander is a pseudonym.

46. Helen Steward, "Report to Vhimba Consultative Committee," 20 May 1997, p. 4. The British organization Voluntary Service Overseas paid Steward's salary.

47. Ibid.

48. Interview, Harare, 8 July 2000. Walker had never been to Harlem.

49. Interview, Chipinge District, 28 July 1999. Terry Eagle is a pseudonym.

50. Interview, Chipinge, 2 August 1999.

51. Much of the area is currently cultivated or under crop rotation, and the soil, rainfall, and agro-ecological classifications are equivalent to those of the banana plantation (Bromley et al. 1968: maps 1, 2, and 4).

52. Interview, Chimanimani, 12 July 2000.

53. Chimanimani Rural District Council, "Draft Tender Notice," 1999, p. 2.

54. Mazambani (1999:29, 32). The conversion rate for 1 August 1999 is 38.4.

55. The aggregate figure derives from the fifth-year estimates of the revenue and expenditure (Mazambani 1999:29, 32–35). I have excluded local salaries from expenditure and—generously—used the exchange rate at the time of the writing of the report (38.4) rather than the rate as of late 2000 (55.0). The per-hectare figure assumes a compound equivalent in size to that proposed by the hotelier above. David Mazambani himself gave no estimate of the amount of land required for tourism.

56. Farai Mutsaka, "'Tourism Recovery Plan Doomed to Fail,'" *Standard* (Harare), 23 July 2000. In the most direct threat to the hospitality industry, paramilitary bands composed of veterans of the liberation war occupied tourist lodges in the Save Valley Conservancy ("Farm Invasions Update," Commercial Farmers' Union, Harare, 24 April 2000, 12 May 2000).

57. Interview, Mutare, 9 November 2000. Sixty percent of the guests were businessmen visiting nearby Chipinge town. Such travelers would have no reason to stay in Vhimba. As the only land use within a 250–hectare private forest, the hotel must earn a relatively low rate of profit per hectare even in good times.

58. Interview, Harare, 31 March 2000.

59. Interview, Chimanimani, 13 July 2000.

60. "Report from the Commission for Economic and Social Directives," Frelimo Fourth Party Congress, 1983 (quoted in Isaacman and Isaacman 1983:196).

61. For examples from the natural resources sector, see Booth and Lopes (1994:168) and Hatton and Rocha (1994:212). The former report population density for a three-district zone covering 36,000 square kilometers. The latter cite a figure for Sussundenga District—7,060 square kilometers.

62. Regarding Manica, see MARRP (1993:30, 84–89) and Lubkemann (2000:71–72).

63. My notes of meeting of Gabinete de Coordinação de Desenvolvimento de Mossurize (Gacodemo), Espungabera, 14 May 1997.

64. "Você quer dizer que, aí, em Manica, eles não vivem nas aldeias?" (my notes on Eighth National Meeting on Forestry and Wildlife, Pequenos Lebombos, Mozambique, 19 June 1997).

65. Anglophone expatriate development workers used this phrase.

66. "O pluralismo deve ser respeitado e valorizado" (Lundin and Machava 1995:1:3; cf. Magode 1996).

67. "Mesmo para os que ficaram em casa, a mudança sistemática de nomes em algumas regiões . . . levou a alienação do indivíduo que (só) se reconhece como homen e assim se identifica, enquanto ser social, dentro do seu território" (Lundin 1995:2:89). Jon Unruh (1998:89, 98), a geographer who worked for the U.S.-based Land Tenure Center in Mozambique, reached the same conclusion.

68. "Uma correcta localização espacial de 'quem ocupa quê e aonde.'" Albino Cuna Júnior (1998: 15), of Dinageca, the National Directorate of Geography and the Cadastre, made the comment at a 1998 national meeting on community delimitation.

69. António Ribeiro (1999:91), then head of the Center for Forestry Experimentation, also describes this involvement from firsthand experience (cf. Neumann 1998:209).

70. Respectively, of the Centre for Applied Social Sciences (University of Zimbabwe), International Union for the Conservation of Nature (Harare office), and the Ford Foundation (Harare office).

71. "O que é que vocês caçam?" (my notes from Workshop on Indigenous Knowledge on Natural Resources Management, fieldwork in Sussundenga District, 10 August 1994).

72. "Estes limites carecem de clarificação e registo" (de Sousa, Juma, and Serra 1995:3).

73. For a similar argument with respect to administrative villages in Thailand, see Vandergeest (1996:285, 298).

74. Schafer and Bell (2001); Singh (2001:111); cf. Neumann (1997). Their critiques of community-based natural resource management are entirely warranted to the extent that officials *wish* to project state power. Ana Paula Reis, for instance, initiated efforts to repress bush clearing and hunting within the Chimanimani Transfrontier Conservation Area (Reis 1999:5).

75. "Um zoniamento que nós concordemos" (interview with one of the fieldworkers, Maputo, 14 January 1999).

76. As Schafer and Bell (2001:17) recount, a fieldworker had turned back game scouts who arrived to shoot crop-destroying elephants. That alleged interference incensed some local residents.

77. However, at least one peasant demonstration occurred in Maputo during parliamentary debates regarding the Land Law ("Componeses manifestam-se," *Notícias* [Maputo], 10 July 1997, p. 1).

78. "Áreas piloto com a participação da comunidade na conservação e uso de recursos florestais e faunísticos " (DNFFB 1996:24).

79. The phrase is from Donald G. McNeil, "Thinking Big to Rescue Big Game," *New York Times*, 7 March 1996, p. A4. (cf. Brouwer 1998; Massinga 1996; Tivane 1999).

80. Nelson Chenga, "The 'Forgotten' People of Chinhopo Area," *Herald* (Harare), 28 July 1997, p. 8 (also Nelson Chenga, personal communication, 9 July 1999). Chenga learned of this plan from interviews with local residents.

81. Foloma, Yé, and Wilson (1998:4). Another group of involved individuals, Estevão Filimão, Eduardo Mansur, and Luís Namanha (2000:151), write in the same vein.

82. Interview, Berkeley, California, 30 September 1999.

83. Celebratory material includes Hirschoff (1997–98), Koch (1998), Madope (1999), and two films directed by Lizinio Azevedo: *Tchuma Tchato* (Maputo: Ebano Multimedia, 1997) and *Mariana and the Moon* (Maputo: Ebano Multimedia, 1999). The Ford Foundation funded the films and brought residents of Bawa to the United States in 1996 and 1998. Other organizations paid for a third visit in 1999.

84. Paula Agostini, "The Role of Gaza Safari in the Development of the TFCA Project" (Maputo: World Bank, November 1994), p. 5.

85. David M. Hughes and Filomena Barbosa, "The Socio-economic Impact of the Coutada 16 Hunting Concession on Resident Communities" (Maputo: World Bank, 1995).

86. C. de Bruin, "Transfrontier Conservation Area—Coutada 16: Pilot Project Proposal" (Maputo and Phalaborwa, South Africa: Gaza Safaris, n.d. [1995]), p. 4.

87. The World Bank drew funds from the newly created Global Environment Facility (GEF).

88. The notion faded away in subsequent years. Now the project is known as Gaza-Kruger-Gona reZhou, GKG, or the Great Limpopo (see Hughes 2005).

89. Agostini, "The Role of Gaza Safari in the Development of the TFCA Project," p. 9; emphasis added.

90. My notes on meeting on Transfrontier Conservation Areas Project, Maputo, 3 May 1995.

91. Interview, New York, 28 February 2001.

92. My notes on meeting on Transfrontier Conservation Areas Project, Maputo, 3 May 1995.

93. For descriptions of and contributions to public debate on the land law and related issues (a literature too vast to summarize here), see Pereira and dos Santos Alves (1994), Myers and Weiss (1994), *Extra* (1996), Comissão Interministerial de Revisão da Legislação de Terras (1996), Negrão (1996), Kloeck-Jenson (1997), and—regarding Campanha Terras's massive education of peasants on their new rights—Campanha Terra (1998) and Negrão (1999).

94. "O que é concessão?" (my notes on Eighth National Meeting on Forestry and Wildlife, Pequenos Lebombos, 20 June 1997).

95. "As concessões são uma via de desenvolvimento. . . . A definição da concessão não pode ser só a exploração" (ibid.).

96. "Princípio de Guarda Florestal e Faunística." "Os direitos e deveres . . . controlo e gestão dos recursos florestais e dos animais bravios . . . nas respectivas áreas concessionadas." "Projecto de decreto—recursos florestais e faunísticos" (version 3 [1997], capítulo 1, secção 1, articles 12 and 16).

97. "Nós pensamos que o concessionário é dono de tudo, pois tem animais, pois tem pessoas" (my notes on Eighth National Meeting on Forestry and Wildlife, Pequenos Lebombos, 20 June 1997).

98. "Comunidade local: agrupamento de familias . . . áreas agrícolas, sejam cultivadas ou em pousio, florestas, sítios de importância cultural, pastagens, fontes de água e áreas de expansão" (Lei no. 19/97 [Land Law], article 1.1).

99. "Uma equipa da *DNFFB* já esteve perdida durante algumas horas e mesmo a fotografia aérea que trazia não ajudou a encontrar a saída assim, rapidamente" (quoted in "DNFFB identifica 'florestas sagradas,'" *Notícias* [Maputo], 17 October 1996, p. 6).

100. Projecto de Decreto, version 3 (as of June 1997), articles 63–68.

101. Replacing "community demarcation" in about 1998, the phrase signaled a willingness to consider hand-drawn and other nontechnical maps (Anderson 2000:769).

102. "Áreas livres" (Maputo, 21 October 1996).

103. Interview, Harare, 25 July 1999.

104. "Proteger ou isolar" (Kloeck-Jenson 1998:1).

105. By and large, Swaziland and Lesotho, whose whole territories Britain reserved against colonization in the nineteenth century, would have presented better comparisons to chiefdoms in both the Mozambican and early Rhodesian situations. Doubtless, the fetish of national boundaries blinded conference delegates to these cases: they were examining national policy toward chiefdoms within (not coterminous with) current national boundaries. Among nations, the mostly Maputo-based delegates clearly knew nearby South Africa far better than they did Zimbabwe.

106. Personal communication, 3 July 2001.

107. "A criação de condições favoráveis para a integração da comunidade e o sector privado . . . promover o ingresso de novo capital nas áreas rural [*sic*] para o beneficiamento de todos" (Tanner, de Wit, and Madureira 1998:9).

108. Personal communication, 3 July 2001.

109. In this case, the World Bank and the government of Mozambique actually revived a proposal from the 1970s, presumably made moot by Mozambique's independence (Dutton and Dutton 1973; Dutton 1974).

110. "Criar ambiente político para investimentos privados," "mobilização comunitária" (my notes from official opening of Chimanimani Transfrontier Conservation

Area, Chimoio, 11 July 1997). At the same ceremony, I presented preliminary results of the Italian-funded mapping project in Gogoi (see chapter 5).

111. Well known in Southern African conservation circles, the Botswana-based Bell (1987) had publicized his viewpoints, and Jonathan Adams and Thomas McShane (1992:98–108) had later written about him.

112. Interview, Mutare, 6 August 1999.

113. Richard Bell, personal communication, 17 December 1999.

114. Ibid.

115. "Nós não podemos atrair o sector privado antes do que termos uma definição da terra" (Chimoio, 18 July 2000).

116. Lei no. 10/99 (Forestry and Wildlife Law).

117. Debate glossed over people's use of these areas for hunting, for collecting and, in the vocabulary of the Land Law, for future "zones of expansion."

118. According to Lei no. 10/99 (Forestry and Wildlife Law), article 10, subsection 3.

119. "Estamos a decidir sobre a nossa Bíblia." With even greater gravity—and cultural tact—the Shona translator rendered the last phrase as "upenyu hwedu," or "our life." (My notes from Chimanimani Transfrontier Conservation Area meeting, Chimoio, 18 July 2000.)

120. Ken Wilson, "Ecotourism and Resource Management in the Zimbabwean and Mozambican Chimanimani," memorandum of 31 January 1997, p. 14. The Ford Foundation also funded a feasibility study regarding the sale of mushrooms from the area (Reis 1999:2).

121. This phrase was mentioned repeatedly with respect to tourism in an electronic mail discussion of Bell's draft report, 17–22 December 1999. Bell himself reserved the epithet for timber, as opposed to tourism.

122. "A pressão que a gente sente" (Chimoio, 18 July 2000). A year or two earlier, the pressure had been real. Political doubts with respect to Zimbabwe had prompted Zimbabwean tour operators to consider moving capital to Mozambique. Then, European, North American, and South African tourists were still traveling to Zimbabwe, whence they could cross into Mozambique (Ken Wilson, personal communication, 15 May 2001). Since the crisis began, the Zimbabwean hospitality industry appears to have tried to shift investments to Botswana and northern Mozambique (Richard Bell, personal communication, 18 June 2001), thus tapping into visitor markets independent of Zimbabwe. Precisely because of its dependence on Zimbabwe—due to transport routes, marketing, etc.—tourism in central Mozambique benefited from no such capital flight.

123. Interview, Harare, 8 July 2000.

124. "Actividades que nunca vão trazer um grande benefício para a área" (Chimoio, 18 July 2000).

125. Interview, Chimoio-Mutare road, 19 July 2000.

126. Known as the "Zambezi River Valley" zone, the investment haven stretched beyond the river's entire watershed, including northern Manica and Sofala, all of Tete and most of Zambézia Province. The exemption on business income tax applies until 2025.

127. As part of an advocacy campaign of the Organização Rural de Ajuda Mútua, Calengo (2001) presents the most thorough analysis of white Zimbabwean settlement in Manica (cf. "Zim Farmers Welcomed by Chissano," *Citizen* [Johannesburg], 23 June 2000).

128. Interview, Harare, 11 November 2000. The scheme's toleration of black smallholders within its borders may explain a cryptic report that "Manica Agriculture and Rural Development provincial director José da Graça allayed fears that the Zimbabwean farmers would expropriate land from the local communities" ("Zimbabwean Farmers to be Settled in Manica," Mozambique News Agency, AIM Reports, no. 199, 23 January 2001).

129. "Pachedu, hatina *development*. Hatina" (Bloomington, Indiana, 1 June 2000). At the Ford Foundation's expense, two community representatives traveled to Bloomington for the meetings of the International Association for the Study of Common Property.

130. "Ninguém saí!" (Maputo, 23 June 1997). In the same spirit, a Washington, DC–based World Bank official had even urged that the Transfrontier Conservation Areas Project refuse to assist or promote any form of resettlement, including voluntary movement (my notes from 3 May 1995, World Bank meeting, Maputo).

131. "Não vamos forçar ninguém a saír" (Chimoio, 19 July 2000; emphasis added).

132. Both quotations are from an electronic mail message posted to World Bank's "Land Policy E-consultation," 16 March 2001. Hanlon (2002:2) quotes the head of the National Directorate of Geography and the Cadastre enunciating the same outlook. In a similar vein, Namanha and his colleagues observed, "The role of the Provincial Forests and Wildlife Services evolved [as a result of Tchuma Tchato] . . . to one of facilitator, conflict manager, and promoter of partnerships" (Filimão, Mansur, and Namanha 2000:145).

133. "Se o operador vem de cima, a comunidade . . . que já não dá para dizer 'não'" (Bloomington, Indiana, 4 June 2000).

134. I examined the books of the installation on 11 November 2002 and found earnings of Z$4,000 for twelve person-nights. (The unofficial exchange rate stood at roughly 1,000.) Council paid the bookkeeper and caretaker Z$5000 per month.

135. Adalima (2004:42) reports the refusal of the Mozambican government to grant one large concession to this scheme, preferring instead to issue numerous, smaller ones.

136. "Nós queremos os bons. Aliás, os melhores. Os bons podem ficar lá" (Chimoio, 18 July 2000).

7 / IN CONCLUSION, THREE LIBERAL PROJECTS REASSESSED

1. "Tinorima kwatinoda" (Gogoi, 29 April 1997).

2. "Hatidi!" (Gogoi, 9 May 1997).

3. "Muno unorima zvaanoda . . . Hakuchina ma*stands*" (Gogoi, 17 July 1997).

4. In discussions of emancipation, Cooper, Holt, and Scott (2000) and Prakash (1990:218–25) reassess "free labor" critically.

5. Rubenstein (1975:18) uses this term in a discussion of the ideology of the Holocaust.

6. This law (Lei no. 2/97), however, stipulated conditions that would delay voting significantly in all nonmunicipal areas.

7. Interview, Chimanimani, 20 July 1997.

8. The "village development committees" created in the early 1980s in Zimbabwe did not provide a helpful guide. They existed plainly to implement government policy, and in Vhimba and many other places, hardly functioned all (chapter 4; Alexander 1993:173–74).

9. Interview, Harare, 12 July 1999.

10. For Zimbabwe, see Moore (1996) and Murphree (1994:418). More generally, see Agrawal and Gibson (1999:634–35) and Brosius, Tsing, and Zerner (1998:165).

11. Personal communication, 3 July 2001. Cf. Tanner (2002:42).

12. In theory, communities could decide on proposals for tourism, but NGOs constantly postponed the vote while they "educated" (or tried to persuade) communities about tourism.

13. To the extent that smallholders would become employees of the hospitality industry, such negotiations also bore a resemblance to collective bargaining between labor unions and management.

14. Vhimba, 21 April 1997.

15. Marongwe (2002:47–50) provides examples of this phenomenon.

16. As reported by one of those threatened: "Toku*torcha*. Tokurova mese" (Mutambara Mission, 13 July 2000).

17. Personal communication, 14 September 2001.

18. For other references to this colonial terminology, see Rutherford (2001:81, 83, 85) and Worby (1998a:57–58).

19. Saul (1993) uses this loaded term. See Pitcher (1996) and Plank (1993) for further debate on its appropriateness.

20. "Transfrontier conservation areas (TFCAs)," as described by the organization's first director, John Hanks, play a "role in socioeconomic development, conserving biodiversity, and promoting a culture of peace." Presented to the "Transboundary Protected Areas" conference, Yale School of Forestry, New Haven, Connecticut, 30–31 March 2001 (cf. Hanks 2000).

21. Personal communication, 3 July 2001.

22. Concurrently, various leaders have embraced an "African Union" similar to the European Union and a "growth triangle" involving Mozambique, Malawi, and Tanzania.

23. A Johannesburg-based planner made the remark at a tourism conference in Bulawayo (Mallows 1972:7).

24. Hanlon (1996) and P. Bond (1998) provided the most thorough critiques of structural adjustment in Mozambique and Zimbabwe, respectively.

25. "Manifesto" of the Movement for Democratic Change (2000: sec. 3.3)

26. "Unongobirwa ne*title deed*" (Vhimba, 12 August 1999).

27. Interview, Chimanimani, 12 July 2000.

28. Myers (1989) questions this logic, citing the example of Pintupi-speaking Australian aborigines for whom a relationship with the land is an integral part of personhood.

29. Hayfield B estate, 23 July 1997.

30. See the beginning of chapter 6 for a discussion of the lack of entitlements in resettled areas.

REFERENCES

Aberly, Doug. 1999. "Interpreting bioregionalism: A story from many voices."
In *Bioregionalism*, ed. Michael Vincent McGinnis, 13–42. London: Routledge.

Adalima, Maria Laimone. 2004. "O processo de ocupação de terra por farmeiros
estrangeiros em Manica: O case do Distrito de Báruè." Tese de Licenciatura,
Universidade Eduardo Mondlane, Maputo.

Adams, Jonathan S., and Thomas O. McShane. 1992. *The Myth of Wild Africa:
Conservation without Illusion.* Berkeley and Los Angeles: University of
California Press.

Africa Resources Trust. n.d. "Community-based tourism: A new direction for
CAMPFIRE." Harare: Africa Resources Trust.

Agrawal, Arun, and Clark C. Gibson. 1999. "Enchantment and disenchantment:
The role of community in natural resource conservation." *World Development*
27(4): 629–49.

———, eds. 2001. *Communities and the Environment: Ethnicity, Gender, and
the State in Community-based Conservation.* New Brunswick, NJ: Rutgers
University Press.

Alexander, Jocelyn. 1993. "The state, agrarian policy and rural politics in
Zimbabwe: Case studies of Insiza and Chimanimani Districts." D.Phil. diss.,
Oxford University, Oxford.

———. 1994. "Terra e autoridade política no pós-guerra em Moçambique:
O caso da Província de Manica." *Arquivo* 16: 5–94.

———. 1995. "Things fall apart, the centre *can* hold: Processes of post-war political change in Zimbabwe's rural areas." In *Society in Zimbabwe's Liberation
War*, ed. N. Bhebe and T. Ranger. Harare: University of Zimbabwe Press.

———. 1997. "The local state in post-war Mozambique: Political practice and
ideas about authority." *Africa* 67(1): 1–26.

Alexander, Jocelyn, and JoAnn McGregor. 2000. "Wildlife and politics: CAMP-FIRE in Zimbabwe." *Development and Change* 31: 605–27.

Alexander, Jocelyn, JoAnn McGregor, and Terence Ranger. 2000. *Violence and Memory: One Hundred Years in the 'Dark Forests' of Matabeleland.* Oxford: James Currey; Harare: Weaver Press.

Allen, Tim, and Hubert Morsink, eds. 1994. *When Refugees Go Home.* Trenton, NJ: Africa World Press.

Allina-Pisano, Eric. 2003. "Borderlands, boundaries, and the contours of colonial rule: African labor in Manica District, Mozambique, c. 1904–1908." *International Journal of African Historical Studies* 36(1): 59–82.

Alpers, Edward A. 1975. *Ivory and Slaves in East Central Africa: Changing Patterns of International Trade to the Later Nineteenth Century.* London: Heinemann.

Anderson, Paul S. 2000. "Mapping land rights in Mozambique." *Photogrammetric Engineering and Remote Sensing* 66(6): 769–75.

Andersson, Jens. 1999. "The politics of land scarcity: Land disputes in Save Communal Area, Zimbabwe." *Journal of Southern African Studies* 25(4): 553–78.

Anstey, Simon, and Camila de Sousa. 2001. "Old ways and new challenges: Traditional resource management systems in the Chimanimani Mountains." In Hulme and Murphree, eds., 195–205.

Arnold, A. J. 1908. "O Território da Companhia de Moçambique: Viagem atravez do Buzi, Mossurize e Govuro." *Boletim da Sociedade de Geografia de Lisboa* 26(5): 141–44.

Arrighi, G. 1970. "Labour supplies in historical perspective: A study of the proletarianization of the African peasantry in Rhodesia." *Journal of Development Studies* 6: 197–234.

Asiwaju, A. I. 1985a. "The conceptual framework." In Asiwaju, ed., 1–18.

———, ed. 1985b. *Partitioned Africans: Ethnic Relations across Africa's International Boundaries, 1884–1984.* London: C. Hurst.

Azevedo, Mario J. 2002. *Tragedy and Triumph: Mozambique Refugees in Southern Africa, 1977–2001.* Portsmouth, NH: Heinemann.

Bannerman, James H. 1978. "Towards a history of the Hlengwe." *Native Affairs Department Annual* 11(5): 483–96.

———. 1981. "Hlengweni: The history of the Hlengwe of the lower Save and Lundi Rivers from the late-eighteenth to the mid-twentieth century." *Zimbabwean History* 12: 1–45.

———. 1993. "Land tenure in central Mozambique: Past and present." Chimoio: Moçambique Agricultural and Rural Reconstruction Programme.

———. 1996. "Distrito de Sussundenga, área administrativa de Dombe: Area report." Chimoio: Moçambique Agricultural and Rural Reconstruction Programme.

Bassett, Thomas J. 1993. "Introduction: The land question and agricultural transformation in Sub-Saharan Africa." In *Land in African Agrarian Systems*, ed. Thomas J. Bassett and Donald E. Crummey, 3–31. Madison: University of Wisconsin Press.

———. 1994. "Cartography and empire building in nineteenth-century West Africa." *Geographical Review* 84(3): 316–35.

Bayart, Jean-François, Achille Mbembe, and Comi Toulabor. 1992. *Le politique par le bas en Afrique noire: Contributions à une problématique de la démocratie*. Paris: Karthala.

Beach, D. N. 1970. "Afrikaner and Shona settlement in the Enkeldoorn area, 1890–1900." *Zambezia* 1(2): 25–34.

———. 1980. *The Shona and Zimbabwe, 900–1850*. Gweru, Zimbabwe: Mambo Press.

———. 1994a. *The Shona and Their Neighbors*. Oxford: Blackwell.

———. 1994b. *A Zimbabwean Past: Shona Dynastic Histories and Oral Traditions*. Gweru, Zimbabwe: Mambo Press.

———. 1997. "Oral tradition in eastern Zimbabwe: The work of Jason Takafa Machiwenyika, c. 1889–1924." Paper presented to "Words and voices: Critical practices of orality in Africa and in African studies" conference, Bellagio, Italy, 24–28 February.

Beard, Peter. 1988. *The End of the Game*. San Francisco: Chronicle Books.

Bell, Richard. 1987. "Conservation with a human face: Conflict and reconciliation in African land-use planning." In *Conservation in Africa: People, Policies, and Practices*, ed. David Anderson and Richard Grove, 79–102. Cambridge: Cambridge University Press.

———. 2000. "Management plan for the Chimanimani Transfrontier Conservation Area." Maputo: World Bank and Direcção Nacional de Florestas e Fauna Bravia.

Berg, P., and R. Dasmann. 1977. "Reinhabiting California." *Ecologist* 7(10): 399–401.

Bernstein, Henry. 1996. "How white agriculture (re)positioned itself for a 'New South Africa.'" *Critical Sociology* 22(3): 9–36.

Berry, Sara. 1989. "Social institutions and access to resources." *Africa* 59(1): 41–55.

———. 1993. *No Condition Is Permanent: The Social Dynamics of Agrarian Change in Sub-Saharan Africa*. Madison: University of Wisconsin Press.

———. 1997. "Tomatoes, land and hearsay: Property and history in Asante in the time of structural adjustment." *World Development* 25(8): 1225–41.

———. 2001. *Chiefs Know Their Boundaries: Essays on Property, Power, and the Past in Asante, 1896–1996*. Portsmouth, NH: Heinemann; Oxford: James Currey.

Bhabha, Homi K. 1992. "Postcolonial authority and postmodern guilt." In *Cultural Studies*, ed. Lawrence Grossberg, Cary Nelson, and Paula Treichler, 56–68. New York and London: Routledge.

Bhila, H. H. K. 1982. *Trade and Politics in a Shona Kingdom: The Manyika and Their Portuguese and African Neighbors, 1575–1902.* Harlow, UK, and Harare: Longman.

Bodmer, Richard E. 1994. "Managing wildlife with local communities in the Peruvian Amazon: The case of the Reserva Comunal Tamshiyacu-Tahuayo." In Western and Wright, eds., 113–34.

Bohannan, Paul. 1955. "Some principles of exchange and investment among the Tiv." *American Anthropologist* 57: 60–70.

———. 1963. "'Land,' 'tenure' and land tenure." In *African Agrarian Systems,* ed. D. Biebuyck, 101–11. London: Oxford University Press.

Bond, Ivan. 2001. "CAMPFIRE and the incentives for institutional change." In Hulme and Murphree, eds., 227–43.

Bond, Patrick. 1998. *Uneven Zimbabwe: A Study of Finance, Development, and Underdevelopment.* Trenton, NJ: Africa World Press.

Bonner, Raymond. 1993. *At the Hand of Man: Peril and Hope for Africa's Wildlife.* New York: Knopf.

Booth, Vernon, and Leonel Lopes. 1994. "The feasibility of TFCA development in Gaza Province." In Environment and Development Group, ed., 147–89.

Borges Coelho, João Paulo. 1993. "Protected villages and communal villages in the Mozambican province of Tete, 1968–82: A history of state resettlement policies, development and war." D.Phil. diss., University of Bradford, UK.

———. 1998. "State resettlement policies in post-colonial rural Mozambique: The impact of the communal village programme on Tete Province, 1977–1982." *Journal of Southern African Studies* 24(1): 61–91.

Borstein, Erica. 2003. *The Spirit of Development: Protestant NGOs, Morality, and Economics in Zimbabwe.* New York and London: Routledge.

Bourdillon, M. F. C. 1978. "The cults of Dzivaguru and Karuva amongst the north-eastern Shona peoples." In *Guardians of the Land: Essays on Central African Territorial Cults,* ed. J. M. Schoffeleers. Gweru, Zimbabwe: Mambo Press.

Bowen, Merle. 2000. *The State against the Peasantry: Rural Struggles in Colonial and Postcolonial Mozambique.* Charlottesville: University of Virginia Press.

Bradford, J. E. S., and A. C. Gauld. 1952. *The Geodetic Triangulation and Trigonometrical Survey of Southern Rhodesia, 1897–1952.* Salisbury: Southern Rhodesia Department of the Surveyor General.

Braga, Carla. 2001. "'They are squeezing us!' Gender, matriliny, power, and agricultural policies." In *Strategic Women, Gainful Men: Gender, Land and Natural Resources in Different Rural Contexts in Mozambique,* ed. Rachel Waterhouse and Carin Vijfhuizen, 199–225. Maputo: Land Studies Unit (Núcleu de Estudos da Terra, Universidade Eduardo Mondlane).

Bratton, Michael. 1989. "The politics of government-NGO relations in Africa." *World Development* 17(4): 569–87.

Braudel, Fernand. 1981. *The Structures of Everyday Life*. Vol. 1. New York: Harper and Row.

Broadley, Donald G. 1974. "The Lusitu Forest: A new protected area." *Wild Rhodesia* 3: 17.

Bromley, K. A., R. C. Hannington, G. B. Jones, and C. J. Lightfoot. 1968. *Melsetter Regional Plan*. Salisbury: Department of Conservation and Extension.

Brosius, J. Peter. 1995. "Voices from the Borneo rainforest: Writing the biography of an environmental campaign." Presented to the conference "Environmental discourses and human welfare in South and Southeast Asia," Volcanoes, Hawaii, 28–30 December.

Brosius, J. Peter, Anna Lowenhaupt Tsing, and Charles Zerner. 1998. "Representing communities: Histories and politics of community-based natural resource management." *Society and Natural Resources* 11: 157–68.

Brouwer, Roland. 1998. "Setting the stake: Common and private interests in the redefinition of resources and their access in the Machangulo Peninsula, Mozambique." Paper presented to the meeting of the International Association for the Study of Common Property, Vancouver, Canada, 10–14 June.

Bruce, John W. 1988. "A perspective on indigenous land tenure systems and land concentration." In *Land and Society in Contemporary Africa*, ed. R. E. Downs and S. P. Reyna, 23–51. Hanover, NH: University Press of America.

Burrows, Edmund H. 1954. *The Moodies of Melsetter*. Cape Town and Amsterdam: A. A. Balkema.

Calengo, André Jaime. 2001. "Investigação sobre o programa de fixação de farmeiros zimbabweanos na Província de Manica." Maputo: Organização Rural de Ajuda Mútua.

Campanha Terra. 1998. *Manual para Melhor Compreender a Nova Lei de Terras*. Maputo: Campanha Terra.

Campbell, Bruce M., Bevelyn Sithole, and Peter Frost. 2000. "CAMPFIRE experiences in Zimbabwe." *Science* 287: 42–43.

Capela, José. 1993. *O Escravismo Colonial em Moçambique*. Porto: Edições Afrontamento.

Capela, José, and Eduardo Medeiros. 1987. *O Tráfico de Escravos de Moçambique para as Ilhas do Índico, 1720–1902*. Maputo: Imprensa Nacional de Moçambique.

Carney, Judith, and Michael Watts. 1990. "Manufacturing dissent: Work, gender and the politics of meaning in a peasant society." *Africa* 60(2): 207–41.

Carter, Paul. 1988. *The Road to Botany Bay: An Exploration of Landscape and History*. New York: Knopf.

Caute, David. 1983. *Under the Skin: The Death of White Rhodesia*. Harmondsworth, UK: Penguin Books.

Cheater, Angela. 1990. "The ideology of 'communal' land tenure in Zimbabwe: Mythogenesis enacted?" *Africa* 60(2): 188–206.

Child, B., and J. H. Peterson. 1991. "CAMPFIRE in rural development: The Beitbridge experience." Joint Working Paper, Branch of Terrestrial Ecology, Department of National Parks and Wildlife Management, Harare, and Centre for Applied Social Sciences, University of Zimbabwe, Harare.

Child, Brian. 1993. "Zimbabwe's CAMPFIRE programme: Using the high value of wildlife recreation to revolutionize natural resource management in communal areas." *Commonwealth Forestry Review* 72(4): 284–96.

Child, Graham. 1996. "The role of community-based wild resource management in Zimbabwe." *Biodiversity and Conservation* 3: 355–67.

Chimanimani District Environmental Team. 1999. "Environmental Review Report for Vhimba Eco-Tourism Project." Chimanimani District Environmental Team, Chimanimani, Zimbabwe.

Chingono, Mark F. 1996. *The State, Violence, and Development: The Political Economy of War in Mozambique.* Aldershot, UK: Avebury.

Chinodya, Shimmer. 1982. *Dew in the Morning.* Gweru, Zimbabwe: Mambo Press.

Christopher, A. J. 1971. "Land policy in Southern Africa during the nineteenth century." *Zambezia* 2(1): 1–9.

———. 1974. "Government land policies in Southern Africa." In *Frontier Settlement,* ed. R. G. Ironside et al., 208–25. Studies in Geography, Monograph no. 1. Edmonton, Canada: University of Alberta.

CIES (Center for Information and Education for Development). 1997. "Inventário florestal de Gogoi." Unpublished document.

Clarence-Smith, W. G. 1975. "The Thirstland Trekkers in Angola: Some reflections on a frontier society." *Collected Seminar Papers on Southern Africa,* vol. 6. University of London.

Clifford, James. 1997. *Routes: Travel and Translation in the Late Twentieth Century.* Cambridge, MA: Harvard University Press.

Cobbing, Julian R. D. 1988. "The Mfecane as alibi: Thoughts on Dithakong and Mbolompo." *Journal of African History* 29(3): 487–519.

Cohen, David William. 1992. "The banalities of interpretation." *Public Culture* 5(1): 57–60.

Colônia de Moçambique. 1931. "Territoire de Manica et Sofala sous l'Administration de la 'Companhia de Moçambique'—Cadastre, Service de l'Arpentage." Publication for the International Colonial Exposition, Paris.

Colson, Elizabeth. 1971. "The impact of the colonial period on the definition of land rights." In *Colonialism in Africa, 1870–1960,* ed. Victor Turner, 3: 193–215. Cambridge: Cambridge University Press.

Comaroff, Jean. 1985. *Body of Power, Spirit of Resistance: The Culture and History of a South African People.* Chicago: University of Chicago Press.

Comaroff, John L. 1978. "Rules and rulers: Political processes in a Tswana chiefdom." *Man, n.s.,* 13: 1–12.

Comissão Interministerial de Revisão da Legislação de Terras. 1996. "Conferência Nacional de Terras, Maputo, 5 a 7 de junho de 1996." Maputo: Comissão Interministerial de Revisão da Legislação de Terras.

Companhia de Moçambique. 1902. *O Territorio de Manica e Sofala e a Administração da Companhia de Moçambique (1892–1900)*. Lisbon: Companhia Nacional Editora.

Cooper, Frederick, Thomas C. Holt, and Rebecca J. Scott. 2000. *Beyond Slavery: Explorations of Race, Labor, and Citizenship in Postemancipation Societies*. Chapel Hill: University of North Carolina Press.

Cooper, Frederick, and Ann L. Stoler. 1989. "Tensions of empire: Colonial control and visions of rule." *American Ethnologist* 16(4): 609–21.

Coquery-Vidrovitch, Catherine. 1976. "The political economy of the African peasantry and modes of production." In *The Political Economy of Contemporary Africa*, ed. P. Gutkind and I. Wallerstein, 90–116. Beverly Hills, CA: Sage.

Corris, P. 1968. *Aborigines and Europeans in Western Victoria*. Canberra: A.I.A.S.

Crais, Clifton C. 1992. *White Supremacy and Black Resistance in Pre-Industrial South Africa*. Cambridge: Cambridge University Press.

Crewe, Emma, and Elizabeth Harrison. 1998. *Whose Development? An Ethnography of Aid*. London: Zed Books.

Cronon, William. 1983. *Changes in the Land: Indians, Colonists, and the Ecology of New England*. New York: Hill and Wang.

———. 1991. *Nature's Metropolis: Chicago and the Great West*. New York and London: W.W. Norton.

Crook, A. O. 1956. "A preliminary vegetation map of the Melsetter Intensive Conservation Area, Southern Rhodesia." *Rhodesia Agricultural Journal* 53(1): 3–25.

Crosby, Alfred W. 1986. *Ecological Imperialism: The Biological Expansion of Europe, 900–1900*. Cambridge: Cambridge University Press.

Cultural Survival Quarterly. 1995. Special issue on geomatics. 18(4).

Cumming, David H. M. 1999. "Study on the development of transboundary natural resource management areas in Southern Africa: Environmental context." Washington, DC: Biodiversity Support Program.

das Neves, Joel Maurício. 1998. "Economy, society and labour migration in central Mozambique, 1930–c.1965: A case study of Manica Province." Ph.D. diss., University of London.

Davison, Jean. 1997. *Gender, Lineage, and Ethnicity in Southern Africa*. Boulder, CO: Westview Press.

de Bruijn, H. S., and Louisa de Bruijn. 1991. "Aspects of the early history of Chimanimani." *History of Zimbabwe* 10: 149–58.

de Soto, Hernando. c. 2000. *The Mystery of Capital: Why Capitalism Triumphs in the West and Fails Everywhere Else*. New York: Basic Books.

de Sousa, Camila, Juma Juma, and António Serra. 1995. "Relatório do trabalho

consultativo na área de conservação transfronteira de Chimanimani."
Maputo: Centro de Experimentação Florestal.

de Valk, P., and K. H. Wekwete, eds. 1990. *Decentralizing for Participatory Planning? Comparing the Experiences of Zimbabwe and Other Anglophone Countries in Eastern and Southern Africa.* Aldershot, UK, and Brookfield, VT: Gower Publishing Co.

Derman, William. 1973. *Serfs, Peasants, and Socialists: A Former Serf Village in the Republic of Guinea.* Berkeley: University of California Press.

————. 1995. "Environmental NGOs, dispossession, and the state: Ideology and praxis of African nature and development." *Human Ecology* 23(2): 199–215.

Derman, William, and James Murombedzi. 1994. "Democracy, development, and human rights in Zimbabwe: A contradictory terrain." *African Rural and Urban Studies* 1(2): 119–43.

DNFFB (Direcção Nacional de Florestas e Fauna Bravia). 1987. *Manual de Legis-lação Florestal.* Maputo: Government of Mozambique.

————. 1996. "Política e estratégia de desenvolvimento florestal e fauna bravia." Maputo: Ministério da Agricultura e Pescas.

Dolan, Chris, and Jessica Schafer. 1997. "The reintegration of ex-combatants in Mozambique: Manica and Zambezia Provinces." Refugee Studies Programme, Oxford University, Oxford.

Doyle, Denis. 1891a. "A journey through Gazaland." *Proceedings of the Royal Geographical Society,* n.s., 13: 588–91, map attached.

————. 1891b. "With King Gungunhana in Gazaland." *Fortnightly Review,* n.s., 50: 112–17.

Dreyfus, Hubert, and Paul Rabinow. 1983. *Michel Foucault: Beyond Structuralism and Hermeneutics.* Chicago: University of Chicago Press.

Drinkwater, Michael. 1991. *The State and Agrarian Change in Zimbabwe's Communal Areas.* New York: St. Martin's Press.

Duffy, Rosaleen. 2000. *Killing for Conservation: Wildlife Policy in Zimbabwe.* Bloomington: Indiana University Press; Oxford: James Currey; Harare: Weaver Press.

Dutton, Paul. 1974. "A new national park planned for the Chimanimani Mountains." *African Wildlife* 28(1): 27–31.

Dutton, T. P., and E. A. R. Dutton. 1973. "Reconhecimento preliminar das mon-tanhas de Chimanimani e zonas adjacentes com vista à criação duma area de conservação." Lourenço Marques: Direcção dos Serviços de Veterinária, Estado de Moçambique.

Dzingirai, Vupenyu. 1994. "Politics and ideology in human settlement: Getting settled in the Sikomena area of Chief Dobola." *Zambezia* 21(2): 167–76.

————. 1995. "'Take back your CAMPFIRE': A study of local level perceptions to electric fencing in the framework of Binga's CAMPFIRE programme." Harare: Center for Applied Social Sciences, University of Zimbabwe.

————. 1996. "'Every man must settle where he wants': The politics of settlement in the context of community wildlife management programme in Binga, Zimbabwe." *Zambezia* 23(1): 19–30.

————. 2000. "Migration and the future of CAMPFIRE in the Zambezi Valley, Zimbabwe." *Commons Southern Africa* (University of the Western Cape, South Africa), 2(1).

Edwards, Pat. 1991. "Early settlers in Chipinge." *Heritage of Zimbabwe* 10: 159–62.

Effler, Dirk. 1995. "Land use and tenure issues in selected areas in the districts of Gondola and Mossurize, Province of Manica." Unpublished paper.

Eldredge, Elizabeth A. 1994. "Delagoa Bay and the hinterland in the early nineteenth century: Politics, trade, slaves, and slave raiding." In Eldredge and Morton, eds., 127–65.

Eldredge, Elizabeth A., and Fred Morton, eds. 1994. *Slavery in South Africa: Captive Labor on the Dutch Frontier*. Boulder, CO: Westview Press; Pietermaritzburg, South Africa: University of Natal Press.

Environment and Development Group, ed. 1994a. "GEF transfrontier conservation and institution strengthening project." Oxford.

————. 1994b. "GEF transfrontier conservation areas and institution strengthening project: Preparation studies." Maputo: Direcção Nacional de Florestas e Fauna Bravia.

Erskine, St. Vincent. 1875. "Journey to Umzila's, south-east Africa, in 1871–1872." *Journal of the Royal Geographical Society* 45: 45–128.

————. 1878. "Third and fourth journeys in Gaza, or southern Mozambique, 1873 to 1874, and 1874 to 1875." *Journal of the Royal Geographical Society* 48: 25–56.

Escobar, Arturo. 1995. *Encountering Development: The Making and Unmaking of the Third World*. Princeton, NJ: Princeton University Press.

Extra. 1996. Special issue on "Anteprojecto da Lei de Terras em debate público." (Maputo), no. 17 (June).

Fairhead, James, and Melissa Leach. 1996. *Misreading the African Landscape: Society and Ecology in a Forest-Savanna Mosaic*. Cambridge: Cambridge University Press.

Feierman, Steven. 1990. *Peasant Intellectuals: Anthropology and History in Tanzania*. Madison: University of Wisconsin Press.

Ferguson, James. 1990. *The Anti-Politics Machine: "Development," Depoliticization, and Bureaucratic Power in Lesotho*. Cambridge: Cambridge University Press.

————. 1999. *Expectations of Modernity: Myths and Meanings of Urban Life on the Zambian Copperbelt*. Berkeley: University of California Press.

Ferraz, Bernardo, and Barry Munslow, eds. 1999. *Sustainable Development in Mozambique*. Oxford: James Currey.

Filimão, Estevão, Eduardo Mansur, and Luís Namanha. 2000. "Tchuma Tchato: An evolving experience of community-based natural resource management in

Mozambique." In *Proceedings of the International Workshop on Community Forestry in Africa*, 145–52. Rome: Food and Agriculture Organization.

Finnegan, William. 1992. *A Complicated War: The Harrowing of Mozambique.* Berkeley and Los Angeles: University of California Press.

Flower, Ken. 1987. *Serving Secretly.* London: John Murray.

Flynn, Donna K. 1997. "'We are the border': Identity, exchange, and the state along the Bénin-Nigeria border." *American Ethnologist* 24(2): 311–30.

Foloma, Marcelino, Sérgio Pereira Yé, and K. B. Wilson. 1998. "Transcending boundaries of scale: Experiences in Mozambique's Tchuma Tchato program." Paper presented to the meeting of the International Association for the Study of Common Property, Vancouver, Canada, 10–14 June.

Fortmann, Louise. 1995. "Talking claims: Discursive strategies in contesting property." *World Development* 23(6): 1053–63.

Fortmann, Louise, and John Bruce. 1988. *Whose Trees: Proprietary Dimensions of Forestry.* Boulder, CO: Westview Press.

———. 1993. "Tenure and gender issues in forest policy." In *Living with Trees: Policies for Forestry Management in Zimbabwe's Communal Lands,* ed. P. N. Bradley and K. McNamara, 199–210. Washington, D.C.: World Bank.

Fredrickson, George M. 1981. *White Supremacy: A Comparative Study in American and South African History.* Oxford: Oxford University Press.

Frelimo. 1982 [1978]. *History of Frelimo.* Harare: Longman.

Garbett, G. Kingsley. 1966. "Religious aspects of politics succession among the Valley Korekore (N. Shona)." In *The Zambesian Past,* ed. Eric Stokes and Richard Brown, 137–70. Manchester: Manchester University Press.

———. 1977. "Disparate regional cults and a unitary ritual field in Zimbabwe." In *Regional Cults,* ed. R. P. Werbner, 55–92. London: Academic Press.

Geertz, Clifford. 1980. *Negara: The Theatre State in Nineteenth-Century Bali.* Princeton, NJ: Princeton University Press.

Gengenbach, Heidi. 1998. "'I'll bury you in the border!' Women's land struggles in post-war Facazisse (Magude District), Mozambique." *Journal of Southern African Studies* 24(1): 7–36.

Gersony, Robert. 1988. "Summary of Mozambican refugee accounts of principally conflict-related experience in Mozambique." Unpublished report, Washington, DC.

Gibson, Clark C. 1999. *Politicians and Poachers: The Political Economy of Wildlife Policy in Africa.* Cambridge: Cambridge University Press.

Gibson, Clark C., and Stuart A. Marks. 1996. "Transforming rural hunters into conservationists: An assessment of community-based wildlife management programs in Africa." *World Development* 23: 941–57.

Godwin, Peter. 1996. *Mukiwa: A White Boy in Africa.* New York: HarperCollins.

Goodier, R., and J. B. Phipps. 1962–63. "A vegetation map of the Chimanimani National Park." *Kirkia* 3: 2–7.

Goody, Jack. 1971. *Technology, Tradition, and the State in Africa*. London: Oxford University Press.

Gordon, Donald L. 1993. "From marginalization to centre-stage? A community's perspective on Zimbabwe's CAMPFIRE programme." Master's thesis, York University, North York, Ontario, Canada.

Gordon, Robert. 1989. "Can Namibian San stop dispossession of their land?" In Wilmsen, ed. 138–54.

Grant, S. C. N. 1893. "The Anglo-Portuguese Delimitation Commission in East Africa." *Scottish Geographical Magazine* 9: 337–47.

Gray, John. 1995. *Liberalism*. 2nd ed. Minneapolis: University of Minnesota Press.

Groen, Gerrit D. 1974. "The Afrikaners in Kenya, 1903–1969." Ph.D. diss., Michigan State University, East Lansing, MI.

Grundy, Isla, and Gus Le Breton. 1997–98. "The SAFIRE MITI Programme— a new approach to natural resource management in communal areas of Zimbabwe." *Rural Development Forestry Network* (Overseas Development Institute, London), Network Paper 22e: 15–28.

Guha, Ramachandra. 1997. "The authoritarian biologist and the arrogance of anti-humanism: Wildlife conservation in the Third World." *Ecologist* 27(1): 14–19.

Guinier, Lani. 1994. *The Tyranny of the Majority: Fundamental Fairness in Representative Democracy*. New York: Free Press.

Gupta, Akhil. 1997a. "Culture, power, place: Ethnography at the end of an era." In *Culture, Power, Place: Explorations in Critical Anthropology*, ed. Akhil Gupta and James Ferguson, 1–29. Durham, NC: Duke University Press.

———. 1997b. "Discipline and practice: 'The field' as site, method, and location in anthropology." In *Anthropological Locations: Boundaries and Gounds of a Field of Science*, ed. Akhil Gupta and James Ferguson, 1–46. Berkeley and Los Angeles: University of California Press.

Gupta, Akhil, and James Ferguson. 1992. "Beyond 'culture': Space, identity, and the politics of difference." *Cultural Anthropology* 7(1): 6–23.

Guyer, Jane I. 1993. "Wealth in people and self-realization in equatorial Africa." *Man*, n.s., 28(2): 242–65.

———. 1995. "Wealth in people, wealth in things: Introduction." *Journal of African History* 36: 83–90.

Haas, Peter M. 1992. "Epistemic communities and international policy coordination." *International Organization* 46(1): 1–35.

Hancock, Graham. 1989. *Lords of Poverty*. London: Macmillan.

Hancock, W. K. 1958. "Trek." *Economic History Review* 10(3): 331–39.

Hanks, John. 2000. "The role of transfrontier conservation areas in southern Africa in the conservation of mammalian biodiversity." In *Priorities for the Conservation of Mammalian Diversity: Has the Panda Had Its Day?* ed. A. Entwistle and N. Dunstone, 239–56. Cambridge: Cambridge University Press.

Hanlon, Joseph. 1991. *Mozambique: Who Calls the Shots?* London: James Currey.

————. 1996. *Peace without Profit: How the IMF Blocks Rebuilding in Mozambique.* Oxford: James Currey.

————. 2002. "The land debate in Mozambique: Will foreign investors, the urban elite, advanced peasants or family farmers drive rural development?" Oxford: Oxfam.

Hansen, Art. 1979. "Once the running stops: Assimilation of Angolan refugees into Zambian border villages." *Disasters* 3(4): 369–74.

Harley, J. B. 1988. "Silence and secrecy: The hidden agenda of cartography in early modern Europe." *Imago Mundi* 40: 57–76.

————. 1989. "Deconstructing the map." *Cartographica* 26(2): 1–19.

Harries, Patrick. 1981a. "Slavery amongst the Gaza Nguni: Its changing shape and function and its relationship to other forms of exploitation." In *Before and After Shaka: Papers in Nguni History*, ed. J. B. Peires, 210–27. Grahamstown, South Africa: Institute of Social and Economic Research, Rhodes University.

————. 1981b. "Slavery, social incorporation and surplus extraction: The nature of free and unfree labour in south-east Africa." *Journal of African History* 22: 309–30.

————. 1994. *Work, Culture, and Identity: Migrant Laborers in Mozambique and South Africa, c. 1860–1910.* Portsmouth, NH: Heinemann; Johannesburg: Witwatersrand University Press.

Hart, Gillian. 1997. "Multiple trajectories of rural industrialisation: An agrarian critique of industrial restructuring and the new institutionalism." In *Globalising Food: Agrarian Questions and Global Restructuring*, ed. David Goodman and Michael Watts, 56–78. London and New York: Routledge.

Harvey, David. 1990. *The Condition of Postmodernity.* Oxford: Blackwell.

————. 2000. *Spaces of Hope.* Berkeley and Los Angeles: University of California Press.

Hatton, J. C., ed. 1995. "Status quo assessment of the Chimanimani Transfrontier Conservation Area." Harare: IUCN—World Conservation Union.

Hatton, John, and Aurelio Rocha. 1994. "The feasibility of TFAC development in southern Manica Province." In Environment and Development Group, ed., 191–234.

Hawthorne, Walter. 2001. "Nourishing a stateless society during the slave trade: The rise of Balanta paddy-rice production in Guinea-Bissau." *Journal of African History* 42(1): 1–24.

Helmsing, A. J. H., N. D. Mutizwa-Mangiza, D. R. Gasper, C. M. Brand, and K. H. Wekwete. 1991. *Limits to Decentralization in Zimbabwe: Essays on the Decentralization of Government and Planning in the 1980s.* The Hague: Institute of Social Studies.

Herbst, Jeffrey. 1990. *State Politics in Zimbabwe.* Berkeley and Los Angeles: University of California Press; Harare: University of Zimbabwe Publications.

Hiatt, L. R. 1989. "Aboriginal land tenure and contemporary claims in Australia." In Wilmsen, ed., 99–117.

Hill, Kevin A. 1996. "Zimbabwe's wildlife utilization programs: Grassroots democracy or an extension of state power?" *African Studies Review* 39(1): 103–21.

Hirschoff, Paula. 1997–98. "Planning with the ancestors: Conservation officials learn that you can't do much in Mozambique's bush without the village spirit medium." *Worldview* (National Peace Corps Association, United States) 11(1): 63–66.

Hobane, P. A. 1993. "A socio-economic report on Haroni and Rusitu Reserves." Harare: Centre for Applied Social Sciences, University of Zimbabwe.

Hogendorn, J. S., and Paul E. Lovejoy. 1988. "The reform of slavery in early colonial northern Nigeria." In Miers and Roberts, eds., 391–414.

Holleman, J. F. 1952. *Shona Customary Law.* Cape Town and London: Oxford University Press.

Hughes, David M. 1989. "Non-governmental development organizations and peasant political history in Zimbabwe." Bachelor's thesis, Princeton University, Princeton, NJ.

———. 1995a. "Community-based forest management in the Lucite (Rusitu) Valley: People and policies of a proposed Mozambique-Zimbabwe transfrontier conservation area." Maputo: World Bank.

———. 1995b. "Draft of two appendices for appraisal document of transfrontier conservation areas project (GEF)." Maputo: World Bank.

———. 1996. "When parks encroach upon people: Expanding national parks in the Rusitu Valley, Zimbabwe." *Cultural Survival Quarterly* 20(1): 36–40.

———. 1999a. "Frontier dynamics: Struggles for land and clients on the Zimbabwe-Mozambique border." Ph.D. diss., University of California, Berkeley.

———. 1999b. "Refugees and squatters: Immigration and the politics on territory on the Zimbabwe-Mozambique border." *Journal of Southern African Studies* 25(4): 533–52.

———. 2000. "To spread opportunity across space: Smallholder-led resettlement in eastern Zimbabwe." Harare: SAFIRE.

———. 2001a. "Cadastral politics: The making of community forestry in Zimbabwe and Mozambique." *Development and Change* 32(4): 741–68.

———. 2001b. "Rezoned for business: How eco-tourism unlocked black farmland in eastern Zimbabwe." *Journal of Agrarian Change* 1(4): 575–99.

———. 2001c. "Water as a boundary: National Parks, rivers, and the politics of demarcation in Chimanimani, Zimbabwe." In *Reflections on Water: New Approaches to Transboundary Conflicts and Cooperation,* ed. Helen Ingram and Joachim Bitter, 267–94. Cambridge, MA: MIT Press.

———. 2005. "Third nature: Making space and time in the great Limpopo Conservation Area." *Cultural Anthropology* 20(2): 157–84.

Hughes, David M., and Melanie H. McDermott. 1997. "Reclamações comunitárias sobre o uso e aproveitamento da terra: Metodologia de uma documentação na zona do Régulo Gogoi, Distrito de Mossurize, Manica." Maputo: Centro de Informação e Documentação para o Desenvolvimento.

Hulme, David, and Marshall Murphree, eds. 2001. *African Wildlife and Livelihoods: The Promise and Performance of Community Conservation.* Oxford: James Currey; Harare: Weaver Press.

Humane Society. 1997. "CAMPFIRE: A close look at the costs and consequences." Washington, DC: Humane Society of the United States and Humane Society International.

Huntington, Samuel. 1996. *The Clash of Civilizations and the Making of World Order.* New York: Simon and Schuster.

Hyden, Goran. 1980. *Beyond Ujamaa in Tanzania: Underdevelopment and an Uncaptured Peasantry.* Berkeley and Los Angeles: University of California Press.

Iliffe, John. 1987. *The African Poor: A History.* Cambridge: Cambridge University Press.

———. 1990. *Famine in Zimbabwe, 1890–1960.* Gweru, Zimbabwe: Mambo Press.

Innes, Duncan. 1984. *Anglo: Anglo American and the Rise of Modern South Africa.* Johannesburg: Ravan Press.

Isaacman, Allen F. 1972. *Mozambique: The Africanization of a European Institution, the Zambezi Prazos, 1970–1902.* Madison: University of Wisconsin Press.

———. 1976. *The Tradition of Resistance in Mozambique: Anti-Colonial Activity in the Zambesi Valley, 1850–1921.* Berkeley: University of California Press.

———. 1996. *Cotton Is the Mother of Poverty: Peasants, Work, and Rural Struggle in Colonial Mozambique, 1938–1961.* Portsmouth, NH: Heinemann.

Isaacman, Allen, and Barbara Isaacman. 1975. "The prazeros as transfrontiersmen: A study in social and cultural change." *International Journal of African Historical Studies* 8(1): 1–39.

———. 1983. *Mozambique: From Colonialism to Revolution.* Boulder, CO: Westview Press.

Isaacman, Allen, and Anton Rosenthal. 1988. "Slaves, soldiers and police: Power and dependency among the Chikunda of Mozambique, ca. 1825–1920." In Miers and Roberts, eds., 220–53.

Jacobs, Susie. 1983. "Women and land resettlement in Zimbabwe." *Review of African Political Economy* 27/28: 33–50.

Jansen, D., I. Bond, and B. Child. 1992. "Cattle, wildlife, both, or neither: Results of a financial and economic survey of commercial ranches in southern Zimbabwe." Project Paper no. 27, WWF Multispecies Animal Production Systems Project, Harare.

Jeater, Diana. 1993. *Marriage, Perversion, and Power: The Construction of Moral Discourse in Southern Rhodesia, 1894–1930.* Oxford: Clarendon.

Júnior, Albino Cuna. 1998. "Levantamento cadastral de Monapo." Paper presented to the Seminário Nacional sobre Gestão e Ocupação de Terras pelas Comunidades Locais, Beira, Mozambique, 12–14 August.

Junod, Henri A. 1962. *The Life of a South African Tribe.* Vol. 1. New Hyde Park, NY: University Books.

Kain, Roger J. P., and Elizabeth Baigent. 1992. *The Cadastral Map in the Service of the State: A History of Property Mapping.* Chicago: University of Chicago Press.

Kambudzi, A. M. 1997. "Zimbabwe-Mozambique border." In *Zimbabwe's International Borders,* ed. Soloman N. Nkiwane, 25–41. Harare: University of Zimbabwe Press.

Katz, Cindi. 1998. "Whose nature, whose culture? Privation productions of space and the 'preservation' of nature." In *Remaking Reality: Nature at the Millennium,* ed. Bruce Braun and Noel Castree, 46–63. London and New York: Routledge.

Kawadza, Emmanuel, and Cathy Rogers. 1993. "A report on the Haroni-Rusitu Botanical Reserves." Memorandum. Department of National Parks and Wildlife Management, Harare.

Kennedy, Dane. 1987. *Islands of White: Settler Society and Culture in Kenya and Southern Rhodesia, 1890–1939.* Durham, NC: Duke University Press.

Kinsey, B. H. 1983. "Emerging policy issues in Zimbabwe's land resettlement programmes." *Development Policy Review* 1: 163–96.

———. 1999. "Land reform, growth and equity: Emerging evidence from Zimbabwe's resettlement programme." *Journal of Southern African Studies* 25(2): 173–96.

Kjekshus, Helge. 1977. *Ecology Control and Economic Development in East African History: The Case of Tanganyika, 1850–1950.* Berkeley: University of California Press.

Klein, Martin A. 1988. "Slave resistance and slave emancipation in coastal Guinea." In Miers and Roberts, eds., 203–19.

Kloeck-Jenson, Scott. 1997. "Analysis of the parliamentary debate and new national Land Law for Mozambique." Maputo and Madison: Land Tenure Center, University of Wisconsin.

———. 1998. "Uma breve contribuição à Reunião Nacional do Ministério de Agricultura e Pescas sobre a delimitação de terras nas zonas rurais." Paper presented to the Seminário Nacional sobre Gestão e Ocupação de Terras pelas Comunidades Locais, Beira, Mozambique, 12–14 August.

Kloppenburg, Jack R. 1988. *First the Seed.* Cambridge: Cambridge University Press.

Koch, Eddie. 1998. "Our forests, our wildlife, our wealth." *Ford Foundation Report,* Winter, 12–15.

Kopytoff, Igor. 1987. "The internal African frontier: The making of an African political culture." In *The African Frontier: the Reproduction of Traditional African Societies*, ed. Igor Kopytoff, 3–84. Bloomington: Indiana University Press.

Kopytoff, Igor, and Suzanne Miers. 1977. "African 'slavery' as an institution of marginality." In Miers and Kopytoff, eds., 3–81.

Kriger, Norma J. 1988. "The Zimbabwean war of liberation: Struggles within the struggle." *Journal of Southern African Studies* 14(2): 304–22.

———. 1992. *Zimbabwe's Guerrilla War: Peasant Voices*. Cambridge: Cambridge University Press. Repr., Harare: Baobab Press, 1995.

Lamar, Howard, and Leonard Thompson, eds. 1981. *The Frontier in History: North America and Southern Africa Compared*. New Haven, CT: Yale University Press.

Lan, David. 1985. *Guns and Rain: Guerrillas and Spirit Mediums in Zimbabwe*. Berkeley and Los Angeles: University of California Press; Harare: Zimbabwe Publishing House.

Larson, Pier Martin. 2000. *History and Memory in the Age of Enslavement: Becoming Merina in Highland Madagascar, 1770–1820*. Portsmouth, NH: Heinemann.

Lattimore, Owen. 1962. "The frontier in history." In *Studies in Frontier History: Collected Papers, 1928–1958*, 469–91. London: Oxford University Press.

Leach, Melissa, Robin Mearns, and Ian Scoones. 1999. "Environmental entitlements: Dynamics and institutions in community-based natural resource management." *World Development* 27(2): 225–47.

Leonard, David K. 1991. *African Successes: Four Public Managers of Kenyan Rural Development*. Berkeley and Los Angeles: University of California Press.

Leverson, J. J. 1893. "Geographical results of the Anglo-Portuguese Delimitation Commission in South-East Africa." *Geographical Journal* 2: 505–18.

Li, Tania Murray. 2001. "Boundary work: Community, market, and state reconsidered." In Agrawal and Gibson, eds., 157–79.

Liengme, G. 1901. "Un potentat africain: Gougounyane et son règne." *Bulletin* (de la Société Neuchâteloise de Géographie), 13: 99–145.

Liesegang, Gerhard Julius. 1967. *Beiträge zur Geschichte des Reiches der Gaza Nguni im südlichen Moçambique*. Doctoral diss., Cologne University.

———. 1975. "Aspects of Gaza Nguni history, 1821–1897." *Rhodesian History* 6: 1–15.

———. 1981. "Notes on the internal structure of the Gaza kingdom of southern Mozambique, 1840–1895." In *Before and After Shaka: Papers in Nguni History*, ed. J. B. Peires, 178–209. Grahamstown, South Africa: Institute of Social and Economic Research, Rhodes University.

———. 1986. *Ngungunyane: A figura de Ngungunyane Nqumayo, rei de Gaza, 1884–1895, e o desaparecimento do seu estado*. Maputo: Arquivo do Património Cultural.

Longden, H. W. D. 1950. *Red Buffalo: The Story of Will Longden, Pioneer, Friend, and Emissary of Rhodes*. Cape Town and Johannesburg: Juta.

Lubkemann, Stephen C. 2000. "Situating wartime migration in central Mozambique: Gendered social struggle and the transnationalization of polygyny." Ph.D. diss., Brown University, Providence, RI.

Lundin, Iraê Baptista. 1995. "Relatório de trabalho de campo realizado nas Províncias de Sofala e Manica no âmbito do projecto 'A autoridade tradicional e suas bases de legitimidade.'" In Lundin and Machava, eds., 2: 37–93.

Lundin, Iraê Baptista, and Francisco Jamisse Machava, eds. 1995. *Autoridade e Poder Tradicional.* 2 vols. Maputo: Ministério da Administração Estatal.

Lunga, S. L. 1999. "Migrants and experienced impacts to the CAMPFIRE programme." Paper presented to the International Conference on Natural Resources Management, University of Zimbabwe, Harare, 26–29 January.

MacArthur, Robert H., and E. O. Wilson. 1967. *The Theory of Island Biogeography.* Princeton, NJ: Princeton University Press.

Madope, Afonso. 1999. "Community participation in wildlife management." In Ferraz and Munslow, eds., 217–22.

Madzudzo, Elias. 1996. "Producer communities in a community based wildlife management community: A case study of Bulilimamangwe and Tsholotsho District." Harare: Centre for Applied Social Sciences, University of Zimbabwe.

Magode, José, ed. 1996. *Moçambique: Etnicidades, Nacionalismo e o Estado.* Maputo: Centro de Estudos Estratégicos e Internacionais.

Makuku, S. 1993. "All this for a bug! Community approaches to common property resources management." *Forests, Trees and People Newsletter* 22: 18–23.

Makuku, S., F. Matose, and P. Mushove. 1994. "Local people's usage of natural resources around the Chimanimani Transfrontier Conservation Area in Mozambique." Unpublished report.

Makuku, S., J. Clarke, J. Ncube, and P. Mukwenhu. 1994. "Village-based woodland Management in Ntabazinduna." In *Building on Indigenous Natural Resource Management: Forestry Practices in Zimbabwe's Communal Lands,* Jeanette Clarke, ed. Harare: Forestry Commission.

Malkki, Liisa. 1992. "National geographic: The rooting of peoples and territorialization of national identity among scholars and refugees." *Cultural Anthropology* 7(1): 24–44.

Mallows, E. W. N. 1972. "The physical planning of the environment for tourism." Paper presented at the "Tourism and environment" conference, Bulawayo, Zimbabwe, 5–7 October.

Mamdani, Mahmood. 1996. *Citizen and Subject: Contemporary Africa and the Legacy of Late Colonialism.* Princeton, NJ: Princeton University Press.

Manungo, Kenneth D. 1996. "The plight of the 'migrant workers' in the commercial farms of Mazoe." Paper presented at the International Conference on the Historical Dimensions of Human Rights in Zimbabwe, University of Zimbabwe, Harare, 9–14 September 1996.

Manyarureni, Graciano C. 1995. "Ministerial control of rural district councils:

Extent and effects on decentralization." *Social Change and Development* (Harare), no. 37: 14–15.

Manzou, Chrispin. 2000. "Communal fruit production and processing: The case of the Rusitu Valley in Chimanimani, 1980–1999." Bachelor's thesis, Department of Economic History, University of Zimbabwe.

Marongwe, Nelson. 2002. "Conflicts over land and other natural resources in Zimbabwe." Harare: Zimbabwe Environmental Research Organisation (ZERO).

MARRP (Mozambique Agricultural Rural Reconstruction Programme). 1993. "Mossurize District re-integration, resettlement, and reconstruction project." Chimoio, Mozambique: GTZ.

Martin, David, and Phyllis Johnson. 1981.*The Struggle for Zimbabwe.* New York and London: Monthly Review Press.

Massinga, António. 1996. "Between the devil and the deep blue sea: Development dilemmas in Mozambique." *Ecologist* 26(2): 73–75.

Masuko, L. 1995. "Rural district councils' financial dilemma." *Social Change and Development* (Harare), no. 37: 9–10.

Matikinyidze, L. 1995. "Report on a preliminary study to assess the potential of developing a Campfire type project in Chimanimani Rural District Council with specific reference to Nyakwaa Forest area." Harare: Zimbabwe Trust.

Matose, F. M. 1992. "Villagers as woodland managers." In *Forestry Research in Zimbabwe,* ed. G. D. Pierce and P. Shaw, 173–78. Harare: Forestry Commission.

Matowanyika, Joseph Zano Zvapera. 1991. "Indigenous resource management and sustainability in rural Zimbabwe: An exploration of practices and concepts in commonlands." Ph.D. diss., University of Waterloo, Waterloo, Ontario, Canada.

Matzke, Gordon Edwin, and Nontokozo Nabane. 1996. "Outcomes of a community controlled wildlife utilization program in a Zambezi Valley community." *Human Ecology* 24(1): 65–85.

Maurer, Bill. 1997. *Recharting the Caribbean: Land, Law, and Citizenship in the British Virgin Islands.* Ann Arbor: University of Michigan Press.

Maxwell, David. 1999. *Christians and Chiefs in Zimbabwe: A Social History of the Hwesa People, c. 1870s–1990s.* Edinburgh: Edinburgh University Press.

Mazambani, David. 1999. "Community-based eco-tourism development: The Vhimba Community Project, Chimanimani District." Harare: Edit Resource Centre.

Mbembe, Achille. 1992a. "The banality of power and the aesthetics of vulgarity in the postcolony." *Public Culture* 4(2): 1–30.

———. 1992b. "Prosaics of servitude and authoritarian civilities." *Public Culture* 5(1): 123–45.

McDermott, Melanie Hughes. 2001. "Invoking community: Indigenous people and ancestral domain in Palawan, the Philippines." In Agrawal and Gibson, eds., 32–62.

McGregor, JoAnn. 1991. "Woodland resources: Ecology, policy and ideology—an historical case study of woodland use in Shurugwi Communal Area, Zimbabwe." D.Phil. diss., Loughborough University of Technology, UK.

———. 1994. "People without fathers: Mozambicans in Swaziland 1888–1993." *Journal of Southern African Studies* 20(4).

———. 1997. "Staking their claims: Land disputes in southern Mozambique." Paper no. 158. Madison: Land Tenure Center, University of Wisconsin.

Meadows, Donella H., Dennis L. Meadows, Jörgen Randers, and William L. Behrens III. 1972. *The Limits to Growth.* New York: Universe Books.

Meillassoux, Claude. 1991. *The Anthropology of Slavery: The Womb of Iron and Gold.* Trans. Alide Dasnois. Chicago: University of Chicago Press.

Metcalfe, Simon. 1994. "The Zimbabwe Communal Areas Management Programme for Indigneous Resources (CAMPFIRE)." In Western and Wright, eds., 161–92.

Mhlanga, W. 1948. "(1) The story of Ngwaqazi. (2) The history of Amatshangana." (Southern Rhodesia) *Native Affairs Department Annual* 25: 70–73.

Middleton, Nick. 1994. *Kalashnikovs and Zombie Cucumbers: Travels in Mozambique.* London: Sinclair-Stevenson.

Miers, Suzanne, and Igor Kopytoff, eds. 1977. *Slavery in Africa: Historical and Anthropological Perspectives.* Madison: University of Wisconsin Press.

Miers, Suzanne, and Richard Roberts, eds. 1988. *The End of Slavery in Africa.* Madison: University of Wisconsin Press.

Miller, Joseph C. 1988. *Way of Death: Merchant Capitalism and the Angolan Slave Trade, 1730–1830.* Madison: University of Wisconsin Press.

Ministério da Educação (Mozambique). 1980. *Atlas Geográfico.* Vol. 1. Maputo: Ministério da Educação.

Minter, William. 1994. *Apartheid's Contras: An Inquiry into the Roots of War in Angola and Mozambique.* London: Zed Books; Johannesburg: Witwatersrand University Press.

Mitchell, Timothy. 1988. *Colonising Egypt.* Cambridge: Cambridge University Press.

Moore, Donald S. 1993. "Contesting terrain in Zimbabwe's Eastern Highlands: Political ecology, ethnography, and peasant resource struggles." *Economic Geography* 69(4): 380–401.

———. 1995. "Contesting terrain in Zimbabwe's Eastern Highlands: The cultural politics of place, identity and resource struggles." Ph.D. diss., Stanford University, Stanford, CA.

———. 1996. "Marxism, culture, and political ecology: Environmental struggles in Zimbabwe's Eastern Highlands." In *Liberation Ecologies: Environment,*

Development, Social Movements, ed. Richard Peet and Michael Watts, 125–47. London: Routledge.

———. 1997. "Remapping resistance: 'Ground for struggle' and the politics of place." In *Geographies of Resistance,* ed. Steve Pile and Michael Keith. London and New York: Routledge.

———. 1998. "Subaltern struggles and the politics of place: Remapping resistance in Zimbabwe's Eastern Highlands." *Cultural Anthropology* 13(3): 344–81.

———. 1999. "The crucible of cultural politics: Reworking "development" in Zimbabwe's Eastern Highlands." *American Ethnologist* 26(3): 654–89.

Movement for Democratic Change. 2000. "Manifesto." Harare: Movement for Democratic Change.

Moyana, Henry V. 1984. *The Political Economy of Land in Zimbabwe.* Gweru, Zimbabwe: Mambo Press.

Moyo, Sam. 1995. *The Land Question in Zimbabwe.* Harare: Southern Africa Regional Institute for Policy Studies.

———. 2000. *Land Reform under Structural Adjustment in Zimbabwe: Land Use Change in the Mashonaland Provinces.* Uppsala, Sweden: Nordiska Afrikainstitutet.

Moyo, Sam, Peter Robinson, Yemi Katerere, Stuart Stevenson, and Davison Gumbo. 1991. *Zimbabwe's Environmental Dilemma: Balancing Resources Inequities.* Harare: Zimbabwe Environmental Research Organisation.

Mudimbe, V. Y. 1988. *The Invention of Africa.* Bloomington: Indiana University Press.

Müller, Tom. 1994. "The distribution, classification and conservation of rainforests in Eastern Zimbabwe." Consultancy report for the Forestry Commission, Harare.

Munro, William A. 1998. *The Moral Economy of the State: Conservation, Community Development, and State Making in Zimbabwe.* Athens: University of Ohio Press.

Murindagomo, Felix. 1990. "Zimbabwe: WINDFALL and CAMPFIRE." In *Living with Wildlife: Wildlife Resource Management with Local Participation in Africa,* ed. Agnes Kiss, 123–39. Washington, DC: World Bank.

Murombedzi, James C. 1992. "Decentralization or recentralization? Implementing CAMPFIRE in the Omay Communal Lands of the Nyaminyami District." Working Paper no. 2/92, Centre for Applied Social Sciences, University of Zimbabwe, Harare.

———. 1997. "Paying the Buffalo Bill: The impact and implications of external aid on the Communal Areas Management Programme for Indigenous Resources (CAMPFIRE)." Harare: Centre for Applied Social Sciences, University of Zimbabwe.

———. 2001. "Committees, rights, costs and benefits: Natural resource stewardship and community benefits in Zimbabwe's CAMPFIRE programme." In Hulme and Murphree, eds., 244–55.

Murphree, Marshall W. 1989. "Wildlife utilization in the Tsholotsho Communal Land, Nyamandhlovu District, Zimbabwe." Harare: Centre for Applied Social Sciences, University of Zimbabwe.

————. 1991. "Communities as institutions for resource management." London: International Institute for Environment and Development.

————. 1994. "The role of institutions in community-based conservation." In Western and Wright, eds., 403–27.

————. 1997. "Congruent objectives, competing interests, and strategic compromise: Concept and process in the evolution of Zimbabwe's CAMPFIRE programme." Paper presented at the conference "Representing communities." Helen, GA, 1–3 June 1997.

Murphy, Alexander B. 1996. "The sovereign state system as political-territorial ideal: Historical and contemporary considerations." In *State Sovereignty as Social Construct,* ed. Thomas J. Biersteker and Cynthia Weber, 81–120. Cambridge: Cambridge University Press.

Myers, Fred. 1989. "Burning the truck and holding the country: Pintupi forms of property and identity." In Wilmsen, ed., 15–42.

Myers, Gregory W. 1994. "Competitive rights, competitive claims: Land access in post-war Mozambique." *Journal of Southern African Studies* 20(4): 603–32.

Myers, Gregory, Julieta Eliseu, and Erasmo Nhachungue. 1993. "Security and conflict in Mozambique: Case studies of land access in the post-war period." Madison: Land Tenure Center, University of Wisconsin.

Myers, Gregory, and Ricky Weiss. 1994. "Proceedings: Second national land conference in Mozambique." Madison: Land Tenure Center, University of Wisconsin.

Negrão, José. 1996. "Alternativas para o 'sector familiar.'" *Extra* (Maputo) 17: 58–63.

————. 1999. "The Mozambican Land Campaign, 1997–99." Paper presented to the Workshop on the Associative Movement, Maputo, 14 December.

Neumann, Roderick P. 1997. "Primitive ideas: Protected area buffer zones and the politics of land in Africa." *Development and Change* 28(3): 559–82.

————. 1998. *Imposing Wilderness: Struggles over Livelihood and Nature Preservation in Africa.* Berkeley and Los Angeles: University of California Press.

Newitt, Malyn. 1981. *Portugal in Africa: The Last Hundred Years.* London: C. Hurst.

————. 1995. *A History of Mozambique.* Bloomington: Indiana University Press.

Nordstrom, Carolyn. 1997. *A Different Kind of War Story.* Philadelphia: University of Pennsylvania Press.

Noyes, John. 1992. *Colonial Space: Spatiality in the Discourse of German South West Africa, 1884–1915.* Chur, Switzerland: Harwood Academic Publishers.

Nugent, Paul, and A. I. Asiwaju, eds. 1996a. *African Boundaries: Barriers, Conduits and Opportunities.* London: Pinter.

———. 1996b. "Introduction: The paradox of African boundaries." In Nugent and Asiwaju, eds., 1–17.

Nyambara, Pius S. 1999. "A history of land acquisition in Gokwe, northwestern Zimbabwe, 1945–1997." Ph.D. diss., Northwestern University, Evanston, IL.

———. 2001. "The closing frontier: Agrarian change and the 'squatter menace' in Gokwe, 1980s–1990s." *Journal of Agrarian Change* 1(4): 534–49.

Nyoni, Sithembiso. 1987. "Participation in the context of rural development in Zimbabwe." In *The Importance of People: Experiences, Lessons, and Ideas on Rural Development Training in Zimbabwe,* ed. Martin de Graaf and Brigid Willmore, 121–26. Bulawayo, Zimbabwe: Hlekweni Friends Rural Service Centre.

O'Connor, Martin. 1993. "On the misadventures of capitalist nature." *Capitalism, Nature, Socialism* 4(3): 7–40.

Ohadike, Don. 1988. "The decline of slavery among the Igbo people." In Miers and Roberts, eds., 437–61.

Olaniyan, Tejumola. 1992. "Narrativizing postcoloniality: Responsibilities." *Public Culture* 5(1): 47–56.

O'Laughlin, Bridget. 1995. "Myth of the African family in the world of development." In *Women Wield the Hoe: Lessons from Rural Africa for Feminist Theory,* ed. D. F. Bryceson. Oxford: Berg.

———. 1996. "Through a divided glass: Dualism, class and the agrarian question in Mozambique." *Journal of Peasant Studies* 23(4): 1–39.

Olivier, C. P. 1957. *Many Treks Made Rhodesia.* (Originally published as *Die Pioneertrekke na Gazaland.*) Cape Town: Howard B. Timmins.

Omer-Coooper, J. 1966. *The Zulu Aftermath.* London: Longman.

Ostrom, Elinor. 1990. *Governing the Commons: The Evolution of Institutions for Collective Action.* Cambridge: Cambridge University Press.

Palmer, Robin H. 1971. "War and land in Rhodesia." *Transafrican Journal of History* 1(2): 43–62.

———. 1977. *Land and Racial Domination in Rhodesia.* Berkeley: University of California Press.

Patterson, Orlando. 1982. *Slavery and Social Death: A Comparative Study.* Cambridge, MA: Harvard University Press.

Peet, Richard, and Michael Watts. 1996. "Liberation ecology: Development, sustainability and environment in an age of market triumphalism." In *Liberation Ecologies,* ed. Richard Peet and Michael Watts, 1–45. London: Routledge.

Peluso, Nancy Lee. 1995. "Whose woods are these? Counter-mapping forest territories in Kalimantan, Indonesia." *Antipode* 27(4): 383–406.

Pereira, Carlos Raposo, and Rui Baltazar dos Santos Alves. 1994. *Reflexões sobre o*

Regime Jurídico da Terra. Maputo: Helvetas—Associação Suíça para o Desenvolvimento e Cooperação.

Peters, Carl. 1902. *The Eldorado of the Ancients*. London: Pearson; New York: Dutton.

Peters, Pauline E. 1994. *Dividing the Commons: Politics, Policy, and Culture in Botswana*. Charlottesville: University of Virginia Press.

Phipps, J. B., and R. Goodier. 1962. "A preliminary account of the plant ecology of the Chimanimani Mountains." *Journal of Ecology* 50(2): 291–319.

Pinto, Henrique Vieira. 1961. *A Exploração Florestal em Manica e Sofala*. Série A, Científica e Técnica, no. 10. Lourenço Marques: Gazeta do Agricultor Publicações.

Pitcher, M. Anne. 1996. "Recreating colonialism or reconstructing the state? Privatisation and politics in Mozambique." *Journal of Southern African Studies* 22(1): 49–74.

Plank, David N. 1993. "Aid, debt, and the end of sovereignty: Mozambique and its donors." *Journal of Modern African Studies* 31(3): 407–30.

Polanyi, Karl. 1944. *The Great Transformation: The Political and Economic Origins of Our Time*. Boston: Beacon Books.

Prakash, Gayan. 1990. *Bonded Histories: Genealogies of Labor Servitude in Colonial India*. Cambridge: Cambridge University Press.

Pratt, Mary Louise. 1992. *Imperial Eyes: Travel Writing and Transculturation*. London: Routledge.

Rabinow, Paul. 1989. *French Modern: Norms and Forms of the Social Environment*. Cambridge, MA: MIT Press.

Raney, H. 1898. "Gazaland." *South African Pioneer* (Cape Town ed.), 9(6): 275–76.

Ranger, Terence O. 1967. *Revolt in Southern Rhodesia, 1896–97*. Evanston, IL: Northwestern University Press.

———. 1983. "The invention of tradition in colonial Africa." In *The Invention of Tradition*, ed. Eric Hobsbawm and Terence Ranger, 211–62. Cambridge: Cambridge University Press.

———. 1985. *Peasant Consciousness and Guerrilla War in Zimbabwe*. Harare: Zimbabwe Publishing House.

———. 1994. "Studying repatriation as part of African social history." In Allen and Morsink, eds., 279–94.

———. 1996. "Postscript: Colonial and postcolonial identities." In Werbner and Ranger, eds., 271–81.

———. 1997. Review of *Mukiwa: A White Boy in Africa*, by Peter Godwin. *Journal of Southern African Studies* 23(4): 671–72.

———. 1999. *Voices from the Rocks*. Oxford: James Currey.

Reis, Ana Paula. 1997. Presentation to the "Oitavo Encontro Nacional de Florestas e Fauna Bravia," Barragem dos Pequenos Lebombos, Mozambique, 16–20 June.

————. 1999. "Projecto de Conservação Transfronteira de Chimanimani—Relatório Anual, 1999." Chimoio, Mozambique: Serviços Provinciais de Florestas e Fauna Bravia.

Rennie, John K. 1973. "Christianity, colonialism and the origins of nationalism among the Ndau of Southern Rhodesia, 1890–1935." Ph.D. diss., Northwestern University, Evanston, IL.

————. 1978. "From Zimbabwe to a colonial chieftaincy: Four transformations of the Musikavanhu territorial cult in Rhodesia." In *Guardians of the Land: Essays on Central African Territorial Cults*, ed. J. M. Schoffeleers, 257–85. Gweru, Zimbabwe: Mambo Press.

————. 1984. "Ideology and state formation: Political and communal ideologies amongst the south-eastern Shona, 1500–1890." In *State Formation in East Africa*, ed. Ahmed Idha Salim, 162–94. Nairobi: Heinemann.

Rhodesia Forestry Commission. 1968. "Afforestation with exotic coniferous species." In *Melsetter Regional Plan*, ed. K. A Bromley et al., 141–51. Salisbury: Department of Conservation and Extension, Government of Rhodesia.

Ribeiro, António. 1999. "Institutional development for community-based resource management research." In Ferraz and Munslow, eds., 88–96.

Ribot, Jesse C. 1996. "Participation without representation: Chiefs, councils and forestry law in the West African Sahel." *Cultural Survival Quarterly* 20(3): 40–44.

————. 1999. "Decentralisation, participation and accountability in Sahelian forestry: Legal instruments of political-administrative control." *Africa* 69(1): 23–65.

Richards, Audrey. 1950. "Some types of family structures amongst the central Bantu." In *African Systems of Kinship and Marriage*, ed. R. Radcliffe-Brown and D. Forde. Oxford: Oxford University Press.

Riddell, Roger. 1979. "Prospects for land reform in Zimbabwe." *Rural Africana* 4/5: 17–31.

Riles, Annelise. 2000. *The Network Inside Out*. Ann Arbor: University of Michigan Press.

Roberts, Richard. 1988. "The end of slavery in the French Soudan, 1905–1914." In Miers and Roberts, eds., 282–307.

Roberts, Richard, and Suzanne Miers. 1988. "Introduction: The end of slavery in Africa." In Miers and Roberts, eds., 1–68.

Robins, Steven. 1994. "Contesting the social geometry of bureaucratic state power: A case study of land-use planning in Matabeleland, Zimbabwe." *Social Dynamics* 20(2): 91–118.

Robinson, Jennifer. 1996. *The Power of Apartheid: State Power and Space in South African Cities*. Oxford: Butterworth-Heinemann.

Roder, Wolf. 1965. "The Sabi Valley Irrigation Projects." Research paper no. 99, University of Chicago.

Roe, Emery M. 1995. "More than the politics of decentralization: Local government reform, district development and public administration in Zimbabwe." *World Development* 23(5): 833–43.

Roesch, Otto. 1992. "Mozambique unravels? The retreat to tradition." *Southern Africa Report*, May, 27–30.

Rose, Carol. 1994. *Property and Persuasion: Essays on the History, Theory and Rhetoric of Ownership*. Boulder, CO: Westview Press.

Ross, Robert. 1981. "Capitalism, expansion, and incorporation on the Southern African frontier." In Lamar and Thompson, eds., 209–33.

Rotberg, Robert I. 2000. "The final stages of African dictatorship." *Southern Africa Report* 18(15): 7.

Rubenstein, Richard L. 1975. *The Cunning of History: The Holocaust and the American Future*. New York: Harper and Row.

Rukuni, Mandivamba, ed. 1994. *Report of the Commission of Inquiry into Appropriate Agricultural Land Tenure Systems*. Vol.1. Harare: Government Printers.

Rutherford, Blair. 2001. *Working on the Margins: Black Workers, White Farmers in Postcolonial Zimbabwe*. London: Zed Books; Harare: Weaver Press.

Ryan, P. G., R. Cassidy, and T. Salinger. 1984. "The Haroni-Lusitu junction revisited." *Honeyguide* 30: 90–91.

Sachs, Albie, and Gita Honwana Welch. 1990. *Liberating the Law: Creating Popular Justice in Mozambique*. London: Zed Books.

SAFIRE (Southern Alliance for Indigenous Resources). 1994. "A participatory rural appraisal exercise in Mutemanerangu Village, Vhimba Ward, Chimanimani District, Zimbabwe, 23–30 July 1994." Unpublished document.

———. 1996. "Community-based tourist development in Zimbabwe: The Vhimba Eco-Tourism Project." Harare: SAFIRE.

Sahlins, Marshall. 1972. *Stone Age Economics*. New York: Aldine.

Sahlins, Peter. 1989. *Boundaries: The Making of France and Spain in the Pyrenees*. Berkeley and Los Angeles: University of California Press.

Saul, John S. 1993. *Recolonization and Resistance in Southern Africa in the 1990s*. Trenton, NJ: Africa World Press.

Schafer, Jessica. 1999. "Soldiers at peace: The post-war politics of demobilized soldiers in Mozambique." Doctoral diss., University of Oxford, UK.

Schafer, Jessica, and Richard Bell. 2001. "The state and community-based natural resource management: The case of the Moribane Forest Reserve." Unpublished paper.

Schmidt, Heike. 1996. "Love and healing in forced communities: Borderlands in Zimbabwe's war of liberation." In Nugent and Asiwaju, eds., 183–204.

———. 1998. " 'Roads or other notable features do not exist': The Anglo-Portuguese boundary commissions of 1898 and 1905/06." Paper presented to annual meeting of the African Studies Association (USA), Chicago, 29 October–1 November.

Schmink, Marianne, and Charles H. Wood. 1992. *Contested Frontiers in Amazonia.* New York: Columbia University Press.

Schroeder, Richard A. 1999a. "Community, forestry and conditionality in the Gambia." *Africa* 69(1): 1–21.

———. 1999b. "Geographies of environmental intervention in Africa." *Progress in Human Geography* 23(3): 357–78.

Scoones, Ian. 1989. "Patch use by cattle in a dryland environment: Farmer knowledge and ecological theory." In *People, Land and Livestock,* ed. Ben Cousins. Harare: Centre for Applied Social Sciences, University of Zimbabwe.

Scoones, Ian, et al. 1996. *Hazards and Opportunities: Farming Livelihoods in Dryland Africa—Lessons from Zimbabwe.* London: Zed Books.

Scott, James C. 1985. *Weapons of the Weak.* New Haven, CT: Yale University Press.

———. 1998. *Seeing Like a State: How Certain Schemes to Improve the Human Condition Have Failed.* New Haven, CT: Yale University Press.

Sen, Amartya. 1981. *Poverty and Famines: An Essay in Entitlement and Deprivation.* Oxford: Oxford University Press.

Shaw, Timothy M., and Julius E. Nyang'oro. 1989. "Corporatism in Africa in the 1990s: Toward a new African studies?" In *Corporatism in Africa: Comparative Analysis and Practice,* ed. Julius E. Nyang'oro and Timothy M. Shaw, 1–15. Boulder, CO: Westview Press.

Shipton, Parker. 1984a. "Lineage and locality as antithetical principles in East African systems of land tenure." *Ethnology* 23(2): 117–32.

———. 1984b. "Strips and patches: A demographic dimension in some African land-holding and political systems." *Man,* n.s., 19(4): 613–34.

———. 1994. "Land and culture in tropical Africa: Soils, symbols and the metaphysics of the mundane." *Annual Review of Anthropology* 23: 347–77.

Shipton, Parker, and Mitzee Goheen. 1992. "Understanding African land-holding: Power, wealth, and meaning." *Africa* 62(3): 307–25.

Sinclair, Shirley. 1971. *The Story of Melsetter.* Salisbury: M. O. Collins.

Singh, Jaidev. 2001. "State-making and community-based natural resource management: Cases of the Vhimba CAMPFIRE project (Zimbabwe) and the Chimanimani Transfrontier Conservation Area (Mozambique)." Ph.D. diss., University of Washington, Seattle.

Sivaramakrishnan, K. 1999. *Modern Forests: Statemaking and Environmental Change in Colonial East India.* Stanford, CA: Stanford University Press.

Sleigh, R. W. 1976. "Survey and the surveyors." *Rhodesia Science News* 10(1): 3–4.

Smith, Neil. 1984. *Uneven Development.* Oxford: Basil Blackwell.

———. 1996. *The New Urban Frontier: Gentrification and the Revanchist City.* London: Routledge.

Spannaus, Günther. 1933. "Erläuterungen zu Konstruktion und Inhalt der Routenkarte der Leipziger Mosambikexpedition, 1931." *Wissenschaftliche*

Veröffentlichungen des Museums für Länderkunde zu Leipzig, n.s., 2(2): 131–142 and map.

———. 1961. "Das Häuptlingswesen der Ndau in Südostafrika." *Beiträge zur Völkerforschung* (Leipzig: Veröffentlichungen des Museums für Völkerkunde), 2: 630–38.

Spierenburg, Marja. 1995. "The role of the Mhondoro cult in the struggle for control over land in Dande (northern Zimbabwe): Social commentaries and the influence of adherents." Unpublished paper.

Spring, Anita. 1979. "Women and men as refugees: Differential assimilation of Angolan refugees in Zambia." *Disasters* 3(4): 423–28.

Suzuki, Yuka. 2001. "Drifting rhinos and fluid properties: The turn to wildlife production in western Zimbabwe." *Journal of Agrarian Change* 1(4): 600–25.

Swynnerton, C. F. M. 1921. "An examination of the tsetse problem in North Mossurise, Portuguese East Africa." *Bulletin of Entomological Research* 11: 315–85.

Tanner, Christopher. 2000. "Registering customary rights and demarcating customary land in Mozambique." In "Securing customary land tenure in Africa: Local recording and registration of land rights," 2–24. (Background papers to a workshop held on 8 November). London: International Institute for Environment and Development.

———. 2002. "Law-making in an African context: The 1997 Mozambican Land Law." Rome: Food and Agriculture Organization. FAO legal papers online, no. 26.

Tanner, Christopher, Paul de Wit, and Sevy Madureira. 1998. "Propostas para um programa de delineação das comunidades locais." Paper presented to the Seminário Nacional sobre Gestão e Ocupação de Terras pelas Comunidades Locais, Beira, Mozambique, 12–14 August.

Thompson, E. P. 1975. *Whigs and Hunters: The Origin of the Black Act.* New York: Pantheon.

Thompson, Leonard, and Howard Lamar. 1981a. "Comparative frontier history." In Lamar and Thompson, eds., 3–13.

———. 1981b. "The North American and Southern African frontiers." In Lamar and Thompson, eds., 14–40.

Thongchai Winichakul. 1994. *Siam Mapped: A History of the Geo-Body of a Nation.* Honolulu: University of Hawai'i Press.

Timberlake, Jonathan. 1994. "Changes in the extent of moist forest patches in the Eastern Highlands: Case studies based on aerial photographs." Research Paper no. 7, Zimbabwe Forestry Commission, Harare.

Tivane, Atanásio. 1999. "An analysis of eucalyptization." In Ferraz and Munslow, eds., 223–28.

Toulabor, Comi. 1992. "L'art du faible." In Bayart, Mbembe, and Toulabor, 107–45.

Tsing, Anna Lowenhaupt. 1993. *In the Realm of the Diamond Queen: Marginality in an Out-of-the-Way Place.* Princeton, NJ: Princeton University Press.

————. 2000. "Inside the economy of appearances." *Public Culture* 12(1): 115–44.

Turnbull, David. 1989. *Maps Are Territories, Science Is an Atlas.* Chicago: University of Chicago Press.

Unruh, J. D. 1998. "Land tenure and identity change in postwar Mozambique." *GeoJournal* 48: 89–99.

Vail, Leroy. 1976. "Mozambique's chartered companies: The rule of the feeble." *Journal of African History* 17(3): 389–416.

Vail, Leroy, and Landeg White. 1980. *Capitalism and Colonialism in Mozambique: A Study of Quelimane District.* Minneapolis: University of Minnesota Press.

van der Linde, Harry, et al. 2001. "Beyond boundaries: Transboundary natural resource management in Sub-Saharan Africa." Washington, DC: Biodiversity Support Program.

van der Post, Laurens. 1966. *The Lost World of the Kalahari.* New York: Pyramid Books.

van Onselen, Charles. 1976. *Chibaro: African Mine Labour in Southern Rhodesia, 1900–1933.* London: Pluto Press.

Vandergeest, Peter. 1996. "Real villages: National narratives of rural development." In *Creating the Countryside: The Politics of Rural and Environmental Discourse,* ed. E. Melanie DuPuis and Peter Vandergeest, 279–302. Philadelphia: Temple University Press.

Vandergeest, Peter, and Nancy Lee Peluso. 1995. "Territorialization and state power in Thailand." *Theory and Society* 24: 385–426.

Vaughan, Megan. 1991. *Curing Their Ills: Colonial Power and African Illness.* Stanford, CA: Stanford University Press.

Vijfhuizen, Carin. 2002. *The People You Live With: Gender, Identities and Social Practices, Beliefs and Power in the Lives of Ndau Women and Men in a Village with an Irrigation Scheme in Zimbabwe.* Harare: Weaver Press.

Virtanen, Pekka. 1999. "Community in context: Chiefs and councils in Mozambique." Paper presented to the "Workshop on governance, rights, and rules for woodland and wildlife management in Southern Africa," Harare, 23–24 November.

Warhurst, Philip R. 1962. *Anglo-Portuguese Relations in South-Central Africa, 1890–1900.* London: Longman.

Watts, Michael J. 1994. "Life under contract: Contract farming, agrarian restructuring, and flexible accumulation." In *Living under Contract: Contract Farming and Agrarian Transformation in Sub-Saharan Africa,* ed. Peter D. Little and Michael Watts, 21–77. Madison: University of Wisconsin Press.

————. 2000. "Contested communities, malignant markets, and gilded government: Justice, resource extraction, and conservation in the tropics." In *People, Plants, and Justice: The Politics of Nature Conservation,* ed. Charles Zerner, 21–51. New York: Columbia University Press.

Weber, Peter. 1971. *Die Agrargeographische Struktur von Mittel-Moçambique.*

Marburger Geographische Schriften no. 48. Marburg, Germany: Geographische Institüt, Universität Marburg.

Welford, Lucy. 1998. "People, plants and parks: The use of natural resources by the Vhimba community, south east Zimbabwe." Unpublished report prepared for SAFIRE, Harare.

Werbner, Richard. 1996. "Introduction: Multiple identities, plural arenas." In Werbner and Ranger, eds., 1–25.

———. 1998. "Smoke from the barrel of a gun: Postwars of the dead, memory and reinscription in Zimbabwe." In *Memory and the Postcolony: African Anthropology and the Critique of Power,* ed. Richard Werbner, 71–102. London: Zed Books.

Werbner, Richard, and Terence Ranger, eds. 1996. *Postcolonial Identities in Africa.* London: Zed Books.

Western, David. 1994. "Ecosystem conservation and rural development: The case of Amboseli." In Western and Wright, eds., 15–52.

Western, David, and R. Michael Wright, eds. 1994. *Natural Connections: Perspectives in Community-based Conservation.* Washington, DC: Island Press.

Whitlow, R. 1988. "Aerial photography in Zimbabwe, 1935–1986." *Zambezia* 15(2): 137–65.

Wilmsen, Edwin N. 1989a. "Introduction." In Wilmsen, ed., 1–14.

———. 1989b. *Land Filled with Flies: A Political Economy of the Kalahari.* Chicago: University of Chicago Press.

———, ed. 1989c. *We Are Here: Politics of Aboriginal Land Tenure.* Berkeley and Los Angeles: University of California Press.

Wilson, Ken B. 1990. "Ecological dynamics and human welfare: A case study of population, health and nutrition in Southern Zimbabwe." D.Phil. diss., University College, London.

———. 1992. "Cults of violence and counter-violence in Mozambique." *Journal of Southern African Studies* 18(3): 527–82.

———. 1994. "Refugees and returnees as social agents: The case of Jehovah's Witnesses from Milange." In Allen and Morsink, eds., 237–50.

———. 1997. "Of diffusion and context: The bubbling up of community-based resource management in Mozambique." Paper presented to the "Representing communities" conference, Helen, GA, 1–3 June.

Wilson, Thomas M., and Hastings Donnan. 1998. "Nation, state and identity at international borders." In *Border Identities: Nation and State at International Frontiers,* ed. Wilson and Donnan, 1–30. Cambridge: Cambridge University Press.

Wood, Douglas. 1903. "Itinerating work in Gazaland." *South Africa Pioneer* (Cape Town ed.), 16(2): 27.

———. 1905. "Gazaland rediviva." *South Africa Pioneer* (Cape Town ed.), 18(10): 251–53.

Worby, Eric. 1994. "Maps, names, and ethnic games: The epistemology and iconography of colonial power in northwestern Zimbabwe." *Journal of Southern African Studies* 20(3): 371–92.

———. 1995. "What does agrarian wage-labour signify? Cotton, commoditisation and social form in Gokwe, Zimbabwe." *Journal of Peasant Studies* 23(1): 1–29.

———. 1998a. "Inscribing the state at the 'edge of beyond:' Danger and development in northwestern Zimbabwe." *Political and Legal Anthropology Review* 21(2): 55–70.

———. 1998b. "Tyranny, parody, and ethnic polarity: Ritual engagements with the state in northwestern Zimbabwe." *Journal of Southern African Studies* 24(3): 561–78.

World Commission on Environment and Development. 1987. *Our Common Future.* New York: Oxford University Press.

Wunder, Matthew B. 1997. "Of elephant and men: Crop destruction, Campfire, and wildlife management in the Zambezi Valley, Zimbabwe." Ph.D. diss., University of Michigan, Ann Arbor.

WWF (World Wide Fund for Nature). 1997. *Quota Setting Manual.* Harare: WWF, Zimbabwe Trust, and Safari Club International.

Young, John. 1970. "The legendary history of the Hodi and Ngorima chiefs." *Native Affairs Department Annual* 10(2): 49–60.

Zartmann, I. W. 1970. "Portuguese Guinean refugees in Senegal." In *Refugees South of the Sahara,* ed. H. C. Brooks and Y. El-Ayouty, 143–61. Westport, CT: Negro Universities Press.

Zimmerer, Karl S. 2000. "The reworking of conservation geographies: Nonequilibrium landscapes and nature-society hybrids." *Annals of the Association of American Geographers* 90(2): 356–69.

Zinyama, Lovemore, and Richard Whitlow. 1986. "Changing patterns of population distribution in Zimbabwe." *GeoJournal* 13(4): 365–84.

ARCHIVES

Arquivo Histórico de Moçambique (AHM), Maputo:
Secção Especial.
Fundo do Governo Geral.
Fundo da Companhia de Moçambique.
Fundo da Inspecção Nacional dos Serviços Administrativos e dos Negócios Indígenas (INSANI).
Fundo do Governo do Distrito da Beira.
Fundo da Administração da Circunscrição de Mossurize.
Houghton Library, Harvard University, Cambridge, Massachusetts, USA: Papers

of the American Board of Commissioners for Foreign Missions (ABCFM) 15.4 vols. 26, 32, 33, 34, 49a; 15.6 boxes 1–4.

National Archives of Zimbabwe (NAZ), Harare: Public records A, D, L, LO, N, NUE, S, SG, UN series. Historical manuscripts by Machiwenyika (MA), Meredith (ME). Map file "La Rhodesia."

Office of the District Administrator, Chimanimani, Zimbabwe: Ngorima personnel (PER) file.

Scripps Institution of Oceanography, La Jolla, California, USA: Charles Atwood Kofoid Papers, 1862–1951. (Kofoid was the brother-in-law of early missionaries at the Rusitu Mission, Zimbabwe.)

Serviços Provínciais de Florestas e Fauna Bravia (SPFFB), Chimoio, Mozambique: Binder marked "Projecto de Reflorestamento," containing file marked "Repartição de Agricultura e Florestas da Beira, SABRI, Ltda., pedido de concessão florestal, 1970."

Serving in Missions (SIM), Charlotte, North Carolina, USA: Papers of the Africa Evangelical Fellowship (AEF; formerly the South Africa General Mission), boxes of the South Africa, British, and Zimbabwe Councils.

South Africa Pioneer (missionary periodical).

INDEX

Page numbers referring to illustrations appear in italics.

CPSIA information can be obtained
at www.ICGtesting.com
Printed in the USA
LVHW031648130121
676401LV00005B/297

9 780295 988405